War & Peace
at No. 249

BY VALERIE HAMPTON

Published by Country Books
an imprint of
Spiral Publishing Ltd

Country Books, 38 Pulla Hill Drive,
Storrington, West Sussex RH20 3LS

email: jonathan@spiralpublishing.com
www.spiral-books.com

ISBN 978-1-7395824-9-4

British Library Cataloguing in Publication Data.
A catalogue record for this book is available from the
British Library.

Printed and bound in England by 4edge Limited,
22 Eldon Way Industrial Estate, Hockley, Essex SS5 4AD

Valerie Hampton is a Wulfrunian with a passion to pass on the memories of a time gone by. It has taken years to bring this this selection of memories to life and this first edition is just for family and friends. Despite recent health challenges, Val remains an ardent painter, gardener and writer of poetry.

CONTENTS

CHILDHOOD AND BEYOND

(or THEY will get you!)

I am writing this firstly because I would like to leave some history about our sometimes weird family for our children and their offspring, and secondly because I have always loved writing.

The era I'm putting down on paper, wartime and the post-war years, was a time when there were many hardships, a diet ruled by coupons, lots of sadness, but fun too, along with some not-so-good memories and lots of very happy memories. Innocence prevailed in the nineteen forties and fifties.

I would hate to think that our family's life during the war was just forgotten. So, here I am with a few remembered incidents, good and bad, just for the record and, perhaps, a small snapshot of life in Wolverhampton, in the forties, fifties…sixties, and… beyond!

THE WAR AND 249

I was born on Friday 13th of May 1938, a year before the start of the Second World War, in one of three Georgian terraced houses, No. 249 Tettenhall Road, Wolverhampton.

I was the 'baby' of the Lloyd-Davies family. I had three siblings, Tony, then aged eleven, Robin, nine, and Pat, seven. Mum, Maude (she would always say to anyone asking her given name "Maude…with an E") was an older mother, aged thirty-seven. I've always thought I must have been a mistake, because of the huge gap between myself and Pat, but Mum told me in later life that she'd had a miscarriage between our births.

Apparently, Mum hadn't told any of the neighbours that she was pregnant again, having had three children, and now another on the way after a seven-year gap, and being… WELL, thirty-seven… What would people THINK at her age? The postman who delivered letters to 249 heard the news of a baby's arrival, walked next door to 247, and astonished the neighbours, Mr and Mrs Greenham, by telling the startled couple of the arrival of Maude and Cliff Lloyd-Davies' new daughter.

It turns out Mum wore the only outfit for expectant mums, a waist-length smock, a cover-all. Apparently, Mrs Greenham had exclaimed on being told, "Mrs Lloyd-Davies was sweeping the yard off yesterday, so I never dreamt she was having another baby. Nothing showed."

At this time, new mothers had a 'lying-in' period after a birth (according to the bush telegraph, Mum had weeks in bed). Her younger sister Gladys, aged about sixteen, had to stay and look after Mum. There were no gadgets, washing machine, not even a mangle, so Glad had a pretty terrible time. I don't think she ever really forgave Dad and Mum for asking her there to work. She had had to give up her job looking after the children of a wealthy family near Stourbridge to be at 249.

Like most men in those days, Dad never helped in the house and he didn't even know where the teacups were kept, let alone how to cook or wash for six people. So Glad became rather bitter, though I didn't realize this until she spoke about it when she was in her eighties.

The next bit is gleaned from my brother Robin and sister Pat.

When I was only months old, Mum fell down the stairs with me in her arms. (Of course there are lots of jokes about me hitting my head against the grandmother clock in the hall, apparently true!) Mum never DID say anything about any damage to her newborn, but she did regale the family with "I had to walk using an upturned dining chair, having a suspected broken ankle, but I never went to hospital, it was wartime." I'm sure she did do something serious, but Maude was a bit of a stoic, also very stubborn, so she just martyred on. Maude was quite a martyr all her life.

I was christened at St Jude's church, just up Tettenhall Road, minutes away from 249. Rumour has it that Dad wanted to call me Myffanwy, because of his Welsh father, but when they got to St Jude's, neither Mum nor Dad could spell the name correctly, so I was instantly 'renamed' Valerie. (Mum knew a family whose daughter was Valerie, it was a name that she liked, and she liked the friend's Valerie, so that became my given forename.) This is hard to believe, but an auntie said that there was SOME truth in the story about the last-minute naming, literally at the font. Somehow this typifies my mother and father, especially my Dad Cliff.

Clifford Pratton Lloyd-Davies – the Lloyd bit was added for business reasons because there was another Cliff Davies in the theatre managers' world, so Cliff added the Lloyd (his second name) – all hearsay really, but very possible within our very eccentric family.

My sleeping arrangements were even stranger than my naming. We had a cellar at 249, long dark steps led down into the damp, mouldy-smelling 'dungeon' with a long brick shelf, and all the electric and gas meters on the far wall. An archway led into another bigger cellar, even worse than the first, with a coal-hole at the far end. (A mix of truth and myth may come into this revelation. Bits may have become distorted. However, this is the story, gleaned from Mum and later from sister Pat.)

I must have been almost a toddler when war started in September 1939. Because of the threat of bomb attack, a pram body was carried down the steps and into the cellar. There I would sleep, well wrapped up in that damp creepy place. Whether Mum was with me, or whether I was alone, it all seems dreadful nowadays and worthy of a visit from the NSPCC! Did I cry, and was I heard? Questions never to be answered, and I can honestly say it has never bothered me.

We did have an air-raid shelter in our garden, shared by the other two houses in our terraced row, but Mum reckoned the cellar was safer from the bombs that she felt sure would rain down on 249 at any minute, 249 being Hitler's main target!

One day, all the family were down in the cellar, having been alerted of a possible bomb attack by the air-raid siren, an extremely frightening sound. Everyone was no doubt huddled together and anxious… there was a sudden 'tap-tap-tap' on the cellar door. I don't know if panic struck, but it must have struck fear into the assembled huddle. Was it some lone German pilot who had crashed his plane? The 'TAP-TAP-TAP' continued. I suspect that Dad hesitantly walked up the steps and reluctantly half-opened the door…

No German complete with jack boots and uniform emblazoned with swastikas, the opened door just revealed a very frightened fluttering budgerigar. The little bird (no name, if he ever had one!) must have escaped his/her cage and, realizing that they were behind the cellar door, was extremely anxious to join his family. The clever bird alerted everyone by tapping with his beak – amazing, and puts a tin lid on the expression 'bird brained'.

This same budgie tried to go shopping with Mum when he/she became a stowaway on her hat (a hat was ALWAYS worn by Mum to go out anywhere, also gloves). Apparently, the bird made its bid for freedom sitting amongst whatever finery adorned Mum's titfer. It only got as far as the gate before Mum realized she had a passenger aboard and returned to the house! Alas, it did eventually realize its dream of freedom and one day flew out of the kitchen window, never to return.

Gas masks were obligatory, and babies were issued with a full-cover cot or pram-protection 'mask', but an older child or toddler had what I can only remember as a Mickey Mouse facial mask, with ears. (Did I imagine this?) I think I was taught to blow out, then the ears would move and the rubber nose would vibrate… I may be inventing this bit, or going 'doolally tap', to use an old Black Country expression. Later, when at school, everyone had their gas mask strapped across their chest in a cardboard box. This went for adults too: TO BE CARRIED AT ALL TIMES. Very official!

Although Wolverhampton wasn't a prime target for the Luftwaffe, precautions had to be taken. There were aero factories nearby, so Mum conjured up solutions should the Germans target 249. She invented 'in-house' ways of softening a blow on the head from falling debris, should a bomb hit the house. As soon as an air-raid siren went off, all the cushions (home-spun 'corked' by Mum) were grabbed off the chairs and settee and held on the head! Then, we would walk, half-crouching under the weight of our headgear, and make our way to the hallway, and down the cellar steps, into the scary cellar, where no doubt spores of damp would invade our lungs, which I think was almost worse than being flattened in our beds, where at least we would die with healthy chests.

Mum's cushion covers were a sight to behold, all 'corked', which is now called French knitting. Mum was a dab hand at it, producing yards and yards of woollen 'ropes' of all colours, in a rainbow effect. Wool was only bought on coupons, so was scarce. Mum would unravel an old jumper, possibly one that had been attacked by the dreaded moths, so the 'rope' was narrower then fatter in places, as the ply changed.

The actual 'corker' was a cotton reel with four pins around the central hole. Wool was wound around the pins, and the corker would use another pin or crochet hook to slip each stitch over its neighbour! Then the sewn 'rope' was pulled through the hole at the bottom. Pat was also a 'corker' and I joined the ranks later.

The cushions mentioned as our weird anti-bomb 'hats' were yards of coloured corking that had been sewn together and stuffed with anything to hand that could be recycled. They all resembled archery targets.

In our house, all garments were knitted. The wool available seemed to be just shades of grey. Everyone had grey balaclavas, socks, gloves, vests (in a lighter colour, thank goodness.). To my brother Robin's horror, Mum even knitted bathing costumes! Robin remembers his grey one sagging dangerously low when in the water, then shrinking dangerously tight when dry!

Probably, anyone not able to turn a heel in a knitted sock or knit on four needles to make fingers in gloves deserved a shaken head along with a 'tut-tut'. Housewives were supposed to do all these things AND bring up a family. And of course some mothers had to carry out 'war-work' in factories and workshops to help the war effort.

Whilst on the subject of clothes, I have to mention the Liberty Bodice, sported by girls from about four until their teens. They were fleecy on the skin side, but had weird suspender-like gadgets along the bottom edge. I never DID find out what these were! They were rubbery and a nuisance dangling down. Were they worn under vests? I should talk to sister Pat. She, being seven years older, would remember the whys and wherefores. The bodices were buttoned with the rubbery-type button down the front, close fitting and did the job of keeping the cold out. There was no central heating in those days (well, not at 249), just open fires, even in the bedrooms, a pure delight when ill, always with a metal guard around the hearth.

CHILDHOOD ILLNESS

Our illnesses, quite severe at times, were made brighter by the glowing coal fire, smoky smell, and a warm cosy feeling, and listening to *Children's Hour* on the radio, or 'wireless' as the radio was then.

My brother Tony, who was eleven years older than me, contracted scarlet fever. He was ambulanced off to the isolation hospital in Wolverhampton, and kept there for around six weeks. He was probably about seven, so it was before I came on the scene.

This is (I hope) a little bit of family myth, but I do recall Mum telling me that, whilst Tony was in the hospital, unable to be visited by herself and Dad (or indeed anyone), they went on holiday to either Blackpool or North Wales. It sounds terrible now. I can't say this is absolutely true.

Most of his life, Dad suffered bouts of serious illness. (That overshadowed childhood for me. I can't speak for Robin or Pat, but Dad's frequent hospital stays, possibly an aftermath of rheumatic fever in his early twenties, must have cast a shadow over everyone.) Certainly it rather ruled Mum's life.

Tony got over the stay in hospital, but years later, when I was about five and in the 'babies class' at St Jude's School, I also went down with scarlet fever, so was duly carried off by a rather jolly nurse who wrapped me in a bright red blanket. This I do remember vividly, because I was allowed one special toy, and some comics. The well-loved knitted dolly and the comics were never allowed to leave the hospital, as they were deemed 'unclean' and full of germs. Isolation meant everything and everyone was kept behind four red-brick walls. So I never brought my dear dolly home. I felt so upset about this but got over it quickly. However, it is a memory that somehow stands out for me. In today's medical and psychology times this would be a headline in the local paper... almost child abuse.

I should describe the fever hospital here in case it doesn't fit in later on in this saga. This particular hospital is gone, and a housing estate was built where it stood. The regime was pretty awful for a five-year-old. I was immediately bathed, and my long hair cut and washed in black anti-nit soap (I don't think I had nits then, but who knows?). I had a bed in a long ward, all girls, and one older lady, who I recognized from walking to school. She too had the dreaded scarlet fever – the peeling skin and redness, and very sore throat and rash. There were perhaps ten girls in the ward. One who had a bed opposite me was from my school. She was called Bunty Stevens (I have dragged that name back from somewhere) and I was happy to see her. There was also a tiny baby, wearing mittens so that she didn't scratch her peeling skin. The older lady in the ward seemed to keep an eye on the baby, who seemed to cry a lot. Scarlet fever was a horrible disease, and could be fatal, especially for a baby.

In the evenings, boys from their ward would join us, and we would sit around the central stove, very homely and comforting. There were toys to play with (I found out why there were so many, later!) and the *Beano* and *Dandy* comics were there to be laughed over. Somehow it was mainly the boys who read the comics.

In one corner of our ward, there was a corner door, the entrance to the diphtheria ward, and off bounds to everyone except specialized nurses. I never even glimpsed what that ward was like. When the door opened I felt sure that something horrible would leak out.

We were not badly treated. In fact, the nurses seemed quite nice. Bunty and I had fun, jumping up and down on the bed, and, for reasons only known to children, pulling our nighties up at the front and almost over our heads. Whilst doing this pleasurable exercise on our beds, a nurse appeared… "Oh dear, dear. Oh dear… Don't show your little 'Marys', girls, it isn't very nice."

It took years for me to realize that the nurse DIDN'T mean our navels! But to this day, I have a fear of showing or touching my or anyone else's navels – how stupid. NOW, I suppose she meant the lower 'private bits'!

When we girls were feeling better, we were allowed outside in the fresh air. There was a type of veranda, high up, and occasionally a plump nurse would appear with a basket of apples and throw them down to us. I became good at catching… and I still am, along with ALL the family!

(The only way into the 'inner sanctum' of our family these days is to be an able 'catcher'. There is a possibly true rumour that I would throw (empty) milk bottles to the children and expect them to CATCH – which in desperation they always DID. Son Robin swears it's kosher!)

Mum and Dad did stand outside in the front of the hospital and wave to me, but I don't remember feeling homesick or lonely. I did hate the food, though. One particular meat on my plate ended up under the bed. It was a giant piece of liver – absolutely dreadful, so… I popped it out of sight under the bed, hoping that the staff would think I had gobbled it up. Unfortunately, a doctor found it shortly after – I don't think he told me off.

I returned home after about six weeks of isolation, only to go back to school and catch measles and end up very poorly again. I also contracted scarlet fever again in the next year, a rather unusual occurrence, apparently. This time I didn't go away to hospital, but a sheet soaked in Lysol (a disinfectant used a lot in those days) was hung over the door to the bedroom, and only Mum could enter. I believe children can contract a type of scarlet fever now but will have just a sore throat, probably helped by antibiotics if they are really ill, but in 1943 it was a serious illness. Mum said that after I had gone into hospital the first time with scarlet fever, two health workers arrived at 249 and proceeded to fumigate our bedroom. The chaps probably used Lysol.

FONDLY REMEMBERED RADIO PROGRAMMES

Illness wasn't all bad! A rather nice prolonged stay in the bedroom usually ensued, listening to *Children's Hour*, with 'Uncle Mac' (I think he was Derek McCullock. Only now do I feel he had a sinister voice, but in those days he was the voice of an hour of excitement.) I listened to the tales of Henry and Norman Bones, boy detectives, Larry the Lamb, with the wonderful German-accented dachshund Dennis. Strange to feature a German voice, as this was still wartime, but I loved him more than Larry, whose voice was really Uncle Mac's. There was the serial called *Ballet Shoes* introduced with the 'Jewels of the Madonna' music, which was right up my street. *The Swish of the Curtain*, *The Blue Door Venture*… all these simply wonderful radio programmes provided such happy hours. The opening music would send a tingle down my spine, and ill though I may have been, these serials lightened my day and made illness bearable.

There was another favourite programme about a cat and dog called Mompty and Peckham, *Said the Cat to the Dog*. This was introduced with the signature tune taken from William Walton's *Facade*. The very best programme for me, though, was John Masefield's *The Box of Delights*. It was the opening music that was just magical and sent my imagination on a colourful and scary journey. (The opening music was Victor Hely Hutchinson's First Noel, from his Carol Symphony – I have had to look this up). Many hours of pure bliss passed listening to the unfolding story… the Punch and Judy man, and the magic box. I was literally transported from my bedroom into a mystical land, and I can say that listening to this programme was one of the most memorable times of my childhood. The war was certainly no worry, just a part of life.

Later on, when I was allowed to stay up to the heady time of 6.45pm, every weekday there was on the wireless *Dick Barton, Special Agent*, who was ably assisted by colleagues Snowy and Jock. This was listened to by all of us, and each thrilling adventure was rarely missed… The music itself was so exciting.

I do remember another serial, either before Dick Barton, or after. It was called *The Daring Dexters* and was about a family who were in the circus business. I don't think this held us in as much suspense as did Dick and his friends.

Paul Temple, along with his wife Steve, also thrilled, and was a programme on the wireless. I do remember the name of the actress who was Steve, I think it was Marjorie Westbury, Paul may have been Kim Peacock (this is rather a lot of useless information). The signature tune to this programme was wonderfully fitting. I believe it was 'Coronation Scot', again a dragged-up piece of info: but SO evocative of the serial.

All these wireless programmes during the war, including the lunchtime one *Workers' Playtime*, must have lifted the spirits and helped people to forget what was going on around them, a welcome break, especially for the families caught up in the bombing and mayhem.

THE WARTIME HOUSEHOLD

Being so young, I really didn't appreciate what WAS going on, but brother Robin was an avid 'war-watcher'. He collected pictures of the aeroplanes and read magazines about the fighting. There were also balsa-wood models of planes hanging around in his attic bedroom, dangling from the ceiling, and maps pinned everywhere, also newspaper cuttings. Robin shared his bedroom with Tony, who was eleven years older than me. It was a rather sparse attic, with a gable window high up, but the most awful dark and frightening staircase up from the main landing to the attic. There was no light switch at the bottom of these stairs, so anyone going up there had to 'run the gauntlet' of fear until in the room.

Tony was working at Boulton & Pauls factory by this time, making parts for planes. It was a factory that was supposedly on the German bombers' 'hit list'. In fact, the Germans did try to drop a bomb on the factory, but it missed and landed in the nearby sewage works, Barnhurst (see later on in the saga). Tony never came down to the cellar or entered the air-raid shelter, apparently saying, "I would rather get killed quickly up in the attic than crushed to death under the house."

Tony loved his animals, and kept rabbits galore out in the yard in hutches. He bought two hamsters, little animals that hadn't been seen in those days. I think he owned some of the first hamsters brought over to England. We always had loads of cats, and to my shame, I can't remember any of their names. We really didn't love them as much as we do today, they were just THERE… they came and went, had copious numbers of kittens. Tony's job was to drown any that were ill, or if there were too many for mum-cat to cope with. All this (what I think of NOW as cruelty) didn't bother me. As a great animal lover, especially cats, I can only put my indifference down to… actually I can't think of anything that would excuse that… except perhaps my very young age.

Our house was built in the late 1700s/early 1800s. Dad rented it, but hearsay has it that he was offered the chance to buy it (later after the war, probably in the early fifties). The price I believe was £200 – amazing now! He didn't buy it, though, he never had the cash, although he had such a good job working for J. Arthur Rank, the film company. I'm afraid Dad squandered his earnings, leaving Mum with very little housekeeping. He also drank too much, and smoked too much. Now, all these years later, I have begun to understand him, and, I suppose, forgive him…

He suffered rheumatic fever, leaving him with a leaky heart valve, not helped by his smoking and drinking. To our shame, we children never gave him a thought. I certainly never felt any sympathy for him, I think Robin did, but Tony never got on with him. I don't remember Dad and Tony ever speaking, which is sad.

There was a final upset as far as Tony was concerned with Dad, involving money. I will try to put that down in a later chapter. Pat also was cold towards Dad. Being seven years older than me, she saw Mum trying to make ends meet So she formed her own opinions.

Our family house, always referred to as '249' by everyone (even friends and relations to this day). The house was just an end-of-terrace house, but somehow is thought of with love by all… rather strange, on reflection, considering how draughty and cold it was. The number 249 seems to be engraved on everyone's memory. Anyone who ran, danced, skipped, or just walked over the portals somehow remembers 249 as a special place.

There were no luxuries, and certainly no comfort. If, during a very frosty night, Mum put a glass of water on the bedside cabinet for night-time consumption, by morning there would be a thin coating of ice on the top. Sash-cord windows prevailed, and the windows were all criss-crossed with brown sticky tape, in case a bomb dropped nearby and shattered the glass. We had the regulation blackout curtains, a rough material, but dense, to keep the light in. Air-raid wardens would knock on the door if any light showed out into the road. Dad became an air-warden. I can't imagine it, and I certainly don't remember him in any uniform or sporting a tin helmet.

The long, front-to-back hall was covered in red lino and had to be polished regularly. This was a chore Mum hated, and she would occasionally delegate it to one of her offspring. The front door was the typical Georgian-type – no window and heavily panelled, and there was a small porch with a stained-glass inner door leading into the house.

Further down the red-linoed hall was a 'lobby', an added-on bit that joined the main house to the kitchen and scullery. This lobby was where all the bikes were parked. Because it had been (many years before) a yard, there was an ominous dip in the linoed floor where there was a water well. The round outline of it could be viewed. I NEVER stepped on this bit, just in case it suddenly opened up, swallowing me down into a dark hole. (I retain a fear of anything with water pipes and sinister dark holes. There was another well in the back garden, also a great worry!)

There was a latched door leading to a breakfast room complete with chimney breast sporting a great black-leaded grate with lots of fiddly metalwork, and two ovens. Mum didn't use those ovens, just the fire grate.

Like the lino in the hall, the grate had to be polished. That was a job we all did from time to time, as was the lino, which became a bind later in life. (Mum always thought that rubbing, scrubbing and polishing was the answer to stomach ache. Later in life, when period pains took me over, the polish came out, and I would kneel and polish away, hoping that Mum was right.)

Mum was a bit of a task-master. Robin would polish the lino, but when he had finished, having done what he THOUGHT was a good job, Mum would shake her head and polish areas of it again. Not a good move to give your children confidence and a sense of achievement, but that was Mum! Tact was not her middle name, and praise rarely left her lips.

From the breakfast room there was a scullery, very basic really. There was what I think is called a 'Belfast' sink (rather trendy in today's world), shallow and brown coloured. Being ceramic, it was chipped and stained with possibly a hundred years of use.

A latched door led to a back yard, all blue bricks and a flower border filled with Mum's hydrangeas (all stolen cuttings) and a long crumbling brick wall on one side of the garden. The garden was where so many dramas unfolded. A lovely place for playing, climbing the apple trees, and putting a cushion on a bent old damson tree, attaching reins and riding it for miles and miles in one's imagination.

Mum was the gardener extraordinaire. She loved her garden (and the garden in her little cottage later in her life, which she did until her eighties). There was a pond halfway down, just a round of concrete, about two feet deep in the middle. A great deal of fun was had in and around the pond. I can't say 'pool' because it was pretty small. Jumping across it was tried, but proved just that bit too far.

Further down the narrow path were flower beds and, at the bottom, a vegetable patch, a chicken run, with chickens in residence, and a wild area of loganberries and raspberries. It was in this overgrown part of the garden that the treasure was DEFINITELY hidden.

I longed to dig up some hidden chest, spilling over with rubies, diamonds and sapphires. I would dig for ages, not getting very far, and always hoping that my spade or trowel would hit some solid object. Friends were recruited to dig, and happy hours were spent dirty but determined. We did occasionally find something, not treasure, though.

We once uncovered a little china dog with a broken-off ear, which fitted well in into my doll's house. There was a very small Father Christmas, possibly a cake decoration, and oddly, lots of rusty bed springs! These springs strapped to the feet with string would, in theory, bounce us into the air, but in reality they were the cause of twisted ankles and disappointment.

13

We never thought about the dreaded tetanus from all the rust… Knees and shins were permanently grazed and bloodied.

Mum was a treasure seeker too, always looking for hidden 'something'. Not a lot turned up, though, but one day when she was digging by the front gate, to her joy, she unearthed a great pile of oyster shells. Not something usually found in almost the middle of England, so far from the sea, but they were treasure to Mum. She reckoned they were from centuries ago, when oysters were the food of the common man, but we were so far inland, I'm not sure Mum's idea was right? She never DID find real treasure, but the shells were a source of interest.

All this opened up an excited feeling in me for times past, particularly the Romans, and the lives of people living centuries ago. Or it could be a manifestation of a 'nosey gene' – I know I have them, dotted about, occasionally springing to the fore. Tettenhall Road was a road of note. Carriages would rattle along travelling from London to Holyhead centuries before, so it was a road with history and a great stirrer of imagination.

Robin DID find treasure in a strange way, and a very strange place. He was risking life and limb up a ladder cleaning out our front gutters, and amongst the dead leaves and twigs he found an amber and gold oval-shaped brooch, very Victorian in style. It was thought that a magpie had seen it shining and picked it up, only to drop it in the gutter. But we never found out. And I have never grown out of the hope of finding something wonderful, so I search on, rewardless.

When digging in our present garden, my spade hit metal, a tin! JOY… treasure after all these years. The box was lifted, and the rusty lid opened. Inside were two pairs of possibly Victorian spectacles. One was a kind of pince-nez. They WERE gold but a very dubious treasure. Also in the tin was an empty jar of Marmite.

Childish disappointment – no emeralds or sparkling diamonds, just a tin that some child who had lived in our house had buried, in the hope that it would lie hidden for hundreds of years. It was nice, however, to think that the previous owner of 200 Henwood Road also liked our family favourite, tasty Marmite.

There was a privet hedge all along the left-hand side of the back garden at 249, interspersed with elder trees, wild roses, lilac, and anything else that chose to grow amongst the privet. It was in this hedge that a very strange thing happened. I THINK I can recall it, but really I am relying on Mum's version of the event. I was about five, so it was still wartime, about 1943.

Over the six-foot-high red-brick wall across the bottom of our garden was the garden of a large house. This was taken over in the 1940s by the Americans for some of their troops. I have no idea why they were there or what they did. Mum's story goes that I was playing down by the pond, when there was a rustling in the hedge, and there, lo and behold, was a naked, dark-skinned man! Very startled, the supposed US soldier ran down the garden and jumped over the wall and into the garden of their billet. I vaguely remember someone running, but as for noticing his naked body, no, I definitely did not, and oddly, I can't remember feeling afraid, and I was certainly not traumatized by it or psychologically damaged! It was Mum who was shocked – she must have seen the 'happening' from the yard. Several days later, Mum found a candle, half-melted beside our outdoor loo, and she immediately jumped to the conclusion, that the US soldiers were using our lav!! It seems much more likely that Tony may have sat out there, reading girlie magazines. This was a more likely scenario than a soldier vacating his barracks, with inside lavatories, to sit in our dark cold cell of a lavatory (which incidentally never flushed, that was done with a bucket of water. Tony's reading would be manuals on aero-engineering, combustion engines or, for light relief, tales of 'Garth', a character out of a comic, a sort of superman hero, now long gone. 'Cowboy and Indian' kind of magazines, with covers depicting guns blazing, horses falling and general carnage, was more up my older brother's street – he loved all kinds of violent activity.

DOLLY MIXTURES WITH GREAT UNCLE HARRY

The food coupon business wasn't all terrible during the war. In fact, the sweet ration was good. I think it was two ounces per week. This brings me to my Great Uncle Harry.

Uncle Harry was Dad's Mum's brother, so my great uncle. I have looked him up on a census, and apparently he was a 'commercial clerk' over in West Bromwich, which is where Dad's mother Gertrude and large family were brought up. Harry's given name was Henry; however, he was just 'Harry' to us.

I think he must have lost his job, because Mum used to say he didn't work (well, not when he moved with his sister, Grandma Gertrude, and brother-in-law, Grandpa Mansel, to Chapel Ash, an area of Wolverhampton not far from 249).

I loved this old man. He would walk down to 249, I'm not sure how often, and stay for the morning. I think I must have been pre-school age. He was a tall, lean man, always in a long brown overcoat, brown trilby, and brown boots, so shiny that they looked like conkers fresh out of their shell.

When it was cold or raining and we couldn't go out, he would set up my small easel, and blackboard, find some chalk, and try to teach me to read and write. It was a help, and I entered school able to write a little. Numbers were another matter, though, and have always been beyond me.

He also liked our cats, and one morning, Blackie, one of the many cats that roamed around 249, sat on its hind legs up against the sofa, paws together in front of its face. "Look, she's praying to Jesus," he said, his sallow, very lined face breaking into a smile. A poignant simple memory and one that is very mundane, but it has stayed with me.

Great Uncle Harry also taught me to tell the time, so that when I did go to St Jude's at the age of five, I had a small head start. He was a kindly old man, and it wasn't until I grew up that Mum told me that he was a pest, landing on her to be fed as he was always out of work. I just loved his visits, though, and especially when he took me to the sweet shop, down the Tettenhall Road to what is called the Newbridge, which spanned the

Shropshire /Cheshire canal. Harry would make sure Mum had given us the coupons, little squares in a book that were torn out and handed to the shopkeeper.

The lady who kept the sweet shop was a Miss Greenfield. I think her sister (also a Miss) helped out too. Along the shelves were rows and rows of shiny glass jars, all holding the most colourful, wonderful sweeties ever imagined, AND there were Dolly Mixtures! My favourites. Miss Greenfield would take a small piece of paper and, with the speed and dexterity of a magician, twirl it into a cone-shaped bag! I can hear now the sweets as they were poured into that cone. Somehow sweets were never in short supply. I would suck each one, savouring it… but did I ever give my dear Uncle Harry one? I doubt it. Childhood is a naturally self-centred and selfish part of life, and Harry, being too much the gentleman, probably never asked for one. He had his cigarettes, his moustache was brown with the smoke, and his rather wizened cheeks were also brown from smoke.

After the sweet shop, we would make our way down towards the canal. There was (and still is) a small garden leading down to the canal. There's no towpath on the garden side, so I suppose it's quite a dangerous place. There was an iron bench in the garden, and there we would sit, me taking time choosing which sweet to pop in my mouth, and Uncle Harry rolling his cigarettes. He once showed me how to roll one, and I can see him now, licking the length of the white paper to seal it, having laid a line of tobacco along inside, never a neat shape, and sometimes a fire on the tip, rather than smoke!

Here we would sit, watching the great barge-horses pulling the boats along the canal. The horses were huge and powerful, they wore blinkers over their eyes and an array of brasses on their foreheads. There was a 'clinking' sound when they approached, as the horses moved their heads. The boats themselves were almost silent as they were pulled through the very green and dirty water. The barges were usually loaded with coal, and I suppose other goods. Just yards along the canal from the garden was the vaulted underside of the bridge, and as the horse plodded under the bridge (now led by a man), the sounds would echo eerily. The rippling water would cast light on the concrete vaults; it was all something magical to a four year old.

After watching the traffic on the canal, the next port of call would be a ruined farmhouse. A strange place, but a 'must' for reasons unknown! There were all kinds of rusty bits of machinery. Harry said one particular machine had been a cigarette dispenser (why in a farmyard I never found out). I used to turn the handle and watch all the cogged wheels turn, fascinated.

(I have asked Pat and Robin about the farm. They both remember the overgrown gardens, but the so-called cigarette dispenser was never that, just another farming 'something'.) The old gardens had bushes full of redcurrants, and Pat says that she and Robin would pick bags full of the sparkling red fruit. They would play for hours amongst the fallen bricks, rust, and jagged metal machinery. It would be out of bounds today, but somehow it was fun, and a good stir-up for the imagination, with an added bonus of some more fruit to bottle for Mum.

It wasn't until I was telling Robin about those happy days with Uncle Harry that it was pointed out that, in today's world, for a child to go off for hours, hand in hand with an old unmarried man, was suspicious, and there would be thoughts of paedophilia. Well, our days out were truly innocent, just a rather sad and lonely old man taking his little great niece out, and spending happy hours, just watching the world, and the canal, go by.

I must put down the very terrible end to Harry's life. I only found out about it recently, from a cousin, Diane, who lived for some years with our granny Gertrude in the house in Chapel Ash, Wolverhampton. Diane recounted Harry's sad end.

As Harry got even older, and his visits to 249 had stopped, he became depressed and anxious, and in fact went mad. One day, he was found wandering naked somewhere, possibly in the house or out in the road (I hope this last bit isn't true). After being brought back and settled, he then set fire to himself, possibly by accident. Perhaps he had fallen asleep with a cigarette in his mouth. Finer details of this terrible scene don't seem to exist. This was probably the last straw to his sister Gertrude and family, so he was sectioned and sent to New Cross workhouse/hospital – a terrible place in those days, by all accounts. (It's a hospital now, in fact our main one, with loads of modern buildings and a very state-of-the-art cardio-thoracic department.)

Mum said she visited Harry once. There was just a bed, a small bedside cabinet, and that was IT! His only possession was a set of shoe-cleaning brushes. Perhaps he kept his boots conker-bright until he passed away. I'm sure he would. This is a sad reflection on the world, and Harry's family and friends, if he had any, but again, it WAS wartime, and there was so much turmoil in Britain and Europe that a mad old man wasn't a priority.

At the time I was too young to hear any of this and I don't think I would have enquired after my walking companion.

WAR FOOD

I'm going back to food during the war. We were reared on Marmite, and we still eat it on toast or pop some in the beef gravy. Dinners must have been a difficult time for mothers. Somehow Mum seemed to come up with all kinds of weird and wonderful foodstuffs. One make-do meal consisted of something called 'Fritamix', a packet of dry ingredients, very like today's packet stuffing mix, herbs, bread and seasoning. Mum would pour water into the mix, fashion sausage shapes, then fry them until golden and crisp. They were all right, but nothing to shout about.

Sometimes we received food parcels from someone in Canada. These were truly delicious. There was maple syrup, tins of meat (I think corned beef), dried fruit, and I think I remember blocks of margarine. I shouldn't think it was 'real' butter as that was something we didn't have much of during the early forties.

Fresh fruit was plentiful, as we had a William pear tree, two apple trees, damsons, and soft fruit. Mum, like most women during this time, bottled anything found 'not moving' to preserve it for the winter. Even home-grown tomatoes went into a Kilner jar. Tropical fruit was non-existent. It wasn't until a couple of years later when at junior school that a classmate, Ruth, whose father was in the merchant navy, brought a BANANA into class! I don't think anyone had ever seen one in the flesh or 'peel', so to speak. We had seen them in comics (usually with a monkey hanging by one arm to a branch of banana palm). The teacher was impressed too, so she set it on a table, and the class had to draw and paint it, such was its rarity! I still have my effort today, amongst some memorabilia. I suppose Ruth must have eaten it at the end of the lesson. I was friends with her from then on, but I have never asked WHO ate that celebrity banana.

In Wolverhampton town centre, in Dudley Street, there was a shop called Winters. It was a rather tatty old shop and you had to go down some steep steps to get in. It was a strange store, selling dried fruit. I particularly remember dried locust beans, weird long black pods, with even weirder 'beans' inside. These beans were dried and SO smelly, but when eaten they tasted sweet. I think they were from the carob tree (carob being used even now as a substitute chocolate). I haven't met anyone since who has even heard of locust beans.

There was a lovely smell in Winters (apart from the locust beans!) coming from sacks of what I suppose was flour. I think they also sold pet food and chicken feed, but that may be incorrect. Somehow I can picture dog biscuits – or were they for human consumption? – as well as packets of dried peas, and I think I remember a loaf of Harvo (a kind of malt loaf) at the back of the counter, which was probably worth a strip of coupons. There were packets of dried dates and fruit to make Christmas puddings. Two old ladies served behind the counter, their hair wound into 'earphones' scraped back and round behind the ears. They always wore sensible green overall-type pinafores. There would be queues outside on the pavement, and in fact queues everywhere. Nobody minded, though; it was all part of the wartime, and everyone 'just put up with it'! I loved this shop, mainly because of the smells!

One of the mainstays in the food cupboard during those days was something called 'household milk', which came in blue and silver tins. It was just dried milk powder, but it was nice mixed with a bit of water and spooned up. Then there was powdered egg. I never liked the smell of this, but it was so useful. Mum used to make omelettes with it and also used it in cakes (Harold says HE loved it!). Meat was usually Spam. Mum sometimes fried it or used it in sandwiches, and it wasn't bad. I think it is coming back into fashion today in 2013 – amazing!

The chickens, down the garden, laid nice warm eggs and provided meat. I hate to say this, but I do remember Tony chopping the head off a white chicken, and then the poor headless body running up the backyard before collapsing. I am such an animal lover now that I can't reconcile not being hysterical on viewing this act, but I only remember it as a quirky episode of childhood! No tears shed.

Because we kept chickens (as did most households in the forties) the rat families enjoyed the leftover chicken food, so about twice a year all the family would gather around the chicken run, sticks in hand (we children in the outer circle). The rats were somehow flushed out from their holes, and then…well…beaten to death! Tony the brother with all the pets was the chief rat-basher. I even remember Dad dashing about, stick in hand, a VERY unusual occurrence.

(Dad had always just undergone a hernia operation, a bowel op or a stomach operation. He had two thirds of his stomach removed in his thirties. Mum always thought it had been cancer, but we don't know for sure. However he did suffer ill health all through his life.)

The chickens were rarely eaten. I'm not sure about the headless one, but our next-door neighbours, who shared the party wall with us, middle terrace, would give us a chicken that they had reared from a chick to adulthood, and I suppose we did the same back. There isn't anything nice about an old friendly 'chuckie' lying all crispy and steaming on a serving dish, but I expect I gobbled it up with the rest.

Medicines and remedies for aches and pains, sore throats etc. were many. Families had to pay the doctor before the NHS was set up in 1947, so home was a mass of DIY medications. One medicine Mum used for high temperatures was a terrible-tasting 'Fennings Fever Cure'. This came in clear bottle, holding a pale liquid, guaranteed to take your breath away so bitter was it! This was almost a 'hold her nose' job, when I had to have a teaspoonful. Better by far was cod liver oil and malt, which was very acceptable. The aftertaste was a bit fishy, but the malty bit was sweet and it slipped down the throat like a dream, velvety and almost as good as a treat.

There were also Meloids. These were tiny black squares, in a pocket-friendly tin. One of these sucked would soothe a sore throat. These were Mum's personal favourites. "All the best opera singers suck Meloids," she'd say, SO, definitely for us!! Another rather vague memory is of a huge bottle containing a pale pink 'emulsion' tasting of strawberries. The reason for being given this rather nice medicine escapes me, but I almost looked forward to having it – whatever medicinal properties it had, they were surpassed by the taste and the pale-pinky colour.

Chilblains were another ailment during the forties, very painful, itchy red places on the feet and hands. The remedy for these areas was 'Snow fire' rub-on stick. It was a green push-up stick like Vaseline in consistency. It's still on sale today and I have some here! No chilblains now in these warm, central-heated houses.

Constipation was high on the agenda in those days. Mum used to pop a 'Cascara' pill into her mouth most mornings. I suppose it kept her 'regular'. They were white coated with a vile middle of brown hell! I bit through one once (I never told Mum) and I didn't know where to spit it for fear that someone would see it. A strange memory is of a bottle of round shiny pink very delectable-looking pills that Mum kept on a shelf high up over our black range grate.

I often asked what they were for or WHO they were for. "Oh, they're for the chickens, they cure croup," Mum would say. I never saw her give a chicken a tablet, so it's just a tiny mystery, THE pill wasn't invented, so…?

NEIGHBOURS AND AUNTIES

The neighbours either side of 249 were great friends to me. The Greenhams (the chicken-givers) were an elderly couple with no children. Horace Greenham also worked for Boulton & Pauls aircraft factory, near home, but not alongside Tony, who was an apprentice. Horace was an engineer, possibly a pattern-maker. He was an east Londoner, and he looked like a happy garden gnome, with a big nose and pointy chin and bottle-bottom-type specs. He was a rough diamond really, and in his youth had 'bummed' around the United States of America, jumping on and off moving trains, roughing it, and getting up to... who knows? However, he must have met and fallen in love with a very well brought-up young woman, Rose, though he always called her Tita. Our family always called her Mrs Greenham, even Mum. In those days everyone was friendly and supportive but formal with names. I think they were Mr & Mrs right up to their deaths years later.

Tita was an elegant lady, her grey silky long hair loosely tied back. For some unknown reason, she would work in the kitchen dressed in a pink shiny underskirt! Tita's family were from Norfolk. I would guess that they were upper middle class, very different from Horace. Horace was a good gardener; he too had fruit trees galore. His patch was more untidy than ours. Mum would 'tut-tut' about it.

Mrs Greenham (I shall HAVE to call her that) had a VERY ancient cousin living with them, a Miss Laura Leggett. Miss Laura Leggett would appear every day to walk her Pekinese dog, wearing a coat of fox fur and boots of the button-up sort, and a brown pull-down hat with a feather stuck in the crown. I don't remember ever talking to Miss Leggett, she was a sort of shadowy furry-covered person smelling of moth-balls, who seemed to live all her days in the back bedroom.

There was a funny story that Horace told us about Miss Leggett. One day, he and Mrs Greenham had locked themselves out of the house. Miss Leggett was, as usual, in her bedroom, so Horace shouted, "LAURA, LAURA!" towards her window. No reply. He repeated, "LAURA, LAURA, are you there?" Still nothing. Eventually they somehow found a key and went in, only to be met by Miss Leggett! Apparently, she was a spiritualist and was a great believer in the 'other world'. "Oh, Horace, you'll NEVER guess. The spirits have been trying to get in touch with me… I heard them shouting 'Laura, Laura, LAURA! Are you there?' I wonder what they wanted." I don't know if they enlightened her or not.

Although I never ever spoke to Miss Leggett, I did chat a lot to the Greenhams. I realize NOW what a pest I must have been, running round to them, watching dinner preparations. There were three apprentices from Boulton & Pauls who slept in the attic and had full board, so Mrs Greenham was always cooking. Their kitchen was where I first came upon marrow seeds. Mrs Greenham always had a pile drying on the window ledge. Threading them onto cotton made a very pretty necklace to wear whilst skipping around, no doubt getting in the way of Mrs Greenham (wearing her pink rayon underslip) as she prepared dinner, silver wisps of hair escaping from two tortoiseshell combs jammed in her hair, both combs trying desperately to stop hair escaping. (I remembering thinking how strange that Mrs Greenham never got dressed in the day, but the pink slip was worn without embarrassment throughout all the meal preparation.)

Horace Greenham would never address me as Valerie, he always called me his 'little chinaman'. (Harold suggests this may have come from the fact that I was left-handed and cricketers who are left-handers are sometimes called that.)

Towards the end of the war, the Greenhams had a great niece to stay, as an evacuee from London. She was called Ann and was older than me, probably eight. (I suppose this had to be before the apprentices arrived to live in the Greenhams' attic, because Ann slept up there.) We used to bang on the attic walls in the evening to communicate, although I wasn't very keen on Ann because she was a bossy child, an only one, what we at 249 called 'posh'.

Her plummy-voiced mother visited occasionally, and once she noticed that I was eating using the fork in the right hand and knife in the left, which I know now I should have been told about before, but Mum was far too busy to bother about table procedures (this last bit doesn't seem to fit in with the Roberts' etiquette?). However, Ann's Mum didn't take it kindly, I remember feeling almost ashamed. I didn't like her, and she didn't like me either. She probably thought I was being dragged up. There's an element of truth in that.

To my horror NOW, a friend, Linda, and myself once mixed up a filthy mixture of earth, leaves, 'dead things' and water, then stirred it and popped the cocktail into a jam jar, and offered it to Ann as some sort of magic potion. Of course she didn't partake, but what were we thinking of?

Ann was also 'in love' with my brother Robin. I suppose it was her first 'crush'. She would follow him around doe-eyed, and one day she asked him to play 'doctors and nurses' with her. Robin was shy anyway, but he must have dashed for cover to avoid this ardent young lady. No, I never liked her. She had suddenly broken into an already set-up group of friends from school, neighbours, and my brother, AND she had a 'posh' VERY loud voice.

Robin became quite ill during Ann's stay with the Greenhams and Mum had to take his meals upstairs to the attic. Ann would fight everyone off, so keen was she to take the food up to her first love.

We were so glad when she returned home! We have a photo of Ann with Pat and myself, standing on top of the air-raid shelter. Pat remembers her as a 'pain'. We never enquired about her well-being afterwards.

PAT'S UNHAPPY 'HOLIDAY'

Sister Pat was a tomboy, perhaps having to compete for years with two older brothers. She was seven when I was born and, to her disgust (even to this day), she was shunted off to an aunt and uncle down in Hampshire, near the New Forest.

Uncle Stan was one of Mum's younger brothers. He was a very kindly, quiet man. I believe he was a pilot, not actually in the war, but an engineer pilot, who helped set up new gadgets for the air force. He became an air traffic controller later, after the war. His wife was Auntie Peggy to us. She was a school teacher. Pat was sent down to stay with Stan and Peggy for the week before I arrived and also for weeks afterwards. I don't think she was harmed psychologically, but she has never forgotten being almost abandoned.

Pat says that her memories of these weeks, going to a strange junior school, eating boiled fish every day, and only getting a pudding of ice cream when her dinner plate was empty, were sad ones. She disliked Peggy, who was a strict 'school ma'am' and spoke with a very strong cockney accent, which grated. (I remember that, years on, when Stan was dead, Peggy spent holidays with Stan's sister Glad, in Stourbridge. Her voice would be heard above everyone else's.)

I don't think life had been very kind to Peggy, though. Her only baby was stillborn, and the midwife who had attended her was of the old school, and told Stan to just 'bury the little one in the back garden'. This he did, but it appears so cruel nowadays, and must have left a shadow over Stan and Peggy. They were not a happy couple, and unknown to Peggy, later in life, Stan had a girlfriend, who lived with him when he was at work at Heathrow. Mum said they shared a caravan together for years. Peggy did eventually find out. Not long after that, on a very frosty morning, Stan was trying to start his car in their drive when he suffered a heart attack and died instantly.

He was the second of Mum's younger brothers to die. The other brother, Ronald Tristram, died in Germany, a few days after the war had ended, having been all through the six years. He was in a car on a German motorway when another car ran into him and he was killed. He is buried in Germany.

One very strange fact about Ron was that he was born a Roberts, but later on in life, he changed his name to Robertson, for reasons that neither Mum nor any of her sisters would divulge. We have all tried to guess what happened to make him change his surname. We even asked Auntie Glad just before she died, but all she would say was, "Wild horses wouldn't drag it out of me, dear." So we are none the wiser.

Ron's daughter Ann would dearly love to know why she was born a Robertson, not a Roberts. It must have been something terrible for Auntie Glad to keep it a secret.

HOME AND GARDEN

This bit is disputed by Robin and Pat. I do remember being very young and being thrown from one sibling to the other, across the hearth. I can't have imagined it, because the sensation was so thrilling. Knowing I was going to write this, I mentioned the 'throwing' incident recently. Both deny it!!! I have always thought that it was my very earliest memory but perhaps I am wrong… On second thoughts, NO, I am right!

One of my earliest memories of Pat is of her stringing a line across the back yard, standing on the pedals of someone's bike, and trying to take a bite out of a slice of toast smeared with Marmite. It was never very successful but lots of fun and laughs. Usually the cotton would break mid-bite, which probably saved a serious accident.

Pat was also the centre of a smoking incident… Mum grew a lot of Aaron's Rod (better known as golden rod) in the garden. It tended to take over and was everywhere. At the end of one summer, when the stalks were dry sticks (good for making wigwams big enough to sit in), Pat decided to try and 'smoke' a broken-off stick. She put it in her mouth, lit the end, inhaled, and HORRORS, a terrified earwig emerged from its home in the hollow stick and was sucked into her mouth. (Pat was also the one of us to bite into one of our loganberries, look at the half left in her hand, and declare, "There's HALF a grub in this one!" It's the old joke, but true then.)

That was the end of the smoking test, as far as I am aware, but there were other plants in the garden to try out on unsuspecting friends. Amongst the lilac in the hedge were wild roses, and in the autumn the rose hips were plentiful. Lots of fun was had by splitting open the hips revealing inside tiny seeds, protected by a fluffy substance. This fluff was a marvellous 'itching powder', very useful for pushing down people's backs. The tiny hairs in the fluff really DID irritate, and it was a game played out most autumns… to screams and sometimes tears.

The garden at 249 was a haven for children, dogs, cats and the grown-ups, particularly Mum's sisters, the aunts. The three sisters, Maud, Ve and Glad, would sit in deckchairs, faces toward the sun, shiny beads of perspiration on their brow, legs akimbo, eyes closed, a tray of tea balanced on a small table, always draped with an embroidered tray-cloth depicting crinolined ladies wearing poke bonnets and standing with a basket-worked trug over their arms. There was usually a rustic rose arch close by in most of these transfer embroideries. I have some still.

Crocheting, embroidering and knitting were all carried out during a spare minute by Mum and her sisters from Stourbridge. Rather splendid dressing-table sets of crocheted mats would appear like magic. A picture of the Victorian lady would be embroidered from a bought linen square already printed with the pattern. Tablecloths abounded, showing rings of beautifully sewn flowers, and Auntie Ve produced some absolutely fabulous 'drawn-thread' work. This was white linen or cotton with threads pulled out to make a complicated pattern. Ve was a dab hand at this. She had no children, so had more time, as did Glad, who was also childless.

Mum knitted for victory, as needs must, socks, gloves, everything. The label on Mum's wool usually said 'Motoravia'. NOW I know it was the brand name, but back in the forties I thought Motoravia was a country!

Here is a really weird memory, and quite irrelevant: I can picture Mum, arms outstretched, unravelling the hank, swaying side to side as the wool 'ran' round unwinding. Most wool came in hanks and had to be wound by hand. Either the hank would be given to someone to hold whilst the knitter made it into a ball, or, failing that, if no second person was available, an upturned chair would suffice, the hank suspended across two of the wooden legs, and hey presto!

When baby teeth are supposed to drop out, mine never did. They were an intense source of angst for all my siblings as I would go around, the loose tooth dangling out onto my lip, and my tongue would play around with the tooth, making it wobble about, inspiring a great urge in my older siblings to remove this, by hook or by crook. All sorts of ways to get these wobbly teeth out were devised by Tony, Robin and mainly Pat. One day, I was cornered and had to enter into the 'must get Val's very wobbly baby-tooth out right NOW' game, although now she denies all knowledge of it. This entailed tying a piece of cotton around my tooth, then tying the other end to the door handle and shutting the door quickly, hoping that the tooth would be yanked out! Sorry to say, it never worked, the cotton always snapped! Pat wasn't alone in this dental procedure. I can remember Tony somewhere laughing whilst I was being very dramatic crying and blubbing.

Tony could be cruel, I suppose, without realizing it. One night I was getting ready for bed and was just about to hop in, when this hand shot out from under the bed and grabbed my ankle... I was terrified and I cried. I must have done a lot of howling. Pat has said I was a bit of a 'baby' and perhaps I was.

Another bit gleaned from Pat, re my arrival at 249, was that Mum and Dad employed a young girl, a sort of child-minder/nanny. I don't remember anything of her, she left when I was still a baby, but Pat and Robin do. Mum would ask Eileen to take me out in the pram for a walk and Pat would go too. Little did Mum know, but Eileen had a boyfriend and would meet him on the lower village green in Tettenhall, leaving Pat in charge of me. So Pat would push me around erratically, shaking the pram, whilst Eileen enjoyed a kiss and cuddle with her beloved! There are lots of steep slopes on the lower green, but I don't THINK Pat would venture up there with me. I am going to ask her this after I have put this on the page, it's a possibility…

I was probably a horrible smelly, noisy usurper to my older siblings, 'bonding' wasn't invented in those days, and neither was sex! The birds and the bees were never explained or even vaguely mentioned. Babies really DID appear from under a gooseberry bush. The morning after I had made an entrance, Tony was called into the bedroom, before school. He saw a baby in Mum's arms. He had had NO idea that Mum was having a baby and he went to the window, looked out and, according to Mum, said, "There's something funny going on here." What he meant I don't know. Was he looking for the stork still lurking in the front garden? It rather beggars belief, because he was eleven years old at the time.

THE HOPPER FAMILY AT 251

The next piece is about the family who occupied the big white house, number 251 next door. They were the Hopper family. The Hopper family became part of our life in the war, and I look on these snippets of events with great fondness, and sadness too, looking back from an adult point of view.

The head of the Hopper clan was old Harold. He was an Ingleby, being father of Mrs Hopper, née Ingleby. Harold seemed extremely ancient to me, rather like a figure from the Bible. Harold had a wife, who for all the time I can remember was suffering from TB, so a special rustic-work round summer house was erected and, as far as I knew, she resided in there! The little house had a diamond-shaped stained-glass window. I never saw inside, probably because the fear of catching the dreaded TB was uppermost. I don't think anyone ever SAW Mrs Ingleby… was she even there?

It does seem, in hindsight, weird that nobody ever saw or heard the patient. I have enquired of sister Pat and my brothers… no one saw her. Mrs Ingleby was invisible.

Outside the little house, on the ground, were two lumps of beautiful blue glass that looked to me like giant precious-stone jewels. They were about half a football size. I never asked WHAT they were or why they were there. I would secretly walk a bit closer to them, and imagine they had dropped down from the sky, perhaps meteorites. I can only guess that they may have been glass residue, perhaps from a glass factory. Because they were close to the door of this quaint little rustic hospital ward I never lingered long enough to actually touch them. Mum had instilled it into all of us that you could catch TB from just breathing in germ-ridden air.

The Inglebys had a son older than Mrs Hopper, Harold Junior. He was extremely disabled, having suffered from polio as a child. His spine was crooked and a large hump protruded between his shoulders. He smiled a lot, although he had nothing to smile about. Harold Junior walked around with the aid of crutches, and swung his callipered legs, completely relying on his trusty under-the-arm crutches. He wore dark-rimmed specs and cut a very sad figure but was always cheerful.

Pat became friendly with the Hopper's younger daughter June, so went round to play. During Pat's first visit, she heard a sound on the landing and looked up into the gloom, only to see Harold standing silhouetted against a landing window, the misshapen figure silhouetted against the light. This frightened Pat, and it's a picture she always remembers as scary. All this changed when she got to know him. He was an extremely educated man, took a degree by post, being unable to travel, and he even did his air-raid warden duty, a tin hat perched jauntily on his head, above his lop-sided shoulders.

Next in line was Mr Hopper. I think he had been in the merchant navy. He certainly sported tattoos on his forearms. He was keen on growing mushrooms in what had been, years before, a coach-house. I suppose he sold them, food being short in the war. He was tall, very thin, teeth all over the place, with the odd gap where one was missing, and most of his front teeth protruding. But he was also a happy soul (I think, but I was unlikely to notice anything untoward). He hailed from Grimsby, or thereabouts. He had a long rubbery neck, and a very protruding Adam's apple, and a strong Geordie accent. His sparse hair was well Brilliantined.

Mrs Hopper was a very fat lady, who sat every day in an upstairs window sewing. She was a dressmaker, and would sometimes cut down clothes or alter the length of skirts for Mum and us girls. Her hair was always a curly mess, as though she had never put a comb through it or washed it. Mum said she noticed nit-eggs abounding in her curls. (Oh dear, I hope I haven't got that wrong?) Mrs Hopper had two daughters when they first moved in, Barbara and June, then years later, in her middle forties, she gave birth to Wendy Elizabeth.

Barbara was a blonde-haired girl, about Tony's age, very vivacious (Mum thought she was a bit 'common'). She was at Bilston Girls Grammar School, a very good school, so was not a dumb blonde, but she liked her lipstick, powder, and heart-shaped-neck dresses, with cleavage. Tony was tone deaf (the music teacher at St Jude's had told him to mime when the class sang) and he also had two left feet, but Barbara was going to rectify that!

She would run round from next door, roll up the mat in our back sitting room, put a Victor Sylvester record on the gramophone, spread out a 'Victor Sylvester' How to Ballroom Dance', a page cut out from a magazine, and off they would go, slow, slow, quick-quick, slow, matching their footsteps to the black-and-white diagrams.

I think Barbara was 'older than her years' where boys were concerned, a flirt. But very few girls dared to indulge in a serious sexual relationship in those days. The shame of having a baby outside marriage was paramount, so really it was just a friendship between Tony and Barbara (as far as I know, but Tony is gone, so I can't ever ask him, and when he WAS alive, I wouldn't have DARED to ask).

The next Hopper daughter was Pat's friend June. June was a rather beautiful girl with a long thick plait of dark hair. She was completely opposite to her older sister. I know that Pat and June made a rudimentary phone line between the houses. Two cocoa tins, and a long, long piece of string, out of one bedroom, across to the yard, and into June's room. Going to different schools (June attended the Wolverhampton Girls' High School, a prestigious school then and now) was probably why June and Pat never became close friends, but it was nice to have young people next door.

Wendy Elizabeth was a late arrival. I must have been about eight when Mrs Hopper gave birth. I shouldn't think anyone knew that she was expecting. She was a large lady and always wore an overall, so hid the evidence. Wendy was a beautiful little girl, golden haired, and the apple of her parents' eyes. In those far-off days, there was something embarrassing about older ladies having babies. It pointed to the awful fact that they must have 'done it', and as for the view that our parents EVER 'did it', this was something we couldn't ever contemplate!

One of my few memories of Dad was when he talked over the garden wall to Harold Ingleby. There was a poplar tree planted on the Hoppers' side, and the roots had lifted the ground, making a small well-trodden hillock on our side, enabling adults to see over the blue round-topped brick wall. Even Arthur was visible (so the ground over the other side must have been higher too). Under that tree was where all the chatting went on. I couldn't see over, but I would stand fascinated as great long lines of ants would use the dents and twists of the poplar's bark as motorways, it was the equivalent of the M25. Some ants were going up, and some coming down and when they met, they stopped, touched, and went on their busy way. Some ants carried their eggs, I don't know where they were taking them. I think now that the ants were busy collecting the honey-dew secreted by greenfly in the poplar leaves above.

In that part of the border were some self-sown buddleia trees, with pale purple heavily scented spikes frequented by butterflies. This area of garden was where Dad and Harold would discuss the war, politics, and the weather. Probably politics was always high on Dad's agenda.

Mum also used this raised area to chat to Mrs Hopper. A lot of their talk was mouthed or whispered so that I couldn't hear. "Little elephants have big ears," Mrs H remarked once.

The most embarrassing event I witnessed was Mum (who I viewed as old and pure as the driven snow) showing a lipstick off to Mrs Hopper. I DID manage a glimpse as Mum wound the lipstick up – two small 'doors' slid open, and the red phallus-shaped lipstick emerged. There were hoots of laughter and, although I didn't know what it meant, I knew the laughter was over something naughty, and terribly rude, so of course I have remembered it.

That wall was to figure so much in these years. I would be hoisted over it, we all would sit astride it, amongst the pear tree's branches which hung low over the wall. These branches enabled us to climb up and onto the half-moon blue-brick coping stones, then jump down into the Hoppers…

When Wendy Elizabeth arrived on the scene, her Mum would 'post' her over the wall, something that Mum wasn't too keen on, because it became a daily 'post'. Wendy called Mum 'Lally' and would call from behind the wall, "Lally, Lally, can I come over?"

Mum would oblige, and I would be made to play with Wendy, inventing games, pretending the butterflies were fairies (Wendy soon sussed THAT). We would dance around (by now I was aged about nine and still hoping to be the next Pavlova).

Fairies were very much part of my life from a toddler up until the seven-year-old realization! Silly though it sounds, I still have a very special place for them. I think Pat was the first to tell me about the fairies who lived all around the garden. For some reason, fairies had to have a bath!. The metal tops off milk bottles made ideal baths for the little people. So, most days I would carefully carry the tops down the garden, balancing a drop of water in them. Then, finding a suitable place amongst the flowers, they would be lowered into position. Failing milk-bottle tops, the lupin leaves had a wonderful dip in the middle, which usually held a drop of golden dew, so made a natural bath. The dew drops on lupins still thrill. I can't pass without peering to see the tiny diamond droplets and, daft though it sounds, I still feel that the fairies ARE there.

The family will probably have me sectioned (quite right too).

GEORGE MASON, GROCER, AND FRIENDS

One rather nice memory was of George Mason's, a grocery shop in Chapel Ash, a mile or so away from 249. I often went with Mum when she went there to order her weekly groceries. There was always a nice smoky-bacony smell in there. The floor was black and white tiles, and there was a high stool by the counter. I used to climb up onto it and sit there watching.

There was the butter counter, always a lady on that. She would have a great block of butter, take a bit off with a wooden spatula then pat it into shape. Then, when it was the right weight and shape, she would deftly wrap it up in greaseproof paper. Next along the counter was the 'bacon-man'. He was a small ugly man, with greasy hair, and always chewing a bit of fat or gristle off the side of bacon. I thought him horrible. He would swap the fat from side to side of his mouth, masticating for victory! He had a meat slicer, a great round red-rimmed wheel, that would slice off a piece as thin as you wanted, "What number do you want, Mrs Lloyd-Davies?" (chew-chew-chew!). Rashers would peel off the wheel and he'd catch them onto a greaseproof sheet. Sometimes thin, sometimes thick, whatever Mum needed it for. There must have been rationing still, but Mum did seem to be able to get some 'best butter' and a rasher or two of bacon.

The best part of Mason's was the overhead wires, with screw-top metal containers attached. These would be opened and the cash put inside, with a folded-up bill, then a handle was pulled and they whizzed up and along the wires high up into a window where a lady sat. She would open the container, pop the correct change into the little container, and whizzzzz, back it came down the wire to the assistant, who would duly open it and hand Mum her change! (Sadly, it closed in the fifties; another chunk of domestic history gone.)

Mum had her main groceries delivered from Mason's. I think a young lad brought them, an 'errand boy'. He would arrive on his trusty bike, an advert for Mason's under the crossbar. I loved unwrapping the cardboard box full of goodies, especially just before Christmas, when there would be dried fruit, to be used in the Christmas pudding or cake. The sugar arrived in blue bags, plain, with no maker's name on them.

Once I remember Mum had splashed out and bought a Battenberg cake. I'm not sure if this memory is from the war days or after, but the pink and cream squares, wrapped in a coat of marzipan was a big treat whenever it was! Whilst on about food, I must say Mum could make a really tip-top rice pudding – always in an enamel dish, with lots of brown skin around the edges, which provoked fights over who was going to scrape the dish, and get the brown bits off. The skin was golden, and that caused another fight, everyone loving its creamy caramel-like taste. Maude was 'Queen Cook' when it came to rice pud!

Meat was rationed, which curtailed the eating of much meat, but when we did have a joint, it would be beef. Mum had a pantry off the lobby where she put all her perishables into a meat-safe, a wire-fronted box. The meat would reside in there. Then, always on a Sunday, we would have roast. One Sunday, Mum lifted the joint from the safe but, unfortunately, a bluebottle fly must have found it prior to it being placed in the safe (perhaps at the butcher's) and had laid its eggs all over the meat. The eggs had hatched and were now big fat juicy maggots wriggling all over the meat. Without turning a hair, Mum washed the meat thoroughly swished the maggots down the drain, and we all sat down to a nice beef dinner. Food was too scarce to let a few maggots spoil our meal.

I loved my friends, usually classmates. I had a friend called Jane, who was a sturdy girl, but she too was happy to dance the summer away. We'd make crepe-paper dresses and stage rather tame, short plays/ballets, mostly in Jane's back garden to an audience of two, her mother and her little brother.

Jane's mother made all Jane's dresses. Her third bedroom was a sewing room, and whenever I played round at Jane's, her mother would be rattling away on the treadle machine, running up garments. Her mother made a white frothy tutu for Jane, who was attending ballet classes. I thought the tutu was out of this world! Jane's Dad was a bank manager somewhere in Wolverhampton. He was a tall homburg-hatted man, not a bit like my Dad, and I was a bit frightened of him. One day, whilst Jane sat doing a wee on their outside loo, I was also in with her, but had shinned up the wall, feet on one side, bottom against the other. I had managed to get almost to the ceiling. The door was wide open.

Her father must have arrived home from work. He came into the back porch, looked up at me, perched head against the ceiling, chatting to Jane as she sat contentedly weeing down below. "Get down!" he shouted (he might as well have added "you little guttersnipe" because THAT is what I felt like, almost dirty). "Look, you must NEVER do THAT again," he said. "I'm surprised at you, Jane," he added. Jane was red-faced and tearful. I have always remembered this ridiculous telling-off. Was it for the climbing or the fact we were in the lavatory together?

Jane's house had a lovely big walled garden, bigger than 249's, with a swing. We would swing ridiculously high then jump off at high speed. This was a great game, except when one day we landed in the middle of Jane's father's delphiniums. I didn't stay long enough to hear another telling-off by her sombre putty-faced father.

Jane and her family left Wolverhampton, her father having been moved on to manage another bank in Nottingham. I wrote to Jane a couple of times, and she wrote back, but it didn't last, and we lost contact, but her Mum did give me Jane's beautiful tutu.

STRANGE NEIGHBOURS

Getting back to neighbours. On the other side of the Hoppers' large semi were two maiden ladies, the Misses Dace. I don't know the background to these ladies, but Mum and the family always hinted that they were strange – a 'bit loopy'. Completely doolally tap, said Dad.

One day, I looked out of the front bedroom window and saw one of the sisters walking up the middle of the Tettenhall Road, a basket on her head!! The handle was under her chin. The road today is so busy she would have been run over immediately, but there was very little traffic then, nobody had a car – if you DID own a vehicle, you were 'somebody of wealth'. So she continued her crazed walk. It wasn't raining. In fact, it was the summer.

Nobody had anything to do with the sisters, which is a shame, so they went on living in their large house, never having a visitor or talking to neighbours. Years later, when the last sister died, the house was entered (I'm not sure who had that task). All the interior doors had been hacked to pieces and chaos reigned throughout the house. Neighbours had heard loud arguments in the past, but WHAT had happened to these lonely old ladies?

There had been a rumour that one of the sisters had attacked the other with an axe. That was thought of as an exaggerated tale, but it set the neighbours wondering. I suppose these days, social services would have been informed. It's a sad little story.

Next but one to the Misses Dace were two sisters, the Misses Hill. Margaret was the sister I remember. She was thin and tall for those days. She leant forward when walking and looked almost translucent. It looked possible for a gust of wind to snap her in two, so fragile did she look. The sisters were daughters of a vicar, extremely religious ladies, and very much the epitome of what was thought of as 'spinsters', always wearing grey, long coats, almost to the ankle, and never seen without hats and gloves. Their hats were also grey, with a hint of net around the brim, and for some reason, I remember them always carrying an umbrella.

Both sisters particularly seemed to walk everywhere. Margaret, who had splayed feet, rather large for her frail figure, always wore 'sensible' black low-heeled, rather masculine-looking shoes. They never attended the local church, St Jude's, but preferred the main church in the town centre, St Peter's, a 'high church', compared to our local church (St Jude's being rather 'low church' bordering on Methodist).

I don't think they ever mixed with their neighbours, except to wave a gloved hand in passing. But later in my life, when I was about twelve, Margaret's sister died, and Mum was asked if I could go round and stay a night or so with Margaret, just to keep her company. So, I was dispatched forthwith. I rang the bell with foreboding. I was shown 'my' bedroom, a large room with a window looking out onto Tettenhall Road, so I didn't feel too far from 249. Friendly trolleybuses passed by, and the odd car. The bed was a double one and looked rather lumpy to me.

"Now, dear, this is what we have to do." Saying this, my host took hold of the mattress. "Get the other side. We have to shake it. It's feathers, so we have to do this."

So we shook it and pummelled it until it looked almost level. It was hard work.

"Thank you, dear. I hope you have a nice comfortable night's sleep. It's a good bed, it was my sister's." Then on her way out of the door, she turned. "She died in it."

Well, what could anyone do except get in, pull the counterpane up, and hope that the sister didn't come back down from heaven to see who was in HER bed! A touch of the Goldilocks tale, but with a grotesque storyline! I slept all right – no ghostly figures – in fact, a pretty normal night, quieter than at 249.

Next morning I was wandering around on the landing, looking for the bathroom, when Margaret appeared. She escorted me to the small room with a very ancient bath and a small wash basin. There were three white-crazed tiles behind the basin splash-backs.

Margaret put the plug in the bowl and handed me a very small piece of soap. In a half-whisper, she said, "Now, dear, please don't splash any water on to the tiles when you are washing."

I was astonished, at home we splashed around not even noticing tiles. Bubbles would burst on the wall, and the soap was sometimes left in the water and scum around the bowl. This was truly weird, but I duly washed my hands and face with precision.

Breakfast was another eye-opener. A table laid, with crocheted doilies and willow-pattern dishes. There were a few cornflakes in my dish, no sugar anywhere, and the tiniest milk jug, doll's size. So I crunched away on the dry flakes, feeling embarrassed in case I was eating too noisily.

Later, she showed me a very old brown photo of her family home. This was a large ivy-covered vicarage. Outside was a horse and an open carriage.

A forbidding-looking man, presumably her father, wearing clerical garb and two fair-haired girls were all sitting bolt upright and unsmiling in the carriage. The girls were Margaret and her sister, but I couldn't relate this elderly grey lady to the photo of the young teenage girl. Somehow I didn't think she had ever been young!

I think I must have stayed only one night. I do remember scuttling back up to 249, so glad to be home. I did relate the night to Mum and family but it was an experience that just didn't startle any of the listeners at 249. Mum would probably have answered, "Well, well, well, … I never did!" or "Fancy that!" My siblings probably thought I had exaggerated my short stay.

Margaret Hill lived on for many years, and came to St Jude's church to see me get married. During her long life, she probably never did anything underhand or made anyone unhappy. She was true to her beliefs, and I remember her as a gentle soul, very unworldly, an Edwardian maiden lady to the end.

In the last of our three houses, the other 'end' terraced one, there lived a single daughter, Miss Bradshaw, and her elderly mother. Again, nobody would dream of using their forenames, they were always 'Miss Bradshaw and mother'. Now they DID have a car. I don't remember it, but Robin does. Miss B would take her mother for a run now and then. The Bradshaw family actually owned the Greenhams' and our house, so they must have been comfortably off. Mum paid the rent to them.

I would sneak into their garden by walking through the Greenhams' garden. I was intent on picking up some fruit fallen from the trees, but I never did… I was so scared I would make a dash back empty-handed.

(Years later with friend Barbara, we DID scrump some fruit, AND creep up some stairs leading up from the coach-house/garage into a billiards room, complete with paintings of horses and horse racing in the manner of Stubbs – they could have been originals, we would never have known. However, we never stayed long enough to get close, but they were probably prints, Miss B wasn't THAT wealthy.)

I never did get to see her mother, but she was there somewhere.

So these people were our neighbours during the war and for years after.

Neither Mum nor Mrs Hopper went out to work, and the Mrs Greenham probably had never HAD to work, so all the ladies were at home. Arthur Ingleby was unable to be employed, he was too disabled, so had the opportunity to study, and this he did.

My Dad Cliff was home in the morning but gone by lunchtime. Being a cinema manager, he was still busy. I don't think the cinemas shut, even during a raid. He arrived home about 11pm, or after, so I saw more of our neighbours than I did of Dad.

I do have one rather poignant memory, which I haven't told anyone in the family, partly because Dad was rather vilified by Mum, and of course we children picked up the negative view of our father, mainly because of his drinking and his largesse to friends, and lack of interest in his family as well as his inability to hand over any money to Mum, even though he had a very good salary from J Arthur.

DAD: A MEMORY

Now I will talk about Dad and some shared times together. Just some small events but they were memorable and rare. Dad was never at home at weekends. Sunday opening at the Gaumont had started in the late nineteen thirties, so time with him was precious. This is one happy memory of a very elusive father. It's a very simple incident, and to a child who has a father who is part of their life, as opposed to Dad who couldn't be with us in the day or at weekends, it's trivial, but it stays with me as a nice side of Dad.

We were in the garden at 249, I think on the path, by the pond. Dad was holding my hand. I was probably about three or four. He turned to me and sang, "You are my sunshine, my only sunshine. You make happy, when skies are grey. You'll never know, dear, how much I love you, so please don't take that sunshine away."

If I had to take a special memory to a desert island, THAT would be IT.

Another memory is of Dad taking me to Billy Smart's Circus. Dad seemed to know the man who kept the little Shetland ponies. We went 'behind the scenes' where Dad's friend was polishing the pony's hooves with a kind of varnish, not polish. Oh JOY... I was handed a paint brush and painted away. The little ponies stood very still. I suppose they were so used to being 'made-up' for their performance.

There were clowns running around, blowing bugles and sitting in a yellow-painted car, their faces grotesque. I decided I hated clowns. Frightening! I still feel the same.

Small memories, but ones that are forever with me. Rare moments, as Dad was an absentee most of my life, so an afternoon out with him was a treat.

A LITTLE NIGHT MUSIC

Mum's taste in music wasn't too wide, but she did have her favourites. She loved someone called 'Hutch', a coloured man, who sang and played the piano. He was her heart-throb.

She also loved Turner and Leighton, two artistes. One of them sang and the other sang and played the piano. Mum seemed to know a lot about them, and I think she had been to the Hippodrome theatre in Wolverhampton when Dad was a manager there in the late twenties and had seen them in the 'flesh'. One of the duo had a withered hand (or so Mum said) so perhaps he was the main singer. Gossip had it that one of the artistes eventually eloped with the other's wife, so that brought their partnership to an abrupt end.

I think the Ink Spots, three coloured entertainers, were also very popular with Mum too. Years on, when Dad had left the Hippodrome, he took Mum and Auntie Ve to see Louis Armstrong live. Dad had booked seats in the front row, probably free, as he knew the manager well. Apparently, Louis opened up, trumpet blaring, very loudly, and for some reason Mum felt faint with the 'noise' so had to leave with Ve in tow. So that was a damp squib!

I must mention the operetta the *Desert Song*. This was Mum's 'escape' music. I think she imagined being picked up off the sand by the Red Shadow, thrown onto his horse, and whisked off into the sunset. Definitely her favourite. There was a singer called John Hanson. Mum had a bit of a crush on him, I think. He was appearing as the Red Shadow at the Grand Theatre in Wolverhampton in the 1950s. Dad secured two of the best seats in the dress circle for Mum and me. We had eaten some crab for tea prior to the show, and I became ill with the most terrible pain in my stomach during the second act. I knew Mum would be so disappointed if we left, so I endured the stomach cramps and soldiered on. I made it to the end, but the trolleybus journey home to 249 was a nightmare. Apparently, I had become intolerant to shellfish, which is still with me now.

Our very cold front room was only used for playing on the mini snooker table or playing records and, later, cards and Roulette, and the piano.

We had a wind-up gramophone in the hallowed (loosely named) dining room. The gramophone was a thing of beauty. The wood shone like a newly opened conker. Inside there were needles that had to be changed after a few records, and two little doors at the front, which would be opened to let the sound out. Dad had an endless supply of records, where from, I don't know. The make of this wonderful machine was His Master's Voice, so there was their never-forgotten logo, a terrier dog sitting listening intently to his master's voice. We all loved the gramophone.

The 'Laughing Policeman' was one of the records played regularly, and another which had the punchline, 'Suzzanna's a funniful man then snorts of a pig', a daft song, but one that made us laugh.

We also listened to dance music, Victor Sylvester, for ballroom practice. Then there was 'Whispering Somebody Smith', singing soft and low, and all sorts of popular music of that era... Oh and I nearly forgot, 'When Father Papered the Parlour'. These will be consigned to the old music-hall now, along with 'Knees up, Mother Brown'. So we were well off for music of all kinds.

When Mum eventually moved from 249, the great pile of records SHOULD have moved with her, but somehow they have been lost, and nobody in the family can recall them being given away – a small mystery.

Some very different and frightening kinds of noises from those war days were the planes going over at night. I learnt to distinguish the enemy planes, by the 'hum-hum' of their engines. "That's not one of OURS," Mum would say, peeping carefully through a crack in the blackout curtains. I still feel a chill when I am in bed and I hear a plane. The sound of the German planes and the British ones WAS different. The tone of the enemy planes' engines was a sinister drumming, a fearful sound.

One incident that a friend of Tony's related was that he was walking home from school one afternoon, when a very low plane flew over. It was so low that Mike could see the pilot in his cockpit. Suddenly, Mike realized it was a German fighter plane, so he shook his fist at the pilot. This sounds so ridiculous these days!

Another sighting of an enemy plane was when Mum and all of us were on a walk (I was in the pram, I think, and even Dad was with us, so Mum recalled). They had stopped out somewhere about a mile or so from home, when they heard the drumming sound of the engines of German planes. They stood by a gate and watched as the pilot dropped some bombs about half a mile away, probably hoping to hit the nearby factory. (Most unfortunate for the German pilot, but very fortunate for the factory, the bombs landed on a sewage farm, missing their target.)

The supposed target factory was in fact where Tony worked, Boulton & Pauls. It was a very important factory, making either parts for planes or even the whole flying machine. I'm not sure, but it WAS probably high on the Germans' bombing schedule. So sewage saved a lot of destruction and possible loss of life, including a very young apprentice, Tony.

Barrage balloons were interesting, floating above their connecting wires hoping to stop the German pilots flying too low. These balloons were made from silver material, and when one of these monster balloons burst, bits of shiny silver material landed in gardens, and our garden was no exception. I don't think we did anything useful with the bits, but I loved picking them up and feeling them – very exciting.

We didn't have a stray parachutist land near Tettenhall, but recently, a friend who knows I am writing this told me of her family, out in the wilds of North Staffordshire. Her father was a gamekeeper on a big estate. One day whilst walking around in a field looking for rabbits to shoot (great food at this time, Mum could make a rabbit go ten ways, as could most housewives), her father discovered a lone parachute, draped over some bushes, with no body or parachutist to be seen.

He should have alerted the Home Guard or police as an enemy parachutist was on the loose somewhere close by. But the canopy of the chute was made of silk, so within minutes of being told of his find, the silk had gone! There must have been quite a few ladies trotting around in their silk undies near Little Hayward village from that lucky find.

Whilst on the subject of material, I must mention the toilet paper, or lack of it. There wasn't any tissue available, so households had to make do with newspaper. Many a happy hour was spent cutting squares from the *Express & Star* local paper, or, heaven forbid NOW, also a rather risqué paper, the *News of the World*, Dad's favourite paper. These squares were then threaded on a string, the string made into a circle, and deposited over a nail, beside the lavatory. We certainly are spoilt these days with the wonderful scented, soft loo roll.

Newspaper was a very useful thing. My Auntie Vera showed me how to twist newspaper into a tight 'ropes' then tuck the ends into each other, making a ring, Hey presto! Firelighters.

Toilet soap was a luxury. Most soap was an oblong-shaped, yellow and greasy-looking common soap. All cleaning jobs would be done using this. An old lady we knew made her own, using some potentially dangerous chemicals. She survived and her skin looked less lined than her peers. I can't remember which chemical she used, but she would shape the bars by pouring the liquid mix into long containers, letting them set, usually in an outhouse, then, when out of their tins, she had usable soap! (We bought ours from Mason's grocery store. Housewives could get a bar of 'common soap'. I think it had to be cut into manageable pieces.) I do remember Mum rubbing the grime from shirt collars using it. There was also the bright red Lifebuoy toilet soap, which was very clinical smelling.

We thought its antiseptic properties held off the dreaded scabby impetigo or the neck boils that abounded in those days. The bars had an imprint of a little nappy-wearing baby striding across the soap.

It sounds silly now, but newspaper became multi-purpose. It made party hats, aeroplanes, boats. It lit fires and wrapped fish and chips… So newspaper was a valuable commodity. Of course, it could also be read.

No. 249 helped with the war effort regarding metal. There had been some metal railings across the front of the garden, next to the pavement. I never saw them, but the sawn-off bits were still there. They were taken, possibly to make bombs, tanks or some item in the war-machine. I don't think the householder was told; they had no choice anyway. So one morning Mum awoke to a clearer view of the main road, and at least we had added something to help Churchill win the war.

Robin or Dad occasionally had a *Picture Post* magazine. I was lucky, I could peruse all the pictures when everyone was either at school or work. One photograph has stayed in my mind ever since seeing it. It was a black-and-white photo of a row of coffins, all laid out in a school dining hall, in a school somewhere 'down south'. A bomb had dropped on the girls' school, killing dozens of children. Up until then, I don't think I had any concept of what was going on outside the walls of 249. The starkness of this photograph suddenly made me feel afraid, and I couldn't stop thinking of it. These memories are etched in the brain, so terrible were they.

ST JUDE'S SCHOOL

I started at St Jude's C of E school in the September after I was five years old. Unlike today's children, I hadn't been to any nursery school or playgroup. I don't suppose there were any here in Wolverhampton.

My first teacher was a Mrs Brown, a rotund roly-poly lady, very homely and motherly. The obligatory gas mask had to be with us at all times. I kept mine on the strap across my navy gymslip. We were allowed to play outside in the playground, and I think we had to keep the gas mask close, even during play, just in case a bomb fell on OUR school, as I had seen in that memorable photograph. There was an air-raid shelter on the playground. It was brick built, with benches down either side. Every now and then, there would be an air-raid practice and all the children had to walk in a crocodile across to the shelter. I think we were made to put the gas masks on, just to get the hang of it. I don't think a siren ever went off whilst I was at school.

The headmaster, Mr Welsh, was a very religious man, and a bit of a bigot too. The fact that my Dad was anything to do with 'show business' was definitely a blight on me. Pat and Robin echo these feelings. They too had gone to St Jude's and had been rather stigmatised because Dad was in the cinema business. (Pat did, however, play with Mr Welsh's daughter Pauline, so perhaps Mrs Welsh was more liberal.)

Assembly was every morning in the 'big' hall. On Fridays, as a special treat, Mr Welsh would wind up the gramophone and put on a record. The music was usually Handel's Largo, hymns, and religious music. However, one Friday morning, Mr Welsh announced that one of us children could make a request for a record to be played the next Friday and he would find it from his record collection.

"So, children, what music would you like me to play next week?" Hands shot up. "Right, YOU in the second row, stand up. What is your request, girl?" A small figure stood up. "Please, sir, can we have 'The Dickey-Birds Hop'?" Even at my young age, I knew that THIS wasn't the sort of music he meant. There was silence as the girl sat down. Mr Welsh pulled himself up and faced us. Oddly, there wasn't the rage on his face that I had imagined. "Well, we'll have to see if I have THAT particular record. Now, children, we'll have prayer for all those fighting abroad." Mr strict old Welsh hadn't turned a hair! Nobody could wait for next Friday's assembly. We filed in, had the hymns and the prayers, also the usual religious pep-talk… then…

Miraculously, came the rather crackly sound of the well-known voice, and YES, sure enough, the rather tinny tones of 'The Dickey-Birds Hop' rang out across the astonished school! Wonders never cease! So perhaps Mr Welsh did have some humanity in him after all, although in later years at the school, I had a job to find any.

It was about this time in my life, aged about five or six, that I wrote a little book. I remember sitting up in bed with some lined paper, a pencil and a few crayons. I must have heard on *Children's Hour*, or read something about a mysterious house and I carefully wrote a very 'unmysterious' story about two children visiting a house where all the furniture moved and talked. Perhaps it was after a dream or nightmare. I folded it and drew and coloured in a house on the front cover. I 'illustrated' a few pages inside, all on lined paper, and took it in to Mum and Dad, who were reading the Sunday papers in bed. I think Mum was quite pleased with my efforts because she sewed the spine with cotton stitches and said I should put a rhyme on the back.

I have the book now, and the rhyme on the last page was probably all thought up by Mum, who was a dab hand at poetry and verse. Mum must have kept this little booklet safe for all these years. I never thought she was all that proud of me, but perhaps she was on this occasion.

Back to the lavatory paper now. Just inside the classroom doors there was a hook, and on this hook was a loo roll with 'proper' paper (Bronco?). The drawback was that when a child wanted to go to the lav they had to put their hand up, "Please, teacher, can I leave the room?" If the answer was 'yes' THEN, depending on whether you were going for a number one or a number two, you could pull a piece of paper off the roll and proceed outside to the open-roofed lavatories situated in the playground. This threw me into a "I will never 'go' at school" frame of mind. There was always one child who didn't flinch when pulling off that sheet of paper, but I was not that child, and never would be through all the years at school. (This has probably had a serious lifetime effect on my bowels.) So, rather than take the paper in front of the class, I would only wee. But if I seriously HAD to do a number two, I remember using the dead leaves lying around in the damp and leaf-filled cubicles.

Later in life, a friend who was at school with me admitted that she had done the same! (This would be a big problem if Mum had given me a dose of syrup of figs the night before, a regular cure for constipation for all the family.) Bowels were, and are, a big problem to me, probably starting with the lack of loo paper or the embarrassment of the classroom paper. Mum was a bit manic about lavatories, and would make sure we NEVER touched the seat in a public loo. Balancing was an art. If you touched a strange seat, you might "catch something". Mum's warning voice would be ever present (for life!). I had no idea WHAT we might catch, but it made life very difficult at times. I was seven or eight when Mum's word 'numbatoos' became number 2s! Mum never said number ones, so I thought for years that 'numbatoo' was one condensed word! How ridiculous, looking back, but not a lot was spoken about bodily functions. Everything to do with the body was either whispered or silently nodded about. A serious illness such as cancer was NEVER spoken about, the word was not used (if we even knew it). Relations just died, and when asked 'of what' or given certain symptoms, the adults would just raise an eyebrow and nod conspiratorially between themselves.

Giving birth was also a very taboo subject. There would be lots of mouthing of silent words, and "Oh dear" and "tut-tuts". Of course, the way babies were started was even more of a grown-up secret, and even the words 'district nurse' or 'midwife' would be said in a half-whisper. The word 'sex' was never NEVER used! Anyway, what WAS sex? We knew nothing about the birds and the bees but, looking back, we were none the worse for it. I think the fear of getting pregnant and 'letting the family down' was uppermost in the minds of most teenage girls at that time.

I was seven when the war was finally over.

POST-WAR LIFE AND MICKEY

I remember Pat almost carrying me through the crowds thronging in the road. The streamers and balloons were there in force. Otherwise, I can honestly say I never felt relief, happiness, or any of the grown-ups' emotions.

We were lucky as we hadn't really been involved in bombing raids, as in Coventry or London. And I hadn't seen any horrors (except that photograph in the magazine), though I had felt fear when the planes were not 'ours'. There were funny episodes, and sad ones, like when a pet died, but otherwise the war years were a mixture of events, most of them tripped lightly through by a small child whose world revolved around herself, with an occasional nasty intrusion caused by the war, a war I knew nothing about, except that 'Germans were baddies'. So, I don't have memories of elation or happiness that the war was over. Those years were a mixture of muddled emotions, happiness, fear. But I certainly don't think it touched us too much as a family. I suppose in today's world we would be called a dysfunctional family, and life certainly had its harrowing moments. But Pat thinks differently. She reckons we are ALL psychological cripples.

There is SOME truth in that.

People in the 1940s, although kindly, were not inclined to show great emotion, or at least not in public. So there was not much kissing; linking arms was the mode for ladies, or a peck on the cheek for relations returning after a long absence, and even that greeting was a slightly awkward affair. Stiff upper lips had something to do with the lack of obvious emotion; the word 'tactile' wasn't the order of the day.

Mum and Dad rarely appeared together, Dad being out all evening at the cinema. I suppose they did sometimes sit down together, perhaps after I went to school in the morning. I do remember, strange as it seems to me now, Mum actually kissing Dad goodbye in the hall, just once! They were normally at loggerheads, so that intimacy was almost peculiar, and noted by me.

Dad was a great and generous friend to his 'cronies', as Mum would call them, but a very errant father and husband. Even Christmas was 'fatherless' as Dad would strut his stuff in the local hospital, the Royal, giving out toys, books and all kinds of presents to the ill children who had to stay in hospital for Christmas. Dad also supported the Limes, a convalescent hospital for children who had TB. The cinema collected money for the hospital children's appeal and I believe that Dad dressed as Father Christmas on some occasions.

I have just found some newspaper cuttings, and there's an obituary for Dad. Stating (along with a lot of other facts about his life): "L D WOULD SOMETIMES DRESS AS FATHER CHRISTMAS, AND VISIT THE CHILDREN'S WARDS AT THE ROYAL HOSPITAL. ALSO L D WOULD DISTRIBUTE GIFTS TO THE LIMES SANATORIUM."

We children were not neglected present-wise. Somehow, Mum managed to produce some exciting presents. When the war was over, she made Christmas puds (complete with sixpences inside). I loved stirring and tasting the uncooked mixture. There was always a wonderful tree, decorated with strings of glass and silver balls, which, when unravelled, exposed some scraps of Chinese newspaper, and also shiny silver birds, bouncing on metal springs sporting shiny hairs of glass for tails, all magic!

One Christmas in particular really shone for me, however. After opening my stocking, still in pyjamas, I went into our back room to see if there were any more presents there. Mum was already in the room, standing by the Christmas tree. Under the tree was a cardboard box. It was moving. I pulled the flap up, and there was a tiny black puppy! This is where Dad seemed to score – he had heard of a puppy going for free, so he had secured this dear little thing. Where he got it from, or how, I never bothered to ask – I had my very OWN dog. That dog, who we called Mickey, became my dearest companion and friend, and he was MINE.

During this time, my brother Tony had been 'called up' to do his National Service. He was first sent to Ireland, somewhere near the mountains of Mourne, probably where they 'swept down to the sea'. So Tony missed the arrival of Mickey. When he came home on leave, there was this little Labrador-cross spaniel dog ensconced in the household. I don't know why, but although he was an animal lover, Tony never spoke kindly to Mickey, calling him 'a yellow-bellied, lily-livered hound' and much worse! I suppose he was fed up. I think he had wanted a dog of his own and had never been allowed one. That might be the reason, but it always hurt me greatly, and I didn't like my big brother. (It took me perhaps forty years to understand him. He was a very complex man, unforgiving of Dad, and often saying derogatory things to Robin by calling him 'Rabbit', seemingly to put his younger brother down.)

To Pat, who was very feisty, he was more tolerant and respectful; he had more than met his match. Pat said only the other day that one day she had had enough of Tony's bad language, so she got up from the table and tipped his dinner over his head – plate, gravy and all! He looked surprised through the gravy, but took it well. Tony's language could be ripe when rattled, but I think he was startled and lost for words, even his usual German swearwords were not said. Pat said it was so GOOD! She never let Tony get the better of her. Pat was the bravest of us all.

After training in Ireland, Tony was posted to Palestine. He joined the unit that tested motorbikes, which was right up his street. All his life Tony loved messing about with motor engines. He and a friend Mike made a primitive car in later years. I was taken out in it once, down Tettenhall Road. The floor of the car was my old blackboard, and there were no seats, just a cushion, so the road surface could be viewed passing by under the floor. There was no vehicle testing or MOTs in those days, just the open road. Tony loved speed (not that the little home-made car went fast). So the roaring across the desert must have been manna from heaven. Also, he had, at last, a dog! A small mongrel was found by his colleagues all caught up in some barbed wire. This unnamed dog became Tony's 'mate' and would zoom around on the petrol tank of the motorbikes, enjoying a lot of fuss and love. We have photos of the two of them, dog between Tony's legs on the tank, both looking happy! What happened to this little dog, I don't know. I think Tony told me that he/she had a sad end, but I'm not sure. Tony may have made the demise up to upset me. Sometimes his thinking was disturbed. That was my troubled brother.

When he was home from Palestine once, I heard something that was, to me then, so terrible: Tony was in the kitchen distributing little gifts from his travels, and I was just within earshot. "Well, there's one thing I learnt whilst in the Middle East… and that's I DON'T BELIEVE IN JESUS OR THE BIBLE! I went to Bethlehem, and it was all just a tourist place, with a star on the floor where they SAID Jesus was born. IT'S ALL A STORY."

I was shocked and thought we would all be struck down there and then by a thunderbolt sent from heaven! I don't remember Mum's reaction, but I don't think anything could shock her, and she probably thought the same as Tony, but would never admit it. (She DID admit it, however, when in her seventies. She asked our religious sister-in-law (Tony's wife) how Adam and Eve's sons COULD have sired children of their own. There was only Eve, their mother and no other females present. I don't think incest was in the 'good book' but there is no other explanation. That was a well-thought-out fact, which really puts paid to any Garden of Eden theory! Mum's observation must have shocked Tony's wife, who was, and still is, is a very ardent churchgoer. I never heard what our sister-in law answered, so it's hard to say, but I'm sure she did say something implausible. Faith is a wonderful thing.

Religion came into our lives propagated at St Jude's school, whose headmaster was a religious bigot. However, we did have a chance to sing, and once took part in the Easter section of the Messiah staged in St Jude's church. Mr Welsh, who had a lovely tenor voice, was Jesus risen from the tomb, and Mrs Welsh was Mary standing outside the tomb. We 'songsters' were the chorus. This helped start my love of music, so Mr Welsh did something good.

AN ANGEL AND TWO SINNERS

The Angel

The teachers at the school were a mixed crew. A very gentle Miss Walters and a "hit you on the knuckles with a wooden ruler" Miss Kingsley, a single lady. So many were single; I should think the First World War took all their menfolk away. There was a married teacher, a pretty smiling woman called Mrs Goodman. She was SO different. She had been recently widowed – her husband had died fighting somewhere in Europe. Her lessons were magic. I remember her teaching us to sing "Look for the silver lining when clouds appear in the sky". I don't think she had any silver linings at that time, but she instilled happiness into all of us. I can remember her face now and her fair curly hair. We all loved her.

The Two Sinners

I have left these next two male teachers until last but definitely NOT least. These two men were 'war-trained', but that should never have affected the way they treated their pupils.

I am writing this down as I remember it. I did hesitate for half a second, but I think I should expose these teachers who made me afraid of school and so scared that most nights I would cry with fear. Their behaviour probably ruined quite a few children's lives. These two men did nothing to help children learn and thrive. They terrified and belittled most of their charges and were truly wicked. They abused physically and psychologically.

The first was a Mr GW. I didn't go into his class until I was a bit older, but I will put this down whilst on the subject of St Jude's. He was a brute who liked to thump children on their backs, between the shoulder blades, so hard it sounded hollow. He would bring pupils out to the front of the class to do this beating, his fist clenched. I saw a lot of children, particularly boys, traumatized by his thumping. These sadistic acts were usually just for incorrect answers, rarely for bad behaviour. (Very badly behaved boys were sent to Mr Welsh's room to be caned. I think the caning was on the palms. I never witnessed a caning, but I did view the results on one classmate, red streaks across his hands.)

When in Mr GW's lesson I was so frightened of getting the answer to a question wrong, that I couldn't think of the answer! I was never beaten by Mr GW (I'm not sure why, because I didn't do all that well in class), but I witnessed his beatings, and it has stayed a horrible memory for all my life. My friend Ruth Brickman's mother played bridge with him, so I don't think Ruth had the 'thumps' either.

Mr GW was a coward, a controller, and I couldn't wait to leave when I reached eleven. I can picture his red face now. What pleasure he derived from these beatings is hard to find. Perhaps he was a sadist. He had a family, so did they suffer too? I really hated this man, he put the fear of God into the class, and made lessons unbearable for me and I would think for a lot of my peers. One unfortunate child who had difficulty spelling the word 'aluminium' correctly was verbally beaten by this man. His face would go red to purple with rage and he would snarl at the 'wrongdoer' in front of him. Another child when asked where the coal-fields in Britain were just answered, "England, sir." Well, this provoked a thump and a snarl. In today's world he would be imprisoned for his sadistic behaviour.

The other dreadful teacher was a Mr H. He was younger than Mr GW. He was dark-haired and only in his thirties. His methods of control were more sinister. He liked to torture children who he thought had transgressed.

There was a very pale and ill-looking little boy called Ray (I DO remember his surname, but won't put it in). Ray had what I can only describe as odd hands. The ends of the fingers were flattened out frog-like, and the fingers were distorted, and he also had a rough flaky rash on his skin, possibly eczema. Ray must have done something that displeased Mr H, so poor Ray was hoisted up on to the top of the easel and blackboard, sat astride it, and made to hang on with his deformed hands, Mr H castigating him from below. I can't say how long Ray wobbled about, clinging on, being giggled at by the more fortunate of us.

Another time, a girl called Dorothy was made to crawl under a desk/table and crouch there on all fours for some misdemeanour. There Dorothy stayed, I hate to think how long, but it was a truly terrible thing to do to a young girl, and may have left her psychologically disturbed. Who knows?

I hated both these teachers. Did I tell Mum? I don't know. What would she have done anyway? Teachers were held in great respect in those days, and Mum had enough on her plate. Dad was, as usual, not part of our everyday life, so I wouldn't have had the chance to tell him anything. I may have told Pat or Robin, but they probably thought I was being dramatic. And anyway, what could THEY do?

Looking back, though, how DID these men get away with it? Why didn't Mr Welsh and the other teachers not know that this was going on? Surely the nice Mrs Goodman would have known, or would SHE be scared to tell the head? I have often wondered why someone didn't 'blow the whistle' on Mr GW and Mr H for carrying out this regime of terror.

I can't say these teachers were paramount in my not passing the eleven-plus exam, but they didn't help ensure a happy class of children eager to learn. Some very bright and tough pupils obviously let this go over their heads, but for the more nervous and sensitive, their prayers would have been like mine.

"Please God, please make someone else take our class today not Mr GW or Mr H …please…please. PLEEEEASE." These prayers I said nightly, but they didn't work. Well, not for me anyway.

Above my bed there hung a wooden picture of lady wearing a crinoline dress and poke bonnet. Ribbons abounded and she had a criss-cross basket on her arm. She stood in a garden full of flowers, mainly hollyhocks. Under the picture was a poem all written in 'hot-poker work', letters burnt into the wood. It read: "DO NOT SPOIL TODAY'S BLUE SKY WITH TOMORROW'S CLOUDS". I never took any notice of this sensible verse! Ever a pessimist, I follow the reverse saying: "EVERY SILVER LINING HAS A CLOUD".

POST-WAR SCHOOLING

I usually walked to St Jude's with my best friend at the time, Linda. We used to pass a long-dead, hollow oak tree whose roots had split the tarmac pavement. We thought this tree was somehow connected to fairy-life. We would write little notes, fold them up until very tiny, then, when nobody at the nearby bus stop was looking, we would post them into the centre of the tree. Next day, we would look to see if they had been 'taken' by a fairy. The fact that they NEVER disappeared didn't put us off trying. I don't remember what we put on the notes, and I suppose eventually we moved on!

The way home from school was interesting to me. There were a couple of yew trees alongside a gate. The red squashy berries would HAVE to be smashed! What I appeared to be doing when I was jumping around stamping all over the pavement, I don't dare think, but it was a 'game' that had to be played… all the berries 'killed'! Once they were 'dead' and flattened, the rest of the journey back to 249 would be taken with my eyes closed. Well, this was necessary 'just in case' I went blind. It wouldn't be possible today; it would now be a suicide attempt, but then there were just a few cars and trolleybuses, and anyway I would secretly open one eye to see if I was near the kerb. I suppose the worst hazard would be to step in some doggy-poo, often done, and usually traipsed into the house, so that everyone accused the other of being the culprit.

There was one very exciting day in the juniors when we all had to dress up as flowers. I was to be a rose. Mum did come up trumps with the outfit. I'm not sure how as the war was probably only just over. However, I was decked out in a frilly dress, which Mum had decorated with real pink roses from the garden. My headdress was a coronet of roses too, and a train swished behind my dress decorated around the edge with the roses. I felt the 'cat's whiskers' in this lovely rosy get-up. Mum must have worked hard, but I wouldn't have cared; all I could think of was how beautiful I was!!

Mum walked to school with me, and I think basked in the glory, as neighbours came out to admire her handiwork. What we did when we got to school is a bit of a hazy mystery. I think we all had to kneel down then slowly 'unfold' like burgeoning flowers. The boys were the gardeners and walked past with watering cans to make us 'grow'. There was a drop or two of water in one of the boy's cans and it trickled down my neck, but I liked this particular boy so I felt 'special', almost as though he had chosen ME to anoint. One of the nicest memories of school.

There were other brighter happenings at St Jude's, though. One of these was a day out in a 'charabanc' (a coach). We all piled in, bubbling with excitement. The destination was the Wrekin, our local Shropshire hill. I had never been on a 'chara' before. I had possibly by then been on a Crossville green bus, to get from the station in Wales to Nevin, but this was an adventure.

The coach park was under a great cliff. We disembarked, and the ascent began. I don't think it was a hard climb, far from it, because suddenly we were at the top, thirsty and hot. Like a mirage, there was a small shed, with a counter and a man dispensing drinks! I think we had to pay a penny or so to this red-faced smiling man and he handed down a paper cup of pale pink liquid. This was probably only watered-down blackcurrant juice, served in a paper beaker, but it was the NICEST drink in the WHOLE world! I have NEVER tasted such a taste since.

Sports days were also something to look forward to. I enjoyed running, and the sack and egg-and-spoon races. One of the sports days, towards the end of my time at junior school, there was a classmate called Y. She hated losing, and if she was trailing or likely to be second, she would fall down, rolling about on the playground with a 'stitch'. She featured in a fancy-dress party too, given at school for the pupils about to go up to the junior part of the school from what was called the 'babies'. Y was Peter Pan, in a see-through bit of net with floating wings. Even THEN, I felt she was under-dressed, and showing her chest, not at all fairy-like.

We had names pinned to our chests. 'Cinderella' had to find 'Prince Charming', and 'Cleopatra' looked for 'Caesar'. I can't remember WHAT I went as… probably another fairy. I can't imagine that Mr Welsh organized this, it doesn't seem religious enough. So possibly one of the nicer, gentler lady teachers was behind this very enjoyable party. There was no food, but it was fun anyway.

Years and years later, I met Y again, but I still thought of her pretending to be in pain hating to lose. (She actually went out with Harold years later, but that is not to be written down, too lurid.)

Life at home was much happier, in spite of bickering between Dad and Mum. Pat was attending the municipal grammar school, Whitmore Reans, and Robin had left school (St Peter's boys' school, then the Art School). At fifteen he joined a poster artist firm in Chapel Ash, Wolverhampton, as an apprentice. This was what Robin did all his life, until he was in his seventies. He became very proficient at all types of posters, boards and billboards. His script was free-hand, and I think very good.

He had saved up for a pushbike, and this trusty steed was his mode of transport, as it was for most men and boys in those pre-car days. He was my favourite brother, always a gentle boy, caring, very different from Tony. They looked very different too. Robin was dark, as was I, and Tony was quite fair. Pat was also fair, and I always joined Tony and Pat together in the family, but Robin was on the same peculiar wavelength as me, and always has been.

Robin's little gifts to me were always thought out and fitted the bill with me. One of his presents was a book on nature, going back to the start of all life on earth, pre-dinosaurs. I loved this book, and I still have it today. I think this book started my interest in all things natural, the animals, plants, flowers. So a much-treasured present.

PAT AND SCHOOL

Pat was a tomboy, and an optimist. She DID pass her eleven-plus exam: she sailed through St Jude's (pre the beatings era). Her time at the municipal grammar school is a bit of a haze to her now. I think she was a rebel, though. She recently told me that she had spent 'most of her evenings in detention'. One story she related was that a rule of the school was that no pupil was to leave any money (if they had any!) in their coat pockets in the cloakroom. Prefects would go round checking… One morning in assembly, a teacher called out Pat's name and made her stand up at the front of the crowded hall, for all to see. Once there, Pat was severely told off in front of all the school for leaving tuppence ha'penny in her coat pocket.

Another time, she got into VERY hot water…

There was, on the opposite corner to the school, a small shop which sold buns and cakes. This shop was out of bounds, but one well-remembered lunchtime, Pat ventured out to the shop, bought a cake and was eating it IN THE STREET when a teacher saw her. All hell was let loose, and once again, she was held up as an example of bad behaviour in front of the assembled school. "Pat Lloyd-Davies, you are nothing but a guttersnipe!" shouted an irate teacher.

Oh well, I don't think it had any great impact on Pat. She was, and still is, a very strong character, not easily bowed by criticism. She could take trouble squarely on the chin.

The same ghastly teacher also told Pat off for letting her hair touch her blouse collar. Pat retaliated with, "But, Miss, I have a short neck."

"Well, you must cultivate a LONGER neck, then," was the angry retort. How unfair.

Pat was very good at sports, and still is. She 'matriculated' in her what are now called A levels and there was some debate with Dad, though, as he wanted Pat to be a doctor. He had never contributed in kind to Pat's education, but to Dad, to be a doctor was a status symbol. Pat wasn't having any of it! She joined Boots the chemist, and was an assistant dispenser, enjoying life as Pat could always do, and still does.

(She has just told me that she changed all her A levels from science subjects, solely because she had not the slightest intention of becoming a doctor. A wise choice, as it turned out, particularly for her would-be patients, as she admits her memory is, and always WAS, bad.)

DANCING TO THE SHOPS

L ife at 249 was unusual, but good. The Hoppers were still next door in their white-painted semi-mansion. Old Harold Ingleby met a rather tragic end. He was badly burnt whilst doing something in the garage by the back yard. His daughter, Mrs Hopper, poured water over him to put the fire out. Mum always said that this was the wrong thing to do, and I think in those days using water on burns WAS frowned on. It's not the case today, though. Anyway, all this went unnoticed by me, I was too busy dancing and tap-dancing around in the back yard. There were also roller-skates lying around. They were really Robin's and Tony's, but I would strap them on and try my hardest to skate. The centre piece of the skate did push in to shorten the skates, but they were never small enough. That's my excuse.

I did, however, have a wooden scooter – my pride and joy. I would whiz down the pavement on Tettenhall Road to the shops. These shops had flats above them, and a friend, Pat Arthur, used to live above Cavendish grocer's.

Pat was keen on ballet too, so we shared a pair of ballet shoes. It was Dad again! He had access to some VERY used block-toed ballet shoes, so he duly delivered them. We girls would pirouette and leap around Pat's small flat. I don't remember her mother being there but I suppose she was somewhere, probably working.

Those shoes were a gateway to all kinds of imaginings. I was definitely going to be a ballet STAR! I danced, skipped, and tapped through the days. I even included my best friend Barbara in the cavorting, something that I think was alien to her, but she joined in with fervour. Acrobatics featured, as did long-jumping on the lawn. We performed handstands against the loo wall, bounced endless tennis balls against any brick structure. We drew with chalk on the blue bricks in the yard and hop-scotched our afternoons away. Boiler cleaners, metal spikey balls, made very good 'jacks', and when skipping, we used any bit of old washing line. The words 'SALT, MUSTARD, VINEGAR, PEPPER…' echoed around the yard, as the skipping rope whizzed through the air. I don't remember ever being bored; outdoor activities reigned.

Newbridge shops were our local shopping venue. We had our newspapers from a newsagent's called Mounsey's. Mrs Mounsey's daughter Renee served there, a little dark-haired frightened-looking person. The shop sold everything and Mum used it regularly.

Next to Mounsey's was a haberdashery shop, run by a Miss Minette. The wonderful smell of wool, twisted into figure of eights, somehow made this shop special. The shop was cosy, a 'ladies only' area. The glass-fronted counter held ribbons of all colours, safety pins, knicker elastic, and knitting patterns. I didn't go in there often, but I think Mum bought her wool from Miss Minette. (Our wool was never anything exciting during the 1940s, just grey wool for socks.) I loved that shop, and Miss Minette, plump and lacy-collared, was gentility personified. She always wore a lavender cardigan, sporting buttons to match! No doubt all hand-knitted!

Next to Miss Minette's was a hairdresser's, I think called Gabriella's. I was sent there to get my hair cut. The hairdresser, a non-chatty woman, just cut it whilst I stood there, no chair, just a cape around my shoulders. Mum had given me sixpence, so I suppose I got a 'sixpenny one-minute standing trim'. (It looked ragged afterwards, and I cried on the way back up the road to 249.)

The end shop in the row was a general grocer's. I think it was called Foster's. It was nothing too memorable, mainly because Mum shopped at Mason's.

Opposite was a cobbler's shop run by a man called Mr Roberts. He had a thickened eyelid, rendering one eye almost shut. He always wore a cap and sometimes a black eye-patch… I was somehow wary of him, I have no reason to say that, but he was creepy.

Oddly, there was yet another smaller greengrocery business, a shop that was always busy. It had two ladies serving, wearing green overalls and the rather old-fashioned wound-round plaits of hair made into two buns, secured around the ears – 'earphones' to us.

There was a man there who drove a little van, so you could have your greens delivered. I'm afraid to say I thought he looked like a pig, with shiny smooth pink cheeks and a flattened nose, sporting big nostrils.

The antique shop run by Chas Brickman added a bit of class, sandwiched between the cobbler's and the leeks, turnips and potatoes displayed outside the greengrocer's.

All the men in the area had their hair cut by Mr Jones the Barber, the striped pole was above his doorway. I never got to see inside this male domain, men's barbers were secretive places, and definitely NOT for little girls.

Last, but very important, was the 'electrical repairs' man. Everything from radios to light bulbs were stocked, and an advert in his small window told all customers that "I will come to your home to repair radios and any electrical equipment, no extra charge!"

The owner was a tall, very thick-lipped young man sporting a Brylcreemed mass of lank dark hair. He was very popular with local housewives. When visiting homes, he would carry a portmanteau-type case and looked more like a doctor than an electrician.

I was sent on many errands to these shops. The quickest mode of transport was my trusty scooter. This I loved. I could shove off with one great push… and this would suffice for the whole of the way down the hill. Apart from my dog Mickey, this scooter was my greatest joy. It must have travelled miles up and down Tettenhall Road. It was a wonderful vehicle that lasted years, until one day it just fell apart! The wood had perished and the narrow rubber tyres no longer fitted and were worn out. I knew the death of this red-wheeled steed was imminent, but when Tony said it was 'past repair', I had to accept it was gone forever. It was consigned to the bonfire.

These few shops were venues for many little trips, and we all got to know the assistants. It was still surname only, of course, no familiarity; that wasn't the 'done thing' then.

NEWBRIDGE SHOPS UPDATED

Newbridge shops are still there. The difference is that they NOW comprise a shop called Booze, where Mounsey's the newsagent's was, a video shop, hideously lit in garish neon lights, and a shop called the Fish-n-Chip Plaice. There is also a fashionable hairdresser's, and a Co-op. (Mum wouldn't be seen dead in a Co-op, she really was a snob at times, but I don't know why.) Alongside the Co-op is a dingy shop called Cost Cutters. There is one nice shop right at the end of the row, a tiny shop with about eight feet of frontage, which is called The Olde Sweet Shoppe. It sells all the wonderful old sweets, the liquorice strands, red fireman's hoses, stripy humbugs, and its shelves are lined with jars full of all colours of the rainbow. So ONE good shop.

I believe they still sell liquorice wood, so loved in the war days, but probably slightly toxic so the Health and Safety crew will add it to their list of banned substances!

(Since writing that last bit, I hear that the sweet shop has gone, where to, we don't know, but that is the last of the 'Olde Worlde' shops anywhere near here.)

Mum would be so upset about the demise of the rather posh row of Newbridge shops, particularly as they were replaced by the Booze one. Nobody in Mum's family would dream of calling alcoholic drink 'booze' – too crude. (Later on in Mum's last years, someone mentioned their baby's 'bum'. Mum shuddered at such a 'common' expression. "Why don't they call it a BOTTOM?" she asked, tight-lipped.)

FRIENDS, A GOAT, AND MISS TILLY

My friend Barbara was the girl I played with most, and we stayed friends until Barbara died in 2000.

Barbara was a very big well-made girl, so tripping the light fantastic around the lawn or yard pretending to be a fairy didn't really do her any favours. She was always well developed in the bust area, and it showed in contrast as I was very flat-chested. However, we spent many a happy afternoon pretending to be anything and everything. Pat says she remembers Barbara bouncing around the garden flapping her arms as wings, looking so much older than her years… a very developed fairy.

Mum's garden was her pride and joy, with its primulas, purple in great clumps, amongst daffodils and crocus. The garden had already been set out before we arrived. There was the top lawn, with two rose arches, and against the wall, an old William pear tree, and beyond that, a garden. Unfortunately this bit was overrun with golden rod (Aaron's rod). Mum had a battle every year trying to pull up clumps of this but it just spread regardless.

There was a circle of small paths around a central garden, all edged with stones, mossy green ones. Lily-of-the-valley also ran amok in this bit, and although wonderful, they took over other plants. A little round pond came next, surrounded by a little grassy area. Here were the apple trees, the damson, plus gooseberry bushes. Raspberry canes filled the lower end of the garden. This is where the chicken house and wire-netting run was. The garden was too much for Mum, but she loved it and did her best. Dad was always suffering from hernias and ruptures so was a stranger to any digging. Mum bottled all our fruit in Kilner jars. Even our tomatoes were bottled. Pears were too, and the pantry shelves were always full with jars courtesy of a hard-working Mum.

The air-raid shelter took up most of the top lawn, its rounded 'roof', which became covered in grass after a few years, was a wonderful place to run up to the top of and try to FLY! So many leaps, runs, falls, cuts and bruises were caused by this endeavour to take to the sky, I wouldn't believe that I COULDN'T. Wings were made out of anything flimsy… but why couldn't we FLY?

That shelter was also very useful to the goat. One night, Dad arrived home leading a huge, hairy and smelly billy goat. As usual, he had been drinking with his 'cronies'. How he got the goat, I don't think anyone, even Dad, knew. Mum became the martyr, grumbling and talking under her breath.

Of course I loved the goat. He would run to the top of the shelter, then take a leap off into the air. His leaps didn't last long, though. In fact, he 'leapt his last' in less than a week. Where did he go? I woke up one morning – no goat! I can't remember any explanation being given by either parent.

Dad's collecting of animals didn't stop there. Someone had a Pekinese dog called Chang. Dad took him under his wing, but kept him at the cinema (I hate to think what the dog did when he wanted to 'go out'). Chang was a snuffly bundle, and not greatly liked. Dad had a secretary called Miss Tilly. She lived near to the Gaumont with her aged father, so perhaps Miss Tilly took the dog home with her? I would sometimes visit Dad at work. He would be in his office, always smoking, and Miss Tilly would be tapping away on a typewriter in a little side office the size of a pantry, in a haze of smoke. Chang would be there, sitting under Dad's desk. I remember putting my hand down and stroking Chang's back and receiving a snapping bite. It bled a lot, but Miss Tilly administered a bandage. (This was very acceptable to a child – anything that looked as though you had 'something wrong' with you gave you credibility with your peers. Sticking plaster anywhere on the body was a sure way of gathering attention from school friends.)

Chang, it turned out, had lumps around his back and tummy, so after this painful episode, like the goat, Chang just disappeared. I didn't bother to ask where he had gone.

Miss Tilly was very kind to me. When Mum felt she couldn't take me to the dentist (too traumatic), Miss Tilly did! I had a tooth extracted, with a general anaesthetic, a most frightening time. Nobody prepared me for it. I was just put in the chair, a mask popped over my nose, and the most weird and awful feeling came over me as the gas took hold. Everything shrank up towards me, then, of course, I woke up, but I was so scared. The dutiful Miss Tilly held my hand and walked me a few yards back down to the Gaumont.

To look at Miss Tilly was pretty grim. She wore too much panstick make-up, a slash of bright red lipstick disclosing what looked like false teeth with traces of lipstick on them, and had orange-dyed and permed hair. But looks aside, she was nice, and must have had a heart of gold.

There was some talk about Dad and Miss Tilly, but nothing concrete. His secretary before Miss Tilly, called Eileen, was a married lady. There had been talk about her too, and this WAS true, according to Mum, but Mum only told me this when she was in her eighties. It was Christmas Eve, and I remember thinking, WHAT a blooming time to tell me THIS. Mum reckoned that Eileen was Dad's mistress and had given birth to a son, who was "definitely your father's baby, because he had your father's EARS!" So could there be someone my age (Mum said the baby's birth was around the time I was born) walking (or hobbling) around, our half-brother. We will never find out, it's far too late. We all have our doubts. Mum could be fanciful at times, but it might be true. Mum's sister Glad said there was some truth in that story.

DAD AND THE THEATRE

Dad had been a manager of theatres and cinemas since his early twenties. I think the first cinema was in Kilburn, in London near Hyde Park. This may have been the end of the silent film era, the 1920s. He married Maude Eleanor Roberts on Christmas Day, at St Thomas's C of E church, Stourbridge.

Mum had not been long married to him when he took the job in Kilburn, and I would think the stay in London was traumatic for her. She spent the time alone in an upstairs flat, hearing the underground railway thundering below. Dad must have been fond of his drink even in those days, because Mum remembered him arriving home late one night very blotto, unable to get up the stairs, so she had to drag him up a flight of steps unaided, terrified that someone would see or hear them. This must have put a damper on their early life together.

After London, Dad moved to Wolverhampton to the Hippodrome (mentioned later). I think it may have been called something different back in the 1920s. Then to the Queen's cinema, in the centre of town. A lovely cinema, with a tearoom, where they held tea dances in the afternoons. I think he enjoyed his time there, as did Mum, who would sometimes venture into the tearoom. This was well before I was born, so I have to go on what I've been told by Mum and the family.

Dad met royalty twice. First, the then Duke of York, who became Edward VIII, then the Duke of Kent. They both visited the Queen's cinema, and Dad did the shaking of hands and probably stilted chat.

Cinemas were places of comfort, red-plush seats, the fairy-tale curtains. There was very little television, certainly not for the majority of people, so the 'flicks' were well attended. Queues would build up outside, with the commissionaires keeping everyone in order. This certainly applied when Dad eventually became manager of the Gaumont.

We were really privileged, not having to queue. Friends have told me how when they were too young to be admitted by themselves, they would go up to someone in the queue and ask if they could go in with them. It usually worked. Another dodge would be to enter by the side doors, opened at times between pictures.

Robin has told me recently that J Arthur Rank Co. would organize a day out for the staff of their picture houses. Everyone from the Gaumont, a multitude of cleaners, usherettes, managers, organists, would all pile into a 'chara' and set off for Trentham Gardens in the Stafford/Derbyshire area. Here there would be a J Arthur Rank sports day.

Apparently, there were crowds of other J Arthur employees there too, from all over the Midlands. There were tug-o-wars, running races, and all kinds of athletics. Somehow I can't imagine this happening today. Nobody had sports gear then, so Robin said they were a motley crew, all shapes and sizes of shorts and running shoes, i.e. pumps. There wasn't the class distinction during and after the war as there is today. I think everyone was on a par in those days. Robin, who went with Dad, said a good time was had by all.

That was just a little bit about life working in the cinema business. Dad worked for J Arthur Rank from about 1928 until 1961.

WINTER 1947

The winter of 1947 was wonderful for children but must have been a terrible time for adults. Snow fell upon snow. Tettenhall Road was impassable and householders had to dig trenches up the middle so that pedestrians could get to work. Our back yard was about six feet high with snow, so the way to the back loo was a challenge, and a channel was dug out. But the loo was probably frozen up anyway.

We did get to school, though, made possible by everyone helping to clear the way. Brother Robin, I remember, helped me up the road and into the school road. The trolleybuses must have been grounded. There weren't many cars in the forties, but they would have had to stay in the garage.

All the teachers lived within a mile of St Jude's, so they all turned up. To my knowledge, the school never closed, even during the war. The open fires were already lit when we arrived, clothes draped over the fire-guards, and steam everywhere. Snowball fights, slides, snowmen – a happy time at last.

The small milk bottles, which arrived in a crate, had cardboard tops, and in the icy weather, these tops would pop up, pushed up by frozen milk. Delicious, especially as the top of the milk had a creamy layer. I don't think I had ever eaten REAL ice cream, but that was a delight.

(Mum wouldn't have let us buy an ice cream anyway. There had been a case in the national newspapers about a man in a seaside resort down in the south of England who was making ice cream in a chamber pot! Some poor soul had picked up typhoid, which was traced back to the ice-cream maker AND his potty, so ice cream was definitely suspect in Mum's eyes.)

After the winter had gone, during the spring and summer, skipping was a very enjoyable pastime, especially in the playground. Sometimes the dinner ladies would hold the ends of the long rope. All the old rhymes were chanted, as we jumped in. If a crowd jumped in, it was 'ALL IN TOGETHER, GIRLS, THIS FINE WEATHER, GIRLS, O. U. T. SPELLS OUT!'

Conkers was played mainly by the boys, dangerously exciting (not allowed today in some schools, which is such a pity). The conkers were soaked in vinegar to harden them. This was not classed as a game, more of a competition, an extremely serious one. Robin said that the battles became almost violent, and there were rumours and suspicion about competitors hardening the conkers by 'underhand means'.

Somewhere around this time, the Hopper family decided to go 'home' to the north- east, to their origins in Grimsby, I think, possibly because of financial problems. A big house, and the girls grown-up (except for Wendy Elizabeth), prompted them to go back to their roots. I was too young to know why they left.

Mum missed the 'over the garden wall' chats, and I certainly missed the chats to Arthur Ingleby, who rather fascinated me, and the play and pretend with Wendy Elizabeth. As I mentioned before, the family had undergone a tragedy, when Mr Ingleby senior, Harold, was severely burnt in a fire. I don't think poor Harold survived much longer after that, and his unseen wife, who resided in the summer house, also miraculously disappeared. I certainly wasn't aware of a funeral, but Mum would probably keep something like a death a hush-hush secret, so these old folk just became 'no more'! (Whether the deaths had anything to do with the Hopper family moving, I don't know, but they were missed. Mum corresponded with Mrs Hopper right up until they both got too old to write!)

UNCLE REG AT THE WHITE HOUSE

The house wasn't empty long. It was bought by Dad's older brother, Reg, who had been visiting us a few weeks earlier. Now I gather it was to view the house with a hope to buying it. Reg brought with him his partner. I thought in my ignorance that she was his wife, a true Auntie.

They had turned up at 249, Reg wearing a huge almost furry coat and dark-rimmed glasses (a bit Orson Wells) with Elizabeth, also called Betty. She was thin and smiling, and had dark hair and was just 'different'.

My exciting moment was showing them the air-raid shelter 'sump', a hole in the ground to drain water away. Why I did THAT, I don't know. I was almost proud of it, but a bit frightened too, as it was full of clay and water that smelled musty. They seemed surprised, but were too polite to ask just WHY it was SO important?

Reginald Bernard Gittoes-Davies and Elizabeth (Betty) Tay, a well-established journalist from the *Daily Mirror*, arrived in a Ford V8 car and set up home in what they would call very grandly… THE WHITE HOUSE HOTEL.

Reg's older daughter Joy came to help out. She was the daughter of Reg and his first wife, Ivy. I was told by Mum that Ivy resided in a 'mental hospital'. She was never mentioned again, and I thought she was a dark secret, someone to be whispered about.

Reg's three other children were by his ex-partner Mabel, so post Ivy. Betty Tay was 'post Mabel' so number three. She had a crooked smile, and teeth to match, but I loved her immediately.

This time of (particularly my) life became a rather wonderful release from the dreaded school, and I look back on the hotel years fondly, and with feelings of happiness, even though, in a way, Reg and Betty's lives were even more disastrous than my parents'.

Reg was a very bright and clever chap. He was two years older than my Dad. We know nothing of my Dad and his three brothers' schooling, but it must have been pretty good because both Reg and Dad had very good jobs and were musicians. Reg became the editor of a newspaper in Leicester, at the young age of twenty-four, one of the youngest recorded (in *Who's Who*).

71

He then moved to Cardiff. I'm not sure if he was an editor there, or sub-editor. (I have old newspaper cuttings somewhere, with all this info, but can't find them at this time.) After quite a few years in the newspaper business, Reg became a managing director of a large company, Ames Industries.

Pat remembers visiting Reg and Betty down in London when she was about sixteen. Reg's younger son Barry took her to see Reg at the office. Pat was astounded. It was a huge office, with a gigantic desk, and Uncle Reg sitting behind it. After meeting Reg there, the others in the family joined them, and they all went for a meal, not in a café, no it was the RITZ. For a young girl, all this wealth and upper-class life was thrilling! These post-war years were all 'coupons and austerity', so this opulence must have been very welcome to Pat, an impressionable teenager, probably still in ankle socks. There were no stockings around in the 1940s, except probably lisle ones for the older ladies. There had been 'black-market stockings' around during the war, or presents of 'nylons' from the American GIs. But no respectable girl would have received a pair from the 'yanks', NOT in our house anyway. Too risky. The black-market 'stocking police' would surely cycle up and frogmarch any woman wearing 'see-through' NYLON stockings to the local lock-up.

Pat had fun too with Reg and family back home near London, a smart mansion in its own grounds. There was larking around at night – apple-pie beds and revenge attacks involving Gorgonzola shoved down a bed, with everyone taking part! Pat has very happy memories of her stay with the Gittoes-Davies family. (Although Reg and his siblings were born just plain Davies, Reg added his Mum's maiden name of Gittoes to the Davies, and my father added Lloyd to ours. I think they had what Midlanders would call 'a bob on their head', but they were jolly and knew how to enjoy themselves, which in those days was a difficult thing for people to do.)

Both Betty and Reg had endured working in London during the bombing. Their tales of fires and wrecked buildings, and the 'doodle-bugs,' the rockets fired from German planes, the sinister noise of their engines coming nearer overhead… then the seconds of silence as the engines cut out, before descending onto streets of houses, wreaking chaos and great destruction, made me feel that my aunt and uncle were heroes.

I was too young to grasp all the terrible happenings in London and other big cities. Reg and Betty told me that they were running along Fleet Street with fires all around them, bombs falling and everyone dashing for cover. They went on reporting the news right through those years, which must have had a massive influence on them and perhaps led to their post-war years of what Mum would call 'frivolity' but what we at 249 considered fun.

Just a small piece about Mum's words to Pat before Pat ventured down to stay with Reg and the family of cousins. "I have something to tell you," Mum whispered. Pat was startled and wondered what terrible deadly secret was coming next. "You see… Auntie Elizabeth and Uncle Reg … aren't MARRIED." This didn't really make any impression on Pat, who couldn't have cared less about their marital state. But for Mum, their co-habiting was something to be whispered about behind locked doors! Mum always had the feeling that if you didn't conform, 'THEY' would get you… whoever 'THEY' were. This ruled her life to a degree, and our lives too.

Reg's family life was complicated, and I think his loins ruled his head where the ladies were concerned. Having no information on his early life in Smethwick, I can only talk about his life after 1918. After doing his stint in the First World War, not abroad, but no doubt something clerical, he was living in London. He met and married Ivy (also in the army in those days). They had a daughter, Joy. Not long after Joy's birth, a sad event took place. Ivy became ill with a psychological illness. Nowadays it would probably be diagnosed as 'baby blues' depression and you would be prescribed anti-depressants, but in the 1920s, you were sent 'away' and isolated in some sort of institution, which is where Ivy found herself.

Meanwhile, Reg was having an affair with another lady, Mabel, and they produced three more offspring. The four cousins were brought up very liberally and were 'free spirits'. The two boys from Mabel and Reg's union, Mansel and Barry, were sent to a boarding school in Hampshire called Beltane. There they had a wonderful, free and happy time. The third child, Ruth, I'm not sure where she went, but she was rather 'posh' (well, we thought so). We didn't have too much to do with Ruth, but Mansel and Barry would appear at the White House when holidays arrived. Ruth stayed occasionally.

By now, Reg had also left Mabel, but stayed on good terms with her, so his partner when they came to live next door was Elizabeth, a lovely lady, not in looks, but in her friendly manner. We all came to love Betty or 'Auntie Elizabeth', to give her our title.

As far as I knew, poor Ivy was still incarcerated in the mental institution, somewhere near the New Forest in Hampshire, with no contact with her daughter Joy or husband Reg. I thought she had stayed in there for all her life, if you can call it a life.

(This next bit is rather upsetting. I recently looked up Ivy's death. She seems to have lived on into old age, and NOT in the mental institution, as we all thought. I feel this is disturbing, knowing that she was alive, and possibly well again. We don't know if anyone visited her whilst she was incarcerated. Ivy was never spoken of, a reflection of those times, and of a husband who must have almost forgotten her.)

73

The raised garden by the wall between 249 and what was now the White House Hotel now became a 'climb over' place for me. Not quite so much chat going on between Mum and Elizabeth as there had been with the Hoppers but memories of Arthur Ingleby's rather sallow face and horn-rimmed spectacles topped with a 'tin hat' peeping over the wall have stayed with me all my life. I can still hear the creak-creaking sound of leather from his under-arm crutches as he positioned himself so that he could see over the wall.

The ant-watching on the trunk of the poplar tree stopped as soon as Uncle Reg and Auntie Elizabeth moved in. There was FAR too much going on at the White House.

MAKING DO AND MENDING

Back on the 249 side, things between Mum and Dad were pretty poor. Dad was a great spender, and a cheerful giver, but only to his friends, not to Mum. There was still rationing, so clothes and food were in short supply.

One memory, and I hope I haven't enlarged this, was Mum buying me shoes for school that were BOYS' shoes, toe-caps, the lot! I hated them. When they showed signs of wear, or sprang a leak in the sole, that's when cardboard from a packet of Kellogg's cereals would be cut by Mum into the shape of my foot. Mum would draw all round my feet, whilst I stood still, then snip-snip, a new inner sole was born! I trotted around with rather colourful 'inners'. THAT didn't matter to me, nobody would see them.

My clothes were really just school uniform and hand-me-downs, formerly worn by Pat years before, or from Mrs Hopper, who gave Mum some of her older daughters' dresses, all home-made.

Gabardine macs became a trial and tribulation for a schoolgirl. Mum would go to a shop in town called Bedford & Williams, where the school uniforms were to be bought. Mum would make sure that the mac would fit me as I grew, so she bought two sizes too big. It would be almost on the ground, and the sleeves well over my hands. "This will last," she'd murmur as she turned the bottom hem up, likewise the sleeves… I know NOW that this 'make do and mend' was essential in the forties, and into the fifties too, but I sometimes hated wearing long coats and the boys' shoes.

Dad carried on his smoking, drinking with his 'cronies' and was rarely seen at home. He would catch the last trolleybus home in the evening. The bus started off from Wolverhampton town centre at 11pm. He would SOMETIMES arrive at 249 carrying a paper bag… his supper. So Mum had to cook whatever was tipped out of the bag. Often there was a red and orange crab, sometimes a mackerel, occasionally what were called (probably still are now!) chitterlings (I think they are cow's intestines) and, for a real treat, sweetbreads, not the testicles of an animal as Dad hinted at, but the pancreas of the poor beast. So, well after 11 o'clock Mum would start supper. Sometimes Tony, Robin and Pat would stay up to see Dad. I was nearly always in bed, but could hear all the talking going on in the kitchen, or hear the radio in the back room.

There was *Penny On The Drum*, or a programme where, if they didn't get a question right, the contestant had to conduct the studio orchestra!! I was sometimes allowed to listen to that quiz, and OH HOW I wanted to conduct that orchestra! There was SO much going on downstairs, I felt left out, and would try to creep down, only to be shouted at by everyone! I remember crying quite often about being out of the jollities downstairs. I felt that being what THEY called the 'baby' of the family was somehow a penance for arriving late, after my brothers and sister had become friends with each other, Robin and Pat in particular. Tony was a loner.

I think the age gap between my siblings and me made me cling on to neighbours and relations… and now that I am penning this saga, I can recall much more of life around 249 than Robin or Pat can. Although Robin does remember quite a few 'gaps' in my memory, I don't think Pat would mind me putting down on paper that she can't remember or visualize much of life at 249 or Dad's behaviour. She didn't get on with Dad, and hasn't changed her opinion of him now that she is elderly.

The Greenhams were still at 247, and I still used to pop round ad nauseam. I liked the gentle Mrs Greenham. She had a Norfolk drawl, and I liked the way her long silver-grey hair was sometimes loose, other times in a round bun, with lots of hair-pins sticking out. She still wore her pink chemise-type underskirt most mornings, then would change into a dress, which was promptly covered with an apron. To go out shopping, she would wear a navy hat, brimmed, with net, a long grey coat, and black smart but sensible shoes. Yes, a very nice old soul, she would talk to me when the family wouldn't (which was quite often!).

To Horace Greenham, I was always 'his chinaman', which felt nice. How he and Tita met and got together I can't hazard a guess, they were so different. Tita, refined, quiet, and from quite a well-off family, Horace the east-ender, rough, bulbous-nosed and loud, complete opposites. I suppose they got on. In those days, there was no show of affection or tactile behaviour, which would probably be thought of as 'cheeky'. So families rarely kissed in greeting, and married couples reserved 'all that' for the privacy of their bedroom or for the time that the children were at Sunday school.

Sunday school for me was brief. Barbara invited me to attend a Methodist one, quite near to us. We would call for a school friend called Margaret. Margaret lived in an area of shocking squalor, just off the Tettenhall Road. I do remember feeling shocked at how they lived, which sounds awfully snobby now, but the conditions were dire. The houses there were back to back, with a main communal yard for washing and mangling. We called one day to find Margaret's mother in the front paved area. She was wearing a turban-style headscarf wrapped round some curlers. The hair sticking out from the turban was dyed orange, and her make-up was clown-like! A slash of red on her mouth, black around the eyes, gaps in her teeth, and a 'ciggy' hanging out of her crimson lips.

The kitchen appeared to be just a fallen-down room, with children's heads peeping out, their faces dirty, clothes the same. The worst sight, for me, was Margaret's mum's legs. They were covered in scabs with open sores. I wondered where I had seen her before, then suddenly realized I had been in town shopping with Mum when she had walked past. Her walk was a kind of 'goose-step', probably because her (what I know NOW as ulcers) would open up and seep if she bent them. Even then, I wondered why people had to live like that. It struck me as cruel.

The Sunday school didn't last long. I thought it boring! We just had to crayon religious pictures, then say a prayer, and walk home. My friend Barbara stuck it out for months longer. She remained a great believer right up to the end of her life, something I haven't been able to do, however much I have tried.

ANIMALS AT 249

The joy of my life was Mickey, my mongrel dog. He was all mine! Although of course Mum had to do all the looking after. We didn't have cat or dog food available in tins, so now I wonder just WHAT they all ate. Leftover dinner scraps were given to the cats, of which there were quite a few, as they were all having love affairs with the local moggies. However, dogs had, I think, Bob Martins dried biscuits and the odd butcher's bone, possibly after it had been boiled to get the goodness out of it for stew. Rationing was still around in the late forties, but I think that meat was the last foodstuff off the ration. I'm not sure exactly which year. Perhaps dog biscuits were not rationed?

I used to secretly eat the black dog biscuits. They were supposed to be mostly charcoal, which someone had said on the wireless was 'good for the digestion'. I just like the crunchy feeling, Tony said they were just 'crushed flies'.

Leftovers were probably in short supply. I don't think we were expected to leave anything on our plates, but the cats always appeared well fed. The cats were always pregnant, and the cardboard birthing-box was sometimes put under the kitchen table. One meal I remember Mum pulling up the corner of the tablecloth. "Oh, look, she's had two kittens… oh no… there's three." There would be little squeaks from below deck, and we'd all duck down to peer. "Oh dear… another two. I hope she doesn't have too many!"

We ALL hoped that too, mainly because if the little mother gave birth to too many, Tony would drown the very newborn 'extras'! This does sound SO cruel, but in a way it relieved the mother cat of a huge family, and, more importantly, there were fewer kittens to try to give away to friends and neighbours. To my shame, I watched Tony armed with a bucket, and I don't remember feeling terribly distressed.

The animals did cause Mum a lot of hassle, I realize now. We arrived home one day from school to find Mum vigorously scrubbing her hands in the sink. She breathlessly told me that, having a moment to spare, she thought she would shake the dog's bed out (it was the cats' bed too as they all got on well). She had looked down under the table, saw one of my skipping ropes in the box, so pulled it out, To her horror, it wasn't a skipping rope, it was a dead rat's tail, with a dead rat on the other end! One of the animal crew had dragged it in, so she had it dangling by its tail. No wonder she was scrubbing!

Mickey was a gentle dog, but one day fell foul of Mum …and everyone! One of our cats had recently given birth to some kittens. We had dragged her birthing-box out from under the breakfast table and settled it nearer the fire grate to keep the little family warm. Mickey's paternal feelings came to the fore, and he would lick them and watch over them when mum-cat went out for a break. As usual, we had lots of visitors, strangers to the cats. Nobody noticed anything unusual until everyone had gone home, and we went to inspect the kittens…

Mickey was sitting by the box, looking sheepish, his tail down… no kittens!! No mother cat either. Mum bent down and put her head against his side. "Listen to this… can you hear a noise?"

We all knelt down beside the empty box, and Mickey (who by now thought that something nasty was afoot) got up. Mum grabbed him and put her ear to his tum. "I can hear squeaks. He's EATEN them!!" Sure enough, we all heard squeals and squeaks coming from Mickey's stomach. He gave a little wag of his tail, but Mum held him down. We all shouted at him as he lay there. Panic reigned and the poor dog was frightened and panting with fear.

Even I believed Mum, and was thinking how COULD my dearest friend DO such a wicked thing? He'd always loved the new arrivals. Just as Mickey was about to be slung out into the yard, the cat-flap opened and mum-cat slid in. But seeing all the hullabaloo, she pretty smartly pushed her way out again. We all dashed out after her. She leapt over a small wall into an old outbuilding (the ancient pigsty). A torch was produced, and there, lying amongst some rubbish up a corner, were the little kitten family, snug and warm. Mummy cat lay over them defensively. We did feel silly to even THINK that Mickey would or could do such a terrible thing. No wonder his stomach was gurgling and squealing having been dived upon by a lot of savages! We installed the cat and kittens back near the fire.

It was thought that all the new people milling around her box in the kitchen had made mum-cat nervous, so she must have picked the kittens up and, one by one, carried them to what she saw as safety. We hugged Mickey, gave him his favourite drink of tea, (with sugar!) and apologized to him. It was Mum's turn to look sheepish. Mickey wasn't a mass murderer.

Another time, we were all eating supper late one night, when out from the skirting board walked a mouse (we had many, running along out of view behind boarding and in holes in the crumbling plaster). WE ALL saw the mouse. Mickey didn't. The mouse walked round Mickey almost defiantly, and we all shouted "GET IT!", but a mere mouse wasn't really important to Mickey (small fry), so he just watched it as it circled round him then disappeared back into the small hole in the skirting board and the floor.

No… Mickey was no mouser, and Tony made it very plain on many occasions, "That dog is a cowardly yellow-livered hound," he would say. But Mickey was my best friend. (I even have a tiny photo of him in a silver locket, just Mickey, no parents gaze out from the little heart… which must say something?)

BOOKS

Books were very important in our lives. Robin read books on Marx and political subjects, as well as the good old *Beano*, *Dandy* and the *Hotspur* comics. (He and Dad would argue for hours, late at night, putting forward their theories on government, particularly communism. These discussions, to put it mildly, would drive Pat mad. She could never stand them and would make herself scarce.)

Tony had his mechanical engineering and American Western-type cowboy books.

I'm not sure what Pat read; there's a small hole here in information! For me, Enid Blyton reigned. *The Wishing Chair* flew me off to a land of fairies, elves and everything that was fantastic, as did Enid's Famous Five, Julian, Dick, Anne and George, not forgetting Timmy the dog. Somehow the five lived the life that children in those days (and even more so these restricted days) would have liked. Freedom to go off across lakes, make camps on islands, look for treasure (this was my favourite bit). It's only now that I realize how snobby the books were. Gypsies were always dirty and illiterate. Circus performers and anyone NOT a white-collar worker were definitely in a lower class! (Oh dear!) However, I loved them all, and spent happy hours being transported by boat to isolated islands, caves, and every kind of adventure with the Famous Five or the Secret Seven.

Comics did figure in our lives, and annuals, particularly Rupert Bear were a favourite. Dad was the provider of these at Christmas time. I think they may have been left over from his Christmas collection for the hospitals. Rupert's adventures with Bill Badger, Edward Elephant and Tiger Lily, all roaming around in Nutwood, were usually in rhyme, as in the DAILY EXPRESS paper.

There were also film annuals, again from the Gaumont, I suppose. I remember poring over one particular film star, I can't think WHO now, but he was of interest to friend Barbara and me, mainly because we had read somewhere that he had had his private parts shot off during the war! This unlikely fact fascinated us; he looked so handsome. I don't suppose this injury was as bad as we thought, and it may have been completely untrue, made up by some magazine or newspaper. He continued to appear mainly in cowboy films for years later, seemingly normal and just as handsome.

Anything and everything was read. Sunday papers cover to cover, and the *Picture Post*, but no women's magazines. I'm not sure they were around in the 1940s. I received a copy of *The Pilgrim's Progress*. The illustrations are beautiful, and I have the book now. I have to admit I have only read bits of it, as it's a bit heavy going and wasn't really my sort of reading. I was only about eight, so Enid still ruled.

One vivid memory was at Christmas, when very small, possibly five, Robin came into the bedroom and gave me one of his old annuals. It was Christmas Eve, and I was bursting with excitement. The first illustration was of Mickey Mouse, and underneath were the lines, "It was the night before Christmas, and all through the house, nothing was stirring, not even a mouse." Somehow that summed up the Christmassy feelings. I kept reading it and watching the window, hoping to see Father Christmas riding by. A magical time, even during the war. I hope today's children have that same excited, wondrous sparkly feeling on Christmas Eve.

HOTEL 'HAPPENINGS'

The White House opened officially as a hotel around 1949. The main guests had bed and breakfast, cooked by Betty and cousin Joy, who had moved in permanently with her dad and Betty. There was also dinner, in a long dining room whose walls were covered in photos of Reg's charges when he worked for Paramount Pictures. Each photo was behind glass, neatly framed in passe-partou, a black sticky tape. I don't think Uncle Reg did anything towards the guests, except talk to them and drift around, cigar in mouth. (The tobacco was always a brand called 'Baby's Bottom', something I would blush over when Reg told me; it was very rude in my eyes.)

I became, what I can only think of NOW, as a pain in the neck… I would take a running jump at the wall, pull myself over, straddle the smooth curved blue-capping bricks, then drop onto the ground. There WAS an easier way round, though bushes in the front garden, or EVEN the front gateless-gate. But the wall was a challenge, and quicker.

Once there, I would tap-dance or *jeter* my way into the kitchen. There would usually be confusion, Betty frying some chops (perhaps meat WAS off the ration now?), Joy would be dabbling with mint sauce, whilst a myriad pans of vegetables were pushing their lids off with steam. I must have got in the way, but nothing was ever said. In fact, Betty and Joy were chatty and always friendly. I was once asked to carry two plates of food into the dining room, where a few men sat – usually commercial travellers.

The photos of Reg's film-star friends from his Paramount days were all very smart, dark suits and ties. Cary Grant sent his love. Mae West also loved Uncle Reg… lots of kisses. Gary Cooper, just best wishes from HIM. These photos and lots more were plastered over the walls. (A post script to this is that we had those photos at 249 when Reg had gone. Mum kept them in our damp pantry, so most of them became spotted with mould or brown marks. When Mum eventually left 249, we had a great bonfire and these photos ended up burnt to ashes. We really regret that as they would be collectors' items nowadays, but we were not too impressed with them at that time. The famous were of no interest unless they had suffered 'war-wounds'!)

There was a sitting room for guests, and this was where the TV was. I had never seen a television in my life until Reg and Betty arrived next door. The TV set was massive, a light wood cabinet, a tiny round screen, and switches down the side. I believe it was a Peto Scott model? (It was moved into 249 after a few years; I remember it well.)

The first programme I watched at Uncle Reg's was a documentary about nature, dung-beetles, in fact. I watched intrigued as these beetles rolled the manure around in great balls. Then there was the news, starting with the television mast and radio waves encircling it, reading 'Nation Shall Speak Peace Unto Nation' whilst the signature tune was played. I was spellbound; it was a marvel… difficult to see, though, the screen was only very small, probably about eight inches square!

There was a round half-moon-shaped conservatory on the side of the house, where Reg had his wonderful tropical fish. He spent a lot of time with me, showing me the guppies, and the Siamese fighting fish. There was something magical about these fish. Again, I had never seen anything like them. Sticklebacks and minnows were what we would catch in our nets in the park pool, but these were exotic, with neon-coloured flashes of electric blue and turquoise with red around the face. The guppies were rather plain, but nice to watch, and (like the cats) always appeared pregnant. I helped Uncle Reg clean the glass, using a razor-blade on a stick, a very pleasurable task, as the green algae would be very easy to get off, leaving the glass sparkling. Also in the conservatory were some pelargonium plants, another first! I have still got some petals from these flowers pressed between the pages of my *Pilgrim's Progress* book.

Another of Reg's hobbies was growing tobacco plants, unheard of in the UK, I should think. The plants resided inside in pots, then when large enough, the leaves were picked and hung on a washing line across the conservatory to dry. These we would inspect every day. They had to be dried slowly, apparently, until crisp and crumbly. I never DID see the end product of the tobacco-growing exploit – the Baby's Bottom tobacco was probably smoother.

I think being able to pop over to Betty and Reg made me forget school for a few hours, especially the dreaded maths, which I hated and couldn't do. I hated 'sums'. Tony, Robin and Pat ALL kept telling me HOW to subtract and add, but THEIR way, which was different from the way I had been told to do it at St Jude's. I cried daily and lay awake at night worrying and praying that there wouldn't be a mental arithmetic test tomorrow. I could never fathom out if there were ten men digging a hole, and they took five hours to dig an area of 100 square feet, how much did they dig in twenty minutes!! Anyway who cared? Same with algebra. What WAS the use of THAT? I loved 'composition', writing an adventure story, or learning some poetry, but maths was a waste of time in my way of thinking… So the White House became a refuge for me. No. 249 was too full of well-meaning but bossy siblings.

JOY, AND A WEDDING

Cousin Joy was probably twenty years older than me. She was a very complex character, a good water-colour painter, a fantastic piano player, especially jazz, or, in those post-war days, boogie-woogie. Long before she came to live next door, she had had an affair with a gypsy. I only know the bare bones, but Joy DID buy herself an authentic gypsy caravan, which she 'parked' in the car park next door. It was a splendid caravan, with lots of wood carving, colourful paintings and a dear little room inside. The back few feet was a pull-down bench/bed, not big enough for one, let alone a family.

Joy helped Betty with the cooking and housework in the hotel. She cut a strange figure, very masculine, hair cut like a man, a cigarette bouncing around on her bottom lip, and clothes that were always trousers, and a tweedy jacket. She could have been taken for a young man, and some people probably did. Her shoes were men's lace-ups. I suppose she would be 'butch' in today's world, but although she looked it, I don't think she was... she had the romance with a male gypsy, and I think would have loved to have met someone and settled down.

I'm not sure my family think the same, as she was extremely odd and eccentric. Joy suffered with 'nerves', was going deaf, and had very serious continuous tinnitus. (This was a very sad part of her life, as we found out many years later.) Her 'nerves' were tested one day when doing her round of cleaning bedrooms and bathroom. Joy walked in unannounced on a male guest just stepping out of the bath... It seems nothing terrible today, but poor Joy had the shakes about it, and couldn't face the guest next morning. (Betty told me this little tale, Joy was too embarrassed.) Betty saw the funny side of it, as she always did.

To complete the Gittoes-Davies family residing at the White House, Betty rescued a little Labrador-cross. Betty named her Minnie. Betty decided that my Mickey and their little Minnie should marry. So, with a straight face, she carefully put a small piece of white net stuck to a hair-band on Minnie's head, also a flower. I had to bring the 'groom' over through the gate, to meet his bride. So a very solemn ceremony was performed by Betty, the 'vicar'(I don't think I was a 'bridesmaid'). The two dogs were then made to face one another and attend to their vows. (I have since realized that Mickey had once pushed his way through the laurel bushes in the front garden and wooed little Minnie… so perhaps Betty was doing the honourable thing and marrying them before an embarrassing event took place!) So my dog became a married one. But I don't think the two dogs met again.

Tony brought a new little 'girlfriend' to 249, for Mickey to commit adultery with. Her name was Flossie.

FLOSSIE

Flossie was a mongrel too, a long-haired terrier cross, black and white, an appealing little dog. I liked her, but couldn't forget a stray dog that Tony had brought to 249 a year or so before Flossie arrived in our midst. This dog was named Buster. Buster was brown, smooth-haired, bouncy and a super young mongrel. Tony loved him, and Mickey tolerated him.

One day, I was walking home from school with friend Barbara when she suddenly grabbed my arm. There was a squeal of brakes… "Isn't that your Buster who has just been run over?"

Sure enough, there was a removal van, stopped, driver out of his cab, looking in the gutter, and Buster lying there motionless. I am tearful now remembering that day. I held Buster and I knew that he had died. A trickle of blood was coming from his mouth… The driver was "very sorry but the dog just ran out right in front of me". The accident was only yards from 249's gate. Buster just looked as though he was asleep.

Everyone cried. I think Mum came out and we all trooped in carrying our lovely little golden-coated dog. Buster was only about nine months old.

There was a much gentler and nicer side to brother Tony. That night I was in bed still crying, and Tony came into the bedroom. He had red eyes, so he had been upset and weeping too. He held my hand, and said how much better it was that Buster hadn't suffered, and that he had just gone to sleep and wouldn't have known anything. So there WAS a softer side to a brother who, at times, rather frightened me.

So Flossie was number three dog, a welcome little rough-haired, black-and-white-coated friend.

Always 'tinkering' with anything that had an engine, Tony had put together a car along with his friend Mike. (Mike and Tony always referred to each other as 'Bill'. I have never found out why!) So Bill and Bill would take the two-seater out onto Tettenhall Road for a ride, to test it.

One day, Tony decided to have a longer run out into the countryside. He put Flossie into the passenger seat and set off. Apparently, whilst driving along a narrow lane, Tony looked across at Flossie, only to find that she had GONE, there was just an empty seat! Panic. He glanced in his mirror, and there she was, running along in the lane trying to catch him up. She had fallen out of the Perspex flap/window, but she was none the worse for her fall!

Flossie lived on for many years, in fact outliving Mickey. I'm trying to remember if Mickey and Flossie had pups. I know they had a tempestuous love affair. Unfortunately, I saw them behaving in a very unseemly manner, in the front garden of a house a hundred yards from home. I ignored them both, but they saw me and started to move towards me. I just dashed home and told Mum, who, as usual, had to go and sort them out.

There was also another even MORE embarrassing moment, when Dad's under-manager, a handsome man called Mr Fullelove (yes, true) came to visit us at 249. I think I was in the house alone, because I had the rather uneasy job of trying to make conversation, no adults to the rescue. In desperation as my chatter dried up, I thought I would introduce Mr Fullelove to the dogs. I flung open the kitchen window and we both peered out. There amongst Mum's hydrangeas, her pride and joy, were Mickey and Flossie in full swing, tottering around joined together. I wished the ground would open up!

Mr Fullelove became a regular visitor in spite of the sexual exploits of our dogs, and fell in (and out) of love with a young woman who stayed with us… but that story is later.

HOLIDAYS AND PICNICS

As a family we did occasionally go on holiday, usually to Rhyl or, better, Nevin, in North Wales. The Nevin holidays I liked. There was a steep road down to the beach, and on the left was a house, not all that big, that belonged to Mr Atlee, our prime minister at the time. On two occasions we stayed with an old Welsh lady and her son who had Downs syndrome. He was always smiling, his cap over one eye.

We had full board, coming in for dinner after a day out (we were not allowed back into the house in the day whatever the weather!). One year, the other people staying in the house were circus performers, an eastern European family, who were 'dare-devil horse-back-riders', the men dressed as Cossacks apparently. Where their horses were stabled is still a mystery. The mother and her son slept in the attic, so that they could accommodate at least two families. Each night, I would hear the couple creaking past on the stairs, then up the ladder into what must have been more of a loft than an attic.

Somehow they frightened me. The mother had large warts or moles on her face and a whiskery chin. Out in the back yard were ferrets. I crept out one day to see them and the son came up and stood looking and smiling at me. It's a terrible thing to admit, but in those days, anyone who was 'different' was almost ignored and given the fish-eye. I didn't speak to the lad and just ran in.

What I didn't know until recently was that Dad couldn't pay for the 'digs'. Mum must have died a thousand deaths. I'm not sure HOW that was resolved.

On another holiday to Barmouth, much later (I was probably ten), Robin ended up paying out for our stay, as Dad had run out of cash. This was Dad, it must have been difficult to forgive him, but I suppose Mum may have done, but it made her more of a martyr than ever.

Robin often came to Dad's rescue in more ways than one, but that was years on.

The carefree holidays were spent with my aunties in Stourbridge. I stayed with Mum's sister Vera (everyone called her Ve) or sometimes with Glad, Mum's much younger sister. Neither auntie had any children so indulged all of their nephews and nieces. They both spent time with me, which was difficult for Mum to do, with a big house, four children, and a husband who never helped in any way... not to mention all the menagerie!

Auntie Glad drove, which was so unusual in those days. She had learnt to drive when she was a nanny/nurse to three children of a wealthy family in Worcestershire. They had allowed her to drive their little car, so she did, driving just round and round the drive, but this start gave Glad many happy years of motoring.

COUSINS

There were many happy picnics on Kinver Edge, a beauty spot in Worcestershire, where the aunts would play hide-and-seek with their nieces and nephew. All three aunts were big in height and in girth, so behind a bracken leaf WASN'T a good place to hide, but they DID...

On one particular picnic, Marj's son Mike was 'seeking', and he glimpsed Auntie Ve crouching behind a leaf. He crept up. "GOT YOU, AUNTIE!" An embarrassed Ve stood up, pulling up her pink to-the-knee knickers. She had been caught having a quiet wee. She laughed about it later, her face red with embarrassment.

Staying in Stourbridge was a time I loved because there were cousins to play with. Mum's younger brother Doug had two girls, Wendy and Judy. Wendy became a good friend, and still is, although now she lives in New Zealand.

There was fun of a sort down in Ve's cellar. Cousin Mike from Fulham asked us girls if we would like to join his 'gang'. (There was only Mike in it, but that seemed irrelevant at the time.) Of course we would, it sounded exciting.

"There is an initiation test to take first," said a serious Mike.

Not put off, we walked down the steep dark stairs into a cellar even bigger than 249's. Ve's husband, Uncle Bill, kept all his tools and turning devices down there. To this day, I don't know what the bit of equipment WAS, but whatever it was, it had a very rusty kind of needle, which lowered down onto an object when a handle was turned. The 'test' involved putting a finger or thumb in line with the needle, then Mike would lower it onto (or into) our fingers!!! I haven't asked Wendy over in NZ lately, but I don't think our skin was penetrated. I think it was a test of braving what might happen.

The days in Stourbridge were good. We could get away with doing things we couldn't do at home, like leaping from chintz-covered chair then onto a settee, and a clamber over the back. This took place in the front room of Auntie Ve's.

We girls were regularly chased by Richard, a cousin on Uncle Bill's side. Richard was a rather nice handsome boy (who always seemed to be in school uniform). We all three took it in turns to slide down the long shiny banisters. The end bit was a curl of wood, rather like a snail-shell, so you had to stop before you hit it in full slide…

Ve's house was a quite large Victorian semi, ideal for running through, hiding, and trying out the soft water pump in the back kitchen. This pump was wonderful for washing hair, as the collected water was so soft – bubbles formed at one drop of water.

Auntie must have developed Popeye-type muscles pumping away before any water arrived then shot into the brown sink. I don't think it was ever used in drinks, though.

There was an incident with Richard in the bathroom. We girls decided to dare Richard to wee in front of us. We never thought he would take us up on it, but he did. So amidst lots of giggles, and covering our eyes with our hands, brave Richard DID. (We both agreed afterwards that we hadn't 'seen anything'.)

About forty years later, at a family funeral, I saw Richard again. He didn't recognize me, which is just as well. But I felt so sad because he had 'let himself go'. He had gone through a nasty divorce, a very bad car accident, and was bringing his two children up single-handed, so no wonder he was rather unkempt. However, I shall remember the handsome lad, fresh-faced, and without a care in the world, carrying out our dare in Auntie Ve's very Victorian bathroom.

VALLEY FARM

Whilst still on summer holidays I sometimes went to stay with Wendy's Auntie Seonee in deepest Worcestershire, in a place called Fockbury, not far from Bromsgrove. Seonee and husband Henry were farmers. The farmhouse was gigantic, with lots of polished wood floors, a vast farmhouse kitchen with an Aga-type range, and a scrubbed wooden table, big enough to seat eight easily. In the dining room was an even bigger table of polished dark wood, the sort that has to have the condiment sets zoomed from one end to the other on castors!

Henry was not a very handsome chap. He was red-faced and very large, with eyes that were slits peering out from above fat cheeks. I didn't get to talk to him, though; he may well have been erudite, but I never could tell. His family owned farms in the district.

Seonee was named by the doctor who delivered her, who had just returned from India and had spent a pleasant time in the Seonee mountains in India. He suggested to Seonee's mother she name the baby after the wonderful mountains – very novel! – and the baby's mother agreed.

Seonee was a lovely woman, as fair as Henry was dark. She had a pale skin too, and was a jolly person. (Apparently she wasn't, being extremely unhappily married to Henry, but to us she was always smiling, and she did a good job of hiding her sorrow from us children.) Henry was her second romance, her previous boyfriend had left her at the altar, something that had blighted her life. Shortly after that sad event, Henry had arrived on the scene, a well-off man of property, so Seonee had married him for better and for worse.

I heard years later that she would have liked to leave Henry, but where would she go? So she stuck it out, as did a whole host of women. No single-mother benefits or pensions in those days, these were the latter years of the 1940s.

To us, though, life was just fun with the hay barns to play in. We would squeeze between bales of hay into a gap, and chatter in our warm sweet-smelling den. We were found once, knickers round our ankles weeing away, into the hay! To climb down and go into the house was far too much trouble. Henry was even redder in the face than usual, "How would you like YOUR food wee'd on? My cows won't like it at all."

Henry DID love his herd of cows, but not so the chickens. They were battery ones. Long lines of cages, more than one poor chicken to a cage, heads out pecking from a long trough filled with grain and a trough for water. Wendy told me quite matter of factly that the electric lights were left on all night, so that the hens would think it was daylight and produce more eggs! I don't remember flinching or feeling any pity for these poor creatures, and it was many years later that I suddenly thought of those hens. It's a shuddering thought now, but I must have been tougher then than I am today.

The village of Fockbury was, and still is, a small collection of houses and farms in a very beautiful area of Worcestershire. (I suppose today there would be wry smiles at the name, but the 'F' word wasn't in our vocabulary. Not that we were goodie-goodies, but nobody used it, and if someone HAD muttered THE word we children wouldn't have guessed what it meant.)

The house opposite Valley Farm was Housmans (originally Valley House, I believe), a very attractive house where Housman the poet was born. The owners of the house were a family called Pugh. I think Mrs Vera Pugh was a doctor and Mr Pugh a lawyer, practising in Bromsgrove. I never met them, but we did meet their son John. A tall lanky teenager, he would pop over the lane and chat with us and play a game or two of table tennis when he was home from college or school. Wendy and Judy knew him well. They would stay for weeks at the farm, as Seonee was their mother Dorothy's sister, so a real auntie (I was a sort of niece-in-law) and they became very close.

I loved staying at the farm. How I actually got there, I can't remember. Mum's sister Glad did have the use of a car, but I must have travelled by bus. There was so much to do. We did try to help with a few jobs, especially jobs around the cows. The milking shed was a place of peace, just the slurping noise of the milking machines.

The resident colony of cats would suddenly appear in the shed door, and whoever was doing the milking would pull a teat out, point it at the cats, and squirt a jet of milk into their mouths. I don't suppose there was such a thing as Health and Safety organizations then. Every cow had a name, and they knew their names and positions in the stalls. Afterwards, the slope into the shed was a mass of sloshy cow-muck. We would brush with vim and vigour, smelly though it was. We thought we were helping, and we never minded the pong!

On dry days in late summer, Seonee picked mushrooms from the 'top field' She would carry a trug, and we would all hunt through the grass.

Usually the trug was full at the end of our labours, and we would march home. The mushrooms appeared for breakfast next morning, fried and crispy.

Early on, when I first stayed at the farm, there were two German prisoners of war still billeted there. Hans and Rudi, I remember them well. Seonee would always include all the farm workers when cooking a meal.

On weekdays these meals were around the scrubbed wooden table in the kitchen, which sat well over ten people. Sunday dinner was a more formal 'do'. The Germans were not excluded from these meals. I would think they thanked God that they had landed on such a nice bunch of English people. Wendy has just told me that Auntie Seonee quietly told her nieces to be aware that Rudi wasn't to be chatted up; he was rather dark and moody. Hans and Rudi were only boys and must have been homesick for their homes and families. Seonee made them very welcome.

The odd thing was that somehow the two soldiers were allowed guns! We cousins would watch them hang a dead rabbit up by its back legs having shot it, then cut the fur close to the ankles and pull the skin down, peeling it off like a jacket – it really became the phrase 'skin-a-rabbit' when taking a child's vest off! Again, I saw nothing cruel about this procedure, and in fact I had witnessed it many times at home when Mum was given a wild rabbit. Rabbits were the staple diet in the war and afterwards. (Underground poultry was what Ve's husband Bill always called bunnies.)

I hope the soldiers eventually returned home to Germany and had good memories of their stay at Valley Farm, and the nice kindly Seonee.

Later on, when I was about twelve, and beginning to get crushes on boys, we developed a crush on a farm hand called Leslie Pepworth. (Wendy says she never DID do what I am about to tell, but I will question her on that.)

The farmyard was usually wet and manure ridden, but sometimes it was all right to play ball or vague pat-a-ball tennis – we never could work out the scoring. I wasn't exactly about to swoon, but out from the dairy came Leslie, overalls, muddy boots, and a lot of spikey blond hair. Not a Greek god lookalike; however, I DID have a fluttering heartbeat, and I was definitely going to 'zonk' the ball and show how very good I was at tennis. I zonked, and Wendy dived forward and – well I hope she doesn't mind me putting this in – she let out a great loud trumpet of wind. She then shouted across the yard. "Oh, VAL, was that YOU LETTING OFF?" We have discussed this lately and Wendy insists that it WAS me, but I will beg to differ. Whoever it was, I don't suppose Leslie turned a hair, or even heard. He may have thought it was a cow.

One abiding memory of life on the farm was the bull. He was a bruiser, with a head that appeared wider than his great bulky body. He had style! His eyelashes were long and fair, he had a metal ring through his wide nostrils and he looked out from under his eyelashes with a superior but kindly gaze. Once a year, the bull was brought to the 'ladies'. He would be led out from his stall and taken into a fenced-off area. There was a five-barred gate and on this gate we would climb to watch. So green was I that I never really caught on. I suppose I may have guessed. After all, I had seen our dogs mating, but so busy were we chatting that the actual 'business' went over our heads…

I remember lots of grunting and shouting as the farm hands tried to direct the bull in the right direction towards his ladies. I feel a real dope now! What had I thought WAS going on? Somehow country life was more 'raw' and yet events such as this were never spoken of. Well, not within our earshot, but we were allowed to view all the animal 'goings-on'.

The summer would usually end with the plums being picked. I only went once. The field was down the lane. There were people up ladders, some shaking of trees, and fat red plums to eat. Along the drive we rattled in the old farm cart, up to the farm and through a brick archway, and were deposited onto the farmyard. The smell of cows and dried mud summed up the wonderful day out. I wanted to marry a farmer.

Henry had lambs, but I never saw any. Perhaps they were in a faraway field.

Judy went back to the farm when in her late teens, to live there with Auntie Seonee and Henry. They bought her a horse. Horses are still Judy's life.

We visited Valley Farm and Housmans last year. Everything appeared the same. We couldn't get a good close-up of the farmyard, it would have been too nosey of us, but the Pughs' house was just as it was.

I have happy memories of those holidays, and the smell of hay brings the thought of our den back, the giggling, the TOP secret talks about boys, big red-faced Henry, and the fair, pale Seonee.

Childhood at its best! Long sunny summer days, making our dens, getting filthy, watching animals in the raw, laughing and giggling as girls do. Wonderful memories.

THE GAUMONT AND CELEBRITIES

Back at 249, I had a job to do. Dad had quite a few visiting film stars, perhaps advertising the film currently showing. One such star was Jean Kent, a well-known actress. She was due to appear at the Gaumont, and someone had to present her with a bouquet of flowers. That was me. Then the worry began for Mum: what could I wear? Mum had a peach-coloured lacy evening dress, I can't imagine where from, or if it was even hers. Well, she decided that she would cut down and alter her rather faded ball gown and I was kitted out one evening in THE dress, and around my shoulders was a white fur cape. Again, where THAT appeared from, I don't know. Mum really didn't have many clothes, and a white fur cape was definitely not one of HER fashion items. (She did, however, have some horrible furs, fox, I think. She would wear them over her shoulders and the mouth of the fox would snap shut and fasten around its tail. There were tiny tails hanging down too. Horrible.)

I met Jean Kent and presented the flowers. The local newspaper was there, so there was a picture in the *Express & Star*. She was nice, glamorous, and the photo turned out well, except for my buck teeth, and what appeared to be Dad looking right down Jean's cleavage, half-smoked cigarette in his hand.

Not long after, Petula Clark the singer also came to the Gaumont. She would be about sixteen. Someone else presented her with the flowers. I don't remember feeling miffed. I was there and thought Petula's midnight-blue velvet full-length cape was so beautiful.

The Gaumont was host to many stars of the time: Michael Rooney the actor, who Pat met and was bowled over by his green eyes; David Whitfield, a singer; Hylda Baker, the comedienne, with her long-faced 'stooge' and partner. Dad said she walked around with two little pet monkeys on her shoulders – not all that hygienic as the monkeys would wee on her, so the smell wasn't of violets.

Dad also started a talent contest. This went very well, and I believe it launched quite a few singers into stardom. I stood at the side of the stage during one contest and became almost stage-struck when a young lady, dressed in a billowing orange dress, ran onto the stage and sang, "I was walking along, minding my business, when out of an orange-coloured sky, CRASH, BANG, ALAKAZANG, I took one look at you…one look and I yelled TIMBER!" Well, it went on, and I thought she was wonderful, the lights, the stage, the applauding audience, the looped see-through gold curtains, glowing… Everything!

Well, I was heading for showbiz.

The feeling didn't last. Ballet was everything, so I went on tapping and twirling around, probably driving everyone mad.

Years later, Dad had Joy Beverley of the Beverley Sisters appearing at the Gaumont. Billy Wright, the captain of the Wolves football team, was a regular picture-goer (as were most of the Wolves team). According to Dad, Joy was chatting in his office before the show when Billy popped in, and Dad introduced them. Well, Dad became a matchmaker, because that introduction turned into marriage for Joy and Billy. I think they lived happily ever after.

FRIENDS AWOL IN THE PARK

The weather in July and August was always sunny! Well, I suppose it wasn't, but looking back, I don't remember many rainy days.

The local park was a venue for fishing for tiddlers, red butchers and sticklebacks. One summer's day I set off with my friend Linda early in the afternoon, fishing nets and jam jars carried with purpose. We had a wonderful few hours, catching the fish, watching the boating on the lake, just sitting talking on the grassy area. Suddenly, a bell rang out, a sign that the park was closing… it must have been eight o'clock. We had never been out that late, not alone! With jam jars swinging, water spilling and little fish being hurtled around, we ran to the nearest gate. I suppose we ran most of the way back to 249. I do remember feeling sick with worry. Just as 249 loomed into view, we were set upon by Pat and Robin, plus a flustered Mum. We had been out for seven hours or more, and the search parties were out.

Mum didn't often get angry, but she did on that occasion. Linda was dispatched home with Robin, and I never knew what her parents said or did. They were probably out searching too. The 'catch' was tipped into the pond. They most likely died, as most tiddlers did after being in a hot jar, swung about for hours in the heat, then tipped out into the pond, only to die in the night or be half-eaten by dragonfly larvae.

Linda's family lived in a crescent close to 249. Her mother, also Linda, was from the North-East, as was her father, who was a jobbing builder, but he wasn't around very much. They lived in a ground-floor flat in a large row of terraced houses. I don't think I ever went into Linda's bedroom, I only remember their sitting room. Linda senior was much younger than my Mum, but was much stricter. If Linda did anything naughty or didn't toe the line, her mother would shout, "I'll thrash you!" This was a word that we wouldn't have used and it struck me as cruel. However, I never saw Linda being thrashed, so I think it was just her mother's North-East expression.

Instead of playing outside, when I went to Linda's we were given football pool coupons to fill in – not to be sent off, but just as an exercise. All the squares would be neatly crossed and filled in by us – a strange pastime and rather useless!

There was also a game involving stockings. As there weren't any about at this time, I wonder where they got them from? Linda's mum's sister was a conductress on the trolleybuses, only a young woman in her twenties, so perhaps she had a nice boyfriend, possibly an American left here after they had been sent back home to the USA? We were given a stocking, already laddered, then we were allowed to ladder the rest, watching as the ladders ran up the leg. I've only now, whilst writing this, realized what a strange lot they must have been, how unimaginative.

Linda played round at 249 quite often. It was possible to buy plastic-coated wire in an array of colours. These were marvellous for plaiting into bracelets. The strands were plaited or woven, then joined into a circle, a decorative item of jewellery. For unknown reasons, Linda would hide some plastic strands in her pocket and take them home. I knew she was doing this, but felt helpless to tackle her about it. I told Pat and Mum, and we watched her as she pocketed some. We did nothing, hoping the stealing craze would abate, but it didn't! In fact, it got worse, in a silly way.

Mum kept our precious hand-picked apples under her bed in newspaper-lined boxes and, after asking Mum, we could take one to eat. However, Linda would pretend to go to the lavatory, nip past the bathroom into Mum's bedroom, and fill her pockets with apples. She would reappear with bulging coat pockets obviously full of apples, thinking that we hadn't noticed. The daft thing was that if she had asked, she could have taken some home anyway.

We still stayed friends, however, and during a conversation when sitting in the little park by the canal, the one that years before my Great Uncle Harry had taken me to (we were allowed to play, unsupervised in those days, even by the canal), Linda told me she thought her mother was very ill and probably dying. How she had found out was that her mother had to use a potty for some reason (probably a urine sample). Linda had viewed the contents, which were dark with blood. So, her mother MUST have been very seriously ill and dying! We stared at each other. Linda wasn't tearful or particularly sad, but I was shocked. I had never ever thought that mothers could die.

Linda's mother didn't die, and she did years later give birth to a son, so perhaps she was having tests, but it filled me with fear that Mum COULD die. I had never encountered the death of a parent. Dad was always ill, but again I never associated his many illnesses with dying, so this was another step towards growing up.

I didn't stay friends with Linda for long after that. We had a different clique of friends. When eleven, she passed for the high school and did very well indeed, ending up in a very responsible job.

(Oddly, years and years later, Linda suddenly called at 249, having had no contact for years. I was very surprised when she asked me to be her bridesmaid. She was teaching and had met a young chap teaching at the same school, and they were about to plight their troth at St Jude's. Her fiancé was a member of a famous tea family, a very likeable man. The wedding went off fine, and I didn't think we would meet up again for another few years, but we DID.)

SAVED BY MY TONSILS!

The end of summer holidays was always dreaded. I still hated St Jude's school. I would get anxious and nervous at the thought of it. One year, though, nature stepped in, and I had to have my tonsils and adenoids removed. Even this operation was a let-off for me, no school for weeks.

I went into the Royal Hospital in town. No informal and comforting talk before the operation. Nothing was ever explained in those days; everyone had to face it all in ignorance. I was in a two-bed ward. I had the operation, nothing terrible to recall, but afterwards was different. I felt ill, and very sore. Dad nipped in from the Gaumont, which was round the corner from the hospital. He had managed to get a carton of ice cream, the sort that the usherettes sold in the intervals. As usual, Dad appeared and was my saviour. Never mind that I never saw him when life was flowing along nicely, but here he was, and the ice cream was wonderful and soothed my raw throat a treat.

The worst bit of my stay was the little girl in the other bed. She had had a brain tumour removed and her head was all bound in bandages, with draining tubes sticking out all over the place. She was SO ill, I suddenly felt death, and a fear of dying when young. Death was surely for the very old?

The little girl's father came to visit most days. Visiting times were restricted. I think family were only allowed to visit twice a week and that was two afternoons. Whether this little girl was so ill that her dad was allowed more time, I'm not sure. Her father was deaf and dumb, another rather frightening sight. He signed to his wife when she did visit, which was rarely. I would lie in my bed watching the girl's father, tears in his eyes, as he sat by her bed. My dad thought she would not survive. I felt very frightened because a child only a year or so older than me could die!

All this was made worse because, for some reason, I began to bleed. As I lay on my side, a trickle of blood must have run across my cheek and down into my ear. I was looking at the bloody pillow when I heard footsteps in the corridor, then voices. It was Mum! I felt all excited … I looked expectantly at the doorway…

I SAW Mum's head pop around the door, THEN THUMP, I saw a pair of feet being dragged past and out of sight. Apparently, Mum had seen the stray blood, thought I was haemorrhaging from the ears, and passed completely OUT. I don't think she came back in to the ward.

I returned home in about a week. No school for a couple more weeks, thank goodness. The nice news afterwards was that the little girl in the next bed recovered. I don't know how well, but she went home to her loving dad.

My dad saved a film annual book that had been collected for the Christmas charity, and walked round to the girl's house, which was in a street behind the cinema. That was Dad, he was either very good or very bad.

The post script to this saga is that I ate a walnut straight after arriving home. This lodged in one of the scars, and I had a throat infection of grand proportions. More time off school.

The Christmas after my tonsil operation was memorable for me. I had a sweet shop given me as a present, I think from Mum and Dad. There were little tiny jars on the shelves, holding either hundreds and thousands or a seed-like sweet. They were all edible and, when bitten, those small round seeds would explode with a spicy flavour. It was many years later when I was making a curry that I realized the seeds were just coriander. That little cardboard shop was almost out of this world. It wouldn't excite a child today, but it made my Christmas, and I played with it for hours. Only a simple thing, but I can still feel the thrill of delight when I saw it, complete with sweeties. Of course it couldn't match up to my best present of all time, Mickey, but it was very special. Eventually the cardboard got squashed, the sweet jars were lost, and it gathered dust under my bed. I don't suppose I even noticed it had gone, thrown in the bin.

About this time, my Grandad Davies, Dad and Reg's father, came to live at the White House.

GRANDPA DAVIES

Grandpa Mansel Bernard Davies was born in a little village in west Wales, a place with rather a famous name, Bethlehem! He was one of nine children, his father a tailor, I believe.

Mansel was bright and would have loved to be a school teacher, but it wasn't possible to keep him at school, so he went to work in his sister and brother-in-law's grocery shop in 'the valleys'. Robin said that he progressed to being his own boss and having a horse and cart to visit people in outlying places in the Black Mountain area, selling just about everything.

Margarine was just appearing in shops, and for some reason, Grandpa had problems selling it, which put him into financial trouble. The customers still liked 'real' butter, not this substitute.

Later, he met Gertrude, moved to Cleobury Mortimer, a Shropshire village, and opened a shop/post office. But I don't think Grandpa was a worldly man. He got into debt and was declared bankrupt years later. I think from Cleobury he opened or worked in a shop in Bishops Castle, also a tiny village in deepest Shropshire.

He was a gentleman in the true sense. Robin thought that Grandpa would let customers have goods on the 'slate' but they would be reluctant to pay him back. I suppose he didn't make much money, or might have been in debt. So, he moved into the Midlands and worked as a grocer in West Bromwich.

West Bromwich is where he and Gertrude, née Gittoes, raised their family, before moving to the Chapel Ash area of Wolverhampton, 15 minutes from 249. They lived there until Gertrude passed away. I was taken to see her just a few days before she died. She lay in bed, eyes closed, her skin a shade of yellow, hair still jet-black. She had cancer.

I had never had much to do with my Grandma Davies. She was always a little bit 'witchlike' – very foreign-looking. Her family, the Gittoes, were also from Wales, from villages near the Shropshire borders. I stood in her bedroom, aged about eight, knowing nothing of death. To me, she was just 'old and poorly'. I was more interested in the little mantelpiece ornaments than my dying grandma.

Years later, when I was told the story of Grandma taking on Bette, Mum's Downs baby sister, I felt very sorry that I had rather dismissed her

104

as just a sour-looking, pointy-chinned woman without teeth. In fact, she must have had a kind heart beating in a grim exterior.

Grandpa Davies settled in with Reg and Betty in the White House Hotel next to 249. So now I had an extra excuse for scaling the wall. He was a very gentle man, Welsh speaking until the age of seven.

So by now there was Reg, Betty, Joy and Grandpa, all jogging along. The odd thing is that neither Robin nor I can remember Dad visiting Reg next door! The two brothers had never fallen out so this is very strange. However, Mum must have ventured round one day. Her story was that Reg made a pass at her! I know he was a Casanova, but I do think she was taking him too seriously. Perhaps I'm wrong. Who knows?

Betty battled on with the cooking, whilst Joy and Reg sat contentedly smoking in the conservatory amidst the drying tobacco leaves. By now, Reg had bought a smaller car, an Austin seven. Betty painted it white, as an advert for the White House. It looked good to me, but probably raised a few eyebrows as it drove out of the drive.

One particular day, I was sent by Mum to buy something from the post office around the corner. The postmaster was a creepy man called Mr Walmsley. (I was told later that he used to watch children swimming in the town baths. I can't call him a paedophile, but I do believe he was strange, and a bit spooky.) I gave him the money that Mum had given me, and for some reason, I will never know why, Mr Walmsley accused me of not giving him the correct money. He wanted another three pence… Well, I hadn't got three pence left over. He made me feel like a criminal, and I rushed home thinking the police would be knocking on our door: 'THEY' were after me. I was crying.

I told Mum, who was flustered, but wasn't too bothered and said, "Forget it. He's a weird chap." But still feeling I had committed a crime and was dishonest, I jumped over the wall to tell Auntie Elizabeth (Betty was only used by the grown-ups). Without hesitation, Betty got the car keys, got me into the passenger seat of the little white car, and roared off to confront him before he closed. She put the car into full throttle, and we roared round the corner, with me shaking. I had never been in a car before. Betty strode into the shop. To my relief, she tore a strip off the horrible man and left him cowering behind the counter. Then she marched out, holding my hand and slamming the door so that the bell jangled loudly. In my eyes, Auntie Elizabeth was a champion.

It was about this time that I did actually join a ballet school. It was the Vera Hildreth School of Ballet. Looking back, how did Mum afford the lessons? She never had enough housekeeping from Dad, so this was a very nice thing for her to do in the circumstances.

I was so besotted by dance, I couldn't wait for the Saturday morning to arrive. The studio was in the centre of town, in Waterloo Road. (Many,

many years later, when Vera had moved down to Tettenhall, these rooms were taken over by a firm of quantity surveyors, and Harold was one of them! So, where we children had strutted our stuff became offices where Harold could strut his stuff, in a different way.)

I took one exam, and attained 85 out of a 100 points. I had criticism of my shoulders lifting, but otherwise I did well.

(Meanwhile, back in Stourbridge, cousin Wendy did REALLY well, and took an exam to enter the Sadler's Wells Ballet Company in London. She got in! Recently she told me the reason she never took up the offer of a place was that she knew her dad, Doug, couldn't possibly afford to keep her in London… so she gave up her dreams. I think this says something for the feeling in post-war Britain. Only the well-heeled could aspire to those kind of dreams. I think it was a very unselfish act on Wendy's part.)

I didn't carry on for long at Vera Hildreth's, although I think I was doing all right. But I would only ever have reached the back row of the corps de-ballet, if that.

However, I still tapped danced and pirouetted around, especially in the kitchen of the White House. I must have driven Betty mad, but she never showed any irritation with me. Or perhaps she DID, but I certainly didn't notice any.

Reg's sons, Barry and Mansel, would visit now and then, Ruth very rarely. Ruth upset Mum, after one of her visits to her father. On leaving, she said, "What a pity Auntie Maude didn't come round to see ME." It probably hadn't passed through her mind that SHE should have visited Auntie Maude.

I think that is what has coloured our view of Ruth. She later became an eye surgeon, but the family completely lost touch with her, and, of all four cousins, she was the one we never really got to know, but brother Robin said how nice she was to him.

Mansel and Barry were very different, though. Friendly, outgoing and fun to have next door. They had lived mainly with their mum Mabel near Southampton. Mabel kept on very good terms with Reg and Betty, in spite of everything. I never met Mabel, but Mum corresponded right up until her eighties. Mabel was a founder member of Amnesty International.

All four of Reg's offspring were very musical, particularly Joy, as I've mentioned. I think Ruth played the cello, but I'm not so sure about the boys. However, Betty told me that when Reg first brought her home to meet the family (this is where I took it that they were just married!), the happy pair were met in the living room by a quartet who serenaded them in! What a weird and quirky happening… but nice. No animosity from the children, who might have been very upset that their errant father had left their mother and taken a young partner. No! Just a musical soirée.

THE COUSINS AND AUNTIE VERA

This was the unusually liberal life the Gittoes-Davies family lived. Beltane School was a free-spirit establishment, and so Barry and Mansel were just that.

I have scars on the back of my hand to this day from being dared by Mansel to ride my bike backwards around the car park of the hotel. I crashed, of course, my hand scraping against THE wall between 249 and the White House.

There were tales of Barry, when aged about five, coming downstairs in the morning and finding spirit bottles left lying around after a party thrown by Reg. Barry drank all the dregs out of the bottles, and was found completely inebriated lying asleep under a table. I don't know if it had any after-effects – they could have been fatal – but it was all taken in good spirits (oh dear, an accidental pun).

I think sex was something more open too, not having the taboo that reigned at 249…

There is one story, I remember Mum told it to me later on in her life. It involved Mum's sister, Auntie Ve.

Ve stayed with Mum and Dad regularly, and on one occasion Reg and Betty invited her round to tea. According to Mum, Ve got all dressed up in her purple outfit, navy hat and white gloves, the lot. Ve waved goodbye to Mum and set off down our front path and up next-door's drive. (Ve wouldn't have squeezed through the laurel, as we did. Dignity was everything to a very elegant Vera.)

Mum didn't expect Ve back for at least an hour, but, only five or so minutes later, Ve arrived back, puffing and red-faced, crochet-edged handkerchief in her hand, a hot flush in full swing. After Ve had sat down and got her breath back, she told Mum what had happened…

When she arrived at the front door, she had rung the bell. Nobody came, so she walked round to the kitchen door. Barry was there, unexpectedly home from school.

"Oh HELLO, Auntie," he said, with a grin as he shook her gloved hand.

Ve explained to him that Reg and Betty had asked her round for a cup of tea. Barry looked a bit flustered… but burst out laughing, grinning like a

Cheshire cat. "OH, Auntie Vera… Oh DEAR. I'm SO SORRY. They must have forgotten you were coming round. I'm afraid they're 'on the job' at the moment…would you like to wait?"

Well, a terribly embarrassed Ve retreated back to 249, all red-faced and flustered. She may have even pushed her way back through the laurel hedge – a quicker 'getaway'. She had her cuppa, but not with Reg and Betty.

Such openness was typical of Reg's family, all privately educated, erudite, musical, and SO different from us next door, but I loved it there. They seemed free spirits compared to us.

Joy became a regular visitor to our house. We had a piano. It was bought for me by Mum, who paid on the 'never-never' for it. Looking back, I feel I was lucky. Mum must have sacrificed quite a lot for me and my interest in all things arty. As the last child, I was spoilt in a lot of ways (I can hear Pat and Robin saying that now). So having a piano was a generous gift. I loved it. I made up tunes, including a lullaby (which I have passed on to my granddaughter Anna). My piano was the second-nicest gift I ever received. Mickey, my black mongrel, was still top-gift. The piano was installed in the front room. It was shiny and black and was a joy for years, even moving with me when I married.

Like a lot of houses then, the front room in 249 was a place where visitors were invited, where snooker could be played (on a very small table), and the piano could be played. Joy would sit, a ciggy always dangling on her bottom lip, bouncing up and down as she strummed the keys, one eye half shut as the smoke rose. She never played from music, although I think she could read music, but she was fond of anything with a bit of 'kick' to it. She taught me boogie-woogie, tunes that were in the hit parade, mainly film music and lots of ditties, and jangles. I liked her, she was very unaffected, so different from her half-sister Ruth. Joy's nose was pointed, with a flat tip, a strange shape, and I remember staring at it! Not only did Joy play piano, her artwork was good, AND she could write.

We still have a typed-out booklet, in a folder, a children's story written by Joy. She too loved animals, so the story was all about a village of dogs who drove vehicles with giant taps attached, and, as they motored, water would pour out, and the streets would be washed clean. Sounds batty, but it has a unique feeling about it. I honestly don't think anyone in the family has ever read it, or even knows of its existence, except me.

Joy's love of books was another side to her life. She read avidly, mainly autobiography, or the lives of politicians and historical figures, I don't recall her reading any fiction or paperbacks. Books delving into religious faiths also interested her, and she dabbled with the idea of becoming a Roman Catholic. A rosary miraculously appeared, given, we think, by her gypsy lover… but this may be hearsay.

At some time during her stay with her father, Joy got a job. It was working at the Eveready battery factory. Not a nice job in the offices, but a job on the shop floor, on piecework, a horrible task, I think she had to pour in the liquid tar that topped the batteries. I know she came home dirty, with a green overall still on, and a scarf/turban over her short very manly hairstyle. Why she did that awful conveyor-belt job was probably to get some money in. She was reliant on her father, but he was far from well off by these days.

Prior to moving in, she had been in the WAAF or WRAC. She liked uniforms and perhaps the company of other women. She may have served in the latter part of the war, I don't know. Her deafness was getting worse and she suffered from tinnitus, not helped by the noise of a factory. Nothing was done, which is such a pity, because Joy had bouts of depression, not helped by constant 'noise' in her ears.

PIANOS AND HEART-THROBS

Having had fun on the piano, I asked Mum if I could have music lessons. Mum had heard of a very 'good' teacher not far away and within walking distance.

So I started lessons with Miss Ponds. The Ponds family were well known in the Wolverhampton area as a 'musical family'. Again, Mum must have saved to pay for these lessons. None of my siblings had any interest in piano or dance.

I walked to Miss Ponds' house, nearby. She was a strict teacher, and I was afraid of her. She wielded a pointer, which looked dangerous to me. She was probably an excellent teacher but, although I loved playing, the hour with her was not a happy time. She was grim and unsmiling. No doubt a brilliant teacher, but too strict.

Miss Ponds moved soon after I began lessons and set up in a house quite a long distance from home. I walked it many times, on my own, which nowadays would be frowned on. I was about ten, going on eleven. I never did take any examination. I had a feeling that I couldn't keep on attending, and she was getting aggressive if I made a mistake, the odd rap on the knuckles would be doled out, and I began to hate going...

That was the end of lessons, but I have continued to play (albeit only for my own ears) ever since, and it's something for which I am indebted to Mum.

The Greenhams were still at 247, Mrs Greenham baking and cooking like mad to feed the three paying guests and making a little go a long way. The Three Musketeers were Clive, Dermot and an unknown chap (for some reason, I have forgotten his name, but I do remember his very clapped-out old motorbike).

I had a bit of a crush on Clive. He was tall, fair haired, and, I thought, handsome, and also well spoken. I would appear in the front garden, just by the long privet hedge between our houses, and watch him set off for work. I hoped he would notice me, but he never did.

I was lurking about one day while Mum was out gardening, and Mrs Greenham came over to the dividing hedge. "Clive has had to go into hospital today. They've found out he's got TB." Mum almost backed off from the hedge...

TB was such a serious illness, and sometimes sufferers would have to stay in a convalescent home for years, being subjected to the 'open-air' treatment. That meant living out on a veranda, in all weathers, having their lungs deflated and reflated, and a weird diet.

I was heartbroken… for at least two days. I never saw Clive again, and I never knew what happened to him, but he was my first 'heart-throb'.

BIRTHDAYS AND BETTY

After the war, I was allowed a birthday party, and in fact a few more later. I would invite school 'chums'. The garden had lots of tiny paths around flower beds, so near to May 13th a whole gang of school friends were invited to 249, not particularly to eat

much, but just to run amok, around the garden, trying to push each other into the pond, which, during the late forties had a host of wildlife in it, newts, frogs, and the pupae of dragonflies, plus mud.

Even at the age of eleven or so, everyone wore ankle socks and navy knickers with pockets in them and elasticized legs. Only girls were invited to my birthday parties, the boys were aliens. I remember one party particularly, I would be about seven.

A mother of one of the girls brought her daughter round to 249. She also brought Mum a gift, a bunch of freshly picked white lilac. It might as well have been a bunch of hand grenades. Mum accepted them, smiling, then, when the door had closed and the mother was off down the front garden, Mum rushed hell for leather, through the house, out into the garden, up to the dustbin, and WHAM! in went the lilac. "White lilac is TERRIBLY unlucky" was her explanation.

Bad luck also applied to lily-of-the-valley in the house, opening umbrellas indoors, walking under ladders, and people whose fingers could bend dangerously backwards, especially their thumbs. Bendy-thumb people were prone to lying AND slyness. There was also an unlucky song – 'Tosti's Goodbye', which, if it came on the wireless, Mum would jump up and switch off. This was something to do with the death of her mother when Mum was seventeen. So THAT was a no-no. It may have been her mother's favourite piece of music (I never asked).

Pat didn't have any parties, only later when she became twenty-one. However, she was once invited to a fancy-dress one. We didn't have anything to dress up in! Material was expensive and out of the question for a mere party outfit. This is where Betty stepped in. She had previously run-up a magician's costume for Joy, so when she heard that Pat needed an outfit, Betty kindly revamped the magician's black cloak and pointed hat. She sewed silver moons, stars, and magical signs on the hat and cloak, so Pat went to the party looking good. Betty had stayed up half the night sewing all this. She was a clever woman, a brilliant journalist and animal lover, and was happy to do anything she could to help her 'foster' nieces next door.

Betty seemed to understand children, and to me she was a magical auntie (Elizabeth to us when the family were around, but Betty Tay when she was working on the *Mirror* newspaper).

Elizabeth Tay had been brought up in central London. Her father was a vet, mainly to horses, and in the 1800s and early 1900s, horses were thronging the streets, so I think he was a very busy man. Betty rode. We have a battered photo of her riding through the city, wearing a jaunty trilby hat and hacking jacket.

Betty had a face that slightly drooped on one side, the result of a serious accident years before. I don't know if it was a fall from a horse, though I think I remember Betty telling me it was a car accident. She didn't wear it when she arrived next door, but apparently the left side of her mouth had to be held up with some sort of chain. I think that the facial nerves were damaged. She wasn't a beauty, but to all of us at 249 she was a star.

School was still a worry to me, but I became tougher during the last years at St Jude's. The bullying male teachers were still frightening, but there were lighter times. I liked poetry; we would learn a poem by rote as we did tables.

Years later, when married, I met a girl who was in my class. She had been a very bright pupil and her mother was a dinner-lady so there were no thumpings carried out on HER – not that she warranted any. She was always the first to shoot her hand up and shout, 'Please, teacher!' AND then get the answer right! She was a star at maths. When we met, her first recollection of the top class was that I stood up and recited a poem about a steam train, making the words fit into the rhythm of a train. She thought I had made it up but, for the life of me, I don't remember doing that. I do vaguely remember it, but it was gratifying to hear that someone remembered something good about my time there. (I hope I DID make it up but it's doubtful.)

There was a shop round the corner from the school. It sold delicious liquorice root, a soft wood that was chewed and sucked but made your teeth yellow, and lumps of liquorice that had to be chipped off a large lump, bashed with a tiny toffee hammer. The shop also sold ice-lollies of what must have been watered-down blackcurrant cordial. They were pink, and SO wonderful. I must have had some pocket money to spend on the delights of that shop, but I don't remember ever holding money. It must have been just a few pennies.

There were lots of arguments now, verbal and easily heard in our bedroom, between Mum and Dad. One seemed to involve Tony recently back from Palestine. Mum told me this next bit, which was brave of her.

Before Tony left to do his National Service, he hid some money under a loose floorboard beside his bed in the attic. He told Mum about its whereabouts, in case anything happened to him whilst away. As usual, Dad was stuck for cash, having loaned some to a friend. He was desperate for ready money, so Mum did a dreadful thing. She told Dad where Tony's money was hidden. Of course, Dad took it, with the promise that he would replace it before Tony arrived home. But he didn't, so Tony's hard-earned savings had gone. Tony and Dad never really spoke to each other again after that.

TRANSPORT AND A GHOST

My trips to the Gaumont cinema were frequent. I loved the 'buzz' of the whole place. The box-office ladies got to know me. They sat behind their glass-fronted booths, friendly and cheerful. On the front doors were two commissionaires, old men wearing uniform, grey jackets with copious amounts of gold braid and military-style peaked hats. I believe these men were oldies who had seen service in the 1914–18 war.

The whole foyer was bright, with a shiny floor resembling marble, and on the walls a gold rococo design in plaster. This grand type of showpiece building has long gone. Live theatres have that grandeur, but the cinemas have not. I was privileged to be part of all this 'schmaltz' and glamour. I would walk up the 'marbled' steps to visit Dad. I suppose I only saw him at work, as home was not his real abode. The Gaumont and the pub were his home, so any time I could, I would take a Tettenhall bus up to town, the ticket of about a penny-halfpenny dispensed by a conductor wearing a navy uniform, with their ticket machine strapped to their waist. Ting, the ticket would pop out. There was always a number on it, and for some reason, you would be 'lucky in love' if the numbers added up to twenty-one.

Trolleybuses were open platformed, so when they had to stop at the lights, passengers could just leap off. When the bus had to turn a corner and so change wires overhead, the conductor would leap off, pull a handle attached to a lamp post, than jump back on board. There was one change of direction, in Darlington Street round into Waterloo Road, in central Wolverhampton, that was manned by a disabled man, one side of his body drooped and looked paralysed. He stood there in all weathers and pulled the lever with verve. He wore a navy transport uniform, so must have been employed just to do this task, a necessary one, though. It saved us all being swung round the corner and off to unknown areas. He seemed to be carrying out his job for years, and I remember his blue, windblown rather distorted face. Even now, I can visualize him. At the time, though, I didn't feel any empathy with his plight. I do now.

Upstairs on the bus was where all the smokers congregated, and if you could get a front seat in the upstairs, you felt you were almost driving the bus! On frosty days, blue sparks would emanate from the overhead wires. I loved the trolleys, so going to Dad's was an adventure in itself.

Dad's office, full of smoke, was a sanctuary for me, with Miss Tilly bashing the keys of the typewriter, and Dad dressed in evening attire, complete with tails. The front of his starched shirt had a 'dickie.' He always wore a black bow-tie. (Dad's shirts, dickies, all were sent to a local steam laundry. Mum never had the luxury of a washing machine or a mangle. The muscles in her upper arms, developed from wringing sheets out, were enormous, and would do a shot-putter proud! Tamara Press (Russian shot-putter and discus thrower) had nothing on Mum and her biceps.)

There was a Saturday-morning film show, especially for children. The organist would play his signature tune and rise up into the auditorium. Then we would all sing the Gaumont British Saturday Morning Club's song. "We come along on Saturday morning, greeting everybody with a smile"… it goes on. I can remember it all.

Dad called himself Uncle Edgar. Before the show (two films usually), the gold transparent curtains would open and Dad would walk on, dragging along a microphone on a stand. He was in just a suit – mufti – for the children's show. There would be some clapping, but some boos… which I took personally! He'd announce what was on that morning, and retreat to clapping and boos. Why the booing? I couldn't work it out. After Dad had gone, the films would begin, mostly cowboys and Indians. There were whoops, whistles, and jeers and I think a good time was had by all.

Sometimes the projectionist had trouble with the reel of film, so there was a hold-up. This REALLY sent the children wild… stamping their feet, and slow hand clapping. That also happened some evenings when the film broke down, but the clapping and jeering was louder, adults being impatient.

The Gaumont had a splendid organ, not a Wurlitzer, but just as fine. There was a resident organist, who would slowly emerge from beneath the floor in front of the stage playing at the same time. Dad had quite a few organists. One called Bill Davis took a shine to me and showed me the complicated mechanisms below ground. Then, as a special treat, I was invited to sit beside him on the long bench, and WOW! up we went, right into the auditorium. There wasn't a film showing at the time. It was fun, though, and as an added bonus I pressed the 'flaps' that made the sound of trumpets, drums, bells, whistles – a truly magical few minutes.

There was a restaurant at the cinema. Dad would always have his lunch there. All the waitresses were in black maid's dresses and white aprons, with frilly caps. I sometimes appeared at lunchtime, and there Dad would be, sitting alone at his usual corner table. Although surrounded by staff, he always ate alone, a meagre meal because of his stomach trouble. His lunch was usually fish. It looked anaemic, and was probably boiled. He cut a lonely figure, and I think he was.

I found a newspaper cutting when thinking about writing this epistle. One yellowing piece of paper was from the *Express & Star*, the local paper. Dad was interviewed and asked what items people left behind after a show. According to Dad, the cleaners had found full sets of false teeth, more than one corset (how did they wriggle THAT off during the film?) and the usual jewellery, handbags, and, of course money – probably not a lot, in those days only pence.

Then there were FLEAS – the human variety. It appears fleas were quite common and would jump off people into the warmth of the red-plush seats. Every night, after the curtain was down, the cleaners would fumigate the seats and areas. Not all the fleas were killed, however, as more than one escaped its fate at the cinema and ended up at 249. More than once, I had popped into Mum and Dad's bedroom to find them on a flea-hunt, sheets thrown back and lots of pouncing going on. Then the sheets would be examined closely and if there were any signs of blood, however small, there was a shaking of clothes and the sound of the bathroom door banging closed! No astonishment on my part, just a sense of relief, though, that a rogue flea hadn't made it into MY bedroom. I can safely state I NEVER had fleas.

Dad's friends, or 'cronies' were a source of irritation to Mum, as they goaded LD (most friends and colleagues called him just that) into drinking too much. Dad never drank at home. We didn't have any alcohol, except perhaps a bottle of port at Christmas, so all Dad's imbibing was in a pub, and later in the Fireman's Services Club, Snow Hill, yards from the Gaumont.

His health was always dodgy. His operations for duodenal ulcers left him very frail. Mum couldn't grasp that being a patient in hospital, without much time for visitors, must have been hell. Visiting times at the Royal Hospital were confined to two afternoons and weekends, and an hour each visit. All Mum could do was say that it was "far worse getting to the hospital and visiting than being a patient in bed". I suppose her point of view was because she had to get a trolleybus into town, then walk a fair distance to the Royal Hospital. Mum had never been a patient so couldn't understand how desolate Dad must have felt. Of course, his drinking didn't help his ulcers, so perhaps Mum was cynical rather than sympathetic.

I do remember one particular night moans from their bedroom, clanking of metal containers, men's voices on the landing outside my door, then footsteps thudding down the stairs. Dad had suffered another haemorrhage, a bad one, after his duodenal ulcers burst. Mum had to stay with us, so Dad was carried off into the ambulance. I didn't hear a bell, but I would think the driver had to put his foot down. Next morning, Mum told us she had been up most of the night, and that she'd emptied almost a full bucket of blood into the bath. Dad survived, and I am sorry to say that I was neither heartbroken when he was driven off nor at all joyful when he appeared again weeks later. I may have shown sympathy, but somehow Mum was slowly eroding away our kind feelings towards him.

Their arguments in the next bedroom were commonplace. I could hear quite well as their headboard was against mine, behind the wall. I never really knew what these arguments were about, probably money. I would strain my ear to the wall… Of course, drinking may have been the trouble.

One memorable night, I was woken by a staggering white-clad figure. It tottered towards me, then it was beside me, fumbling and swaying… the figure tried to get INTO my small bedside chest of drawers. The strange man was followed by Mum, nightie flowing, arms outstretched. I thought I was in a rather peculiar dream.

"GET OUT, CLIFF!" The white spooky figure retreated, with Mum marching him forward, muttering. It turned out not to be a zombie, an 'undead' or scary ghost, just Dad, wearing white long johns and full-sleeved vest! He must have been completely blotto!

Mum directed him towards the door, no explanation, no "sorry", or "go back to sleep". Nothing! I didn't realize at the time that Dad THOUGHT he was in the bathroom /loo.

It WAS frightening, but not a word was said the next morning. I can't remember any of Dad's weird behaviour being discussed… it had become the 'norm'.

The cellar became almost redundant now. It was very damp and had a strong musty smell. The gas meter was down there, and so the gasman had to negotiate the hazardous steps in semi-darkness. So Mum decided to utilize part of the cellar. She had so many fruit and vegetables that, after bottling most of the fruit, she embarked on making her own wine. Pop bottles were used, and some wine bottles from Reg.

She made parsnip, rose petal and anything going. Every now and then, a cork would be jettisoned out of its bottle. We would be eating a meal, and BANG! … another cork exploding. The liquid in the bottles tended to settle down when the fizz had gone. I don't think there should have been a fizz in the first place, but Mum swore it was all right. So the wine fizzed and popped away, along with the odd frog and creepy-crawlies.

Another use of the cellar became popular – it became a very spooky ghost-house. Josie, an honorary cousin (Mum's best friend's daughter), often came over to play and we would have hours of fun setting up white spectre-like sheets, string and cotton for cobwebs, flapping paper, and weird sounds. This artistry would take all afternoon. Then Robin and his friend Fred would have to walk down and submit to a scary few minutes. Of course, Robin had to pretend he was frightened, but years later, Robin told me that Fred WAS frightened! (Or was he having us on?)

We tried these ghostly happenings on all and sundry. Tony's friend Mike was a regular customer but he was a bit more critical and dismissive. Anyway, the cold damp air would get us in the end, and we would abandon all 'hootings' for another pastime.

This was easier in a way. We would cadge an empty chocolate box off someone, fill it with stones, and leave it on the pavement outside 249's gate. Then we would keep watch from Mum's bedroom window. The JOY of seeing someone, stop, look round, then furtively pick the box up and go on their way was wonderful. The next stage in this game was to attach a cotton or string to the box. Then, when the unsuspecting person went to pick the box up, we would jerk it away. It was sound in theory, but not in practice. The string was never strong enough, and really too long to have any 'pull', so this was abandoned, but not until after one attempt almost worked. We would nearly wet ourselves laughing over the chocolate-box ruse. It certainly wouldn't work today. It would probably be blown up by the army. But there were no suspicious parcels in those far-off days.

MOUSE

Josie's mother was my mum's best friend. They met before they had both married. Violet was an astonishing woman. When young, she had been troubled with heart problems, and the doctor had advised her "never have children, your heart won't stand the strain". However, Violet married a butcher, and had four children with no ill effects. Josie was the last child, a little younger than me. We were good friends, never falling out. We are still good friends sixty-five years on. When Josie was about five, her father died, leaving Violet to bring all four children up.

I loved going to their house, two bus rides away from 249. Tea was always Marmite sandwiches, which was great for me. Violet must have had a dreadfully hard time making ends meet, so it was good of her to have a guest when food was short, but there she was, always smiling, dishing up the sandwiches, with not a hint of her struggle.

I have to pop a late piece of news in here.

I received a call from Bill (Billy when young) Freear, Josie's one remaining brother. I told him I was typing this and he told me a little bit more about my mum and MARMITE. Bill was once asked to tea at 249. The wonderful spread wasn't known to him then. Mum put a dark-brown jar on the table, and we all began dipping our knives into it. Bill did the same, but, thinking it was chocolate spread, he put lashings on. He remembers the burning throat and mouth. However, it didn't put the Freears off – and seventy-six-year-old Bill still enjoys his Marmite on toast now. What an advert.

After tea, Auntie Vi would entertain us by playing the piano. Not just playing a piece from memory, but reading a page of a book chosen at random, and afterwards repeating what she had read. She would also sing. She was such a marvellous character, greatly loved by her children, who called her 'Mouse'.

The garden at the Freears was a child's paradise. The small lawn was where all the games of badminton took place, a net strung across to the fence. The grass was hardly visible and was mainly just earth patches where everyone served.

Brother Billy had a shed, full of cages holding guinea pigs and white mice. At one time, wild mice had managed to 'break and enter' the pet mice's cage. Then they had a bit of 'rumpy-pumpy' with the lady mice. They then raced round the wheel, and left, leaving a few female mice in an 'interesting condition'! So Billy's baby mice were born all colours.

The hallway at the Freears was always piled up with tennis racquets, shoes, pumps. Josie and her brothers all played tennis. (Josie became a very good player when in her teens and twenties.) Upstairs, the three brothers all shared a bedroom, chaotic, but a teddy was always propped up on (I think) Billy's bed.

The strange part of my relationship with the Freears was that I THOUGHT we were blood cousins! So, when a game of postman's knock was played, which was most times I visited, the game was a real fizzle-out, mainly because Josie wasn't going to go into the hall to kiss her brothers, heaven forbid… and although I was chosen all the time, I thought it very indecent to kiss a blood relative!! So that game lost its interest.

In the back room was a small gas fire. We would gather some windfall apples from the garden, stick an apple on the prongs of a long toasting fork and hold it in front of the fire and watch as the green peel bubbled and became brown. Then… they would burst! "Oh GLORY!". We never ate any – too revolting – but it was good warm fun.

Also, whilst playing at Josie's, we met up with a 'gang' of lads. They congregated around the shops down the avenue. They weren't rough, although I sometimes felt they were, but there was the usual rivalry and verbal bullying. Billy wore glasses, so the gang would call him 'four eyes', nothing really awful, and certainly today it wouldn't make number one in the bullying stakes, but it was behaviour I had never come across before, and I made my mind up that I didn't like the boys in the gang… well, except one, who was called 'Decca'. He was blond-haired, smooth-skinned, plump, but nice, if not a little cheeky.

I lost track of Decca, except to say, that only this year I heard that he had died years ago. Oh well, not a very fruitful tale.

GRANDPA AT THE WHITE HOUSE

Grandpa Davies seemed to be at home with Betty and Reg. He liked the laid-back lifestyle of his oldest son. He would sometimes walk round to 249 to listen to the Welsh home service on the radio in the corner of the back room. None of us could understand a word of it, it was BBC Welsh, and Grandpa didn't hear much of his native language, so he was an avid listener. Grandpa didn't speak English until he was seven, so his mother tongue was Welsh. He taught me a few words and sayings. I know a 'black dog' would feature in one of the bits he taught me.

I'm not sure why we didn't have a great deal to do with Grandpa. He was a gentle soul, so different from Grandma Gertrude, his late wife. One memory I DO have of Grandpa is his awful hernia. I never dared ask what it was, but his trousers bulged with a massive lump. He never had any surgery on it, unlike Dad, who had a double hernia removed or repaired.

This brings me to the period of searching for anything of an 'interesting' nature in Mum and Dad's drawers. Mum was keen on her make-up. Never over the top, but lipstick would double for rouge, a smear on a wash-leather then smoothed into her cheeks, and her everyday dollop of Pond's Cold Cream. All this went on at her dressing table in their bedroom. I wasn't supposed to play with anything, it was far too precious, but I did! I mooched about, opening drawers, rifling through the contents, and smelling nice aromas. One very weird item used to make me shut the drawer quickly. I know now that it was a hernia truss. It consisted of an elastic belt, with a pear-shaped solid piece of what I assumed was leather. Of all the items I thought were taboo and 'adults' stuff", this belt was the most viewed of all the contents of Mum's drawers. I stared at it many times, as I tried to work out just WHAT it was used for. I think by now I knew that 'something rude went on in the bedroom' and I convinced myself that THIS was a rather naughty find, and I would feel guilty afterwards, as I crept downstairs.

Christmas presents were also sought out. I would search for ages, hoping to find something wrapped in pretty paper. The top of Mum's wardrobe lifted off, and for years I think the presents were hidden up there, far too high to look, even when perched on a bedroom chair. This I did many times, never successful. I tried everything, though, but Mum changed her hiding place every now and then. The sound of the rustling wrapping paper, the restrained bubbling of excitement, everything about Christmas was a joy, a wondrous time of the year for all four of us. I'm not so sure about our parents, though.

The last few months at St Jude's were full of changes. Mr Welsh retired and a new head arrived called Mr Mott. He was a dark-haired moustached man, I suppose quite young, but I thought he was in his dotage! I can't say too much about Mr Mott. He hadn't got the religious fervour of Mr Welsh, but there was one very scary incident one day, initiated by the newcomer.

Someone must have had some money taken from somewhere. I think it was a sixpence. Mr Mott strode into our classroom, told us of the theft, and that he thought one of us was guilty. He then told us he was going to take each pupil's pulse and that he could tell by how quick the heartbeat was whether HE or SHE was the felon!! My heart immediately began to beat its way out of my chest, as did (I suspect) everyone else's! True to his word, he walked amongst us feeling our wrists, frowning and looking at the potential criminals with a deranged stare. I don't know if he found the culprit. He just walked out of the classroom and we never heard anything more about it, but it was a very unnerving few minutes, and he did exactly what he intended to do, frighten the life out of us.

I must have condensed this time a bit (unless Mr Mott was only head for a few months) before I left to go to senior school.

One of the teachers at St Jude's became head. This was a Mr Harris-Jones, who had previously taught art. What a difference he made to school life. He was fair, softly spoken, small with large protruding front teeth, rather rabbit-like, but he was, for the short time that I was at St Jude's, a saviour. If only he had been in charge for the previous years, I would have enjoyed school and never experienced the feelings of absolute fear each night, especially when I knew we were having a maths test next day.

I had always dreaded being thumped by GW, or held up as an idiot, which is what Mr H did. I never DID get thumped or shown as a sloth in front of the class, but I remember these two teachers with something next to hatred, for spoiling what should have been a treasured part of childhood, for me and probably hundreds of children in their so-called-care.

However, my earlier prayers WERE answered (a bit late) with the coming to the headmastership of the kindly Mr Harris-Jones, and I think Mrs Harris-Jones joined him too later in the term.

I didn't pass my eleven-plus, so was sent off to Whitmore Secondary Modern school. I did feel the lowest of the low for a while, as Pat had done so well at the municipal grammar, but I never expected to rise to great heights, and neither did the family. Dad probably didn't even enquire where I had been seconded to, and Mum was silent, accepting that I would fail anything involving numbers but I was good at literature and art, so the secondary modern would be adequate for me. The eleven-plus exams did instil in me a feeling of great failure and they always have.

Holidays before I began secondary school were turbulent, especially at the White House. I didn't know of any discord between Betty and Reg, I was far too busy showing off dance steps, and complicated ball games or skipping to take any notice of their personal problems.

The hotel was never really successful. It relied on commercial travellers, who would be passing through Tettenhall on their way to demonstrate their wares. The bedrooms for these men were small, partitions having been erected to make one room into two. The sitting room, with the television set, was comfortable enough, and Betty was always welcoming, as was Reg. He still walked about, king of his castle, doing nothing very much but charming the guests with tales from his years at Paramount Pictures.

Reg had been quite a big-cheese in the years prior to buying the hotel. Where his money had gone, no one seemed to know. He had given Ruth and his two sons a good and expensive education, but he certainly needed the money from his guests.

(He was particularly friendly with Archie Leach, who changed his name to Cary Grant, the film star. Archie asked Reg to be his best man at his forthcoming wedding. Reg was delighted, so did the honour. Cary had two or three more weddings after that.)

The white paint on the hotel walls became a bit tatty, as did the hand-painted little car. Reg and Grandpa would sit out in deckchairs wearing what can only be described as Mexican sombreros, possibly a gift from some film star or from a film set. They would both have a cigarette stuck to their lip. All this whilst Betty, and sometimes Joy, dashed around baking, washing, changing beds and everything that had to be done, to keep the place going... and of course looking after Grandpa, who was failing mentally.

About this time, Reg suffered a slight stroke. He wasn't too badly affected, but it did make him rather slurred with his speech, and one side of his mouth drooped slightly. I still helped him in the conservatory with the fish tank. The tobacco-making idea was not a success, so there were no leaves hanging on their strings. I think the tropical fish must have died, because the water in the heated tank became cloudy and the glass greener than ever. Uncle Reg couldn't cope with all his hobbies, so my job as glass-cleaner-in-chief was over.

The guests still arrived at the hotel in their little cars.

We had a strange occurrence at 249 one autumn. It was November 5th, Guy Fawkes night. The family usually celebrated by having a huge bonfire and a very Worzel Gummidge type of guy, stuffed with newspapers no longer needed for toilet paper as we had rolls (always crispy Bronco).

This particular day, we had hollowed out swedes or turnips and the boys had managed to get some fireworks, and everyone had collected garden rubbish for months, so that we could have a good bonfire. Tony always played around with ways of scaring us, using bangers lit under dustbin lids, jumping-jacks set off behind our legs, and rockets sticking out of a milk bottle sideways, all very precarious. I hate to say it, but I think some fireworks were home-made, very dangerous, and in today's Health and Safety times, illegal and usually pointing in the wrong direction, making for terrifying 'swishes' as they ploughed along the ground, everyone having to run for safety skipping over a fiercely burning rocket zig-zagging across the lawn.

The hollowed lanterns were lit and hung around in trees. Once Tony had lit the bonfire, Mum and Pat would come down and pop potatoes into the base of the fire, where they would burn, the skin crisp and charcoal tasting. It was at one of these parties, where lots of our friends gathered to lark around, that a funny thing happened.

We finished all the excitement outside, so settled into our living room, the two-bar electric fire was doing its bit, and we all crushed up on the settee and easy chairs (dilapidated with horse-hair hanging out). Mum asked if we wanted a cup of tea, so off she went, coming back with a tray and special home-made bonfire night treacle flapjacks. Everyone was talking, laughing, and having a happy time. After the tea, about 9.30, a 'friend' of one of our family suddenly stood up. We all looked at him, surprised.

"Well, I had better go and get my things from the car. Could you show me to my room?" There was silence. "This IS the hotel, isn't it?" he said, looking somewhat bemused at our astounded faces.

How the young man had EVER thought that our very modest house was a hotel, when the great white house loomed large next door, we never found out. Whatever he thought, he must have put us down as the most welcoming hosts in the world – bonfire fun, food, a party, then 'afters' with tea and merriment. Of course, we all wondered how WE had not realized there was a stranger in our midst, but that was our family. So many various friends, Mum never knew who or what they were. She didn't enquire about anyone, she was far too busy looking after Dad and sometimes his cronies! No cronies in sight that happy night.

SOME CRONIES

D ad's friends were part of my life.

One of these, Dr Terence Brady, a twinkly-eyed, curly-haired Irishman, played quite a big part in my early years. There was no NHS before 1947, so doctors had to be paid. To call a doctor out, Mum thought you had to be dying, mainly because of the money and the inability to pay, but also because doctors were like gods to Mum, and were not summoned lightly. The family doctor, who lived a few doors away, expected a fee to be in place on the mantelshelf when he visited, a constant worry for Mum. And so it was that Terry Brady stepped in on many occasions when I was ill.

After drinking in a pub at night with Dad, Dr Brady would be asked to have a look at me. I don't think the fact that he MAY have been a bit tiddly came into it. Apparently, he had genuine concern. So, when poorly, I often woke up to find Dr Brady standing by the bed or feeling my forehead. He was nice, kind, and jolly, and I never felt fearful as I would with a GP (especially as Mum would practically spring-clean the bedroom, remake the bed, and prop me up like a wooden model before the GP came). I won't even guess how good a doctor Terry was. His prescribing was, Robin tells me, erratic. I was prescribed the very new M&B tablets by him. I think they were one of the first antibiotics, the M&B standing for May & Baker. I was one of the first children to receive them, so I was either very dodgy and ill or Terry Brady was impressed with these new drugs, so wanted to try them out! This 'first' is a rather dubious triumph.

Terry was a bit of a ladies' man. He had many girlfriends, and no wonder. He was tall, dark and handsome, with wavy dark-brown hair. Also being a medical man, he was quite a catch.

Terry must have owned a car, although I never saw it, because he came after I was in bed. Mum told me a story of a trip in his car, out into the Staffordshire countryside. A crowd of friends went too, and the venue was a manor house owned by an eccentric lady who called herself Lady Smith (can't verify this). She lived in a huge farmhouse out in the wilds. It was Christmas time, and she was putting on a buffet for her guests. The entrance hall was palatial, but what impressed Mum more than anything was a great ball of mistletoe hanging from a chandelier. About four feet across, it dominated the hall, and somehow to Mum it was the eighth wonder of the world. Lady S had put on a good spread. In what was described as a barn off the kitchen, a table was laid with the most gigantic side of ham with all the trimmings. In those post-war days, Mum had not seen anything so opulent (meat might still have been rationed). No doubt also there would have been lots of drink.

Mum didn't have too many such adventures out of the house, so she would tell the story of this particular evening with pleasure. I have no idea who this Lady Smith was, or if there was a Lord Smith around, but it was a happy episode in Mum's life.

Terry Brady popped in and out of our lives at 249, and the family were friends for many years. Terry eventually married, a very nice Irish girl called Julie, and they had two boys. His soft Irish brogue and twinkling blue eyes would still make the ladies' hearts flutter.

Another of Dad's friends was Teddy Polkinghorne. He was rather like Toad in *The Wind in the Willows*, with a chequered cap and tweed jacket, his upper lip covered by a 'handlebar' moustache – very RAF! Like Toad, he owned and drove a small red two-seater sports car. What he did for a living, I will never know. He always seemed to be around and in Dad's drinking circle. Mum had to make supper for Teddy and friends. Sometimes Dad would bring a crab home, late at night, or a pig's foot – all these Mum would cook or prepare. She was a dab-hand at dressing a crab, mixing the body contents (having removed the 'dead-mans-fingers', the mere name terrified me) with salad cream and sometimes mustard, salt and pepper. The small legs were just right for an apostle teaspoon. The spoon was good for shoving into the leg then pulling out the white meat The very best were the big claws! Fat, pieces of white meat would just appear when the claw was cracked open. So often Mum would martyr away after 11pm, then Dad and whoever he had asked back or had given him a lift back from the cinema would get stuck in.

Tripe, pig's feet and chawl (which I think is the cheek of a poor pig) would all be wobbling around in either milk, for the boiled tripe, or a jelly from the trotters. A horrible sight, but Dad said that the tripe and trotters were good for his tum. I mentioned chitterlings earlier on. I think they were a 'treat' for Dad, as were the sweetbreads. I learned later that chitterlings are the flattened intestines… vile whatever they are, but Dad enjoyed them, and they might have been good for his stomach.

Mum did tell me of some stupid behaviour between the 'cronies'. I'm not sure who was with Dad on this occasion. The friend was bragging about a certain part of his anatomy. Dad and his friend were probably sozzled at the time (more than 'probably', more like 'definitely'). This unknown man boasted that his 'member' was bigger than Dad's. So, they took them out and slapped them on the table! Mum was sent to find a tape measure, and both men then measured their privates. I never heard from Mum which man won, but she did actually let a tiny smile and a chuckle pass her lips when she told me the tale. (That last bit will be a revelation to Pat and all our family. I just HOPE Mum wasn't making it up to shock...) Mum was never great on the smiles, and I suppose who could blame her, but that story seemed to tickle her fancy. I never really wanted to hear WHO won the competition. It would have been too embarrassing to ask, but I have a feeling it was Dad.

BROTHER TONY

Tony was rarely part of the suppers. He didn't eat with us very often. I will write a few lines about him here.

He was what would be called today psychologically disturbed. This manifested itself in his love of weapons, knives and guns. He collected knives, all shapes and sizes. He became good and quite accurate at throwing the knives, letting them spin in the air, then catching them by the handle in his hands. The knives would be thrown too at targets, sometimes tree trunks. It sounds really mad now, but he would use these knives to show off, prove himself, and frighten all and sundry. I hate knives now because of this.

Guns were swivelled on his trigger finger, then back into his holster. He must have watched cowboy films, where someone like John Wayne would spin his gun, and shoot red Indians dead, all in a split second. The films were definitely viewed somewhere, certainly not the Gaumont. There was a fleapit cinema not far from 249, so he may have gone there.

His air rifle he would shoot INDOORS at a target attached to the kitchen door. Too bad if someone was trying to get in. Ping-ping… he would also set up targets against his beloved tool shed, an old converted pigsty. Inside he had all his tools, and a work bench, very neatly laid out.

The William pear tree had more than its fair share of pellet holes. Tony would shoot with abandon, sometimes missing so that the pellet struck the wall. There was nothing else behind, thank goodness, but the wall often 'bought it'! He loved to look at his collection of lead pellets embedded in the poor tree's bark. He was also known to suddenly 'whing' a knife into something close. He was quite good at all this, but it was an obsession that should have been talked over, but there wasn't anyone to talk to. Mum would tut-tut. If we complained about something, her favourite saying was "Well I never DID!" Every worry was met with that, then a shake of her head as though shaking the intrusive thoughts away. Mum never listened. Tony did behave oddly, but it all went over Mum's head. She had Dad to contend with, so other matters were shrugged off. But I did feel upset and embarrassed when friends called round to play.

He also used bad language, which upset everyone, even Dad. It wasn't so much the swearing, although that shocked, it was the pseudo-Germanic terms: 'swine hundt' and 'goten-himmel' were two, but there were many more. Also, getting into the cowboy-gunslinger mode, bad animals were 'critters'.

One evening, it came to a head for me. Our parents were out, and so were Pat and Robin. Tony was in charge. I must have carried a plate of cooked beetroot into the back room, but I slipped and the red-staining juice spilled all over the hearth-rug. Tony hit the roof. He exploded. "Clean that up NOW!!!" I may have back-chatted him and said I would do it later but suddenly he went ballistic! He had a knife in his hand, and he chased me through the house with it. What he would have done with it, I didn't know. (I know NOW he wouldn't have hurt me.) We had just had a telephone installed, so I dashed, scared to death, into the dining room, grabbed the receiver, and said I was calling the police! That thankfully did the trick, so I didn't ring (I wouldn't know how!), and by the time everyone came back to 249, Tony was back in the kitchen, and I was hiding in bed. I don't think I ever told anyone about the 'happenings' that night. There didn't seem any point anyway…

Robin was too quiet to interfere, Pat would escape most dramas by jumping on her trusty bike and racing off to Stourbridge to visit the aunties, and Mum and Dad were really not in a position to tell Tony off, because of the 'stolen' money, and all the events around that. Perhaps Tony cleaned the stain off the rug, because nobody noticed.

Life went on as usual but, today, Tony would have had to visit a psychiatrist to find out why he could be so aggressive. Collecting knives and guns certainly wasn't a healthy pastime. He did love any article in his books and comics that were set 'Out West', as well as country and western, hillbilly music. He wore his gun belt like John Wayne, low on the hips. He had a slight limp, one leg shorter than the other, so it was easy to walk the walk of a 'gun-slinger'. His shorter leg came about (according to Mum) because when a youngster, he would never be off his wooden-wheeled scooter, pushing off with one leg! That was Mum – very bizarre thoughts. However, Tony did have a slight limp, probably from birth. Tony was a maverick, everyone knew it, but it was not mentioned. Many years later, a friend from schooldays told me how scared she was of him.

LIFE AT 249 AND A DEPARTURE

The big day arrived when I was due to start at the senior school. I was kitted up with uniform from Bedford & Williams, and the far-too-big mac, and STILL boys' shoes with toe-caps, but minus the Kellogg's cardboard insoles.

I was so disappointed because I was in a different class to my friends. In fact, a lower class, 'A' as opposed to 'A plus'. I suppose I must have done really badly, and I resigned myself to my lower status. But within two weeks, joy of joys, I was put up into a class with my friends. Perhaps the head thought my exam results didn't echo my class work. Nobody told you anything so I just got on with the move.

Everything was so much better – the teachers were quite kindly and the work not very stretching but interesting. St Jude's was a mere cloud that had blown away, and I settled in well.

I don't think Dad knew I had left the juniors, although I might be doing him an injustice here. In the August before, Mum had had a meeting with Mr Thomas, the headmaster. Mr Thomas was Welsh, a fair and good man, so different from the St Jude's head.

Dad never visited any of our schools, nor attended any plays or open days. He gave me no feedback on my failure to pass the eleven-plus. Mum opened the letter and scanned it but didn't show that she minded me not passing. I don't think she commented, but she DID have 'well I never thought you would pass anyway' written all over her face. I suppose underneath she felt very disappointed with me, but you mustn't show your feelings… So I didn't either.

Pat was going out with boyfriends, none of whom Mum got to know or asked about. No. 249 was a very easy establishment, no real rules about friends coming, or times to come in by. Oddly enough, my brothers and sister were rarely out late. They toed an unseen line, that line existed all our lives, so Mum must have done something right.

There were arguments, many of them, with lots of door slamming and riding off into the sunset for Pat, and tears from me. The big arguments were between Dad and Mum, usually in their bedroom, not too loud, but loud enough for us to hear. Mum never cried. I did see her tearful when her younger brothers died.

One particular phone call I remember particularly. It was Mum's sister, Ve. She was crying, something the Roberts siblings didn't do often. I now realize how sad it all was. But I just barged in to Mum and said, "Uncle Stan is dead." Mum crumbled, but I didn't go over and put my arm around her, I just left her there to cry. It was as though our emotions were always on 'hold', but this time Mum let her guard down. But I didn't. I just did what we were expected to do, keep a stiff upper lip at all costs. I wish I could have flouted the unwritten rules but, to my shame, I didn't. I should have hugged Mum, but that intimacy didn't cross my mind.

We were not a tactile crew, no kisses or cuddles. We weren't made aware that showing one's feelings was wrong, but there was this glass barrier up, especially between Mum and all of us 'children'. I think she would have liked to show more emotion but just found it very difficult, probably the result of her strange upbringing. This was a shame, because it has had a great influence on all our lives.

Life was not going well at the White House. Mum and Dad probably knew something was afoot. I came home from school one day to be met with "Don't go next door. Auntie Elizabeth has gone. She's run away."

What a shock, especially as all the adults kept quiet about her disappearance.

Eventually, it all came out into the open. Betty had packed her belongings, with the help of a friend who cleaned for her, and the two women had gone to London. The cleaner, a Mrs Wellsbury only went to help Betty carry her cases. I think she came back to her family the next day. Who could blame Betty? She had been looking after Grandpa Davies as well as a frail Reg, plus trying to run a hotel with all that entailed.

Cousin Joy was left there to close the hotel and be a carer for her father and Grandpa Davies. I missed Auntie, her sense of humour and her interest in what I did at school and elsewhere. Now the wall between us was no longer scrambled upon or climbed over. I did go round but through the laurel bushes in the front garden. Easier but somehow I was at the end of a chapter.

The wall was still nice to sit astride, though, and view the gardens, dreaming about being grown-up, and would I ever own a bike? (I did eventually, when I was in my teens, but it was a super one, a racing bike, shiny, and a shade of purple. It was second-hand, but that didn't matter.)

Betty Tay went back to journalism, reporting for the *Mirror* newspaper. She also helped set up the IFAW, the now huge animal rescue charity. I heard a radio programme a few years ago about a Brian Davies, who helped to start the charity (mainly aiming to stop the culling of young seals in Canada) – he was a journalist friend of Betty's. He spoke about meeting Betty in a pub one evening. They were shocked to read and see photos of the cruel way the Canadians beat these little pups and their mothers to death. The wicked crew would sometimes skin a pup whilst the poor thing was still alive, just for its pelt. So Auntie Betty (or sometimes Elizabeth) was still the caring animal lover.

Years later, Mum ventured up to London to visit her sister Marj. Whilst there, she looked up and found Betty's address. It was in Dolphin Square, a block of rather up-market flats. Surprisingly for Mum, who was timid, to put it mildly, she went up to the flat and was welcomed by Betty with open arms. Betty had a partner by then, who also wrote for the *Daily Mirror*, quite a well-known chap (his name escapes me). Mum came home to relate that both were "drinking a lot" and the chain-smoking was going well.

I think Betty did the right thing leaving Uncle Reg, but at that time we were all sad. I never saw Auntie again.

Much later, when Mum was in her eighties, she corresponded with Mabel, Reg's ex- partner, mother of the three 'children'. In one of her letters to Mum, Mabel says "What a shame Betty had such an awful death." We never found out what had befallen the lovely Betty. It may have been drink, but we don't know for sure. I do know now that she and another journalist wrote two children's animal books, relating to the *Daily Mirror*.

All of us agree now that she was a lovely honorary auntie who made life (especially MY life) much more exciting. She became a sounding board when worries about school loomed, a champion for a young person's rights, and a lover of animals – a truly 'good sport' all round.

Grandpa's mental health was deteriorating, and he became confused and rather rude. Well, I thought so. From where he sat in the kitchen of the hotel he could see a window of a house three or four doors away, and he was convinced that some of the 'maids' working there were shaking their dusters out of the window, TOPLESS. It rather shocked everyone at 249, because he had been, up to then, the soul of decorum and gentility, so seeing all those bosoms hanging out of the windows proved to all that he was going senile. He had started to go a bit barmy well before Betty fled the house.

Once we were in the kitchen, all round the table eating, when Grandpa started to laugh. He pointed up to an oil painting of a rather voluptuous bare-breasted girl holding a rose "See those," he laughed. "THOSE" being her bare breasts. "Well, SOMEONE has put some jam on the ends of them." He pointed to her nipples. Betty quickly tried to distract him away from the painting and even Reg was embarrassed that his father had suddenly become a dirty old man. "Val's here, Dad… don't say things like that." But Grandpa went on chuckling.

The girls carried on waving their dusters at him for some weeks. They afforded him some hilarity during what were to be his last months. During his last days, Robin sat with him until almost the end. Then, when he slipped into a coma, Grandad was taken by ambulance to the dreaded New Cross Hospital, where he died.

A much-loved grandpa, a bright intelligent man, who never had any chance of becoming what he wanted to be, a school teacher.

A GOODBYE

So Joy and Reg jogged on together. Joy had sold the old brightly painted gypsy caravan some time ago, having slept in it for a few weeks one summer. The White House sign was down and the house was looking neglected.

How Reg took Betty's escape to freedom, I wasn't party to. He was ill, his sight bad, and he had experienced another slight stroke.

I would like to say Dad would squeeze through the laurel bushes and sit with his brother in his last years, but I don't remember that happening. But I don't know for certain. I don't think there was much contact between the brothers. They had never fallen out, so that is strange. His sons came over from down south a few times, probably Ruth too, but they rather abandoned him to his fate. Joy, who had always suffered with deafness and her nerves, must have found her father difficult to look after, so the inevitable happened. Reg, who was once such an erudite, clever and amusing man, was taken to the same hospital where my Great Uncle Harry and Grandpa Davies had died, New Cross. It might have been a bit better than a workhouse-type building by then, but Robin thinks not. Reg was bedridden by now, suffering with the last stages of lung and heart failure, added to by mini strokes.

As usual, Mum did her bit and visited Reg. Her account of his life in the ward was depressing. Just a row of beds, poor facilities. Like Great Uncle Harry, Reg had just a bare bedside table. He was lying completely paralysed, the only movement was in his one eyelid. What an end to a glitzy life, great houses, wonderful offices, mixing with the stars, playing the piano, even having a piece of piano music published, and lots of carousing, now all gone.

I don't know who paid for his funeral. Joy certainly had no money. I will have to be kind here and say perhaps his sons and Ruth paid, but somehow I think it would have been Dad, although he would have had a job to scratch up a few hundred pounds.

Some years earlier, Joy had become a convert to Catholicism, and just months before Reg died he must have made it plain that he would convert too. How he was 'converted' in the short time, I don't know, but there may be a special clause for people who are dying to be accepted into the Catholic religion on a 'fast-track'.

I hope a priest visited Reg in the hospital and sat for a while. I like to think one did. One nice thing came to light recently when looking through Mum's letters from Mabel. I read a poignant few lines. Mabel wrote, "I always send Reg some nice sweets. I don't know if he ever receives them though". Reg had treated Mabel very badly by running off with Betty and leaving Mabel with sole responsibility for the children, but she must have been very sorry for him. A few sweets doesn't sound much, but it was a kind thought and showed she had forgiven him.

As a PS, Mabel called Reg "Robin". In an article I read about her death it stated "wife of the late Robin Gittoes-Davies". Could they have ever married? Joy's hapless mother Ivy lived on for several years. Perhaps "Robin" and Mabel could never marry so were partners. I never met Mabel, but she strikes me as a bright and generous soul.

Reg was buried, on a snowy, cold day, high up in Bushbury cemetery. Only Mum, Dad and Robin went from 249. Joy was there, and Robin thinks Mansel and Barry were too. His service was conducted in a Catholic church in Wolverhampton, by an old doddering priest, who mumbled quickly through the rites. He then said a few words of Latin over Reg's grave. We think the priest was one of Dad's 'cronies', a Father L, a well-known drinker, who was priest in charge of a RC church that was very close to the Gaumont cinema.

There was always lots of talk about Father L and his housekeeper. But to be fair, it was 'hearsay'. Whoever the priest WAS, Robin's thoughts were that he couldn't get the whole job over quick enough. So poor Reg was laid to rest with speed but no feeling. Robin thought it was a wretched funeral.

To me, Uncle Reg was a kindly friend, a guru, and I look back on him as wonderful company for a rather dance-mad little girl.

We recently researched where his grave was in the local crematorium. The old graveyard area is at the top of a windy slope. The grave is just a number, no headstone, not even a mound now, sixty years on. I hope I can get the stone mason to make a little cross, it is such a sad lonely grave, not worthy of a very interesting, clever and knowledgeable man, if a bit naughty with the ladies!

The White House was once more put on the market, and after a few months, a family called Taggart moved in. The Taggarts were from 'up north'. I think Tony took a shine to one of the family, June, but I don't know if June was the daughter or the mother! I have a feeling it was the mother!

Joy moved in with us. I know Mum really couldn't keep anyone else, and at this time Joy wasn't working. I think Reg may have been in debt at the end, so I shouldn't think there was any money from the sale of the house. More's the pity, because Joy could have done with some extra cash. She still lit one cigarette from another, although she suffered with chest trouble.

The piano sessions were loud and prolonged. I loved it seeing her ciggy moving in time with the beat, one eye half shut to escape the smoke. Joy was a character, a nice one, but life wasn't good to her. She lived with us for some time, and when she contracted pleurisy, Mum looked after her as well as Dad and all of us.

I think Joy left 249 after about a year. I know I missed the fun on the piano and even her smoker's cough. Where she went, I'm not too sure. I think to London. Mum was heartily glad she had gone, one less to look after. Now I understand, but THEN I thought Mum rather heartless.

This is rather confused, but I know Joy had been in the forces at one point in her life, the WRACs, and after Wolverhampton, she stayed in an ex-forces hostel. Mum received a letter years later, from a manager of the hostel, saying that Joy was now totally deaf and had given Mum's name and address as next of kin … and could we have her here to stay? It sounds so awful and cruel, but Mum had so much on her plate, so she never replied. It wasn't very sympathetic of Mum, NOT to reply, but she knew she would be looking after another invalid, Dad not being well, plus all of us 'children', so I mustn't judge.

We could never work out why Joy's half-brothers and sister didn't get keep in touch with her and help. They all had very good jobs, so could have supported her to a point, but they didn't. We know this, because much later, years on, when Joy died alone in the hostel, the witness to her demise whose name was on Joy's death certificate was a matron cum supervisor.

Mansel, Barry and Ruth disappeared from our lives, and didn't even get a headstone for their father. His grave in Bushbury cemetery is unmarked still, with just that number. Rather selfish considering Reg paid for all the children to attend very expensive schools and bought cars, at an early age. So I must say in their terms, and in their rather plummy posh southern accent, "jolly bad show, chaps!"

GAMES, AND WEIRD POSSESSIONS

I must mention Robin and Pat's friends. There was Fred Collins, who was known as 'Colley' (the friend supposedly frightened in the ghost-house), as well as Dennis, Pauline, and many more. If it snowed, there would be a huge snowball fight lasting hours in the back garden. I was allowed to take part in those. Then there was a weird game where something was written on the backs of pictures that hung around on the picture-rails. I never DID find out what that was all about…

When it wasn't snowing, the evenings were spent crowded around the backroom table playing cards and board games. Monopoly was a serious game played for hours and sometimes carried over and continued the next day. Our dining table became a ping-pong table. It was small but doubles could be played on it without doing too much harm to the surrounding furniture. Not that there was much of any value. Our furnishings were a hotch-potch, with some weird objects that Dad had somehow acquired. One was an ashtray made from moulded plaster, a skull and cross bones with the Latin inscription, "Memento Mori". Sinister but fun.

One of its colleagues was a small crocodile-skin, bony and brittle but regularly polished by Mum. As far as I can remember, it hadn't got its head, but it took pride of place in the front-room fireplace.

In the attic there was a moose/stag head, large glass eyes staring out through the dust, its antlers dangerously pointed, but oh so useful to hang pants and vests on, which Robin and Tony did. This stuffed head was Mum's first bit of 'furniture', bought by Dad and his mother Gertrude, when on a search for furniture to start Dad's married life.

Mum had nothing to do with the choosing of her furniture. Grandma Gertrude was a very strong character!! So mother and son went out on shopping trips, arriving home with anything that took their fancy, nothing practical.

Gertrude's youngest son Leslie was the apple of her eye. So much so that he wasn't encouraged to work as his older, and smarter, brothers did. He did try piano-tuning, but that came to nothing, and some time later he got a job in a local shop. One day Gertrude was walking past the shop, and there, in broad daylight, was her son Leslie, sweeping the pavement outside the shop front. Well, it was a blow… she stormed into the shop and tore a strip off the owner. "My son wasn't brought up to sweep pavements," she ranted, so poor Leslie had to leave. He didn't work again to my knowledge for the rest of his life, but I may be wrong. He certainly wasn't in a job for long.

He married, but on his wedding night, Gertrude wouldn't let the newly weds sleep together. Leslie slept on the sofa downstairs, Marjorie upstairs in a bed. Little did Grandma Gertrude know that she was 'shutting the stable door after the horse had bolted', because Marjorie was already pregnant with her first child, my cousin, also a Reg (now a vicar, living in Australia!). Leslie and Marjorie went on to have a son, Mansel, and a daughter, Diane.

Uncle Leslie's last years were dogged by ill health. When walking along an underpass in Wolverhampton town centre, he was mugged and left bleeding and distressed. People passed him by, possibly thinking he was just drunk. The only help came from a Sikh gentleman, who helped Leslie to his feet and then took him home. A really good Samaritan. I believe Leslie was never well after this attack.

Mum and Dad would 'go on' about Leslie, but we now realize that his life was ruined by an overbearing mother. We always thought he was 'the black sheep', but we have found out more about Grandma Gertrude. She had lost two children in infancy, and 'adopted' Mum's Downs sister Bette, an extremely kindly act, but she was reluctant to let her youngest son go out into the world of education and work.

THE ATTIC

The attic at 249, where Robin and Tony slept, was quite a large room, with a sloping roof, and a high-up small window looking out over the roof. Under this window in the wall was a door. This 'door' was just a square piece of hardboard, wallpapered and jammed into the wall, not easily pulled out, but not impossible! Behind the wall was a room. Friends always found this 'secret' room fascinating. I did too and there were many stealthy creepings up the dark unlit stairs to the attic, having made sure first that Robin and Tony were out.

On one such visit with a friend, having managed to pull the square out, without much difficulty, the board just fell out, we didn't have to peer in, because there, right in the 'doorway' was a great white owl, just sitting there facing us looking menacing. We didn't stop to see more but hurtled down the stairs screaming, only to be met by Mum, who had heard shrieks and come to investigate…

What a let-down! The 'owl' was nothing more than a white washstand and water jug, recently put in there by Mum, who had no safe place to put it.

Owls were part of another superstition perpetrated by Mum. I have no idea when this happened. I do know I had been, and still was, ill in bed, the fire lit and guard up. It was dark outside. I had heard owls hooting and squealing and one particular owl was sitting on the roof or chimney. Mum looked out of the window and proceeded to tell me, "They say that if an owl lands on your chimney, there will be a death in the house." I was SO frightened. I think it confirmed to me that even children could die. Mum just walked out, not knowing what awful seed she had embedded in my head… That did have an effect on my life.

Some time before the owl episode, Ruth, the friend from junior school, came round to play. We were standing on a chair craning our necks to peer out of the small attic window which overlooked the White House (I must have gone back a bit in time here because it was still a hotel). Always scared when in the attic, worried that Robin or Tony would find us playing in their bedroom, and also frightened of the dark unlit stairs, we were in a giggly, jittery mood… So, when we looked down onto the car park and saw a HEARSE, right there below us, complete with coffin, we jumped down and fled down the stairs almost hysterical. Dracula, teeth out and dripping with blood, was after us. Later, we found out that a funeral director and driver were on their way 'up north', so had spent a night next door, body and all.

SENIOR SCHOOL AND MATHS

Amazingly, I did well at school, except for maths. Our maths teacher was a Mr Glaze, a red-faced, balding man, stern, as nearly all teachers were. I sat next to friend Barbara, who wasn't brilliant at maths, but better than me, as were most of the class. My mind really did shut off where numbers were concerned, so when Mr Glaze asked for the answer to some mathematical question, there was probably a show of hands, but for some reason, he picked on me to answer, although my hand had stayed on the desk, firmly down.

"Well, Valerie, what's the answer?" I must have just stared back at him, pleading to be let off, because he said, "Don't look at me with those big blue eyes, because my heart is a swinging brick."

I think from that moment Mr Glaze wrote me off from his teaching. He was head of the school library, and not long after this realization, he asked me to be a student librarian. My duties would be mostly when his maths classes were going on elsewhere. I suppose he was either glad to see the back of me, or there's a slight possibility that he knew I loved books and literature, so it would suit us both.

I was into Louisa May Alcott's *Little Women*, going on to *Good Wives* and *Little Men*. I loved these stories. There was some romance in them, and I had a crush on Laurie, the handsome young man in the books.

My school was co-ed, which was fine. To me, boys were just 'boys'. Coming from a two-brother family, it would have been strange to go to a girls-only establishment. There were rules for the boys about caring for us. If a girl had no chair, boys were expected to give her theirs and fetch another from wherever. There were indignities, though, such as having to play games out in the playground wearing our navy-blue knickers. Most self-respecting girls would roll the legs under, to make them tighter and more streamlined, but there was always one or two who just wore them *au naturel*, elastic edges showing, hankies bulging out of knicker pockets, the original 'droopy-drawers'.

After games, netball, or gym, we were made to have a shower. This was the end for me as I hated getting undressed in front of everyone then having to run round the communal shower room. You were not expected to

stop under a shower, there were too many girls, so we RAN…round and…
out. I hadn't developed a bust, so my chest stayed put, but poor Barbara
had developed early, as had a good many of my class, so there were a lot
of breasts bouncing around and bottoms wobbling.

Our dressing area was a cloakroom on line to the dining hall. The snag
with this was that the male teachers would have to walk through from the
boys' playground to have dinner or make for home. I feel sure now that
they could have made a round trip, but they didn't, and many times we
girls were getting dressed when three or four male teachers would walk in,
unannounced, pretending to shield their eyes from any half-naked bodies.
Looking back, this was wrong and of course it wouldn't be tolerated in
today's schools. Although I must add, nothing undesirable ever happened
– well, at least I hope not.

One or two of the boys in the class were disruptive. They were usually
dealt with with a mixture of understanding and force! One Christmas term,
there were a trio of boys doing their level best to spoil an RE lesson. The
teacher that day was a Miss Weaver, a tall willowy lady, usually very much
in control, but this time the talking and laughing behind open desk lids
had gone on too long. She suddenly stopped mid-sentence. "You, you,
and YOU, come out here IMMEDIATELY!" She pointed at the chatterers.
They trooped out and stood in front of her. Instead of raising her voice,
or for that matter banging their heads together, she turned to the class,
who were watching all agog. "These boys are so fond of their own voices
I suggest they sing for us. As it's Christmas soon, how about 'We Three
Kings of Orient Are'?"

It must have been the equivalent of being put in the stocks to be jeered
at, a punishment to remember. The three looked sheepish, red-faced and
embarrassed. Their voices just about to break, the three began singing to
a silent audience. However, after a terrible first verse there was giggling
with laughter and slow hand clapping. So the carol was brought to a much
welcomed halt. They walked back to their desks, heads down still flushed.

"Now, class, let's get on with our work." Miss Weaver had won.

There were the crude boys' innuendos and gestures which I didn't
understand at that time. They were gestures not aimed at us girls but
between themselves. One lad, who I will call JT, was always geared up to
cheeky signs and lavatory humour. He wasn't going to learn anything, so
he made it his job to play the fool. All kinds of rumours percolated around
in the class about JT. The one that sticks in my mind wasn't a rumour as
it happened during an English class. Whatever he had done, instead of
being sent out to stand in the corridor for all to see, or if the offence was
really bad, to go to Mr Thomas's office for a telling-off (he probably had
been through all of this), this misdemeanour must have pushed the English

teacher over the edge. This particular woman was never able to keep control, and sending pupils out into the corridor was a daily event. But that day, she almost burst with anger. She frogmarched JT up through the class and into a large walk-in store-room, where all the paper, chalks, exercise books were piled up. There was also a great pile, hundreds of sheets, of blotting paper. JT was propelled into the store-room, and the door was locked! The lesson progressed with no sound from the store-room.

We were then dismissed for our dinner break. Quite truthfully, I never thought of JT, nor did any of my friends, but the boys did, and, on the bush telegraph they found out what JT did whilst incarcerated in the room. When he failed to turn up for the afternoon lessons, there were whispers, smirks, and shoulder-raising suppressed laughter. We managed to get the boys to tell us what HAD happened in there. JT, feeling bored, with nowhere to sit down except the floor, had decided the window was too high to escape, so he stuck the time out. That is, until he suddenly felt his bladder filling up. The perfect way of getting back at school, the teachers, and learning in general, not to mention his bursting bladder… So he relieved himself on top of the hundreds of sheets of blotting paper, therefore ruining the LOT, as his water gradually got blotted up, soaking down the stack! We never heard what punishment he eventually received from Mr Thomas.

JT stayed right through the school, leaving at fifteen. What he did after that, I daren't think about, but I hope he settled, married and had a happy life.

So school for me became less of a 'dread' and more inviting, with lots of art and drama. Mr Thomas was very keen on that. We had some wonderful times playing 'shipwreck' in the gym. (Something that did make me fed up was that I could never shin up a rope. No matter how I tried, I never got more than three feet off the ground. I just never mastered it.) If I was to be asked what I liked best at senior school, to my shame, I would probably have said 'playing shipwreck'! That says it all.

The school dinners were awful. Although cooked on the premises, they tasted vile. Puddings were bearable and sometimes even pleasant. The dining hall was a purpose-built sort of Nissan-hut. True to form, the cabbage was always khaki, the potatoes were supposed to be freshly mashed or powdered. The dinner ladies did their best with the ingredients they had. We took it in turns to be 'table monitor'. This entailed removing half-empty plates and clearing the messy table. This was a job I hated!

MANAGING DAD, AND THE 'THING'

Back at 249, Dad was getting more irritable. He had always just stood still when getting dressed, whilst Mum would rush around to his commands of "Collar stud, my dear…get the cufflinks, come ON!"

Mum would do her duty, fastening cuffs and the intricate back-collar stud. "Socks, my dear." Again she would open a drawer and select the obligatory black ones (Like his mother, Grandma Gertrude, Dad was colour-blind so socks were a problem. Once, to his dismay, he wore one dark-red sock and the usual black one, and went through his whole day in the public eye 'odd socked'.)

Grandma Gertrude had gone one further in the colour stakes. She chose a big black hat for a relative's funeral (back in the early 1900s), and, apparently, when she arrived at the church, her family and all the congregation were taken aback – her hat WAS black, but, sitting on top was a full-flowering silk rose, bright RED!

So Dad would be dressed by Mum. "Handkerchief… hurry up, my dear." Mum would realize she hadn't ironed his hankies, so would drag the ironing board out and press one whilst Dad did nothing to help.

As for his shoes. These were ALWAYS cleaned by my martyring Mum. Because of his job, he was always on view, and appearing in the 'front of house' at the cinema, all his clothes had to be perfect, shoes polished to the brightest 'Cherry Blossom' shine.

Dad always called Mum "my dear" in all circumstances. I found that term of endearment odd even when I was very young.

I think the many illnesses, complicated by his smoking and drinking, made Dad less tolerant. In a way, he escaped household duties. When Mum had to go to an old auntie's funeral in Stoke, he had to find his own socks and try to fiddle with his studs and cufflinks. I remember helping him on a couple of occasions. The sight of Dad, arms out crucifix-style, hands waving, is memorable. Whilst Mum was away, even making a cup of tea became a great drama for Dad. He had no idea where anything was because he'd always had his food put before him and tea handed him. He did try during Mum's absence and actually seemed to enjoy the unfolding delights of the cupboards. He would whistle happily as

145

he searched, and strains of 'Bread of Heaven' would be sung. Dad had a very nice voice.

"Oh shut up, Cliff, we don't want it to rain," Mum would sometimes say. But being more than half-Welsh, Dad enjoyed a good old sing-song or hum.

Pat remembers helping him on another day, when Mum was off to some family 'do', probably another funeral. Dad was, as per usual, standing, arms outstretched, shouting "where's this?" and "where's that?" Being a strong character, Pat replied, "Find them yourself." On this occasion, making his own cup of tea was quite an event at 249. The remarkable thing is that he DID... AND he found the cups and saucers, and made a cuppa. He had been very spoilt by Mum, and by his mother years before.

He did, on a few occasions, cook himself a fish. Silver foil had just come onto the market. One night, after a bout of heavy drinking, he arrived home, accompanied by a friend called Richard. Richard's hobby was fly-fishing, and he obviously had to do his own cooking. He knew exactly what to do. I think the fish was a trout. He tore off some silver foil, popped the prepared fish in it, with a blob of 'best' butter and salt and pepper on top, sealed the parcel up and popped it into the oven. And the two men sat down and enjoyed the meal. So from then on, if Dad had a fish given him, he could and DID cook it, an amazing achievement and, for Dad, a learning curve. But alas, that was ALL he could do in the culinary line!

Years later, Dad was given a completely different type of fish. He walked in from the Gaumont late one night, having been dropped off at the gate by a friend. He carried a great lumpy-looking sack – it was obviously very heavy and bulky. We all stared. Mum ventured forward. "What is it, Cliff?"

Dad let the sack drop onto the floor in the kitchen. "It's an EEL, my dear, an EEL. A big one and I think it's still alive."

We all jumped back. Dad just slumped in his chair. Where he had got it from and WHY was always a mystery. He didn't seem to know anything about it, so tiddly was he. The only answer was to take the sack, complete with its contents, down to the canal and let it gently slide into the water. This was done at the dead of night. (This was carried out by a friend of Robin's called Harold, who was a frequent visitor.)

I also walked down to the canal helping Harold to drag the sack along. We got on to the towpath, then we didn't take the 'beast' out of its hessian home, we just tipped it into the murky water. The top was open so the sack filled with water and sank! Anyone seeing this would probably have called the police. It must have looked as though we were disposing of a body. There hadn't been any visible movement whilst lugging it through the streets so we presumed it was D.O.A.

HORACE AND ROSE GREENHAM

The Greenhams from 247 were going through a tough time. Mrs Greenham had been ill with some serious illness. Horace was perky, but every time he looked up, he almost fell over, a kind of vertigo. The apprentices had all gone, and Miss Leggett was bedridden. But for some reason, to add to their worries, they acquired a dog, a golden cocker spaniel. He was lovely, a friendly chap, middle-aged when they got him. They named him Rusty.

Mrs Greenham must have felt much better because she made two little drawstring waterproof bags for his long dangly ears! This meant that when Rusty had his nose in the bowl drinking or eating, his long curly ears stayed gravyless. They loved him, and he gave them a lot of happy times. Well before the arrival of Rusty, Binky, their ginger tom cat, had died. He wasn't my favourite cat. I went to stroke him once whilst he rolled on our front lawn, and WHAM... he not only bit me, but hung on to my arm kicking and scratching with all his might. I still have the scars on my finger today! He was some fierce pussycat

The White House owners, the Taggart family, were never too close to me.

The garden where so many conversations, laughs, and jumping overs took place earlier was now full of Mum's hydrangeas, huge bushes heavy with blue lace-cap flowers, all the result of Mum's covert activities whilst walking past someone's garden, or even whilst walking around a stately home. There were peony bushes, their red petals always lying around in a carpet underneath, and the age-old gnarled buddleia tree, its mauve flowers still full of butterflies. So the wall was almost out of sight behind the plants. Some of the smooth blue coping stones had fallen off, never to be stuck back on, and the TWO-hundred-year-old (and more) bricks were crumbling, leaving sandy piles below.

There never WAS any treasure to be dug out, but it didn't really matter, the real treasure was the open space, the old grassy air-raid shelter, and the long blue-bricked yard where so many happy games were played, involving Marmite on toast, a headless chicken, plus two dogs doing what dogs do! A kaleidoscope of events, enjoyed by all (except that poor white chicken).

Then Horace Greenham became ill. He had always looked sallow and yellow, so I don't think anyone noticed much change. He still visited and was as cheerful as ever. After dark one evening in the winter, I was sitting in the back room alone in the house, probably watching the television rescued from Reg's house. I had left the curtains open. Suddenly, there was a loud knock on the window, and the most terrible face was pressed up against the glass... It frightened the life out of me....

Why Horace had done such a silly thing, I will never know. Perhaps he thought it was funny pressing his face (which was rather ugly at the best of times) so that it was squashed and distorted. He went off chuckling, leaving me shaking.

There began a few years of ill health for the Greenhams. Mum would go round and sit with them, drinking a cup of tea and putting the world to rights. Poor old Rusty the cocker spaniel had died, leaving them sad. Their chickens had also gone, the last one killed (I think we were supposed to eat it, but Mum found coal in its crop, so the last chucky had not been fed properly.) I don't know what we did with it. Waste wasn't something that came easily in the post-war days.

Miss Leggett was still alive but upstairs in bed. I think the doctor was informed, but rarely visited. She was old, so that was enough for some doctors to write you off.

Tita (Rose) Greenham became very ill with some stomach trouble, an illness that was unspoken, but heads were nodded when the symptoms were explained. One afternoon, her sickness must have become unbearable, so an ambulance was called to take her to the Royal Hospital in town. For unknown reasons, I was instructed to accompany her to the hospital in the ambulance. I was only about eleven. I sat in the back with Mrs Greenham, looking out of the darkened windows, suddenly realizing that, although the ambulance windows were black from the outside, the people inside could see out – it was one-way glass – so I watched the houses and trees flash past. Mrs Greenham hardly seemed to know I was there.

I had her handbag, and was told by Mum to "Hang on to it, DO NOT let ANYONE take it off you." So I hung on, and still kept clutching it when Mrs Greenham was wheeled into A&E.

I think Mrs Greenham underwent an operation to relieve some pressure. She arrived home weeks later, a pale very frail lady, always being sick and feeling nauseous.

The next bit is something that was so ridiculous, but Mum believed it and nobody could make her change her mind, so even years later she repeated this story. Mum would go round for a chat to the ailing Mrs Greenham. The two ladies would sit in the 'best' front room, sipping tea out of china cups, tea that had been made by Horace. Mrs Greenham was still being sick and had lost weight. After one of these tea-and-sympathy afternoons, Mum felt ill, and had violent stomach pains. She was also sick. After her sickness was over, some weird idea struck her, like a beam of light.

"Horace is slowly poisoning Mrs Greenham. I thought that tea tasted awful. He must have given me Mrs Greenham's by mistake." Did she think Horace was performing a 'mercy' killing by poison?

Whatever we said, nothing would sway Mum from this extraordinary idea. So as Mrs Greenham got slowly worse, Mum would never drink anything in their house, even when once again the poor ill neighbour was driven off to hospital for a bowel operation, to fit a colostomy bag, Mum wouldn't retract her thoughts about Horace.

Horace was also admitted for a while into the Royal, I'm not sure what for, but he was away a few nights, leaving Mrs Greenham alone, except for Miss Leggett upstairs. Whilst Horace was in hospital, I heard POOR Mrs Greenham crying, "Where are you Horace?" Her bed was downstairs, and they shared the party wall between our hall, so I could hear her plainly weeping and calling out. It did make me feel sad, but I suppose life went on. Perhaps Mum went round, but I don't suppose she did. I didn't lie awake worrying, I suppose it's part of being a child. I hope I wasn't any more selfish than other children of that era.

Horace did return and he did what he could for his wife. The nurse would come in most days to change the colostomy bag. I would sit with Mum by the bed, hating the smell that surrounded us. Mrs Greenham had let her long silver hair down; loose, it was almost to her waist. Her false teeth had been taken out, probably because she was being sick, or because she was so thin that they no longer fitted her mouth. Whatever the reason, I found the lack of teeth very degrading, making her look chin up against her nose and not the pretty lady I had known all my life. Doctors seemed low on the ground, although there was now the NHS, so treatment was free.

Mrs Greenham died a few weeks later. I went with Mum to her funeral. Afterwards Mum whispered that she had experienced a 'whiff' of that dreadful smell when the coffin was brought down the aisle and past us. I didn't smell anything, thank goodness.

Horace coped. He still looked wizened and sallow, but was in good spirits. Unknown to us, Miss Leggett was completely bedridden. Horace would take her food upstairs, but it was all he could do to look after himself. I know that a Dr Brown was called one day to see Miss Leggett. When we asked Horace what he said about her, the answer shocked us, and beggars belief now. "Just leave her up there, give her access to water, but nothing else."

So that is what poor ill Horace did.

Miss Leggett lingered for a while, lying in a urine-soaked bed, until death was her relief. After Horace had also died and the house was cleared, the bed in Miss Leggett's room had been so soaked that the urine had dripped through onto the floor. The boards were impregnated with the stale smell, the result of months of neglect and they had to be replaced. But who could blame Horace? He had no back-up from the medical people, no doctor to turn to who had any empathy. Miss Leggett was old and forgotten.

Not long after Miss Leggett's death, Horace was rushed into hospital. He had an operation. I never asked exactly what it was, but he seemed to recover. We expected him back, but one morning the phone rang. Mum answered it. It was the Royal Hospital saying that Horace had died that morning.

According to the sister on his ward, he had had a good night, sat up for breakfast and was eating an orange, but then had suffered a heart attack mid-bite.

I did miss him. I was always his 'chinaman' and had a special friendship with him.

So 247 was empty, and a whole crowd of relatives descended to look through their furniture and knick-knacks. Ann's (the niece who had stayed with the Greenhams a few years before) mother from 'down south' appeared, and a Scottish lady who had helped occasionally at the house, a Mrs Lloyd. The two ladies came round to Mum with some linen and a chair, a Norfolk woven-backed one. It's an heirloom, and it's in our dining room today. I do think about Tita and Horace when I pass the chair. I suppose because I was the youngest child at 249, I had a lot more to do with them. Pat doesn't remember them really. Robin does, but doesn't have the same intimate memories that I have. Lovely memories.

TEACHERS

School was going well. I no longer lay awake praying that there wouldn't be some bully in the classroom next day to teach us. There were some odd teachers, particularly in the boys' department, woodwork and metalwork. One strange teacher was a Mr K, metalwork was his subject. I believe he was a German Jew, who had either come over to England before the war, or just after. Apparently, nobody was safe from his hammer throwing. He would 'whing' anything to hand at a boy who was misbehaving. I thought at the time what an awful man he was, but since (in fact last year) an old school friend, John, said how very good Mr K was at chess, and that he had run the chess club successfully, and without any anger. John liked him. I had to deliver a message to Mr K in the metalwork room once. I got ready to duck, but the hammers were kept on the bench.

Every girl had a crush on the sports master. He lived in the same road as Barbara, so his house was casually walked past many, many times. He didn't teach the girls, we had a Miss Yates, a rather masculine lady, but friendly and a good teacher. That was until I had an infected blister on my heel. I was away from school for a few days, and it was so infected that one night, after going to church with Barbara (choirboy watch), I looked down at my leg and saw it was sore and red, with a red line progressing up my calf. The poison had started to go elsewhere – very frightening at the time. All this dashing around ended up with the doctor being called, who immediately lanced the offending pus-filled area. So that I could go to school next morning, Mum had to cut a U-shaped piece out of the heel of my sandal and send a letter to Miss Yates excusing me from sports. That didn't go down well. She thought I could still carry on and made me feel a 'slug' for trying to get out of the lesson. The fact that it was one of my favourite lessons seemed to elude her, so I went off her. Barbara, however, had a girlie 'crush' on her and still thought Miss Yates was "super".

Mr Gwynne -Thomas was an amiable man, a Welshman with the Welsh love of music and drama. The drama group were flourishing, and all years put on a play. The top class acted out *David of the White Rock*, a very Welsh operetta, with lots of pretend harp playing and rather dour. I wasn't too impressed. It was a bit too serious for me, and no dancing in it. That wasn't right.

Our class put on several dramas. One sticks in my mind, purely because I was asked to don a tutu (I still had Jane's tutu, the dress her mother made all those years ago, it was fleece lined and beautifully made). It had to be worn over a bare body, and I remember stripping off somewhere in the wings of our small stage and suddenly realizing that I was in company. So eager was I to be asked to dance that I had just thrown modesty to the wind. Nobody appeared to notice anyway. So I tripped onto the stage and became the fairy in Hansel and Gretel. I had to skip around a pile of leaves that the 'birds' had dropped to cover the sleeping children. I feel embarrassed now all these years on. I didn't have any steps worked out, I just danced and pranced about, wand in hand, then aged about thirteen. The dance teacher Mrs Parker seemed thrilled with my efforts, and I truly had not a nerve in my body, I just 'did it'. I have never just 'done it' since.

The domestic science teacher was a Miss Pring, very much the dried-up old spinster. Everything had to be just so. No wooden spatulas or spoons put straight back in their drawer. "They will go black, class. Leave them out to dry in the air." Once, for a kind of test, we had to make an afternoon tea of sandwiches for members of the staff. The only sandwiches I could make were of Marmite, so that was on the menu. At the last minute, I managed to find a piece of celery, so chopped that up finely and added it. According to the teachers who ate them, they were a hit.

I never liked Miss Pring, and many years later, I joined an art class run by the Education folks. There was a large gathering of ex-teachers in the main hall, and when I came to get into the car outside, some idiot had parked in behind me, so I couldn't get out. I had to find the driver, so I hesitatingly entered the darkened main hall. There was a film being shown (educational of course). An announcement was made and the driver stood up. In the semi-darkness, I came face to face with Miss Pring. She might have been good at domestic science, but she was a bloody awful, selfish car-parker. She didn't recognize me, thank goodness.

How ridiculous to feel like that. I suppose in MY young days, teachers and their sharp remarks and total authority became engrained into one's brain. We were more naïve in those days, more so than children today. Teachers were held in great respect, and sometimes fear, like my terror of Mr G W, the child beater. Thank goodness teachers today are so much more amiable and approachable. Perhaps, though, the wheel has turned a little bit too much.

School days rolled on, the birds and the bees were talked about in the playground, and one girl admitted going out with bus drivers! This shocked most of us, who knew nothing of sex, but she did, and she talked about it, not to me, but to other friends, so of course it came zooming back on the bush telegraph.

There was one sad scandal involving a girl who was in the remedial class. She became pregnant. Nobody could believe it, especially when the father of her baby was said to be her own father. This terrible news didn't make sense to me or to most of the class. We couldn't imagine what kind of life she must have endured at home. She had to leave, and we never heard of her again. I don't think we had ever heard the word incest, let alone knew what it meant.

RELIGION AND THE CHOIR

Back at 249, Dad had been ill – I'm not sure what his illness was, but he had to go into hospital. Mum would trek up on the bus to town, then walk to the Royal, quite a jaunt. She still maintained that being a visitor was much more of a trauma than being a patient. I suppose she would think like that, but she had never been in hospital, so wouldn't know the feeling of loneliness when the bell rings to tell everyone to leave. I didn't go, child visitors were not allowed. The visiting hours were dire, just Wednesday afternoon for an hour (possibly two) then Sunday afternoon, no visiting in between these times, excepting patients near to death. At one point, I did write a letter to Dad telling him that the cat had given birth to yet another lot of kittens. I found that letter a few years ago.

By the time I was thirteen, choirboys had become very interesting to Barbara and me. We began attending St Michael's and All Angels, Tettenhall. I think we were also going through a teenage religious period. I did believe in God, in spite of what Tony had said years earlier. We went three times on a Sunday, twice in the morning and to Evensong at night. After the service, the choirboys would race out, and we would all gather outside. Occasionally, Josie joined our God-fearing group. She liked a boy called David, so set her sights on him. Barbara fell in love with Frank, who was head choirboy, sang alto, and played the organ and piano.

Unfortunately, Frank asked me to go for a walk with him around Tettenhall one evening. There were fields and stagnant pools. The whole area has been built up and now the Regis /King's School stands there. So, we met. I felt it was all right for me to meet him because he wasn't going out with Barbara, but I knew she liked him. It must have been about early evening winter time, because it was almost dark (I wouldn't have been out late at night). Frank wheeled his mauve racing bike along, and we held hands. We came to a five-barred gate, and were looking at a white horse standing in the gateway, when Frank tried to give me a kiss on the lips. It missed because I turned my head, and the kiss landed on my cheek. Well, it might as well have been a sexual assault, I was SO upset. I remember vividly saying "What would my mother SAY, if she knew what you had just done?" After that rebuke, we walked back quickly, not speaking, and I couldn't get back up 249's path fast enough.

The crux of my worry, my mother, was a bit of a farce, because she wouldn't even ask where I had been, let alone about any 'goings-on'. She rarely wanted to know where any of us had been, or who with. I could have been going wild with boys, smoking, and getting into all sorts of trouble, but Mum never wanted to know. If I DID try to tell her anything then, or in later years, the same standard 'Mum saying' would annoyingly be said: "Well, I never did!" or "Fancy THAT!" would nearly always be her reply. I gave up later in life, she was so wrapped up in her life, particularly Dad. So it was easier for her to just let most things go over her head. That was Mum's only way of dealing with life's minutiae.

Another of Mum's many sayings that have stayed with me all my life is: "If you want to do a job, do it WELL!" I wish she hadn't always instilled THAT rule. I can 'hear' her saying it now. Consequently, I have tried to do any and every job to the best of my ability, but it is an albatross around my neck at times.

The church-going carried on. I made friends again with Frank and his friend Clive. We had post-service meetings. I joined the AYPA, the Anglican Young Peoples Association, and we met once a week (rather boring, in fact). One of the group was John, a boy from Whitmore secondary school. I had had a crush on him earlier, so was happy to see him in the choir. He played the organ very well (and still does).

We were going to get confirmed at St Michael's and All Angels. We started confirmation classes, and were given a red booklet, 'IN HIS PRESENCE', to write details of who we were praying for. I seem to have written just about everyone in Tettenhall who would benefit from a prayer – family, aunts, uncles, doctors, cronies and some teachers, in fact 'Uncle Tom Cobbley and all', even the dogs and cats. I hoped they would all benefit from my devotion. The confirmation classes were given by the vicar, Mr B, in the large vicarage. (I remember a large coach-built pram in the dark hallway, something I couldn't equate with Mr B, who was a middle-aged, stiff-necked man – somehow him actually having children… well, it was a ghastly thought. Begetting wasn't something I would like to think about where Mr B was concerned.)

Amongst our confirmation group were three boys from Tettenhall College, a private school. One young man called David was my heart's desire! I don't think I ever said much to him, but he was, to me, so handsome, with a sparkle in his eye. Nothing ever came of it, but my heart would miss a beat when he walked into the room at the vicarage. There was also a Christopher, and a Craig, both David's pals from Tettenhall College. They were all rather nice and rather 'posh' and impressively polite. I think their politeness was a draw to us girls. They would all stand up when we girls came into the room, not altogether unusual in the 1950s, but somehow very romantic.

We got confirmed one Sunday. I don't think Mum came to church, and I know Dad wouldn't have even known I was about to become a member of the church. I think we wore white veils and a light dress. The Bishop of Lichfield confirmed us. I don't remember any food or pop afterwards, I think we all just went home, in my case not feeling any different, and certainly not blessed.

We lost contact with the Tettenhall College boys, but years later, we heard that Christopher had been killed in a car accident, and Craig had become a fighter pilot, and was landing or taking off from an aircraft carrier when his plane didn't quite make the deck, and it crashed, killing him. As for my heart-throb David, I never heard anything about him, and to this day, I have no idea what happened to him. Anyway, I always thought he was too 'posh' for me and he probably would have thought likewise.

JOSIE

Josie was a frequent visitor, and we still had great fun…

We would catch a bus up to the Gaumont. Josie loved the 'glitz' of the cinema. I can't imagine how we were allowed to come home after seeing a film, late at night, but on one occasion it must have been after the shops had shut, because Josie, who had set her heart on becoming a policewoman, would dart into every shop doorway and try the door handles, to test if they had been accidently left unlocked. Her grandfather had been a chief constable, so perhaps policing was in her blood. (Josie DID eventually join the police force, so her sleuthing into unlocked doors may have been handy.)

I remember walking down the road heading for 249, arm in arm, really happy friends. When at 249, we would test our breath underwater. We'd fill the wash basin to the brim with cold water and plunge our faces into it, holding our breath, and see who could stay down longer. There was still the ghost-house to be set up, Marmite on toast for tea, then for Josie, two buses home.

One Christmas, whilst waiting with Josie at the St Jude's bus stop, we cooked up a plan to get a bit of extra money. We went carol singing. No songbook, no music, and certainly no mastering of the words, but we did. Unfortunately, the houses we went to were almost opposite 249, and I suppose the householder may have recognized me, but we sang as best we could, and I think made about sixpence each, so quite a good return for our efforts. Sixpence was about five bus rides to town.

I was scared to tell anyone at home about our carolling, and, as far as I know, nobody mentioned it to Mum. She probably wouldn't have let THAT episode go over her head, mainly because she would have thought I'd 'let the side down', and the neighbours would know. Mum was honesty personified. So this was money not well earned. There wouldn't have been the Maudie trademark saying, "Well, well, well. Fancy that. I never did!" when an 'offence' broached the status of our family!

THE MAN IN NUMBER 9

About this time, my friend Ruth's uncle had opened an hotel opposite 249. He asked us if we would help, making beds and general tidying. It seemed a good idea. The weekend we started, her uncle was opening a cocktail bar. He had bought the next-door house and amalgamated it into the hotel. We served all the guests with buffet food, and one of the little finger-held savouries was canapés.

I had never seen or heard of them, but they looked good. We did our waiting and some washing-up, then walked across the road to 249. Mum was away at a funeral in Stoke that weekend, due back on the Sunday evening. How nice, we thought, to make some canapés for Mum's homecoming…

We got some aspic jelly from the hotel, set out bits of tomato, celery and anything that would go in, cut our rounds of toast, and admired our handiwork.

Mum was due home along with two of her sisters, so we pulled out all the stops, best cups and saucers, doilies, napkins, the lot, and laid it all out on a wooden dinner trolley.

We waited, and at last the aunts and Mum arrived home. What a damp squib. I can't remember any great surprise or even praise for our efforts. I was SO disappointed, and so was Ruth. The aunts were usually forward with compliments, so perhaps they DID say something, but I don't think Mum said anything, almost as though she expected it.

Our foray into the hotel was short, but sweet. We made the beds of some quite famous actors who were appearing at the local theatre in rep. Apparently Kenneth More was once in rep in Wolverhampton, and there were a few I can't put a name to who became well-known film stars.

One chap had his greasepaint set out on the dressing table, a great colourful array. We knew his name but never saw him. There was also a room, a double, where the occupants were a long-stay couple, possibly actors. They never wanted to be disturbed, so we didn't have much chance to go into the room, although we were dying to, as we had a sneaky feeling that 'something' was going on. WHAT, we didn't know. Our chance came one morning when we had to take a bottle of milk up to their room. Not wanting to miss out, we both went up and knocked. There were shouts of 'come in' so we did. The couple were in bed and somehow looked as though they lived in there. They smiled, and we put the milk bottle on the floor. I don't know WHAT we expected to see in that room, but it was a bit of a let-down, nothing weird going on. I think we expected them to be in a naughty clinch!

The nicest guest was a Mr L. He was a tall distinguished businessman who seemed to live at the hotel. He was so jolly and friendly, so we felt we should brighten up his dull room. We picked some wild flowers and stuck them in the only available container, an empty jam jar. This we arranged on the dresser in his bedroom. The flowers looked rather beautiful. The next morning our nice Mr L had already had his breakfast and gone off to wherever he worked. Our job was to make his bed, but on one previous occasion, we obviously didn't do a good job because lying on his pillow was a little poem, especially for us. It was witty and made us laugh. The gist of the verse was that we never tucked the sheets in at the bottom of his bed. I have kept this, and it's amongst my keepsakes. He could have complained to the management, but this was a nice gentle way of pulling us up. This is his note.

THE BLOKE WHO'S UP IN No. 9
HAS WONDERED FOR SOME CONSIDERABLE TIME
WHO PENS THE LITTLE BILLET DOUX
ABOUT HIS SOX AND SHOES.
BUT NOW HE KNOWS, AND WONDERS IF,
THE JAM JAR AND THE FLOWERS WERE 'GRIFF'
TO PUT HIS BOOTS (AND SUITS)
INSIDE THE WARDROBE "OK TOOTS"
BUT FAIR ENOUGH, THERE'S GIVE AND TAKE,
BY TIDYING UP I'LL MAKE THE BREAK.
BUT IF BY THE NOSE I MUST BE LED,
HOW ABOUT TUCKING IN THE SHEET,
AT THE BOTTOM OF MY BED?

Mr L had written this on the other side of his weekly bill.

Weekly board	£	s	d
	4	12	6
Afternoon tea		2	6
Early tea		1	9
Meals in Bedroom		1	0
TOTAL	£4 17 shillings and 9d.		

I have this poem still, with the bill on the underside. The year would be about 1952.

We didn't last long at Uncle Johnny's. It was a short but eye-opening episode.

Months passed. It was Easter Sunday morning. The phone rang and I answered it, as I was the only one up early so that I could go to church. The caller was Ruth's Uncle Johnny, asking me to "pop over and do a bit of washing-up, as the staff hadn't turned up." I didn't want to, and for once, Dad seemed interested and said I shouldn't go over, but I felt obliged to…

So church was off, and I walked across the road to the kitchen. When I opened the door, I was astounded. All the surfaces were buried under dirty dishes, cups, cutlery, the lot. Uncle Johnny said that they had given a party the night before, and now they had been let down by the usual kitchen staff

Nobody helped. I just ploughed through all the washing-up. It seemed like hours, and all I could think of was that it was Easter, everyone was at 249, eating boiled eggs whose shells had been painted. There also may have been an Easter Egg, a chocolate one. I slaved away, finished and Uncle Johnny gave me half a crown. I ran home.

Again Dad was incensed about Johnny's cheek. I never helped over at the hotel again, or even spoke to Uncle Johnny, but I couldn't say too much to Ruth, who held him in great esteem. I later found out he wasn't an uncle-proper but a friend of her Mum's. I think they played bridge together – that sums it all up.

STAYING 'UP NORTH'

My cousin Wendy had moved from Stourbridge to Wallasey on the Wirral in Cheshire. Her father Doug, the youngest of Mum's four brothers, was the manager of a shoe shop in Liverpool's Broad Street. We were good friends as well as cousins, so I was invited to stay at their house in Broadway Avenue

The house was an Edwardian semi, in a nice tree-lined avenue. Wendy's mother Dorothy was a strong character, and very different from Mum, but she had a good sense of humour, and I liked her. Uncle Doug was tall, with a big moustache, curly hair and all that my Dad wasn't, a home lover. He had been very keen on the boy scouts movement when he lived in Stourbridge and rose through the ranks to be in charge of a troop. His ease at making a fire appear from nowhere, when out on a picnic or camping, was admired, and many a cup of tea, brewed in a billy-can, was savoured after his efforts to get a pile of sticks to smoke into life.

Wendy's younger sister Judy was rather left out because Wendy and myself were almost the same age, so probably thought of Judy as a 'drag' when out playing.

Boys were definitely on the scene by now, and Wendy's heart-throb was a George Valentine. Even his name conjures up romance! He lived a few avenues away, so we would purposely take a 'walk-about' around his area, hoping to see him emerge. I don't think he did – well, not when I was visiting, but Wendy always hoped!

When we were not trying to 'stalk' George, we were making plans for a midnight feast. This would entail going to a local cake shop and buying their absolutely gorgeous trifles. The trifles came in a rectangular waxed dish. I just loved them, and they were such a treat, as we didn't have such wonderful confectionery back at 249, so these were the tops. It was the bottom layer that was so tasty. Looking back, I should think that the layer was made up of old stale cakes crushed up and soaked in some sweet fruit juice. The custard topping was itself topped with what I remember as REAL cream! I had never eaten cream before that. I suppose it could have been buttercream, but whatever it was, I adored it! These we would buy (I think Auntie Dot must have paid for them, so not such a secret feast) then hide them under the bed, along with probably Marmite sandwiches (I'm not sure here).

So, at dead of night, we sat there, giggling, talking about boys, hazarding guesses as to HOW babies were made, and did parents actually DO it… and if they DID, how COULD they, they were SO old! We had teenage fun, and happy carefree times, with our lives ahead of us.

We would sometimes make the trip into Liverpool to visit Uncle Doug in the shop. This was a journey over or under the river Mersey. We weren't keen on the train, but we did manage it. Broad Street is one of the main shopping streets in the city. I can't remember much about the shops, probably too boring, but Uncle Doug would take us into the Kardoma, a coffee house. (I haven't heard of any lately, so they may be gone.) I felt very grown-up going in there, having never been into anything like that back in Wolverhampton. A nice smell pervaded the place, and it was cosy.

Back in Wallasey, Wendy sometimes took me to what she called 'the breck', a wild open area of grass with the odd gorse bush. A gang of lads hung out there and were almost lying in wait for us girls. I think there was some verbal banter and a lot of showing off by the lads, who I felt afraid of. At one point, there was a chase, a breathless run across the open ground, and one that I thought would end in violence, and I was very frightened, but I tried to look and behave nonchalantly. Wendy was more stoic, and I think she knew the lads by sight, so I may have been making more of it than Wendy. (This was less friendly, though, than the gang who would hang around Josie's house and call Billy names, a rather alien crowd, and I didn't think much of them either.)

Doug and Dot had a golden Labrador dog, waggy-tailed and friendly. I took to him. He appeared soft and gentle, which I think he was with everyone, EXCEPT the postman. I heard later that the dog had bitten the postman and caused a lot of angst. Dot never wanted him in the first place. I think the dog (can't remember its name) was Judy's as she was an animal lover extraordinaire… she still is!

I know now that Uncle Doug and Auntie Dot had a very hard time making ends meet when they moved in shortly before I stayed for the first time. Auntie had made her front-room curtains out of old sugar bags, hessian material. She had dyed them pink, and to me at the time they looked fine. Doug didn't own the house, it was rented. (This was the case right through their married life.)

How Auntie afforded our trifles, heaven knows. Unlike Mum, Dot wasn't a lady who dressed up to go out, and clothes were not top of her priorities, her girls were. She had a temper that scared me, flaring up when Judy in particular had done something wrong, and I once saw Dorothy in Stourbridge shouting at Judy and actually giving her a wallop… in the street.

The garden at Broadway Avenue was tiny, a yard with a low wall to the right where, true to these times, neighbours would chat, peering over the top, mouthing and miming subjects that were considered 'not for our young ears'. I vividly remember one day, we were sitting cleaning our tennis shoes on the back step out in the yard. Doug and Dot were talking to neighbours who had recently moved in next door, a Ghanaian doctor and his wife, a youngish couple, although I suppose Doug and Dot were only young, late thirties. Snatches of conversation were floating across to us girls. One bit made us sit up and bend an ear.

"So what method do you use?" asked the doctor.

There was a hesitation, then Doug answered in a low voice, "Well, now we use the withdrawal method."

We couldn't believe our ears. So they DID do something. We weren't too sure WHAT, but we had an inkling of what they had said. (It was easier for me to imagine naughty goings-on between Auntie and Uncle, but my parents – NEVER.)

(We were 'green' in those days, and none the worse for it. Later in our lives, the fear of having a baby when not married, and letting your parents down, was very strong, and there was always the 'NO' word. I feel like Mary Whitehouse now, but I still believe that 'NO' has a place.)

Wendy was slightly bigger than me, bust-wise. I never really blossomed. In fact, in my class at school there was just me and a girl called Joy who were flat-chested and didn't have to wear a bra. I was so fed up of being bra-less. I still just wore a vest, and I felt left out in the puberty stakes. But Wendy had an idea. She DID wear a bra, so if she left HERS in the bathroom on a chair, my Mum would see it and realize her daughter, who was fourteen months older than Wendy, needed a bra. It didn't work. Mum couldn't bring herself to even mention bras, periods, sex, or anything blush-making. So I had to ask months later, all flushed and embarrassed. It did the trick. I was taken up to town, to Bedford & Williams and a bra was wrapped up and brought home. I couldn't wait to get it on, even though there wasn't anything to put in it!

School holidays 'up north' with Wendy and family were good times, and are fond memories.

THE BIRDS AND BEES

Pat didn't know about periods, and she has since told me the harrowing story about the day she started hers. She had been for a long ride on her bike, got home and saw blood. She thought she had some dread disease and was possibly dying. Mum just bundled her upstairs, didn't really tell her anything, ripped a bathroom towel into a strip, and that was that!

There didn't seem to be any sanitary protection in those days. There may have been, but Mum would boil the towels, and hang them on a dark part of the washing line, out of view. They were bulky, to say the least, and they were fastened to your pants or vest with safety pins. The time did come when sanitary towels were available in the chemist's if you could dare to ask in front of a queue. They were called 'STs', hushed voices all round, no openness.

I was about fourteen when my period arrived. Pat had never divulged anything, all too hush-hush, and I didn't know much, so it was a shock. When I told Mum, I was taken to one side. "You must NEVER go near a boy, not now you have 'started'."

Did that mean I couldn't sit with a boy, or, heaven forbid, dance with one? I was so unsure. Not long before, I had been told that just kissing a boy would make you pregnant, but now not touching one. Oh dear.

I think it was shutting the stable door for some girls, as in the third year at Whitmore, we were given 'sex lessons.' We were split from the boys, who had theirs later. Mr Glaze, the maths teacher, erected a screen, sat behind a projector, and, amongst nervous giggles, the film began.

By then, most of us had heard via classmates who were 'going out' with boys what the birds and bees were all about. So we sat through a lot of technical stuff, diagrams, all very formal and biological. Nothing new! There was a piece for us girls about periods, telling us we shouldn't wash our hair at that time of the month, and bathing was not on the agenda, all so ridiculous.

I don't think sex held any mystery for one or two of our classmates. The girl who went out with bus drivers was probably well into sex and all its complexities. One girl in the class actually came to school sporting a 'love-bite'. I think she tightened her tie, so that her blouse collar obscured it. We were allowed to view it, though; she viewed it as a rite of passage into the adult world. All her classmates just thought she was 'common'.

BARBARA

Now a bit about friend Barbara.

Barbara lived just off the Tettenhall Road in a terraced house with no front garden and a narrow back garden. To play, we used to go out into the street and play there on the pavement and watch the world go by. There were games played on the pavements, hop-scotch and jacks. These were usually boiler cleaners made of spiky metal, thrown down and as many as possible picked up in the hand.

Barbara's mother was very different from mine. She had once worked in the box-office at the Grand Theatre, Wolverhampton, and some of the 'stars' were known to her. I think they may have stayed with Barbara's family at some time, as B&B guests.

Barbara's parents went out most nights to a club, so all day her mum would keep her hair in curlers and wear a scarf wrapped round as a turban. She loved her make-up and splashed it on with gay abandon. Her lipstick was almost orange and went over the edges of her lips.

My abiding memory of her was the kitchen mantelshelf piled up with make-up, and Barbara's mum standing there in front of a mirror 'getting ready to go out'. She always appeared to be cheerful and had a good sense of humour. One day, we were perusing one of her bottles of medicine (lots of bottles, all shapes and sizes, all piled up on the mantelshelf). On the label were the letters BP. Not knowing what this stood for, Barbara asked.

"Bloody Poison," was her Mum's quick riposte, with a cackling laugh as she went on painting her face in many exciting colours, dabbing here and there.

Barbara's father was a very tall, thin man, a carpenter by trade, a nice quiet man. He always hung his coat up on the clothes stand in the hall, and one day Barbara decided to look in his pockets. (She had seen her parents laughing at something from his pocket the night before, and was curious.) So she rifled through the coat and emerged triumphant with a small, long book. We huddled over it and opened the very grubby pages… and GOODNESS, it was a pictorial book of what can only be described as pornographic cartoons! Naked men and women in all sorts of sexual positions, with the males' 'privates' larger than life.

We flicked through it, hardly daring to look past the first two pages, before replacing it nervously, hopefully finding the correct pocket. What a terrible surprise. How could they? I viewed them both with different eyes after that, as did Barbara. 'Adults behaving badly'. The crudeness of the book brought us down to earth with a great bump; grown-ups were supposed to set a good example to us, and here they were laughing at THIS.

GOINGS-ON AND A FIRE

For me and most of my friends, childhood was still continuing, in spite of the onset of puberty. We still wore ankle socks and navy knickers, but the liberty bodices had long gone – their cosy warmth was missed.

I still danced and pirouetted around the garden, played endless games of ball in the backyard, sat astride the wall, and dreamed about hidden treasures and my big dream of being a famous ballerina. And spent hours performing somersaults, cartwheels and handstands. I even joined Tony in airgun target shooting at a cardboard target pinned to the pear tree.

I think Tony had calmed a little and was more sociable, but still not speaking to Dad, and not eating with us mortals at meal times.

Pat was at the chemist working and had boyfriends, Robin was hard at work painting posters, Tony was working at a garage, as a motor mechanic, a slightly lighter chip on his shoulder.

Dad was drinking heavily and smoking, and also lending money to friends and drinking 'cronies' but never getting the loan back. I think he liked the fact that he was thought of as a generous giver… "Good old LD, he's a card". He was greatly liked by most. His ex-usherettes would go out of their way to speak to him, even after they had left the Gaumont. Some of the girls had gone on 'the game' and would frequent the road that Dad would have to walk down when the show was over. He always had the night's takings to put into the bank's night-safe. Sometimes Mum would be with him if she had been to the pictures. As they passed the street corners there would be a "Goodnight, Mr Lloyd-Davies," and the young ladies would wave happily, and Dad would wave back. (I can't imagine Mum would be enthusiastic about that.) Dad's staff or ex-staff appeared to respect and like him.

All the hospitals in the area were so fond of LD too, he did so much for them. We regularly received a beautifully iced Christmas cake from the matron of the eye infirmary (it smelled of moth-balls, though). LD was well liked. Pat told me recently of a Welsh saying: "A Welsh husband is an angel at the roadside, but a devil at the hearth." This summed Dad up.

I still attended church, loved the music, and all the responses, we knew them off by heart, and the choir boys were just as interesting. Frank was now going out with Barbara, and they were heavily into romance and love.

Ruth came along occasionally, and we would always end up giggling... Whenever the vicar said, "Let us pray" in that monotone-all-on-one-note, Ruth would say under her breath a long and sonorous "Okay", a rhyme that never failed to make me nearly cry with stifled laughter and still does.

I did go to my first communion, with others from our group, and still had a belief, but that got diluted as I got older. But at this time, life was sunny and exciting. The music, especially the organ recitals, was enjoyed, and the chat to the boys and the flirting when standing in the graveyard was a happy part of life.

In the graveyard there was a place of pilgrimage for the group – a grave of a young woman, said to have sat in a yew tree in the graveyard knitting on a SUNDAY! This was condemned by the local village people. A curse was put on her by the elders, who told her that if she knitted on a Sunday AGAIN, her arms and legs would drop off!

In the spookiest part of the churchyard, we would all troop and gaze at the grave. Sure enough, the flat stone resembled a torso with no extremities. We would all stare at it with a mixture of fear and hilarity... but it WAS there! I suppose it still is, now hidden by the grass of years, and perhaps forgotten by today's young ones, who have more ghoulish happenings on the television. To us it was chilling and creepy wonderful.

I don't know which year, I was about thirteen or so, when the news came in to school that St Michael's and All Angels had been burnt to the ground, only the tower escaping. We made a round trip on the way home from school that afternoon. When we arrived at the lychgate, the fire engines were still there, there was water everywhere, smoke, steam, and blackened timbers... it was a terrible sight. We visited again the next evening and could walk around the debris. There was a crucifix-shaped piece of timber standing upright amongst the still-warm timbers. We took it as a sign, of something, I'm not sure, WHAT, but we took it as a symbol that God had been watching. So why hadn't He stepped in and stopped the fire? This question didn't cross our young minds, we were still full of religious fervour.

The cause of the fire was thought to be an electric fire left on in the vestry, perhaps a surplice or some material had dropped down onto it. The trouble was that, for some reason, the fire engine couldn't connect to a fire hydrant, so the hoses had to be run down to the canal a few hundred yards away, which sounds impossible, but that was the story going around.

A temporary church, a large wooden structure, was built in the grounds of the Rectory. This was St Michael's and All Angels for many years, until the church was rebuilt.

SAD GOODBYES

Not long after the sad demise of our church, a very worrying and awful week unfolded, and a dark cloud descended. My friend and companion Mickey had passed blood in his water and had become stiff in his back legs. He was just as gentle, and patient, rarely barking, his black coat shiny, a result, we thought, of his cups of tea (good for the coat). His urge to lean against someone's legs was suddenly becoming more urgent. We were not a tactile family, so loving and warm Mickey fitted my bill and filled a huge chunk of my life, right from that little puppy sitting in the cardboard box under the Christmas tree. He gave unreserved love. At that time I think I loved Mickey more than anyone in the family.

I have a small silver locket. It was a present from Pat and Ray to their only bridesmaid. I have it still. It's heart shaped and it opens and each side there's a space for a tiny photo. Well, I'm afraid to say, one side is blank, as it always has been, but in the other half is a photo of my dear companion Mickey, with his grey muzzle and sad eyes, taken when he was middle-aged. Psychoanalysts would have had a field day falling over themselves to analyse all our family. No snap of Mum or Dad in the silver locket, just a dog.

I knew he was ill, but I went to school as usual. He hadn't become any worse, as far as I knew. He had still gone outside to do his business, and could still cock a leg. So when I returned home from school, I rushed into the kitchen to check on him. Mum was sitting there, by the table. I asked where he was. She looked up. "He's gone. He's been put to sleep by the PDSA. He had kidney failure."

I can't write down how betrayed I felt. I hated Mum at that moment. How COULD she, without even telling me? I hadn't even said goodbye to him. The poor old chap hadn't even had a member of his family to be with him at his end. He had died, probably frightened, with just strangers. Nobody he knew was there to hold him and kiss him farewell. Apparently, Mum had rung the PDSA, and a van had arrived. The driver, a girl, took him off, and that was that. The only sign that Mickey had lived with us all those years was his old collar and lead, the PDSA had left that, so Mum had just hung it on its peg in the kitchen.

Mum MAY have felt guilty, but all she could say was that he was so ill, it was "all for the best", which technically was right, but someone should have been there to stroke his head during his last moments. A great hole had opened up for me, and even today I have never been able to forgive Mum for that thoughtless act.

Flossie missed him, but she was Tony's dog, and although we all loved her, she wasn't Mickey.

Mum didn't do very well in the 'mothering stakes' that year. She blotted her copybook again soon after Mickey's death. One day I walked in from school and could smell burning. Mum had been burning rubbish in the back garden. The smell wasn't like the usual woody nice smell, this was almost a chemical one. When I asked what the smell was, she replied, "Oh, you know all those toys in the big cupboard, well I've burnt them. WELL, you are TOO old to play with them now, and they had got the moths in them, so…"

All my treasured toys just gone, burnt to death. I burst out crying, then I started to shout at her. How COULD she? The dear little rabbit knitted by an auntie, stuffed animals, old and holey, floppy dolls wearing home-made clothes, all gone up in smoke. There must have been well over twelve, all greatly loved. A chapter of my life became just ash. I think Mum WAS upset, I don't think she had thought enough about it. True, the moths were in the knitted toys, and they were also taking up space in the big wooden-knobbed kitchen cupboard. I was in my teens, so Mum thought "Just get rid of them."

I didn't inspect the remains of the bonfire, I was far too heartbroken. I couldn't have faced a lone glass eye or a bodiless head. The smell of burnt wool pervaded the house for hours.

Psychology was not Mum's best attribute. If you want to alienate your child, get her dear dog put down, and burn all her toys.

I did still have two precious teddies who lived on and escaped being burnt at the stake. I realize, now, that Mum couldn't put herself into anyone else's shoes, so just did what she thought was best, but I would have liked a "sorry". Unfortunately, that was always a hard word for Mum to say. I don't remember her ever saying "sorry", but memory is a strange thing, so I hope I am wrong.

I feel that this episode was the end of childhood. I was lucky to have had wonderful aunties and lovely neighbours and supportive siblings. Even Tony could come up trumps when need be, and the softer side did appear through a narrow chink in his protective armour, but never for long. The war hadn't touched me. I was young and shielded from serious issues, so I floated, or danced and tapped, my way through life with the selfishness that is natural in the very young. I hope I have got most of it right and that nobody has been shown in a less than true light. I have left out one or two happenings that would shock or offend my immediate family. Old memories can change over the years, rather like "Chinese whispers".

So childhood was over, but the teenage years, and beyond, were on the horizon.

TEENS AND EARLY TWENTIES

I left Whitmore Secondary Modern aged fifteen. The years at Whitmore had been eventful, the head master Mr Gwynne Thomas was a good and sympathetic head.

There had been floods down in Devon, Lynton and Lynmouth, and our art teacher Miss Wragge had all the class weave baskets for all the cats and dogs rescued from the houses. The class had learned how to ballroom dance, not very well, but it was quite nice being able to get close to a boy who you fancied. My forte was icing Christmas cakes. Miss miserable Pring didn't say much, but Mr Thomas was most impressed, and thought I should take up decorating cakes as a living. (Art was in my mind, but NOT icing cakes.) I was voted head girl in the last year, and had the unenviable task of giving a pep-talk once a week in girls' assembly. (Lavatories must be left clean, cloakrooms spotless, and taps always turned off, not left running.)

I didn't shed a tear on the leaving day. There were small groups of classmates having a weep in the cloakrooms, lots of hand shaking with staff, autograph books written in and sad farewells. I was glad to be off into the world, and I never looked back.

Back at 249, relations between Mum and Dad were worsening. Mum still managed to appear comfortably off, but behind the scenes she had a job to make ends meet. Her sisters Glad, Ve and Marj, all helped. They would all arrive by car – Glad seemed to have access to one. The aunts always dressed well with hats and gloves (sometimes long to the elbow), almost flat stylish shoes – proper heels were out, due to their height. They were a handsome group of ladies, greatly loved by all of us.

During the summer holidays, I had an interview with the head of Wolverhampton Art College. I was accepted, along with my friend from St Jude's days, Ruth. (Ruth had passed her eleven-plus, so had gone to the same school as Pat, the municipal grammar school). However, here we were together again at the art school. Ruth had not stayed on to take her 'O' levels. I'm not sure why, because she was a very bright pupil, but I suppose she was a bit of a rebel.

I don't think Dad even knew I had left school, let alone got into art college. He remained a very distant figure, because of his absence from the house. His working hours meant he was at the cinema until after eleven at night, and still in the bedroom when we left for our various venues.

Pat was now working in the pharmacy in Boots the chemists, going out with boys, riding her bike whenever possible, especially if there was any argument going on. Robin loved walking, as did Pat, so they joined the Rambling Association. The group would take a bus out into the beautiful Shropshire countryside. I do remember walking with the group to Clee St Margaret, where in the village there was a very old beamed cottage in the front garden of which were long benches and seats. We all sat down, and an elderly lady came out carrying a jug of (I think) ginger beer. Nothing wonderful, but somehow it was magical – beautiful surroundings, the ancient cottage, and an apron-wearing lady, rosy-cheeked, pouring cold fizzy pop.

I also joined the Ramblers one summer's day on a train trip to Wales, Colwyn Bay (I think). It was the seaside, so an exciting day out. Pat came too, and her friend Pauline. I don't remember much, certainly not about the food. We probably had sandwiches, possibly Marmite. In the afternoon, we played on the beach, and somehow our ball games turned into leap frog. Robin's friend Colley (really Fred) was by now very tall, over six foot. I took my turn, but was much smaller than all the others. My hands were wet and so was Colley's back. My hands slipped. I managed to get over but fell flat on my chest onto the hard ridged sand. I felt awful pain, but didn't want to make a fuss, mainly because I was much younger than the others and had been called a 'baby' when I had cried over other issues. I was winded, and shocked, but we all made it to the train, and home.

I felt then that something was wrong. My ribs hurt, as did my chest. Now sixty years later, I wonder if that fall started my bouts of tachycardia. I heard later that compression of the chest cavity could cause heart irregularities, all related to the pressure inside the chest cavity. It's just a thought, but it was a nasty fall. I don't think it registered with anyone and, although I was thought to be a 'cry-baby', I certainly didn't make a scene on that occasion. I can say it now, I was very brave.

ART SCHOOL

I started Wolverhampton Art School aged fifteen. The building was imposing, with stone pillars, a frieze of stone-carved Romanesque figures, and steps up to the gallery itself. Students had a side entrance in an alleyway. There was a hatch-like opening where you could buy all you needed. I bought the obligatory carrying folder, paper, and although I don't recall, I must have bought paints and brushes, all probably expensive. Looking back, Mum must have given me some money. This was still a problem, but she may have had money saved, as Dad still drank, smoked, and loaned money to all and sundry. There was never enough left over to give to Mum for the housekeeping.

Ruth, my friend from St Jude's, was with me on the first day. We walked into the girls' cloakroom to view the loos, only to be met by a tall, heavily spectacled girl running wildly out from the room, shouting "HELP, HELP. I'VE BEEN RAPED!" She ran into the main hallway. Nobody blinked an eyelid or went to comfort her. We just stood amazed, and shocked… even more shocked when the girl began laughing. Goodness knows what THAT was all about? (We got to know her later in the term. She became a well-known potter's wife and mother to two children.) This small episode was our baptism of fire at the art school. Today it doesn't amount to much, but in the 1950s the word 'rape' was a 'no-no'. I don't suppose it shocks these days, but it did then. We were two young 'green' girls, both wearing ankle socks, and in my case, navy knickers, probably with pockets.

We had mixed bag of teachers. One was Norman Thelwell, the artist who drew little girls on horses. He had apparently noted from the window lots of little girls riding on fields opposite his house in nearby Codsall village. Teaching was NOT his forte, however. This is a personal view, though, and other students may disagree with me. He would set a lesson (one I remember was to design a logo for a shipping company) and then once he had got us all started, he would mysteriously disappear. I suppose he was busy drawing the daily or weekly cartoons for the newspapers. He was a very small man in stature, dark-haired, with sharp features and a pronounced Liverpool accent. I never really had any dialogue with him, and I shouldn't think any of my class did either. I may be remembering incorrectly, but I don't think he ever sat through a lesson, and he certainly didn't teach me anything. We just handed our work in at the end of the lesson. I still have my work from that first lesson, a black ink simplistic drawing of a large hook and chain, with a boat floating around somewhere. Mr Thelwell just handed the drawing back, no criticism but no praise either.

Mr Thelwell's colleague at the art school was another cartoonist, Bill Kimpton. He was red-haired and smartly dressed. He certainly did teach us quite a bit about setting up still lifes and mixing oil-paints. I know he would set up a still-life group most lessons. One was a glass of red liquid, supposed to be wine, standing on a draped cloth. However, unlike Mr Thelwell, Bill Kimpton did go from person to person, offering advice about the shadows and reflections. I can picture him wearing a green tweed suit and shiny brown shoes – what a weird recollection! Bill Kimpton went on to found a studio called Rainbow Cards. His cartoons were extremely good, and the cards were sold in the UK, and possibly worldwide. He was a very likeable member of Wolverhampton College of Art.

Life classes were a great surprise to all of us. We entered the studio, sat legs astride a 'donkey' seat, drawing board propped up in front, paper well stretched (this meant soaking the whole sheet in water, then gum stripping it all round, letting it dry, so that any dampness from the paint wouldn't bubble the paper). Mr Sweet, our tutor, walked in with a middle-aged motherly-looking lady wearing a dressing gown. To our utter amazement, the rather plump mother-like figure went behind a screen then emerged completely naked. She was our model.

She mounted a dais draped with material, and Mr Sweet carefully positioned her naked body into a suitable pose, exposing everything. My neighbour Alan Barrett on the next 'donkey' whispered, "I would have thought she'd have shaved her pubic hair." Oh, goodness, 'pubic'. I knew what he was looking at, but didn't know the word for that part of the anatomy. I had never ever said the word 'pubic' to friends, so I just muttered something nonchalantly as if I went around mentioning pubic hair as a matter of course! I wasn't even sure that EVERYONE had it. Did men have it?

I must say, Mr Sweet was a wonderful teacher. He knew every bone and muscle in the human body. We had to draw the skeleton, then build up muscles and skin. The models changed over the weeks – a young lady, very thin, took over from the older lady, and THEN a male model. Well, we girls all giggled away until we were almost hysterical with smothered laughter. Would he or wouldn't he take everything off? The model, a very dark and handsome young man, disappeared behind a screen, and came out… wearing a leather 'posing pouch'! Not even a tiny bit of genitalia in sight! WHAT a let-down!! I never asked WHY females showed all and men didn't. I do know now.

Life drawing wasn't all nude bodies. We had quite a few clothed models who I think were just brought in off the street. Lovely people, mainly elderly, who may have needed the few shillings, hopefully given at the end of the lesson. I still have the drawings of these men and women.

One in particular is a special pencil drawing. It's of an old man, dressed in his army uniform, proudly wearing a beret above a strong but gentle face. I often wonder what he would think of our world today. He would sit quietly in a reasonably warm atmosphere, with a cuppa, and some money at the end of the three-hour lesson. These sessions may have filled a gap for some old soldiers or gentlemen of the road.

We also had models who I realize NOW were possibly 'ladies of the night'. One in particular was middle-aged, with dyed jet-black hair. She wore high black suede shoes with ankle straps, and her eyebrows were pencilled in above the original brow-line. In my mind, ankle straps were a sure sign of low living. A crimson mouth pouted at us. She never acknowledged anyone, and we thought she might be French.

To me, ANYONE who wore ankle-strapped high heels was of dubious character. My cousin Mike had already mentioned seeing ladies standing on street corners in London, but did Wolverhampton have such ladies? I pondered. Also, this sitter was French, so THAT did it.

Although I was at art school, I don't really think Dad ever gave it a thought. Mum was the parent who gave me bus fare money. I would sometimes get off a stop earlier than my stop, as the fare went up a halfpenny if you stayed on. The drivers and conductors on the trolleybuses were often Polish, having fled to the west during post-war unrest. They were usually nice quiet folks (who also became clock repairers).

One conductor in particular Ruth and I called Tenkyu. He didn't say anything else except "tenkyu, tenkyu," as he tinged his ticket machine and accepted the money. We always got on with Tenkyu. Well, that was until one day, when I didn't get off at the Halfway House pub but carried on one stop further, to my bus stop nearer to 249. Tenkyu must have noticed this, so when I was on the platform, he walked down the aisle, horn-rimmed specs almost steamed. It turned out he COULD say something other than "tenkyu" because he told me to pay the halfpenny or "GET OFF"! I didn't possess any money, as per usual, soooo I had to get off, watched by all the other passengers through steamy windows. Oh, the embarrassment.

However, this wasn't as terrible as my little journey some time later. I was instructed by Mum to go to the town hall on the bus to the rates department. Mum gave me an envelope. It held the last reminder, the "YOU MUST PAY THIS OR YOU WILL FACE BEING SUMMONED".

Mum usually tried to gather together money, but it was very difficult, as Dad never had any spare. Today was the very last date for payment. I never worked out WHY I had to do the dirty work for Mum and Dad. When on the trolleybus bound for town I clutched the brown very official envelope as though it was hot coals. It was so humiliating standing in a small queue made up of people who had not paid their dues on time. This was in public view right outside the rates arrears office in the centre of Wolverhampton town. Everyone passing must have been thinking that my family didn't have the money to pay. But it was just the opposite. Dad had a very good job, a better salary than any of my peers' fathers, but he never managed to pay bills for rent or housekeeping. The envelope seemed to burn my hand, and my face felt red with a mixture of fear and embarrassment, and from the effort of running to the rates office having got off the trolleybus this time BEFORE my stop. Nerves made my mind go to jelly. I did it, though, and no doubt Mum breathed a sigh of relief. She always lived on the edge of debt, which for her, a truly honest person, must have been hell. No wonder her constant fear was that 'THEY' would get her. Well, thankfully, this time they didn't get her.

I am bragging, but I did do well in life drawing, though I was not so good at drawing or painting buildings (this is still the case today). I was in my element. For once I felt I could do something, even though I hadn't passed my eleven-plus (I felt shame for years about that, something that would never have happened had the comprehensive schools been around. I took the shame of not passing the eleven-plus to heart for almost all my life.) I loved the life in the wonderful art college. I always felt VERY important walking out of the college, even though our entrance was through the door in the side alley.

Friend Ruth had a crush on a rather weird chap, all bristles and mottled scaly skin, who was always in a buff-coloured duffle coat. Apparently, he knew that sixteen-year-old Ruth was keen on him, so he arranged to meet her on the upper green, Tettenhall! To this day she has never said what happened that evening, but she did 'go off' him pretty quickly after their date. He did have a reputation with girls, so I imagine he shocked Ruth somewhat! Sadly, he died very young, in his early twenties during an asthma attack. He did smoke an awful lot, which wouldn't have helped.

The common room at the college was small, with a counter selling tea and coffee. In one corner was a piano, which was played sometimes by an older chap, and singing along in a sort of double act was another chap, who usually wore a daring pink shirt (men just didn't wear PINK in those days). I didn't know anything about homosexuality, but I gather they may have been an 'item'. There were quite a few nudges and head-shakes. The small room was always thick with smoke and loud chatter. Nothing

177

more intoxicating than tea or coffee was served, by the tea lady who had been there for many years. She always wore a flowery apron, and was a homely-looking woman, who looked quite out of place in the smoke-filled room, with its strange male duo playing and singing melodies from some operetta or another and tinkling the keys of the old piano. She stood there behind her small counter, tea on the go, cups ready to serve. And serve she did! I never even knew what her name was! We were very much the juniors so could never dare ask. I don't think we ever bought a tea. It sounds ridiculous now, but paying for a cuppa might have meant we would have to walk the two miles home. No bus fare… Money was that tight!

Down in the college basement was a pottery room. Mr Willets was in charge. He was a round Mr Pickwick lookalike. Clay modelling was also on the agenda, and I threw myself into it. An old man leaning on a lamp post in white clay was produced, and I went on to model a dog – not exactly a budding Barbara Hepworth, but it was fun. The trouble was that I seemed to break bits off my finished product and rarely took them home in one piece; a lot of my figurines, if not ALL, ended up in the bin!

One of the venues for students was a drinking place called Madame Clarks. I only went in there once. We first years thought it was probably a den of iniquity, the name 'Madame' conjured up naughty 'goings-on', and it HAD certainly been a place of lewd behaviour. Originally, the pub (or bawdy-house) had once had sawdust on the floor and spittoons beside the bar. It was very old, possibly Elizabethan. A lot of drinking did go on amongst the older students. How they afforded it, I don't know. There was a lot of talent amongst the group, and quite a few went on to higher things – pottery, sculpting, and teaching art. I liked them all, I thought them sophisticated and somehow daring.

I had a crush on a duffle-coated boy, Brian. (Duffle coats, usually camel coloured, were the order of the day in the 1950s. One of the group wore a dark green one, Oh mercy, he stood out from his teddy-bear-coated friends.)

WELSH ADVENTURES, AND ALAN

I made quite a few friends during my short stay at the art school. One day, six of us decided to go camping to mid Wales (very Enid Blyton). Where I got the train fare from is still a mystery. It was the beginning of a bank holiday and we all piled into a very crowded train. We had to stand, sit or lean against our very small and quite unsuitable tents and backpacks for the two-hour journey.

Looking back, did Mum say ANYTHING about my going off with a mixed group? What about sleeping arrangements? Mum said nothing to ME, but only recently sister Pat related how worried Mum WAS, and Pat had persuaded her that everything would be all right – what trust!

So here we were, on our way.

The farm field where we pitched our tents was not a campsite, but the farmer just let a couple of tents use his field, charging (I think) two shillings a night. There was a most unhygienic loo, just an Elsan, which had to be emptied, but never WAS, and with six using it, it became full almost to the brim. I'm sure that started my fear of all public loos. As Mum would say, the main thing was NEVER TO TOUCH THE SEAT, YOU DON'T KNOW WHAT YOU WILL PICK UP. So balancing on this terrible hell-hole was worthy of an acrobat.

I shared a tent with Margaret, who was much older than me She had joined the art school after working in a factory, I think on 'piece' work. She was determined to study art, so had saved up to finance herself. She was small, bespectacled, and strangely funny, once confiding to me that she never EVER viewed herself naked! She couldn't bear it. She startled me by relating how, at a party, she was romantically snogged by a young dentist. They were alone in the party-giver's bedroom – the next bit was way above my head, but Margaret and her dentist amour had discussed the 'Immaculate Conception'. I never told her, but I couldn't fathom WHY they had, mid-snog, talked about the Bible.

The others on our camping extravaganza were Terry, a tall thin lad, with slicked-back hair, and a couple who were 'an item' so had ONE tent together – so 'modern'! Oh dear! Then there was Alan, my neighbour in the life-drawing class.

179

Alan became my special friend. He was handsome in a male ballet dancer way. He lived with his parents not too far from me. I met his mum, a kindly caring mother, who had cats all over the place, most of which were usually in 'an interesting condition'. I thought Daisy, his mother, was homely, and I liked her interest in Alan and his older brother's 'doings', so unlike my Mum, who was too busy to notice what we were up to. Alan's father was (according to Alan) an awful man. However, when I met him, he greeted me and was friendly, in spite of his pale blue eyes, in my mind associated with German soldiers, mainly in films viewed at the Gaumont.

Why Alan didn't like his father was something not discussed. My good friend and ally was a boy of many facets; one in particular was a shock. Alan was a thief! I say this with a smile now, but at the time I was appalled. We were strolling around one day in the West Park, where a few years before I had spent many hours fishing for tiddlers and sticklebacks. The tearooms were purveyors of goodies. Although I would never have afforded sweets or crisps, I may have indulged once in a sherbet with a liquorice stick in it!

This particular day remains a shock to this day!! Alan went inside and appeared holding a cupcake, complete with ruffled paper-case and pink icing, very delectable. He handed it to me, without taking a bite himself, so I accepted it, with thanks, and was just about to take a bite when he said, "Don't thank ME, I didn't pay for it, I stole it." I was suddenly stiff with fear. "Go on, eat it. This is nothing. Don't YOU ever take sweets from Woolworths?" (I had NEVER taken one tiny sweetie from Woolworths, 'THEY' would have got me and the whole family would be shamed!!) Needless to say, I couldn't partake, so Alan scoffed it all, and I couldn't get out of the park gates quick enough. I felt that at any minute, I was going to feel a firm hand on my shoulder. I have had that feeling ever since that 'THEY' were after me!

Alan just laughed.

Another petty crime took place one night whilst Alan was kindly walking me home from some art school 'do'. We were passing Wolverhampton town hall, and in front were flower beds all very correctly and symmetrically planted with uniform red geraniums. To my horror, Alan grasped a plant in full flower, pulled it out of the ground, and handed it to me, roots and all. I felt as if I had been struck by lightning!

We walked to 249 with the wilting plant, dirt dropping, so that it was bare rooted when we ended our journey. Once in the house, I crept upstairs and shoved it under my bed. Mum would be electrified with fear, awaiting the early-morning knock on the front door, where 'THEY' would be standing, handcuffs at the ready… Then the next day we would be the headlines in the *Express & Star* newspaper: "CINEMA MANAGER'S DAUGHTER

ARRESTED OVER THE THEFT OF A COUNCIL GARDEN PLANT".

Well, that night 'THEY' didn't get me, but my conscience DID, and the plant ended up wrapped in newspaper and thrust down to the bottom of our dustbin.

Decorating was something Alan enjoyed doing at home, so when I was invited to see his latest décor, I eagerly walked into his back sitting room. In there the walls were a dark, drab green, I had opened the wrong door. "When are you going to start on THIS room?" I asked.

"This IS the room. I've decided that the dark wall shows up the pictures." I wished that the ground could have opened up, but he only laughed. We had the kind of friendship that never ever verged on anything sexual.

Years and years later, I read in the local newspaper that "Alan Barrett, a local man, who trained at the Art College, is visiting his home town, having designed the scenery for a theatre production which is showing this week at the Grand Theatre. Alan Barratt is the well-known scenic designer, famous for his scenic set-ups for the Bristol Old Vic theatre."

My husband tried to get me to contact Alan. "It's easy enough to ring the stage door, and say you were a good friend." Oh glums! I couldn't. I regret that now. I know Alan would have been welcoming as he always was, but my lack of confidence got the upper hand, so I never saw Alan again. Silly scared me! It's one of my biggest regrets.

(Alan is dead now, but happy memories of him stay with me, sixty years on.)

Well, that was Alan, so back to camping. We spent a few very hot, hungry days in mid Wales (I can't remember where). The farmer who let us pitch our tents was unsmiling and grumpy. The infamous loo was a walk away, stuck in a field against a tree, and was absolutely disgusting, and soon filled to the top, so that we were almost sitting in the muck and mire. I believe we washed, but rarely, and what we ate is still a great mystery.

The two friends who were an 'item' were some way off in their own little two-person tent and rarely mixed with us. At the end of the few days, they decided to stay on, whilst we were ready to leave. Unfortunately, there was a rail strike, so no trains to get us home. We decided to hitch. Terry and Alan hid behind a hedge, whilst we two girls thumbed… Sure enough, a driver stopped and opened the passenger door, only to find that two chaps then rushed out from the undergrowth and squeezed in too!

The driver took us some of the way, but then dropped us off the other side Shrewsbury, about forty miles from home. Again we displayed our golden brown, bare legs, and quite quickly a lorry stopped. It was open at the back and had remnants of what looked like agricultural lime. Before we could decide who would sit in the only passenger seat beside the driver,

Terry pushed us out of the way and climbed into the cab! I had never been enamoured with Terry, and now he sank down in my estimation to nought out of ten. So Alan, Margaret and me all clambered up into the back and sat amongst the covering of lime, boiling hot, windblown, and all three hating Terry!

The driver dropped us off still miles away from Tettenhall and comfort. We must have looked like ghosts, we were covered from head to toe in white powder. Our lips stung with it, our wonderful golden tan gone undercover. Terry, however, emerged in Technicolor, having had a very cosy journey! I have always hated him!

To save the day, a very cheerful lady who ran a café close by took us under her wing. Insisting we wash, she took us through to her kitchen, a large farm-type one. We reluctantly stripped off, with some embarrassment. Taking one's clothes off down to a bra was something we very virginal girls had never done in front of others, but needs must, so we half-stripped in front of the boys.

"Don't worry, girls," the lady said, seeing our red faces, "we are ALL the same underneath." How right she was.

Alan, Terry and Margaret all stayed on after I left the art school, but the happy times spent with Alan in particular I cherish. His love of music ignited an interest in me too. He introduced me to the Rite of Spring by Stravinsky. He arrived one evening at 249 with a pile of 78 records. We carried the gramophone into the kitchen, opened all the little doors on the front to give the music full vent, wound the handle until almost breaking point, then let the ritual commence… The music was extraordinary, I had never heard anything like it before. Loud, rhythmic, almost hypnotic. The trouble came, though, when the music took a dive as the gramophone ran down. There was frantic handle winding and then back to the dance… I can't say it was erotic, I wouldn't have known what eroticism was, but it did conjure up dancers mesmerized, chanting and wonderful, tribal mystery…

We flung the windows fully open, and let the air fill with the drumming beat, only to hear an angry voice from a bedroom window at the White House, "KEEP THAT TERRIBLE NOISE DOWN". Mum was probably in, but she didn't intervene, if she even heard. She would be watching our nine-inch television in the back room.

If there was a fashion show given by the students in the dress-designing class, Alan provided suitable music – *Spring Symphony* is the only piece of music I can recall. Alan had brought a new dimension to my life. I learned later that he HAD thought of becoming a ballet dancer. I wasn't sure that I would appreciate him leaping around on stage wearing a pair of rather revealing white tights.

TREADING THE BOARDS

Ruth would walk down to 249 most evenings and weekends, and this is when a very insane ritual would take place during some warm days. The canal was still a great place to wander, the towpaths, barges and water fowl were very pleasant to two teenagers, who talked endlessly about romance, boys and everything under the sun, usually reliving scenes from a current film.

One film in particular starred Rock Hudson. We had gone together to Dad's to sit mesmerized watching Rock forever dragging a very sick fur-wrapped lady across some snowy terrain on a sledge, then carrying her into a log cabin, where he would tend her every need, whilst she gazed up at him with eyelashes moist with tears. These walks never just ended sitting on the nearby grassy bank, discussing Rock's marvellous physique, his dark brooding face, and wonderful performances. No, we would make our way across the tall grassy wasteland. Here, hidden by the weeds and debris, were two overflow tunnels, only full when there was rain or a storm; they enabled the canal to stay at the same level. Once there, we would find the tunnel with the least water running through it (this water would discharge into what was called the Smestow Brook) and it was here that we would search our pockets for a halfpenny. Once found, we'd throw it into the water and make a wish! (Oh dear, a bus fare in the river! What a waste of a halfpenny… four stops on the trolleybus.) The chemical smell in these tunnels was awful as the canal was still being used by Courtaulds factory to dispose of smelly waste.

What all this money throwing had to do with life, luck, or romance is a mystery, and unexplainable. I am almost unbelieving as I write this, but it IS true.

The canal was a very familiar place to all of us. Robin and friends had use of a small rowing boat housed on a stretch of the canal close to the huge waste pipe. To this day, I hate any dark discharging pipe, having on one boating venture badgered Robin to let me steer the boat. The Courtaulds pipe loomed on the right bank, but try as I might, I seemed to be drawn towards it. It came nearer and nearer, and there was much shouting and jostling to get hold of the ropes and stop the boat from floating under the pipe. Fear of dark open pipes has lasted a lifetime. So why we girls went to such a place, to sit talking of teenage doings, and wishing fervent wishes is behaviour I STILL haven't worked out! I can't even remember WHAT we wished for. I suppose it was for dreams and hopes, that a tall handsome man would sweep us off our feet and drag us across a frozen wasteland. Good happy times, though.

This was also the time that Ruth joined a drama group. She was a very good actress and could mimic stars of the day, especially Margaret Rutherford, the elderly double-chinned actress of screen and stage. I had no inclination to act, and was far too scared to stand up in front of strangers. I must have been easily led, though, because Ruth managed to persuade me to join too. I feel a blush coming on when relating this.

The play the company were rehearsing was *The Same Sky* by Yvonne Mitchell. The play is about a Jewish family living in London just after the war. The rehearsals took place in the central library. Ruth was keen, and very good. I was an absolute failure.

We were allotted parts, and because there were only just enough members to fill the cast, I was (probably reluctantly) chosen to play Ruth's sister Renee. Ruth was chosen for the main character, and although only sixteen, acted the part of a much older married woman. This she carried out with acuity and passion, and a real understanding of someone older. Ruth was sixteen, Mrs Brodsky about forty-plus.

She even had to KISS the man playing her husband. Oh, blushes all round! The (for me) most embarrassing bit in the play was a scene where I had to pretend to dance. This 'dance' was hip wobbling whilst singing a Carmen Miranda number. Carmen Miranda was a very exotic 1940s singer. Her headgear was usually a huge mound of pineapples, bananas and grapes, a sort of mobile fruit salad. I can say that this was the most stomach-churning time of my life. I had to wiggle my hips and sing "Aye aye aye I lurrrve yoooo verreeee much. Aye aye aye I think you'rrre grand." I felt flushed and red, in fact about to explode or die.

Eventually, the performance was booked for the local Wulfrun Hall, and Mum and Robin dutifully came along to one of the evenings. I did do it, but felt like legging it out of the place and running red-faced back to 249. But that was the stuff of dreams, so I stayed. I must have put in a performance SO bad that the review in the local paper didn't mention me, and neither Robin nor Mum mentioned it afterwards. Ruth was given a good write-up, as were the other actors. Strutting my stuff was NOT for me.

I still have the programme, however, secreted away in a memorabilia drawer.

LEAVING

Just before the end of our college year, Ruth's father died rather suddenly, having only been ill for days.

Chas Brickman was an antique dealer with a shop near Tettenhall. He was a dark-haired moustachioed man, very Jewish-looking, with dark-rimmed specs and a smiling face. I liked him a lot. Their house was a Victorian semi in Tettenhall village. Because Chas sold antiques, some of the furniture would reside in their home. One minute there would be a large imposing piece, then next visit, it would have gone, sold! However, they had a 'static' boudoir grand piano in their sitting room. Chas would ask if anyone would like a Bach 'fooogooo' for fugue – he could play well and was so cheerful, but unfortunately he was under the thumb of the very aristocratic-looking Mrs Brickman. Dorothy Brickman was a very demanding woman, and not my favourite person.

Chas became ill with what the doctor said was a 'germ' on something he had eaten. I was told by Ruth that Chas was suddenly confused, trying to eat toothpaste, and seeming not to make sense of everyday rituals. A point that has stuck in my mind is that Chas didn't know what to do with a tomato and wasn't sure if he could or SHOULD eat it – a very sad illness.

Ruth's mother was a bridge fanatic and bridge always came first in her life. Not knowing how ill her husband was, she still trudged off to catch a bus to the bridge club, carrying a metal box containing all the packs of cards for the evening. I remember Ruth's older sister Jean saying, "Oh, poor Mummy, let me help you carry the box." Even then, I thought how odd it was that Mrs Brickman was trotting off to bridge, leaving Chas at home looked after by Jean and Ruth.

Two or three days later, Chas died. The doctor told the family that Chas HAD picked up a virus from food that perhaps a fly had landed on. He had attended a buffet the night before he became ill. He was a very jolly, likeable man, loved by his children. He was only in his forties.

With no money coming into the Brickman home, Ruth was told that her days at the art school were over. We were on the upstairs of the bus, going home from town when Ruth said that she had to leave. I also realized I would never be able to carry on, as Mum was desperately trying to keep me, so I answered that I would probably have to leave too. Well, Ruth snapped my head off and shouted, "You'll NEVER leave! You have a daddy, and I HAVEN'T!" And with that, she stormed off the bus.

We did stay friends, however. Ruth was going to apply for a job at the telephone exchange and was due to start a course before she could become an operator. We had both kicked the dust of the art school off our badly shod feet, so we indulged in sewing, decorative belts, even aprons. One warm evening we walked from Ruth's home along the road to 249, the lime and plane trees were in full leaf. We sat on the floor in our front room, the sewing-basket between us, industriously sewing, when all of a sudden, Ruth WENT MAD. COMPLETELY. She clutched at her face, screamed, cried and pointed to an invisible 'something'. I was frightened and thought she had seen the ghost of her dead father. Ruth danced madly, whirling, still pointing and screaming at the sewing box. THEN I saw it!! There, in the box, on its back, legs waving, was a huge may-bug, a giant beetle.

What had happened was that Ruth, who was wearing long dangly earrings, thought that they were tickling her neck so put her hand up to her ear and pulled to adjust the bejewelled earring, and discovered this loathsome creature firmly clinging onto her ear lobe … Its little suckered feet were clamped onto her ear, so in complete panic she had dislodged her unwanted guest and flung it as far as she could. It landed in the sewing box.

Ruth became hysterical. Tony must have heard the screams as he ran in and slapped her across the cheek. (Tony had never liked Ruth anyway, so it was probably quite pleasurable for Tony, though not for Ruth, but it did stop her screams.)

Tony said he would drive her home so distressed was she. The terrifying may-bug was ceremoniously squashed on the front path. I was told later that may-bugs only fly on one day so that they can mate. It was a truly horrible end to a day for Ruth, and an even worse one for the may-bug.

Some years later, I told this story to my Auntie Ve, and she recalled that one night the Stourbridge town clock was stopped by thousands of may-bugs (or, to give them their proper name, chafer beetles) clogging up the works in their orgy of unbridled sex. One-night stands, because the next day they would die, but I suppose they would die happy and fulfilled during their passionate last hours.

Before Ruth started her course, we went to London, just the two of us, much to the tut-tutting of the adults.

The front door of 249. Taken 2021

Grandparents

Me aged 2

Dad

Robin, Tony and Pat

187

Tony, Robin, Pat and me

Pat and I

At a family wedding

Jean Kent, Dad and me

Dad

Picking pears

Still picking pears

Horace and Rose Greenham

Grandad Mansel and Reg

My dog Mickey

My book, aged 5

On the air raid shelter

Me with Tony's rabbits

The rear of 249

Pat with me

Me, Billie and Mum

Tony in the Army

Wendy and myself with Mum Aunts and Uncle

Arthur William Proctor Brograve Beauchamp

191

My 21st Birthday

Colly, Robin and me

Robin Colly's Best Man

Robin, Pat and Tony at Blackpool

Official portrait of me

LONDON, AND EDMUND

An opportunity had cropped up when Mum's sister Marj, who lived in Fulham, was coming to Stourbridge to stay with her sisters, my aunties Glad and Ve, leaving her house in Clancarty Road empty.

What a fantastic chance to see our heart-throb at the time, Edmund Hockridge, who was starring in *Guys and Dolls* at the London Coliseum.

Dad had worked his magic some months before, and because he was a fellow theatre manager, he had procured two tickets for the musical *Carousel*, which was showing at the Wolverhampton Grand Theatre. We had a tremendous crush on Edmund after seeing him and hearing him sing on the radio. We even clubbed together and accrued a few shillings and bought a furry animal. This was sent to Edmund as a 'mascot'. We had received a very nice photo with 'not a very good picture' written in French and a thank-you. Edmund Hockridge was from the French-speaking area of Canada, hence the French, which Ruth, having been to a grammar school, unlike me, translated! So wherever HE was, we wanted to be, and THAT was now London. How we managed to get Mum and siblings to agree to us going, I'll never know, but it must have been tricky, because the aunties, especially Glad, were adamant that we would end up carted off to some eastern flesh-pot, as white slaves, probably bundled into wooden crates and offloaded for men to do what they wanted with us.

However, it was agreed that we would stay at Auntie Marj's, NEVER venture out at night, and remain innocents whilst in the 'big smoke', as London was called in those days (smog prevailed). I feel completely at a loss as to who paid for the train tickets, which must have cost a couple of pounds, and there was food to buy. We had no worries, though – very thoughtless of us, in hindsight.

So two lucky sixteen-year-old girls set off, innocents abroad. We started our adventure climbing onto a train at New Street station in Birmingham. We even managed, goodness knows HOW, to reach Parsons Green in Fulham, then Clancarty Road.

We viewed Auntie Marj's modest Edwardian semi and thought it was wonderful. We two giggling 'greenhorns' settled in, and so began our great adventure, in the hope of seeing our hero.

We DID see Edmund, in fact, after hanging around the stage door, not daring to ask the doorman if we could at least get another autograph. Ruth, being the braver, asked. Well, she asked, and sure enough, there appeared before us the man of our dreams. We were ushered into his dressing-room and chatted to. I suppose we spoke but I can't remember any speech – we were floating around in HEAVEN. My heart thumped with excitement. Edmund Hockridge was a true gentleman, who gave his time to two young fans and made our day, not to mention our lives! He looked as good in the flesh too…

What could possibly follow THAT?

We actually found a café/bar. It was downstairs, and there was a chap playing a guitar, and lots of hippy-look-alikes, all drinking something. Long greasy hair prevailed, and that was just the men. A thick smoke pervaded the basement. It could have been the smoke of 'spliffs', but we knew nothing of drugs; aspirin was the only drug I had ever heard of.

The next-door neighbours at Clancarty Road had been asked to keep an eye on us. We were invited round to meet the family. They were a very jolly bunch, especially the husband, who obviously didn't appreciate how young and impressionable we were, because he regaled us all evening with ghost stories, all true, he said. So we let ourselves back into the darkened hallway feeling that 'SOMETHING' was about to pounce… evil prevailed, it was oozing out of the walls. We didn't stop to have a cocoa, we just ran scared up to our very cold beds, hearing the clanking of chains!

Food was at a premium. Good old Marmite on toast sufficed in the mornings, followed by sardines in oil on toast for our evening meal. As far as I remember, THAT was IT! We walked our feet off most days, but we never did see a Chinese laundry with great wooden boxes stacked up in readiness, their dark confines holding crying young girls heading for China or an eastern harem. We WERE followed one day around Trafalgar Square by two Indian men. They were in dark suits and looked very respectable, but we were suddenly afraid. Were they going to try to take us to the docks and sell us as 'white slaves', as Auntie Glad had feared? I think all the warnings had frightened us so much that we imagined that they were on our trail when they might have been innocently ambling around the Square like us, taking in the glories of London.

A strange thing DID happen, however. There was a knock at the door one day, and it was my brother Robin! We were very pleased to see him, mainly because the loo was stopped up, and each flush made the water rise almost to the seat… Robin hadn't been sent by the family to make sure we were still there and not sullied, he was on his way to Spain for a walking holiday. I can't recall whether he stayed overnight, but it was good to see him, and I think he gave me some money to tide us over. That was very typical of my brother. I was very fond of him. Oh, and YES… he successfully and gallantly unblocked the loo!

We set off for home in the late afternoon. A rather strange event happened on the platform, just before our train was due. A well-dressed businessman walked over and sat down on a bench. He was carrying a briefcase, which he deposited on the seat beside him. A minute later, along came another man, equally well dressed, also carrying a briefcase. He also took a seat on the bench beside the first man. They didn't speak to one another, not even a nod, but, when one stood up and walked off, he took the other man's briefcase!! Shortly afterwards, the remaining man got up and strolled away down the platform carrying the other case. They had swapped cases. Was it Russian espionage? Who knows? We never alerted anyone, but we both thought it weird. But our train was pulling in, so we hopped in, and, to be truthful, we didn't give it another thought.

Neither of us had telephoned our relatives back home the whole of the week. We would have had to use a phone box and the pennies were precious. Robin may have rung 249 to say that we were still in the country and not in Shanghai as predicted by Auntie Glad.

The train pulled into Birmingham quite late at night. The trouble WAS that we had hoped it was a northern destination train, so would pass through Birmingham and land us in Wolverhampton, where we could get a bus home to 249. The reason for not going back to Ruth's has never been clear to me. We panicked when the train announcer said that our train was going no further than New Street! The last train had already departed for Wolverhampton, and anyway, we would have had to pay extra fare. So we phoned Ruth's mother at the bridge club. When we asked if we could take a bus back to Moseley, the answer was a definite "NO! There's a no way anyone can fetch you…I have a club to run…"

So the cards ruled the day, as they always did with Mrs Brickman. Even the fact that we would have to stay all night on the station didn't thaw the heart of a very hard woman. What a MOTHER!

So, feeling more terrified than at any time in London (New Street in those days was notorious for prostitutes picking up clients on the station), we eventually found the ladies' room, and sat there until about 5am.

On the advice of a guard, we boarded what was called the 'milk train', which was destined for Wolverhampton, and home to 249! Our troubles were not quite over, however, because we had to find a taxi, but had no money at all, so the journey from the town was a silent one. We reached 249 and the taxi stopped. I had to explain that I would have to get my family up from bed, or possibly my brother Tony, who was always up very early to go to work. The taxi driver turned and smiled. "Is your brother Tony Lloyd-Davies?" When I replied that he was… "Oh, forget the charges, love. I was in the army with Tony…we got on well, I knew he lived somewhere in Tettenhall." What marvellous luck… and what a kind driver.

The house had never looked so welcoming. There was still no hot water and we had to carry numerous buckets and kettles of hot water just to have a bath. Water still froze in the bedside tumbler, but 249 was home.

So Auntie Glad's predictions about white slavery never happened, and the 'big city' proved interesting and exciting, but it was meeting our idol Edmund Hockridge that topped everything.

I must put something in about Mum's three sisters, my aunts; they played a big part in our lives.

AUNTIE VERA

Auntie Vera, who was eleven months Mum's junior, married late in life, probably in her late thirties. Bill, her husband, had been badly injured in the First World War. He had been shot in the side of his head and shoulder. (My cousin Wendy and I asked if we could view the 'holes'. Uncle Bill was reluctant, but eventually he lifted his shirt and showed us his scars. I never really felt much sadness or upset, but it was a very interesting sight, as was the dent in his head, but curiosity was uppermost.)

Auntie Ve was a big lady, tall, almost six foot, and big boned. She also had a rather large chest. Once when she was staying overnight at 249 she told me that when young she would bind her bust tightly with material to try to hide it! I liked her immensely. She was my godmother and a very nice one too. She and Bill never had children, so we nieces and nephews were indulged. Later in life she told me that Bill had never wanted children. He had a relation who had epilepsy and was frightened that any children of theirs might inherit it. Mum always raised her eyebrows and 'tutted' at this story, but she never said why.

When young, around 1919, Ve worked at a jeweller's in Stourbridge called Blurtons. She earned enough money to buy a bar of perfumed soap, which she hid high up on a ledge in the kitchen /scullery at the family home in Stourbridge. She thought it was safe, but every day it appeared smaller! Her younger sister Marjorie, who wasn't working and was head of house (as Mum had left to get married), really got it in the neck from Vera when Marj owned up. She had found it and used it regularly. It's such a little simple story today, but that soap somehow spoke words about how precious everything was to the family who had never had any finery.

On Christmas Eve Blurtons stayed open until midnight. Poor Auntie Ve would then have to dash through the darkened streets alone and fearful.

The house, 7 Clifton Street, Stourbridge, was only two doors away from her childhood home so she was familiar with everything and everybody. It was a semi-detached Victorian red-brick house, not much front garden, large bay windows and a mosaic-tiled front porch. What always intrigued us children was the water pump in the back kitchen. The soft water from its spout was a problem with hair-washing – too much lather and bubbles . Ve had to pump with vigour for some time before the water poured out. Also in the room was a large 'copper' for boiling the washing. Auntie would amaze us children by telling this tale.

It was here by the boiler that one night Auntie Ve saw a mouse. Auntie Ve was NOT afraid of the four-legged visitor, so she grabbed a yellow duster … and POW! dispatched her victim by holding it in the duster and squeezing the life out of it. Horrible job done, she was just about to pop the body in the bin, when another mouse appeared, a much bigger job. It seemed to be searching for its lost beloved. This second creature Auntie reckoned was probably 'Daddy' mouse. He too was unceremoniously squashed in the unforgiving yellow duster. There then appeared THREE baby mice looking for their parents. Oh disaster. Auntie got them ALL in one swoop and all three were swiftly given 'duster-to dust' treatment. We listened to this tale of murder with amazement. To Auntie Ve's credit, she did say she had to have a swig of sherry out of the bottle after the deed was done!

When in her early teens Vera had thoughts of grandeur! Her mother Ada's sister Maud had married into the Beauchamp family, a family well known, with 'connections' to nobility.

Great Auntie Maud (my Mum was named after her) was a girl with spirit. She would ride a bike wearing bloomers, not done in the quiet village of Hallow in Worcester. She was always different from her Edwardian sisters and friends. A beauty too, dark-eyed and, hearsay has it, a 'bit of a flirt'. I rather like the sound of Great Aunt Maud.

Maud met and married Arthur William Proctor Brograve Beauchamp (son of James, a lawyer whose practice was in Worcester). Maud and Arthur appeared to run away to London, where they found 'digs', and soon after, they married in a registrar office. This was in the early 1900s. Mum said the marriage was a disappointment to Arthur's father, who disapproved of his daughter-in-law, who in his eyes was beneath the high-ranking Beauchamp family. However, the couple did go back to Arthur's home, the Old Rectory in Hallow… and this is where Auntie Ve comes into the picture.

Ve had always fancied herself on horseback. She really didn't know one end of a horse from the other, but when the opportunity arose to STAY with Maud and Arthur, she leapt at the chance. We had a photo of Ve seated imperiously on a fine steed in the grounds of the rectory. I don't know what happened during her stay, but when back in Clifton Street, she decided that Vera was NOT a forename that was suitable for the high life, so she called herself Veronica Beauchamp. She added to this fib by creating a German birthplace – the house in Clifton Street where they all lived was called 'Stuttgart'. (I would have thought NOT a very acceptable house name during or after the First World War; however, Vera didn't let that worry her.) So Vera Roberts suddenly became Veronica Beauchamp, born in Stuttgart, Germany. The Beauchamps' rather noble name didn't gel with anything Germanic, so Vera's school friends must have wondered. Nobody accused her of being a spy, though.

Auntie Ve admitted that the fibbing didn't last long, and soon Vera Roberts returned. But her stay with a family on the edge of nobility thrilled her, and was a high point in her life, spoken about many times.

Not long after Maud married Arthur, he was sent across the world to Australia. (Naughty Mum always said it was his father who paid to rid himself of his rebellious son, whose marriage irked him. After all, Maud was 'only a shop-girl'!) Arthur began sending money to Maud for her fare to sail out and join him in Australia, but Maud never did join him. We think she just kept the money and was happy to stay near her family. I don't know if she EVER considered going over to the other side of the world. Eventually, she met gentlemanly Percy, where, we don't know, They settled in Stoke ('up north' to her family). They remained partners until death. There were no children.

Arthur Proctor Brograve Beauchamp died out in Australia; they never divorced.

I know that one or two of our family thought that Ve had a 'bob on her head'. Yes, she was always very genteel. She never cleaned the front step off with her rear-end to the road, so she always faced the road and the passers-by. However, most of the cleaning was done by her next-door neighbour, a Mrs Dawes, who cleaned for Ve and Bill for many years. Vera was also never seen out of the house without a hat.

Ve was wonderful at crochet-work. She crocheted beautiful tablecloths, doilies and, one time, a jacket, along with a natty crocheted beret. Auntie was also wonderful on our picnics, hiding in the ferns on Kinver Edge, a local beauty spot. Auntie would crouch down during games of hide-and-seek, sometimes just holding a couple of fronds of ferns, hoping not to be seen, but failing, as portions of her ample body would project beyond the fern.

She baked little shortbread cakes with white icing on the top, called 'melting moments'. Everything she did was to perfection; her ironing of even handkerchiefs was meticulous, and to me, who was so used to Mum dashing around, folding rather than ironing, Auntie's ironing was mesmerizing.

Vera and Bill doted on their little green budgie named Paul Philips. Paul would play ping-pong on top of the tea-trolley. He was truly loved. There was a near disaster, though, one day. Paul flew onto Ve's head and got caught in her almost invisible hairnet. It was touch and go for a few minutes as Marj and Bill tried to release him without breaking his wings. He was rescued, legs and beak intact, feathers ruffled. It sounds a very small drama, but little Paul Philips was the baby that Bill and Ve never had. He lived for over twelve years. He fell off his perch one winter's evening, and was never replaced. There was a feeling of genuine love for this little budgie.

Vera and Bill always used silver napkin rings and would never dream of putting milk on the table in anything other than a china jug. Also, Auntie's newspaper firelighters, diligently screwed into a kind of Staffordshire knot, were works of art, and very efficient. She would light the fire using wonderful rainbow coloured wooden spills, always an attraction for us children. These were kept in a triangular brass holder also a magnet for us children.

Afternoon tea was sometimes taken in Cranages, a rather upper-class tearoom in Stourbridge town centre. Dainty cakes on stands, and tea in china so thin you could see your fingers through it.

At home, Ve always had afternoon tea, all set out on a drop-leaf table, with an embroidered tablecloth, and always the same items… all sitting on a blue-decorated plate. A pot of chocolate spread, a pot of preserve and a home-made sponge or cakes. A friend of Ve's, Clare Egan, would be invited for tea, and the two ladies would spend a pleasant hour, all very genteel and cosy.

Clare was a maiden lady, a VERY strong Catholic. Once, on Stourbridge station with friends and members of her family, who were all gathered to catch a train to a friend's wedding, Clare and her sister Ida suddenly became worried and desperate as the train was due into the station. The wedding was a Protestant one. It was a FRIDAY, and fish WASN'T on the menu! Holy smoke! They might be excommunicated. She and her sister tried to ring their priest, to get a 'pardon' should they fall from grace and eat the meat offered by their host. I never found out what DID happen but I'm sure Clare and sister Ida wouldn't end up in the flames of hell! Such was their indoctrinated faith. I don't recall a bit in the Bible telling us that we mustn't eat meat if it's a Friday? How ridiculous, but I suppose we have to admire such a naïve view and strong faith. Both sisters were kindly, good friends to the Roberts family, but their ample bosoms did heave over this meat versus fish debacle.

One weekend, cousin Wendy and I were staying with Auntie Ve. She was about to become fifty (very old we thought) and she appeared at the bedroom door in her dressing gown. "Well, girls…fifty. I may as well…" she broke off and put her dressing-gown belt around her neck in a noose, then laughed, head on one side, grotesque. We both laughed with her, but later in life, I realized that Vera was like a swan, serene on top, but pedalling like the devil underneath, and she was probably feeling terribly depressed, but we girls just laughed at a rather eccentric auntie. Anyway, the milkman had arrived down below the bedroom window, so sanity prevailed again. (This next bit really dates me.) The milkman had a horse-drawn cart. The milk was poured into a jug and left on the step. I'm afraid we became so interested in the horse, chomping its oats from a nose-bag, that we didn't think anything was wrong with our much-loved 'very old' Auntie Vera. The pseudo 'hanging' scene certainly didn't frighten us or psychologically damage us; it made no impact on us young nieces.

The truth was that my nice gentle godmother suffered from depression on and off all her life. Like all the Roberts girls, she would smile her very toothy smile and hide any pessimistic feelings. She faced all kinds of trials in her life. Her physical ones were her teeth, very protruding, and her bust, which had developed rather early in her teens, had become a source of great embarrassment to her. Nowadays, her teeth would be gradually drawn back with braces, and her bust would be viewed with admiration, but in the 1920s, a no bra time, she must have tried desperately to get her breasts under control.

One of her lesser trials was dismounting from her pushbike. She couldn't do it. The only way she could stop was to use the kerb as a brake and almost fall into the gutter, not a ladylike action. This was awkward because at one time she worked for National Savings, and had to visit people in their houses. This she did on her trusty steed. I don't think she ever had an accident whilst pulling up and wobbling alongside the kerb, but her dignity may have taken a fall!

A little brighter piece about Auntie Ve was her juggling. She could juggle three oranges and delighted us children with performances. Whilst on about oranges: Mum was talking to Ve about buying some navel oranges for marmalade. "I wonder why they are called NAVAL oranges. Is it something to do with taking oranges on board when scurvy prevailed?" Ve asked.

When Mum told her that they were NAVEL oranges because the 'hole' at one end resembled a navel, Auntie apparently looked disgusted. "Oh DEAR, Maudie, I will NEVER feel the same about them now that I know WHAT their name means."

In spite of leaving school early, all the Roberts children were well read. Shakespeare was Ve's forte. She could quote whole passages, always in a rather deep droning tone. The same with poetry, some from her scant schooling, and others from her many poetry books. General-knowledge crosswords were done with alacrity. The same went for her sisters, who appeared to have acquired endless knowledge in all areas. Even Greek mythology didn't stump them. We have never worked out how all the Roberts clan, with so little schooling, managed to be extremely knowledgeable.

In middle age and later, Ve accumulated antique furniture, some really tasteful pieces (her best friend owned a very up-market antique shop in Stourbridge High Street), and her home became a haven of comfort. I rather liked polishing her brasses. There was a brass ornament on the mantelpiece, the 'three wise monkeys': "Hear no evil, see no evil and speak no evil." I loved them, and polished them with vigour. "I will leave you those in my will, dear," Auntie pronounced.

Ve's husband Bill became ill. It was a short illness, and he died after a week or two in bed. For some reason, Vera wanted Bill 'on show' after he had been attended to by the funeral director. Ve had his open coffin brought into the front room, and Bill, looking very regal in a purple robe, lay for all his friends and family to admire...

"Do come in and see your Uncle Bill, girls... he looks so nice." (She didn't add, "so well"!)

I was hanging around the front-room door with cousin Wendy. We managed to escape. The thought of a dead Uncle Bill was too much, and so we made our getaway. Later, Mum told me he didn't look a bit like Bill. He even had a sort of choirboy's frill around his neck. Mum didn't want to gaze over at Bill either, but didn't want to offend her younger bereaved sister, so she dutifully took a quick look. Mum thought the funeral directors had put make-up on his face to, in Mum's words, 'perk him up a bit'!

After Bill's death, only twelve years after their marriage, Auntie Ve met an elderly gentleman who told her his wife was disabled, and how unhappy his marriage was... Auntie threw care to the wind and had a flirtation, ending suddenly (we think) because her friend's wife found out! Vera did confide in her sister Marj that she was thinking of sleeping with him, and "was this all right?" We don't know the answer, but it was probably "Go ahead, kid." However, we don't think she DID; it wasn't the 'done thing', and, like her sisters and brothers, she had a very strong feeling that 'THEY' would get her!

Auntie Vera's was always a comfortable retreat for me during the school holiday, and even now I miss her. There is nobody left in Stourbridge for us to visit these days. Everyone has gone. We drive through occasionally on the way back from 'down south'.

Such happy memories of childhood days in Clifton Street. Childhood fun in the summer holidays when it NEVER rained and was ALWAYS sunny and where school worries disappeared as the holidays unfolded.

AUNTIE MARJORIE

We never saw a lot of Auntie Adie Marjorie Roberts, to give her full name. She was the third child, and the third daughter, the boys arrived later.

After Mum left to marry, Marj took on the housekeeper's job, whilst Ve worked at the jeweller's. Their four younger brothers also lived with them still in Clifton Street, but now, for some unknown reason, they were now living at No. 7.

Marj was supposed to be head chef and bottle-washer to them all. The trouble was that Marj was an avid reader. Anything and everything that was in print Marj read. The penny dreadfuls, romantic fiction aimed at young ladies, was her favourite. I am only repeating Ve here when I say that the printed page ruled Marj's days, and the housework was second place on her list of duties! I suppose Ve, who had to dash off to Blurtons every day, became a little jealous of her younger sister's time at home, able to put her feet up and enjoy a quick read when household duties didn't call.

The girls did go out together, though, really on the lookout for prospective beaus. One story of Ve and Marj's romance-seeking jaunts always makes us laugh…

One afternoon, for reasons unknown, the girls set off from Stourbridge Junction train station and ended up in Birmingham. Once there, they had tea in a rather upper-crust tearoom. At one of the tables sat two very handsome well-dressed young men. During tea, a note was passed to the girls. It was from the young men.

According to Ve, it was all in rhyme and indicated that they would like to walk out with them. Oddly, it was signed 'MUTT and JEFF', characters from a film or play at that time (about 1920). After much giggling and discussion, Ve and Marj agreed to have a stroll. So another billet doux was passed via a waitress to the chaps and all was agreed.

So the four set off along the street, the only drawback being that both Ve and Marj were very tall, and Marj in particular was head and shoulders taller than her beau! So, poor Marj decided that rather than have the embarrassment of walking cheek by shoulder to her new friend, she would walk in the gutter, therefore making her the same height.

How it all went, we will never know, except that the liaison didn't get any further, so the girls headed alone to Birmingham railway station. But this wasn't the end of their exciting day out. Once on the station they sat in the ladies' waiting room, as all young women would do, secure from any male attention. Or so they thought. The waiting room was warm, there was a coal fire burning, and soft leather-covered benches were placed around the large room. There was no other lady in the room, so they were alone. Suddenly, the door opened, and a station worker, possibly a train guard, popped his head round and smiled at the two young ladies. He entered, and to the girls' horror, took out a bunch of keys and locked the door from the INSIDE!

Then began a very frightening chase with the testosterone-filled man jumping around the room desperately trying to grab them. Ve said they were even climbing up onto the benches to escape his clutches – hot and scared, fighting for their honour! After some time, the man lunged forward and grabbed Marj in a rugby tackle. A loud explosion filled the air. The 'hunter' had suddenly and violently let out the biggest loudest FART…!!!! He then collapsed, embarrassed and defeated, but laughing, all sexual urge gone with the wind! The hunted 'prey' laughed with him.

So their hour of fear was over. The red-faced man unlocked the door, and they boarded the late-night train to home, none the worse for wear. In today's world, that episode would end in police being called and headlines in all the papers, followed by a prosecution, but Ve and Marj viewed it as just part of life, so they dealt with it and got on with their lives.

Marj met and became engaged to Leonard Read, a teacher. Although engaged, for most young girls, intimacy with your loved one wasn't on the cards. Both aunts said that the fear of an illegitimate baby was the great deterrent, so for Len to walk in when Marj was in the tin bath in the kitchen would have been an unspeakable event. Len DID do this, however. Ve was helping pour in warm water. The girls all shared the tin bath, so would step in one after the other. The bath was behind the outer door…

"Have you seen Marj?" Len asked Ve, not seeing his beloved fiancée shrouded in steam behind the door.

"No, sorry," replied Ve.

"Oh, it doesn't matter. Tell her I called and I'll see her later." And with that, he closed the door.

Ve told me they both burst out laughing, Marj's modesty saved. That last bit sounds so formal and naïve, but that was the order of the day back in the 1920s. Of course, there were a few exceptions!

Marj married Len and left Stourbridge to live in Fulham, the house where Ruth and I had stayed when in the throes of adoration for our hero, Edmund Hockridge. Marj and Len had one son, Michael, now Mike, a good cousin and friend to this day.

I liked Uncle Len – he had a twinkle in his eye, played the violin badly, and sported a coarse-haired moustache, and to me always appeared jolly and chatty. But unknown to me, Len suffered from mood swings, sometimes up very high, then down in the slough of despond. We now know that Len suffered from bipolar problems. In those days, he would just be called eccentric, or worse, a nutcase.

Pat once went with Marj and Len to a London show. Len was on a 'high', which manifested itself in loud clapping and cheering and 'Bravo-ing' louder and with more fervour than most of the audience – something that Pat thought embarrassing.

I don't think Len had any trouble teaching, though. He taught maths and worked until retirement age. Len died in 1956 aged fifty-six. He was greatly missed by Marj and Mike, and all our family.

When alone in Fulham, Mike having married and gone to live in Northampton, Auntie Marj decided to go back to her roots, so she moved to 17 Clifton Street, to live with Ve, bringing very little furniture to Ve's.

Marj was very different from Ve and her sisters. She wasn't 'into' goods and chattels. I don't think she had any feelings about her possessions. Her bits of furniture stayed dust covered for years in the back room at Ve's.

So the two sisters were together again, both very good at crosswords, particularly Marj. Unlike Ve, she didn't play cards, but she knitted and crocheted, as all her sisters did. She loved her books and was always had her nose in one. "Oh, THIS book is SO terrible, all that SEX, DRUGS and dirty goings-on," she would say, having chosen it from the library. "Oh, I DID enjoy it, though!" she would add with a grin.

Always quick with her ripostes, she once received a cheeky phone call. The girl at the other end, amidst lots of giggling, was being very rude about Marj's underwear. Marj listened for a while then asked, "Do you know the ballet Swan Lake?"

"Yes," replied the girl.

"Well, go and JUMP IN IT!!"

Later in life, Marj lost a lot of her hair, so became a wig-wearer, always looking well coiffured and statuesque. She was funny, with a wicked sense of humour, sometimes a bit caustic in her views to her sisters, but a jolly auntie. She lived for many years with Ve, eventually ending her days in her much-loved Stourbridge. She died the night before she was due to move to a nursing home in Northampton to be nearer to son Mike and his wife Val. She was determined to stay in Stourbridge, and this she made sure she did.

AUNTIE GLADYS (GLAD)

Mum's youngest sister, Gladys, always called Glad, was a very different character from her sisters. She still had the 'Roberts girls' rather snobby attitude to some events and behaviour, though.

Not quite so tall as Marj and Ve, but still above average height, dark as all the girls were, she also had the Roberts' Roman nose. (Mum always said it was Roman crossed with Jewish, but since then, a whole lot of ancestry has emerged. The Jewish bit, which we ALL thought was true, has dropped by the wayside, but the Roman bit has stuck. So Mum was right. However there is a great-great grandfather who may have been Jewish, so Mum's nose, and her sisters', were not pedigree appendages, but a cross, Jewish/Roman, somewhat bigger than average.)

Being so much younger than her sisters (about twelve years younger than her big sister Maude), Glad was always required to help out after childbirth (as in Mum's case). She was always a bit acid about helping with our births in Chapel Ash and at 249. She blamed Cliff for not having any aids, no wash-tub or mangle. True to say, she didn't like Dad, and that sentiment stayed with her all her long life.

Glad and young brother Doug definitely had the worst early life of all the Roberts children. When they were still young, their father Ludd left the house and lived with his mistress May in Worcester. Ludd must have had a conscience, so he decided that the two youngest children could live with him and his partner in Worcester. Both little children hated May, and also hated being apart from their siblings, so they decided to run away. This they did. Glad was about seven and Doug five. They walked all the way from Worcester to Stourbridge, probably around ten miles. They arrived home, were greeted by all their siblings, and were promptly taken back to Worcester to the frightening lady who hoped to be their step-mother.

Neither child was sent to school, something that Glad never forgave her father for. Of all the sisters, Glad was the outgoing one. And the stay with her father Ludd's amour, May, in Worcester, and her escape with Doug showed courage.

Glad had such a varied life I really have no timelines about her early teens. She certainly worked at the Courtaulds factory in Wolverhampton whilst living with her father Ludd close by in a rented terrace house. (No May in sight, which is odd.) HOW Glad came to board with Ludd is a mystery. It's a mystery she never spoke about, but Mum let the cat out of the bag once, then told me, "Don't ever tell Glad that you know that she worked in a FACTORY." So I never did. I suppose she was on the factory floor, piecework or such, something a Roberts would hide. It certainly wasn't a 'ladylike' job.

Later (about 1936 or so) she got a job as a nanny to a family in a Victorian mansion in Kinver, a few miles from Stourbridge. The family sound very nice. They treated her well, and in fact that is where Glad learned to drive. The family allowed her to use their little car. Glad told us that she would drive round and round their large front drive. Never on the open road, of course. She took to driving like a duck to water. Her charges, three girls, must have liked Glad – there are snaps in sepia of the girls all dressed in very frilly aprons and poke bonnets.

Glad liked the boys! I can't say exactly what 'went on', but Mum said there were numerous boys buzzing around her like bees around a flower… Later in life, Uncle Doug told daughter Wendy, "Your Auntie Glad, was a VERY naughty girl." From that, we gathered Auntie had been a flirt, and a femme fatale with the chaps.

Sport was never taken up by any of the other Roberts girls, except Glad, who threw herself into swimming. Where she learned, we don't know, but later when we nieces were on holiday and in her care, there were swimming parties down by the river Severn at Grimley Beach, a small sandy patch on the river bank. It was glorious, but NOW I realize how dangerous this swimming was! The currents, the soft river bed, all frightening now, but I loved it all. The cruisers going past were something of a hazard, though, creating waves. But none of us drowned, which was due to luck more than judgement!

Glad could also ice skate and play tennis (although she never did work out the scoring!). She was also a very capable cyclist, and one day, when in her mid-teens, she and Doug cycled all the way from Worcester to London to stay with sister Marj. Quite an ordeal, but Glad had determination, and loads of guts.

She was always the protector of young Doug. In fact, all the girls seemed to feel that 'little Doug' had suffered more than the rest of his siblings. Everyone blamed Ludd's mistress, May. She was, in Glad's eyes, the wicked step-mother, having left her husband and only child, a girl of three, and swanned off with Ludd, who in turn left ALL his children to set up a love-nest with her. Then to add salt to everyone's wounds, May and Ludd went on to have three more offspring, two boys and a girl, David, Peter, and Laura.

Gladys May (she always hated her second name because of the infamous step-mother May) met and married Arthur Barlow in the mid 1930s. Arthur was a choirmaster and organist at the local church. How they met, I'll never know, but we don't think it was in church. Glad wasn't known for her church-going. Arthur was smaller in height than Glad, bespectacled, fair-haired, and quite well-off.

His father, mother, and his two brothers and a sister lived around the corner from Clifton Street. His mother was a publican who brewed her own beer. His father was in the pub, but goodness knows what he did there, as Mrs Barlow senior was the boss. His mother also made hand-raised pork pies, which Arthur told us all were fantastic!

Uncle Arthur told us this little story… it has a moral! Usually after he had been out late at night, he would rush back to the pub and scoff a piece of his mother's hand-raised pies. It was his big treat, and something he would look forward to all evening, especially on a cold winter's night. One night quite late, he was on a train coming home from a concert in Birmingham, and opposite him in the train carriage sat a very pretty young lady. They exchanged greetings and chatted for most of the short journey. When they reached Stourbridge Junction station, Arthur realized a thick fog had descended. It was dark too, a horrible night.

They both alighted onto the platform, and Arthur faced a VERY serious dilemma! Should he escort the young lady home and become her knight in shining armour, OR should he get home quickly to eat his pork-pie supper…? It had to be a quick decision. The young lady was attractive and pleasant, but the pork pie was succulent and he hadn't eaten any tea; he had 'saved himself' for that pie!

The pork pie won! So Arthur dashed off into the gloom, leaving the young lady to make her own way home through the night and thick 'pea-souper' fog. Breathless, he arrived at the pub to be greeted by his mother. "Oh hello, Artie luv… I'm afraid the pork pies have ALL GONE, we had a big rush on them tonight!"

There is a moral to this somewhere, but I don't know where!

Arthur and Glad moved into a semi-detached house, still in Clifton Street. There was no bathroom (they converted the third bedroom into one years later). Their washing facilities were basic but sufficient – they used the deep kitchen sink for all their ablutions. "We have a jolly good 'all over' wash, dear, so we are as clean as the next person," Glad would say, with pride. So they were… always wholesome and smart.

(When, some years later, we children stayed with them, we found the sink a bit embarrassing, mainly because there were often friends chatting in the kitchen whilst we were being undressed, scrubbed down and popped into pyjamas.)

The Second World War arrived and Uncle Arthur was enlisted. This is where he drove his army vehicles in the desert. Auntie coped well. She wasn't alone in the house for long, however, as Doug and his new wife Dorothy came to stay. This arrangement lasted for many years.

Glad still liked the high life. Where THAT was in Stourbridge, we don't know, because Stourbridge certainly wasn't known for its flesh-pots, but she would certainly spend many an evening out.

It was after one of her nights out that one morning there was a knock on the front door. Dorothy rushed to the door, but Glad was very reluctant to put her head round. She stayed hiding in the kitchen. Dorothy opened the door. There was a tall young man, hat in hand, standing on the step.

"Good morning. Does Paddie live here?"

Dorothy thought he had arrived at the wrong house. "I'm sorry, there's nobody called Paddie here."

The young man consulted a small piece of paper. This IS 59 Clifton Street, isn't it? Paddie gave me her address last night." He showed Dorothy the paper note.

The penny dropped. Dorothy managed to look baffled and the unknown man left, reluctantly, very puzzled. A rather shamefaced Glad appeared from her hiding place behind the kitchen door and admitted she HAD met the chap and had told him her name was Paddie Barlow. Why she gave a stranger her address is suspect, and is one of the many unexplained happening in Glad's life which I mustn't dwell on!!

Later in life, Glad was the first one of our aunts to 'throw stones' should anyone in the family go off the rails, or (heaven forbid) find herself in an 'interesting condition'. Mum would whisper, "Talk about the pot calling the blooming kettle black" after a homily from Glad on the lapsed morals of today's girls!

Dorothy told daughter Wendy the 'strange man at the door' story many years later. Dorothy always tut-tutted about her sister-in-law. In fact, ALL her siblings did a lot of tut-tutting about Glad's escapades.

Arthur was away for some years, I believe, so Glad, stuck for cash, took in lodgers! The lodgers in question were two Belgian airmen, Francoise and Celeste, both handsome young men. To say Glad enjoyed their company is obvious. Not only was Glad good at sport, she was also very agile and a 'wow' at cartwheels and handstands. One sunny afternoon, hearsay has it that Glad gave an informal show of gymnastics on the back lawn, her pale green frilly French knickers on display for all to admire… especially the two boys.

Wendy and I would sometimes secretly rifle though Auntie's lingerie drawer, marvelling at the pastel shades of her buttons-in-the-crotch knickers. Glad liked her frilly underwear. Her choice of knickers was

VERY different from her sisters, who favoured the 'passion-killer', to-the-knee pink shiny drawers!!

During the boys' stay with Glad, there was one night a fracas somewhere around the front garden which exploded out onto Clifton Street! (Oh Lordy!) One of the Belgians was indulging in fisticuffs with some unnamed person. We know not what this was all about, but we can imagine. What this brawl, in full view of the neighbours, did for poor genteel Auntie Ve can't be imagined. Fortunately she was at the other end of Clifton Street, but no doubt she would hear of the fight on the grapevine. A Roberts girl involved in a fisticuffs. Oh goodness! Unheard of, truly letting the Roberts family down. Fortunately 'They' didn't get the chaps, and it must have blown over, wartime was not a time to hold grudges.

I met the two boys, and I remember how gentle and kindly they were to me. I was probably only about four. One of them spent his spare time making models of Spitfires out of pennies. He would solder a small safety pin on the back so that it could be worn as a brooch. He gave one to me. I kept it for many years, but somehow it just disappeared, possibly accidentally thrown away when I left 249 to get married.

I hope the boys enjoyed their exciting time with landlady Gladys. If they had any feelings that the English were a reserved race, I'm pretty sure their views changed over the war years in Stourbridge, thanks to cartwheeling Glad.

Uncle Arthur arrived back from the war and was greeted by everyone. Wendy remembers a handwritten poster strung between the apple tree and the gate, WELCOME BACK ARTHUR. He settled back in well and became a choirmaster and organist again, alongside his job in the offices of a large garage.

Auntie Glad then embarked on evening classes in WOODWORK! She had decided that her kitchen was not up to standard, it would HAVE to go! So, never daunted, Glad decided she would update her kitchen. She became a doyen of DIY.

Over the next year, Glad made a complete fitted kitchen. Whilst down in the cellar (the only place she could lay out the wood) she would measure and saw wood for hours, like a troglodyte. She would heave the panels of wood up the very steep stairs every few minutes to see if they measured up and fitted, then down she would go again into the damp cellar to redo and remeasure her work.

Uncle Arthur, Artie to Glad, would sit reading his paper or playing the piano as Glad laboured underground. Amazingly, she did it! The cream units were all her own work, as were a couple of small worktops. The kitchen looked wonderful. We were all taken on a tour of the glossy cabinets and shelves. Nothing would be beyond Glad.

Years later, when sorting some old papers found in a box under the bed, Glad had a shock. There was a certificate. It read: THIS AWARD IS PRESENTED TO ARTHUR BARLOW FOR GAINING HIS CITY AND GUILDS CERTIFICATE IN ADVANCED WOODWORK. Naughty Unc had hidden the fact that he was very capable of constructing kitchen cupboards AND PROBABLY MORE…. We can only guess what Glad said when she eventually found him out.

Glad always wanted a family. She had all kinds of exploratory operations and tests. At one time she fostered a little girl. We don't know how that came about, but she brought the baby to 249, for a B.A.S. (a baby adoration society) meeting. All her medical test results concluded that she would have difficulty conceiving due to 'ladies' problems'. Mum would always raise one eyebrow and shake her head in a knowing way, when her sister's lack of family due to 'down below' trouble came up in conversation.

So, as the 'family' door seemed to close, a very sad time for Glad, she decided not to think about it, she would try to find work. It didn't take her long. She applied for a job as housekeeper to a very rich vegetable wholesaler, who became 'Uncle Fred' to us.

Uncle Fred lived in a very comfortable bungalow, a bus ride away from Clifton Street. I don't know how the arrangements came about, or if Uncle Arthur was happy with the housekeeping job, which entailed days away from home looking after Fred, but usually Glad got her own way. So Glad became head cook and bottle-washer, looking after not just Fred, but a great bull mastiff dog called Rodney.

Wendy and her younger sister Judy plus me would be taken with Auntie on her duty days to play in the garden and play with Rodney. He was huge, a smooth golden colour with a dark snout, a gentle giant. Judy would ride on his back. We loved him, and we thought Auntie Glad did too. It wasn't until many years later that she admitted feeling very scared of him, he was such a huge powerful chap.

Fred was out all day, he had a wholesale and retail vegetable business. So Glad was in charge. She was in her element, cooking and tending to Fred. We have no idea how Uncle Arthur took all this! Uncle was incapable of boiling himself an egg, according to Glad.

Whilst visiting Auntie at the bungalow I had a go at riding a pushbike. It was at Uncle Fred's that I began the process of learning to ride. Glad would hold the back of the saddle whilst I wobbled along the winding path in the very wild, uncared for garden. (There was also a weed-filled tiled swimming pool, possibly well used before Fred's wife and he divorced. Also the war meant no water.)

At the bottom of the garden was a main railway line. One day, Rodney decided that he would go for a stroll, taking in the beauties of the rail track. He liked the warmth of the metal rails, so decided to lie across them in the sun (so good for the coat) and have a little snooze. The train driver must have seen a brown heap on the line in the distance. He applied the brakes in time and a sleeping Rodney was saved from a mangled death. The only trouble WAS that Rodney refused point blank to move from his warm and sunny nest. No amount of cajoling by the driver and his mate could move the giant dog. Poking wasn't an option, or pulling on his collar, just in case… Certainly, Rodney wasn't ferocious, but the men were not going to find out the hard way. I have no idea HOW they contacted Uncle Fred, but somebody did. Fred arrived in his vegetable van and walked up to Rodney. He shook his head at his trouble-maker. "COME ON, RODNEY, you BAD boy." No more was said. The great hound stood up and walked obediently back down from the track and into the garden. Accident averted.

Auntie Glad stayed for some time as housekeeper and general 'everything' to Fred. I can't say too much, but they got on VERY well, which became the source of rumour in the family. Probably lots of tut-tutting and "fancy THAT" and "I never did" from Mum. We don't know if Auntie DID.

There are certain bits of this epistle that are marked TOP SECRET. We know that 'something' went on between Fred and Glad. We cousins all agree little elephants do have big ears, but it HAS to remain a secret that even MI6 wouldn't be able to extract from our sealed lips.

The 'Fred' tables were turned, however, later when Uncle Arthur's church took on lady choristers, and one young lady in particular caught Unc's eye. Rumours are rife in the family about this too, so I mustn't assume that they had an affair, but we THINK they did, something that upset Glad's apple-cart for ages in spite of her liaison with red-faced old Fred!

There were so many facets to Glad. She was the buyer of the latest children's 'gadgets' and toys. She turned up at 249 one day (always an exciting event) and produced from a bag a carton of weird-smelling liquid. This and a bubble blowing pipe enabled the blower to make a huge bubble; however, THIS one didn't burst – THIS was a plastic bubble. This was early plastic, it was acrid smelling and probably carcinogenic.

On another visit, she produced pots of pale-coloured wax She shot out into the back garden, and arrived back in with twigs, lots of them. The wax was then rolled out, and Glad, always very 'arty-crafty', twisted the warmed wax into flowers, usually lily types or morning glory lookalikes! These were delicate and lovely, as they 'grew' out of the twigs, as though real. Another delight much looked forward to were beech husks or 'mast'. They lent themselves to being painted and attached to twigs. We would have happy hours searching for these slightly prickly husks, difficult sometimes because most had been trampled on, so finding an intact one was very exciting. We spent many happy hours with those. She was always experimenting with ideas.

Goose eggs were painted and sometimes made into little containers. Ideal, she thought, for an engagement ring. You opened the decorated egg up and HEY PRESTO, the ring would be there sitting in a nest of satin.

She spent many hours on one particular egg shell. A young man commissioned her to make the duck egg gift hinged, so that it opened up, showing a veritable nest of satin or velvet, ready to bear a ring. The young man was getting engaged to his beloved, so Glad made a very beautiful ring box decorated with flowers, poppies and forget-me- nots to boot – only to be told by a very distraught young man that the engagement was off.

She painted flowers, mainly poppies in water-colour and acrylics, and a pair of tights would end up a flower arrangement too. She would dye the tights delicate colours and stretch them over wire. Petal-shaped 'leaves' would appear looking splendid. Wonderful, but dust gathering, so not a long-lasting gift.

One day, the three sisters, Ve, Marj and Glad, all arrived bubbling over with laughter. They almost fell out of Glad's little old car outside 249. They had been on a buying spree at James Beatties, Wolverhampton's only really 'posh' shop in the town centre. No longer under that name, and no longer the same!

Out from the bag came a packet of what looked like baby tarantulas. Lots of chuckles, as pairs of false eyelashes appeared. Each aunt then got us to fix them to their eyelids. Much laughter ensued… Well, all three could have auditioned for the part of the ugly sisters in Cinderella! Or a part in a scary spider movie! They fell about, batting their eyes at each other, ending in screams of laughter, finishing with watery eyes. Pulling the lashes off brought more shrieks, shrieks of pain this time!

This was when the aunts were in their late sixties. They could laugh at themselves. Mum never could, so she was on the side-lines, half smiling, but very red-faced. To Mum, this was a case of her younger sisters behaving badly.

To Auntie Glad, an idle pogo stick HAD to be tried out on the back yard, followed by a stroll across the lawn on home-made wooden stilts. She mastered both! I don't remember her trying out our roller-skates, though, but as she could ice skate, she would probably have given the roller-skates a good try too.

I know that Mum viewed her much younger sister as a 'loose-cannon', but she was an auntie that many a child would love to have. No children of her own, so she made up for that with all of us nieces and nephews.

Uncle Arthur loved his music. He still played the organ in church, but had a job to practise when at home, as they only owned a piano. Glad was amazed one day when Arthur told her he had bought himself a 'practice-organ'. It didn't worry Glad too much. That is, until she SAW the 'thing'. Three keyboards, pedals, the lot! The only way they could get it into the front room was to take the bay window out. This a builder friend had done, and Unc was the proud owner of a rather rare instrument. Nobody had ever seen or heard of such a piece. (It ended its days in a music museum, somewhere far away.)

This was the start of many musical get-togethers. Every niece or nephew was instructed how to play a few repetitive notes on the bass keys, whilst Unc would play Bach's Toccata and Fugue or Mendelssohn's wedding march from *A Midsummer Night's Dream* on both the other keyboards and pedals. This usually ended up a fiasco with the child being given 'the sack' and Unc carrying on. Rustle of Spring was a favourite of Unc's. He lacked stature in height, but once on the bench seat of this wonderful instrument, Arthur Barlow shone.

Glad and Arthur's house was a haven for us children. There were games of sardines, played with tight squeezes behind settees or curtains. Unc was good at handstands (shades of Glad) and would amuse us all standing on his head, money falling onto the grass from his pockets. He would then assume a lotus position with his legs crossed in the air above his head. He could hold this position for ages.

Their loo was an outside one. It was just a large wooden sculpted seat above a hole that went down (I thought) into the middle of the earth. Apparently, according to Glad, one of next-door's cockerels fell down into the mire. The young son of the bird's owners, who was aged about ten, was forcibly volunteered to rescue the bird. The poor lad was lowered down by his ankles into the smelly darkness. There was a happy ending for the cockerel, though, but not so good for the poor rescuer. He has probably been afraid of dark places and may have suffered all his life after THAT debacle.

I hated going to that lavatory, and so did Wendy. It wasn't good for the bowels, and may have started us on a lifetime of constipation!

MUM'S CHILDHOOD

Most of the family seem to have escaped any bitterness in our early life, probably the result of knowing how much we couldn't do to further any ambitions, funds being scarce. Added to this, Mum would add a few drops of poison about Dad and his behaviour, so we didn't expect to rise to great things.

Mum was definitely a martyr, and had no idea how to react to Dad and his many failings as a husband and father. She would perform menial tasks for him supposedly willingly, THEN later moan about it. She had no guidelines to follow, having lost her mother at a young age, and a father soon afterwards (not to death but to *amour*). It's only in these last few years that I have blamed her dysfunctional childhood for her rather cool and restrained mothering.

Mum was one of nine children. Her father, Ludd, full name Arthur Luddington Angel Roberts, was an architect and land surveyor. These qualifications have never been proved in any document, but he certainly carried out the job, having a hand in the building of Stourbridge library and Bourneville Village, Birmingham.

Ludd was married before he met my granny, Ada Anne, but that is based on information passed down from Mum and her siblings, I have never found any 'first wife' on any ancestry site. However, Ludd was supposed to have two daughters by this first unknown wife, who died of TB. What happened to the two young daughters nobody knows – a mystery.

Ada had Mum, Maude Eleanor, then eleven months afterwards, Vera, and so on. Ada gave birth to nine living children, and one stillborn.

Mum remembers breakfasts at home, everyone around a huge table, eating porridge, Ludd tucking into bacon and egg. After he had finished his meal, one of the children would be allowed to wipe a piece of bread around his plate and mop up the bacon grease, a treat.

The family were quite well off for those days. Each morning Ada would make a giant pot full of what Mum called gruel but was probably porridge. This she would hand out to passing children at the backyard door on their way to school. Many of these little ones were probably ill fed and badly dressed, shoes missing, such were the times (just before the First World

War). Mum remembered children coming into school barefoot.

Ada sounds a lovely person. Mum and the oldest siblings always talked about her with great affection but sadness. The last four children would be too young to remember their mother.

On Sundays, the Roberts children were allowed to play outside in the back garden, a terrible crime in those days. Neighbours complained that it was a 'holy day' when everyone should be inside reading their bibles, certainly NOT running around happily on the lawn. I guess Ada wasn't bothered, and thought fresh air better for the body and soul. I really like her for that.

At the age of forty-two, Ada became pregnant again and gave birth to a daughter. Mum, then in her middle teens, remembers the midwife saying, "Oh dear, this poor baby is all floppy."

Six weeks after the birth, Ada Anne, née Williams, died of a kidney infection. We have her death certificate, and the strange thing is that Mum signed the death certificate as witness to the death, not Ludd, her father, and now the widower and 'next of kin'. We wonder where he was. Or was he not in the family house at that time? It's a mystery.

The new baby girl, Honour Joan, was a Downs syndrome baby. Shortly after the untimely death of Ada, Ludd eloped with one of Ada's friends, leaving Maude in charge of a new disabled baby and seven other siblings. Mum was only just seventeen. They had no income at all.

The bailiffs were called in to organize a sale of furniture, which was put up for auction. Two men were bidding for the beds and general household pieces. Neither of these men knew that they were BOTH bidding to help the family get the furniture back. One, I believe, was an uncle, Ada's brother Philip. The other bidder was a kind friend of the family. The two men didn't know each other, so they bid against each other, putting the price up and up between them. One of the saviours did get most of the household goods back at a price, a marvellous gesture.

All this upheaval took place during the last year of the Great War, 1918.

How Mum coped we never knew. Of course, her two sisters were only two years younger, so would have helped. Who fed Honour Joan and tended to a baby's needs is a complete mystery, but was one that was solved quite quickly.

A near neighbour in Clifton Street, Stourbridge, was mother to four boys, having lost a girl and a boy to stillbirth and miscarriage. So Gertrude Davies, née Gittoes, stepped in and said she would look after Honour and bring her up as her own. This Gertrude Davies did, to her great credit. Honour was quite severely disabled, mentally and physically, so the offer was doubly wonderful and almost unbelievable. Gertrude unselfishly 'adopted' the little girl, and brought her up as her own child; no aids or extra funds from the government in those days. Not to mention Gertrude's husband, Mansel Davies, who must have agreed to the unofficial adoption. We think Honour became the daughter that Gertrude had lost.

Gertrude changed Honour's name to Bette (after Bette Davis, a famous film star). Bette was well looked after until her death aged seventeen. Like some Downs syndrome children, she had always suffered from a hole in the heart and was described by the midwife as a 'blue-baby'.

The very complicated and strange ending to this tale of the family is that neighbour Gertrude's second son, Clifford Lloyd Pratten Davies, eventually married Mum, so little Bette/Honour became not just Mum's blood sister, but also her adopted half-SISTER-IN-LAW. So complicated, but true. But this event took place many years later, when Dad married Mum, in 1924.

Ludd went on to have three more children by his new partner May (Mabel). Most of his children estranged themselves from him for most of his life, all except Mum. Mum forgave Ludd, and he would visit 249 and play with his grandchildren. All three liked him, and thought he was a gentle old grandpa. (I wasn't born then, so never met him.)

In 1936, Ludd took a bus down from his then abode, somewhere in Wolverhampton, and had a game of football with Robin in the backyard of 249. Ludd then set off for the bus and home, a home he never reached. He suffered a heart attack by the bus stop, and was dead on arrival at the Royal Hospital. He was seventy years old.

He left not just his family, who were all married and settled, but also three children with May, David, aged about six, Peter aged four, and a little daughter called Marcia.

Mum and her siblings never knew about Ludd's last child. Peter Roberts died in the Second World War, aged eighteen, in Germany, and Ludd's daughter died with TB aged seventeen. David Luddington Roberts was the only survivor. He lived not far from his unknown half-siblings, in Halesowen. Ludd's partner May seems to be almost forgotten. There was always a lot of ill feeling about her, and she was generally disliked amongst family and friends.

Since I started this saga, I contacted the son of Mum's half-brother David. He didn't know anything about his Grandad Ludd, but passed me on to his sister, who "knew more about their grandparents".

There was a stony silence from his sister when I explained about Ludd and May. They had never married and stupidly I mentioned this – I have never thought it anything terrible. Of course, May was grandma to the half cousin on the other end of the phone. Her answer rather surprised me. "I am shocked that Grandad wasn't really MARRIED to my Granny May. I really don't want to know or talk about them." She sounded angry. With that, she said "Farewell", and the phone was put down.

I was so surprised that anyone in the twenty-first century could be so shocked or upset at hearing of a partnership, not an official marriage, almost a century later, but my strange half cousin no doubt thought her grandparents were sinners. I never got in touch again.

This is just a little saga about Mum's rather sad and motherless teen years. I believe that Ada Anne loved all her children, but numerous child births, only eleven months between each of the first three daughters, and the other rapid births, must have led to her early death. She was only forty-two. From Mum, aged sixteen, down to Honour aged two months, all the children clung together as their parents 'disappeared'. It was a bond that was as strong throughout their lives, and became stronger as they got older.

I think that this disturbed life during Mum's growing-up may have given her feelings that she probably felt but that she could never express towards her own children – somehow she just couldn't let her emotion out into the open.

WALKING WITH GREYHOUNDS

Just after leaving art school, I managed to get a job walking the racing greyhounds at Monmore Green stadium. A friend from college knew someone who trained dogs, so I applied, not all that hopeful.

Jim was a dog trainer who was paid to look after other people's racing dogs. I rushed off, had an interview, and got the job! Jim wasn't nice! He was a rather sly-looking man, in battered trilby and muddy wellies, ciggy on his bottom lip, dangling from the corner of his mouth. He grunted when spoken to, a rather unwholesome character, I thought.

I had to catch two buses to get there, and the area the stadium was in was not a salubrious part of town. I was met by a jolly, very nice girl called Fay. She was on the permanent staff. She was plump, blonde, ruddy-faced and welcoming. The kennels were row upon row of hut-like shelters and chicken-wire runs. The inhabitants were so beautiful! Wonderful, sleek, kind-faced greyhounds, long tails wagging. I fell in love with them.

Our jobs were numerous. In the morning we had to release the dogs from their kennels and fasten on a collar and lead. Their necks were long, I couldn't stop smoothing them, and they responded by resting a damp nose against my chest. I was definitely in love. Every morning, afternoon and evening the dogs had to be walked to do their business. On the first morning, I was almost tearful when I saw blood splashed all over the run and onto the wooden kennel's walls. The poor animal was bleeding from somewhere. I called nice Fay. She took one look at the blood and laughed. "Oh THAT, it's nothing, love, some dogs have to have the tip of their tails cut off."

She nuzzled the tail-wagging bleeding dog. "She's all right, aren't you, sweetie." Fay was someone I could like. I never found out the reason for the tail-tip snip; it seemed brutal to me.

There was a field, fenced and with a closed gate, for the dogs to relieve themselves. The field resembled a battlefield, with piles of poo for land-mines. Stepping in one of those was a regular occurrence, and I never got over the smell.

Next was feeding. There was a great metal drum, almost full to the brim with what looked like gruel. I think it was bread, soaked in something that

219

smelled 'meaty'. This was fed early on in the day, not too near race time, which was at night. The dogs appeared to like the sloppy mix, though, and licked their dishes clean. But to me it didn't seem a suitable diet. I couldn't work out what vitamins were in the dreadful stuff. I felt that old Jim was a mean, money-grabbing chap. I didn't like him at all. He never spoke to me anyway, just grunted instructions.

The evenings were really exciting, I thought (I would think differently now, though). Six sleek graceful dogs were paraded around in a small ring. The vet to the greyhound racing fraternity felt them all over and looked at their coats to see if any owner had put boot-polish on them to disguise a bare patch or sore skin. I found out THIS had been done once or twice, so the vet was vigilant. Six kennel-maids with their slender graceful dogs were gawped at by flat-capped red-faced punters, but I found that I quite enjoyed the limelight. We had to parade the dogs around the track before each race. I was tired, having been there all day, but the excitement of actually being amongst crowds of people, jostling, and queuing up at the bookies, the bright lights of the race track, and the keenness of the dogs, it was very like preparing for a stage show.

My dog was number six so he would wear a striped coat. We had to put the coat on, plus a lead and a collar and parade a whole circuit of the track, under everyone's gaze! The dogs weren't the only ones to wear a coat; we sported long white ones, mine almost touched the track. I think there were only large ones, so not a glamorous get-up. Just before the race, we girls had to undo the dogs' collars. I think the dogs had muzzles on, but I'm hazy about that. Then we would push them into a small trap. This was sometimes a sweat-making job, but once in, the noise was deafening, so excited were they that they let out the most blood-curdling screams.

The artificial 'hare' was started from behind the traps, and as soon as it reached the traps, the dogs were out! Wonderful to watch. It was thrilling, but I felt the racing life was very shady behind the scenes. It's probably more organized now, and dirty dealings not allowed. (I have to say THAT, just in case I feel that firm hand on my shoulder and 'They' cart me off to court for libel (or is it slander?)).

At the end of the race, we stood at the finishing post. The 'hare' would drop off the wire, and there would be a clamber of dogs trying their best to do something dreadful to it, so we would have to extricate OUR dog. If my dog won, there was a lap of honour and TIPS! One flat-capped gentleman gave me a one pound note! I was incredulous – it was more than I had ever earned in my fifteen years.

I loved those smooth-coated, graceful dogs. When one of the dogs who was in our care was thought not to be interested in running and was more into trying to play with his fellow racers whilst on track, something had to be done. Fay told me to get him ready to go to the vet's surgery on site. This I did. We walked over, and Colonel W, the vet, was ready. What I didn't know was that we were taking this dear dog to its death. He was to be 'put down' there and then, not as we know it today, painlessly, or for any of the right reasons; he was just a nuisance on track, not a money-maker, so he had to go!

If I was to count ten of the worst happenings in my life, this next bit would be high up in the wicked stakes. The poor young, frightened dog was trussed up with twine, two front legs together, likewise the back, so that he lay down. Then, without ceremony, the vet injected him. I can hardly type this, but I must. The poor innocent creature immediately began to convulse, eyes wild. Col. W had already pushed off, so we just stood there watching the dog writhe in pain and distress. The terrible torture lasted minutes. I couldn't believe anyone could do that to a helpless creature. I began to cry. I turned to Fay, who was so much tougher than me. She must have seen my tears. "Oh yes, isn't it AWFUL. They are injected with Epsom salts, it goes into their bloodstream. I think it creates bubbles."

The rest is obvious, but I still couldn't believe what I had witnessed, so I crept back an hour or so later, and there, lying at last lifeless, was the dear cream-coated playful but not money-making dog. His body was lying in the same place, bloated in the sun, a victim of the quest for money which overrode any feelings for the animals. Just pure wicked greed.

I never did stay the whole week. I developed some blisters on one palm caused by holding the dogs' leads. The blisters became infected, so I left. I had managed to draw and crayon some dogs, not well, but I have kept them, a memory of some beautiful dogs but some cruel money-grabbing people.

After the greyhound experience, I applied to be a Christmas postie. Miles of walking, all sorts of houses, all shapes and sizes of letter boxes. Two very nice young grammar-school chaps helped me settle and showed me the ropes. I became very rich, earning £4 12 shillings!

AN INTERVIEW

The post over, I HAD to get a job. Mum really couldn't afford to keep me any more. I used to scour our local newspaper, the *Express & Star*. Anything would do, anything that is, except work in an abattoir, funeral parlour or BANK!

One evening I read that a dental surgeon in the town centre was looking for a dental nurse, so I applied. I'm not sure I even told my parents; certainly Dad didn't know. He was becoming even more vague about what we were doing. He was still drinking too much and lending money to his friends, who all loved him. But all this was making Mum's life a hard one, very little cash, and an absent husband and father.

I got the job, with a tall, very elderly dentist, who, because of his great height of about six foot five, was nicknamed Tiny. He was a terrible dentist, as a good many were in those days during the fifties. He was also a heavy drinker. Dad knew him (something I found out later). They had a liking of alcohol in common, and I think Dad would meet up with him occasionally.

Mr K had a very tall dark and (I suppose, in a way) handsome junior partner, Paul Sinclair. He was the partner who interviewed me. A young woman sat beside him, looking me up and down, sporting a huge sapphire and diamond ring. Ellen was Paul's wife, and I suppose, looking back, she was there to make sure he chose an ordinary-looking young girl, not a glamorous blonde bombshell. Well, she need never have worried. Paul was oh so old, about twenty-eight, but ancient to a girl of sixteen.

I was very pleased that I had got the job, as I needed to bring in some money to help with the family finances. The weekly wage was agreed at £2. I thought it was marvellous.

All the family were now working, bringing in a little money for Mum.

Robin was still cycling up to Chapel Ash to paint and write posters for a living. He had been to the art school for a short time, really because he wasn't faring well at St Peter's boys' school. Robin was a very erudite young man, well read, almost a Marxist, and great arguments went on with Dad late into the night. Pat could never stand these arguments, and Mum kept out as best she could, knitting endless jumpers and crocheting delicate doilies, tray cloths and what were called 'Duchess sets', for the top of the dressing table, to pop under pin trays and jewellery boxes. I still have a few today.

Brother Tony was still not talking to Dad and was resentful of everybody. He was (I can only say that this is rather vaguely remembered) working in a garage, not too far away. I think he had a motorbike then. In fact he had many motorbikes over the years, a joy to him. He would tinker around with them, getting spare parts, joined by his friend Mike. They would spend happy hours greasy-handed, out in 249's backyard.

Tony became friendly with a girl called Pat. Her auntie was his boss's wife (I may have that bit wrong). Pat worked in the aunt's pet grooming parlour. Well, Tony fell hook line and sinker for Pat. She must have been much younger than him. He actually brought Pat to one of our November 5th bonfire nights. Before he picked her up, we were in the garden, in the dark, when I heard him say, to all of us assembled there, "Pat has just lost her mother, so DON'T ask her ANYTHING." Well, poor girl, she must have thought we were a dumb lot, because we DIDN'T say much to her at all!! Too scared the word 'mother' would pop out. She probably thought what a heartless bunch we were. That was Tony.

Pat was the first amour to be brought to 249 by anyone. Surprisingly, it was Tony who started the run of possible suitors who would over the years appear and disappear from the rather chaotic Lloyd-Davies house. Of course, all was very above board. Certainly, nobody would dream of taking their girl/boyfriend up the very worn creaky stairs, THAT was never even THOUGHT of. Well, if it WAS, it never became reality, just imagination. Bedrooms were OUT OF BOUNDS to anyone of the opposite sex!

LAUNDRY AND A 'BLEEDER'

Life at the surgery was busy, but great, the patients so diverse and interesting. Mr K had been living above the premises for some time, and I think owned the premises. On the third floor there was an empty flat, all carpeted in bright purple (a later exploratory find). However, his wife lived down in Sussex, 'Something' on Sea. They were parted, but he would go down for some weekends.

Dreadful though it sounds now, Celia, the senior nurse, saw and read a personal letter left in the telephone room (under the stairs). It was from Mrs K to Mr K. It read that she would put something green outside her bedroom door if he was 'needed' that night, and something red if he was not. We giggled like drains. He must have been in his late sixties, how COULD anyone do THAT at their old age?

The thought of red-faced, ginger-haired scaly-skinned Mr K indulging in sex, probably wearing his long johns, his homburg hat parked on the dressing table, was awful, and again a giggling whispering between Celia and a definitely innocent me. We knew he did wear long johns, because we had to prepare them to be collected by the steam laundry.

About once a week, Mr K would leave a bulky bag on an easy chair, in what was our office cum staffroom. The bag's contents had to be gingerly tipped out at arm's length. The contents were almost always terribly filthy! There were vests with long sleeves that had been washed so many times they were yellow. These were all right, as were his striped shirts. BUT the long johns (also yellow) were always stiff with dried blood. Mr K had bleeding haemorrhoids. These vile garments, with bodily fluids caked on them, he expected us to sort through. We had to make them into a parcel to be picked up by the local steam laundry. HOW we did it, and WHY we did it, has long been a puzzle! I must say Celia did most of this dirty work and seemed resigned to it. She had been doing it for some time before I got there.

Occasionally I had to run a little errand for Mr K. This was to trot across the road and enter the Ex-Servicemen's Club, a very impressive stone-columned building. I can't remember if Mr K gave me an empty gin bottle for a refill or another bottle was handed over, but this I did with speed. No money changed hands, so I guess it was on his bill. I gathered that my Dad wasn't the only heavy drinker in town!

Mr K lived in a very beautiful house in Staffordshire. It wasn't his house, it was a country club, a good venue for parties, marriages etc. The owners were friends of Mr K, so let him stay there as a paying guest. It was rumoured that Mr K was having an affair with his host's wife. Again THAT would provoke horrified screams and laughter, and was probably NOT true.

Once a week, the surgery had a 'gas session' when perhaps ten patients who needed extractions had appointments. Paul Sinclair was still very much the junior dentist, and Mr K would carry out most of the work. The gas machine was so basic. I know there was a rubber bag resembling a rugby football inner tube. We had to squeeze this to mix the nitrous oxide with oxygen, the patient had a mask put over their nose, and the savage surgery began…

With shaky hands, Mr K would wait until the patient's eyes went up into their head, then he'd tussle and struggle with the forceps – absolutely no science or expertise involved, just brute force. If the tooth proved difficult to extract, or broke off mid-pull, all manner of twisting and turning went on. Many times the patient's face turned rather blue, so they were brought back to consciousness, bloodied, sore, and disorientated.

How they survived, I'll NEVER know, it was so hit and miss. Heath Robinson would have quaked!

We dental nurses worked hard, long hours. I was going to evening classes and studying to get my Dental Nurse's Examination. Paul Sinclair was one of the tutors at the college. (I have to say, teaching was NOT his forte, and so the whole digestive system is a complete mystery, as I think it must have been to him too! He was not meant to teach.)

One of our patients was Lord B, who resided at a lovely house in Staffordshire, a fabulous country estate. His dentures were gold, a sort of filigree of open-work across the palate. Mr K knew him (he was familiar with all the top-nobs in the county, the High Sheriff also was a patient). However, Lord B was a very down-to-earth gentleman, if I remember correctly. I blush now when I think about the evening he came in to the surgery to pick up his repaired upper plate. The dental mechanic Jim handed them to me, and I promptly handed them over to his lordship, hand to hand, without so much as a paper tissue, just 'au naturel', in view in the hallway. Lord B thanked me and strode out down the steps, his denture in his hand. I did have a rocket about that from Paul, but Lord B didn't seem to think anything was wrong.

Jim our mechanic who made all our dentures, gold inlays, etc. was nice enough. A middle-aged man from 'down south', he liked to be 'tactile' with us nurses. Today, there would be eyebrows raised and a possible 'sexual harassment' case brought against him, but I looked on him as a father figure. He was in his fifties, married with two teenage children.

Jim, however, liked to tell slightly sexy jokes about honeymoons and other what would be called cheeky happenings. "I got married on December 22nd, nurse. It was the shortest day and the LONGEST night!" (wink-wink). He would repeat this to any new member of staff. He also liked putting his hands around slim waists and standing a bit too near, so personal space was invaded. In fact, it wasn't until a few years ago that I realized how cheeky he had been! However, I DID avoid him when he ventured into the X-ray dark room so something must have lurked in my very 'green' mind.

We had scrapes with weird patients and terrible frightening worries.

One patient, who had to have a general anaesthetic had (we found out too late) always bled a great deal when he cut himself shaving. He came in to have nine teeth taken out and dentures fitted. After a few of his teeth had been extracted, we found that we were all 'sloshing' around in 'gloopy' blood. The blood wouldn't clot. It covered the chair and Paul. The floor quickly became a red sea. The anaesthetist who was administering the anaesthetic, plus Paul, managed to carry the patient up a flight of steps, and into a car, before he bled to death. They apparently zoomed away, horn blaring, through the streets, going up a one-way street the wrong way. They managed to get him to hospital, but only just in time. He had to have pints of blood via transfusion and his wife was called and sat with him through 'the crisis'. A tremendous worry for all.

(This blood-bath took place in the small surgery. This room was a special radiation leak-proof room which had been used by an oncologist/radiologist, Dr H, so was lead-lined, with no corners where the blood could escape through. I will say a little bit about Dr H the radiologist further down.)

Getting back to the frightening haemorrhaging... I had to deliver a nerve-racking announcement to all the worried and frightened patients in the crowded waiting room. With dentist and anaesthetist gone, it was up to me to deliver the bad news. I was terrified. By now, all the patients waiting for a general anaesthetic been told to 'spend their pennies' in the upstairs loo, and had been anxiously waiting with a loved one or friend for hours, whilst the drama of the 'blood-bath' was going on. I had the task of explaining that due to unforeseen circumstances, they needed to make another appointment. There were looks of horror. Some were furious, others very understanding, all were VERY disappointed.

The bleeding patient survived, but it was touch and go, and after that trauma all patients who were to have a general anaesthetic were given a 'third degree' about excess bleeding or spontaneous bruising. A low count of platelets was the cause of this patient's bleed.

The radiologist Dr H rented our small surgery so that he could see his private patients and administer radiation treatment for their cancers. I was afraid of Dr H. He never spoke to me, just walked past, no dialogue. He was slightly Caribbean in looks, tall in stature, with short very curly grey hair, and was always extremely smartly dressed. I never saw him smile.

Celia was the nurse who helped the very ill patients to get comfortable on the bed. When she had finished, the room was closed, and the radiation was switched on. Dr H looked into the room through a small window, observing the patient. The only time I heard him say anything was when he peered out of the office window to where a lone dandelion grew. It was sticking out of the drain in the yard, a very tall specimen, well over twelve inches. He pointed. "That flower must be the result of all the radiation, nurse." He gave a small smile. That was IT.

One morning I was standing at the bus stop waiting when a great black car drew up beside me. The driver leant over, the window opened. It was Dr H. "Get in, nurse, I'll take you to the surgery."

With trembling legs, I got in and we set off. What COULD I say to him? There was nothing relevant to say. I felt SO nervous. I needn't have worried, because Dr H didn't say anything to me either. We sat in silence surrounded by the smell of leather. It was a very 'posh' car, and so comfortable and quiet, but it felt like the longest car ride of my life. True to his word, he dropped me off, gave a small wave, and went on his way.

I found out Dr H was married with children and lived very near 249, so would possibly see me standing in the usual place by the bus stop. I hoped he would pass me by, and he must have done just that, because I never saw him driving past again.

MR OATES AND LEMPRIERE

There were very few black or Caribbean people living in Wolverhampton in those days, but we did have one gentleman, a super chap, bowler hat, dark suit, with cataracts dulling his big brown eyes. This was Mr Oates.

Mr Oates had to have a tooth extracted with a general anaesthetic (the Heath Robinson machine had been updated – it was still basic, but I suppose safer). After the extraction, a very wobbly Mr Oates tried to stand up in the chair. He then proceeded to deliver a homily about how lucky he was to have Jesus with him, and how good life was to him and how nice we all were to him. "Thank you… thank you." He almost bowed in gratitude.

He was a sincere man, with a lovely toothy grin that encompassed his whole being. He was a truly nice gentleman; his smile radiated around the surgery. We all felt quite humbled by his outpouring of friendship and faith. Looking back at the rather basic anaesthetics in those days, God must have been watching over the lovely Mr Oates.

Spitting into the bowl was always a source of smiles behind the chair. Ladies spat quietly, daintily dabbing a handkerchief to their mouth. Men were louder and more powerful spitters, but top of the list were the big boy spitters, who would roll the mouthwash around their mouths, gargle making a noise like a growling dog, puff their cheeks, make some more animal noises, before a copious amount of bloody mouthwash hit the bowl. SPLASH!

There were patients who passed out, patients who jumped ship and ran, never to be seen again!

One extraordinary man, a psychiatrist's son, insisted on hypnotizing himself by rubbing his gum with a finger, concentrating on the area around the offending soon-to-be-extracted tooth. The rubbing went on for a minute or two, then, with an "I'm ready" he opened wide for the extraction… without any medicinal aid and no local anaesthetic!

Paul was scared and hesitant. He probed down between the tooth and gum to test if the gum really WAS numb. Then as all seemed well, hey presto, the tooth was out! Phew all round, all except the patient, Lempriere (his name as unusual as his self-treatment), who appeared surprised at our lack of confidence and went on his way minus one tooth, but happy. I don't think he was charged by Paul. We probably made a cup of tea after that. It had been quite an experience, a surreal twenty minutes.

We worked long hours, Saturday mornings, and no lunch hour on 'gas days'. For this I picked up the weekly wage of two pounds, as promised. It was an absolute fortune to me.

A little aside here. I brought my hard-earned cash home after my first week and deposited it in a dish on our sideboard. Next day when I opened the lid to take out my precious money, surprise – it had gone!! I dashed into the hall. Mum somehow knew that I had been searching "Oh dear. It must be those gypsies," she said. "They knocked on the door and asked for a drink of water. I only left them alone for two minutes. Oh dearie me, those blinking gypsy women must have stolen it."

It was years before I guessed just WHO had pinched it. It certainly wasn't a gypsy. A rather dark and sad happening, and again Mum was forced to tell whoppers. So my wages never materialized, but at the time, although fed up, I wasn't heartbroken. I must have developed a suit of armour! I probably still believed in the 'gypsy' story.

So no axe to grind with Dad.

THE WEDDING

Home life was as chaotic as usual, but there was nice news, Pat and Ray, her boyfriend of only a few months, were getting married. I was the only bridesmaid, and Pat, who was very good with the sewing needle, made my dress. It was pale blue, with a Juliet cap to match. Dad had a rather nice restaurant at the Gaumont cinema, so the wedding breakfast was going to be there. Dad's head cook would provide the buffet. She was a small, dark, attractive lady, and Robin appeared to fancy her, although she was possibly ten years his senior, and married! (The jury is out on whether 'anything' happened between them.). Also there was a rumour about Dad and the head cook.

The wedding at St Jude's church went well. It was April, a very windy day. Mum seemed to magic up a grey suit with a black velvet collar, and of course Dad gave Pat away.

Pat looked lovely in a white lacy dress, with veil. She decided to carry a prayer-book with a flower or two attached to a long ribbon. I'm probably being very boring describing all the outfits, but it was the 1950s and fashions were so different to today's, but apparently the 50s' style is coming back, not my favourite period of dress.

The wedding 'do' afterwards was a success. A friend of Dad's was barman and dispensed drinks with a professional touch. I had never been to such a sophisticated affair before; it sticks in my mind as a very happy day.

Dad, although too fond of drink, would never look intoxicated. He always managed to appear all right, that is, until later in life, when his body couldn't cope so well with the alcohol. But at Pat's wedding he excelled, and was a proud father of the bride.

Three months after the wedding, Pat was talking to Mum in the scullery. They were almost whispering. Pat was wearing her 'going-away' suit, a brown pinstriped pleated skirt. I couldn't hear what they were saying, but suddenly Pat turned round. "I'm having a baby in January."

Well, instead of being joyous, it was as though a great secret, almost unmentionable, had been blurted out.

All I could say, was "Does Ray know?" What a daft question!

"Of course he does," she retorted. (Pat might as well have added 'silly twit', but she didn't.)

That's how I was, aged sixteen, I knew nothing about sex. Well, probably just the basic technical side, having viewed that film at senior school, but sex within marriage was something to avoid even thinking about, especially one's own parents. That thought still feels almost unhealthy, and rude, quite different from today's young ones, who know everything, or think they do.

In the films, when a wife was 'expecting', the scene would usually take place in the 'drawing room', the young husband facing his beautifully spoken wife. "I have something to tell you, darling." There would be a pause, then he would say, half whispering, "You're not...?"

"Yes, my darling, I'm having our baby." This would be followed by a kiss on the lips between them and 'AAHHHS' from the cinema audience, and a wriggle of embarrassment from me.

BOYFRIEND NUMBER ONE

Now here comes a bit about my first 'real' boyfriend. We met at a dance in the local Civic Hall. I can't remember who I went with, but within minutes I was asked to dance by a tall, dark, bespectacled boy who introduced himself as Ben.

We danced, sat on the balcony, watching the glittering ball turning around over the dancers. We held hands and talked. His family came from Stourbridge, so that was a good start in my eyes! Ben was training to be an accountant. His father ran a grocer's in the town. The family owned a static caravan in North Wales, again a good point! In the middle of a conversation, Ben turned and whispered, "I hope you are reliable?" Now, to this day, have NO idea WHAT that meant! Well, we arranged to meet, believe it or not. Ben had access to his father's Cortina car. I don't suppose I had been more than a handful of times in a car, so this was exciting, Ben would pick me up from 249, the following week, IN THE CAR! Oh heaven, a proper date, at last!

Just before the day arrived, I had cold feet, and decided that I would hide in the now empty pond. (I had done that once when a very pushy lady from St Jude's church had called at 249, to try to get me to join their bible class. I had seen her stomping up the path, so I shouted to a startled Robin, that I was 'NOT IN' and on NO account tell her I WAS!! With that, I had run hell for leather down the garden, and crouched below ground and out of sight of the house. I crouched there cold and cramped for about twenty minutes. Surely the woman wasn't STILL talking to Robin? I didn't dare pop my head up, so I stayed… and stayed. Eventually, it was no good, I had to break cover. This I did reluctantly, only to find Robin back in his bedroom, having seen the churchgoer off the premises more or less straight away. I think he thought it was funny, as most older brothers would.)

So now the thought of legging it again into the empty pond before Ben arrived was a cowardly but acceptable option. Or so I thought. But I hadn't reckoned with Mum, who was horrified. "You have GOT to go! He will have driven all the way from Kingswinford (all of six miles). What HAVE you got against him?"

That was the trouble, Mum never did really seem to imagine what

COULD happen to her youngest child. I think that might have been because her mother had died when Mum was seventeen, so she never could envisage just what young ones could get up to. So the "you mustn't go near boys" of the earlier years seemed to have faded.

So here I was, driving off with a stranger. A lamb to the slaughter. Ben decided on Kinver Edge, a beauty spot near Stourbridge (scenes of many a picnic with the aunties), a lonely place in the evening, with sandy cliffs and cave dwellings (lived in until about the early fifties, empty for years but now renovated today, with tenants, and owned by the National Trust).

I got into the car, feeling anxious, but excited. How very masterful to be able to drive, and how daring to be going off, just the two of us. I would have a tale to tell back at the surgery tomorrow. I don't think Mum worried or envisaged any hanky-panky.

We parked on the sandy car park and climbed up one of the steep winding paths holding hands. We reached the top and found a bench. It was a lookout point… but Ben didn't want to look at the lights below. He slid an arm around my shoulders and our noses clashed, his horn-rimmed specs slid sideways, but somehow we managed to connect lips.

Sadly, I had a horrible surprise… all I could think of whilst kissing was slugs, slimy and squirmy. My first real kiss was a let-down, I somehow couldn't get the hang of it. I liked the smell of his tweedy jacket, he was handsome, spoke nicely (the Roberts family traits rising there) and he had a decent family, but this kissing and groping (yes, there WAS a bit of THAT too) was not what I expected, so it ended with me saying, "Let's go down, it's getting dark." Trouble was, that it didn't end there. A closed stationary car, in an empty car park, away from prying eyes, was JUST what Ben wanted. I had played into his eager hands, quite literally. Decorum prevails over the next half hour. I did get the hang of the kissing business, but didn't like the groping or windows steaming up.

I thought the 'stop that snogging' police would bang on the windows and we would have our names taken down for some 'criminal offences'. A page in their notebook would be headed: 'INDECENT BEHAVIOUR IN A STATIONARY VEHICLE'.

THEY would get me, as sure as eggs were eggs!

However, Ben seemed pleased with his evening. He dropped me off. I felt a bit like a beetroot, all red-faced, hair a mess, although, to be honest, it was nothing to write home about. I felt a little tarnished, so I waited before going into the kitchen. Mum was there closing the curtains.

"We went to Kinver, and walked to the top," I said, feeling strained and anything but normal.

Mum looked up briefly. "Well, well, I never did," was all she said. NOT a question, nor even a searching look to see if I had love-bites. This was Mum's way of dealing with life. "Well, well, I NEVER did", was her trademark answer to all situations. She was still saying it when in her eighties. It got her through a very dysfunctional life, though… "Well, well, I never did."

The funny thing WAS, I never DID!

I was taken by Ben to meet his parents. I don't think I impressed them. I ate tea there. His mother was a nice gentle soul, but his Dad was a sharp-nosed man, who brought the shop's takings home in the evening and counted the money.

I fell foul of him one day, when I was helping with the drying of the teacups. The wooden bread board was on the draining board, and I just wiped it over and was setting it down as finished, but, oh dear, Ben's Dad pounced. "Look HERE… there are still crumbs in the carved bits." He pointed to the offending crumbs. I was amazed that he even noticed or cared about such a petty oversight. 249 this WASN'T.

Then there was the incident of the tortoise.

Next door to Ben lived two small children who owned a tortoise. Ben asked if he could show it to me, so he was handed it over the garden hedge. He brought it into the kitchen, front end facing me, back-end towards his very smart accountant's suit. Well, the obvious happened, and the tortoise let go a hot stream of bright yellow wee, all down Ben's jacket and trousers. So what would anyone do? I laughed. The laughter didn't go down well in that household… points against me again.

The third and final faux pas came when Ben was about to drive me home from his house. It was shortly before his twenty-first birthday. He suddenly ran upstairs, then, moments later, he reappeared wearing a black, sinister-looking homburg hat, a present from his parents. I must have looked shocked, and slightly unbelieving. I can only say that I was almost praying that he wouldn't wear it out of the house, especially with me in tow; he looked so old and old-fashioned in it. The strange bit here is that I can't remember if he DID drive me home wearing it. I don't think he would have done.

Looking back on those days, I now realize that perhaps his parents were Jewish. I'm not sure about that last statement. I never found out because my amazement at his titfer put the tin lid on our romance. We talked on the phone (249 had a phone, it was only normally used in emergencies though) but, somehow, Ben was never available for a date. He was either playing rugby, or going out with the family, and other excuses, so I knew it was the end.

I apparently hadn't lived up to Ben's question on the balcony of the dance hall. "Are you reliable?" I never knew what that meant, but whatever it was, I obviously wasn't reliable enough.

I did shed copious tears, but nobody had any sympathy. After all, it was just a blip and a broken heart was low on the agenda, and life resumed its chaotic path. "Well, well. I never did." Mum's saying sums that little romance up, I suppose.

Heartbreak over, I was made an auntie when Pat gave birth to a son, Andrew. All went well, so quickly in fact that Pat said when on the birthing table, she suddenly realized her feet were dirty as she'd been gardening up until 'the call'.

Pat and husband Ray were living in a flat not far away, it was part of an old coach-house. A great believer in fresh air, Pat would pop her little son outside in his pram in all weathers. We have laughed since then about Andrew's tiny pink face peeping out from his blankets as snow fell onto the pram. It doesn't appear to have done him any harm – quite the contrary! He enjoys the 'outdoor life', probably the result of exposure to all the elements.

PATITENTS

Life at the surgery was great. I loved nearly all the different patients. Most were nice, polite and a pleasure to look after. The senior nurse, Celia, became a friend. The early mornings were hectic for me, but not for Celia, who would ring a friend up at work, chatting for ages, laughing and giggling about their boyfriends. This was in the tiny pantry/office. I did occasionally feel hard done to as there was such a lot to do before we could open the surgery, and there was only me to do the necessary.

We had paraffin heaters, and it was my job to fill them from a container out in the backyard. Even in the coldest weather, ice, deep snow, I had to be at work early to fill the heaters up and warm the surgeries.

One day I fell up the steps into the hallway, cutting my knees. Blood trickled down my legs. I was startled to see a lady with her young daughter standing there looking fed up. Apparently, someone who worked for the estate agents, who used the upstairs offices, had let them in, so no one knew they were there. Something had upset the mother, I can't remember exactly WHAT, but, regardless of blood dripping and the paraffin container smelling, the mother let fly at me. It was so trivial – something that had been done, or not done, whilst having treatment. I sorted it out, and just went on filling the blooming heaters, knees a bit tattered and bloody. So mad was this patient, she hadn't even noticed the state I was in. That kind of rude patient was in the minority, though.

The main larger surgery was nothing like today's spartan germ-free room. There was a corner seat, all chintz covers, where other members of a patient's family sat and usually chatted to Paul. The ceilings were high with dusty moulded plasterwork, and beside the big bay window was a house phone. No ordinary one, though. It was a Victorian gadget, which I suppose only survive today in antique emporiums. The person trying to contact upstairs had to blow into the mouthpiece, which apparently made the other end whistle to alert the receiver when they picked up their end. You could speak into this contraption. We never DID, though. The estate agents upstairs were very friendly but it would have to be a crisis like a fire or flood for us to try it out.

We really did have all sorts of patients. One young girl asked in great confidence, "Will I be all right…you see I have a period on at the moment?" Even with reassurance, she decided not to have treatment that day. Too risky, even though she was only having a small filling!

There was a tall, lanky young man. I had been to school with him, not that we acknowledged each other. He had a grey gabardine mac and always carried a small black suitcase, and to me looked as though he had crawled out from under a stone. He didn't turn up one day for his appointment, which happened to be the last of the day. I disrobed Paul and cleaned down the surgery. I put my hand round the waiting-room door to put the lights off. Paul was already in the hallway, on his way out to the bus (no car in those days), when suddenly we heard a slight cough.

Oh horrors… there was someone in the darkened waiting room! Everything was reversed. Paul was thrown back into his white, back-fastening coat. He then raced back into the surgery, whilst I had to switch the lights back on. I did, feeling terrible! Sure enough, sitting behind the door, in what had been complete darkness, was the patient, grey mac and case in place.

He didn't say anything, just grinned and followed me in to see Paul, who must have apologized profusely, but I was too busy resurrecting all the instruments to hear. But why hadn't he said something? Once again, he had been let in by the upstairs estate agents. He could have been there all night. It didn't put him off, though; he was a patient for years. We found out later that he was an extremely clever man who had written scientific papers and was well thought of in the science world. I am very ashamed to say that at the top of his record card were two letters, a code only known to us. (I can't divulge what those two letters meant, I wasn't guilty of that shameful bit, but at that time I didn't think it was degrading so went along with it.) The truth was that he was very intelligent, bordering on the 'strange', and not a worldly man.

Our updated anaesthetics were carried out by a very nice doctor, who worked in the local hospital as an anaesthetist. He was very efficient, and I felt the patient would actually LIVE after the extractions were completed. No blue faces, as happened when Mr K administered the nitrous oxide and oxygen gases.

If female patients had perhaps too much 'panstick' make-up on, whilst they were asleep and dreaming, Dr J would gently press a finger across the patient's cheek, drawing a small crack in the panstick. "She's nice looking, so why all THIS?" he'd say, gently filling in the crack and wiping his finger on his green gown, before bringing her round.

I liked Dr J, he was a chatty happy man. He related how, as a youngster, he had had his tonsils removed on the kitchen table, no anaesthetic (this was in France, I think). He loved music, especially Bach, and was taken aback when Paul said he thought Bach was 'too regimented and clinical'. Dr J owned a grand piano, and played. Although I never saw him socially out of the surgery, I used to imagine what a lovely house he must live in.

One morning, whilst a 'gas session' was in full swing, I had a head cold, and my nose was about to drip and I couldn't leave to get a hankie. Dr J glanced over. "Oh don't worry, nurse, what do you think sleeves are for?" He was human, if not too hygienic on this odd occasion.

It was during one of these gas sessions that I dropped a teapot into the basin. It broke, and when gathering up the pieces, I cut my palm very badly. Nobody could look, they were too busy, so I wrapped it in gauze, and after the patient had gone, showed my open wound. It was deep and bloody.

"Oh, don't worry, nurse, it's NOTHING. Keep something tight over it."

That was IT – not even sympathy from my friend Dr J! (I'm just checking as I write … yes, I still have the long scar – it should have been stitched.)

Dr J did have a great deal of sympathy for anyone who WAS ill or had a painful complaint. One particular man, who had curvature of the spine and looked as though a puff of wind would blow him into the air, arrived for an extraction. This was done with great gentleness and success, in spite of the way his head couldn't move into an upright position, his face was almost on his collar. He looked as though he was in great pain, and walked with difficulty. "Thank you so much, very kind, very kind." He walked out with difficulty.

Dr J turned to me and said, "That man suffers with the most terrible pain. His spine will begin to crush his lungs – a very sick man."

The patient didn't keep his next appointment, and we never knew what happened to him, but Dr J's sympathy had rubbed off on us all.

One morning, Mr K appeared even redder in the face than usual. He was in pain, a back molar was giving him 'gip'. SO, he decided to extract his own tooth. I was asked to stay whilst he did the deed. So, peering through his thick-rimmed glasses, he injected copious amounts of local anaesthetic, all carried out with a very shaky hand. Then came the choosing of the right forceps for the job. "You can go, nurse," he mouthed, his mouth probably as dead as a dodo.

Dr P's small 'watching' window had long before been blocked up, so I never DID witness the actual removal. There was silence. I was waiting for a shout or an OOOHHH… but all was silent. (A gin, taken medicinally, would probably have helped.)

However, sound sometimes DID seep out from the surgery into the office. I was used to hearing the tap turned on and water pouring into the basin, but one day, I learned that it wasn't just water.

"Shhh," Celia whispered. "Can you hear THAT… put your ear to the door." I pressed against the door, only to hear the water tap turned on… "It's not WATER, it's Mr K WEEING in the sink, he can't make it up the stairs to the loo, trouble with his knees."

Oh dear, rude awakenings for me, and not hygienic, to say the least.

There had been an extraordinary little scene in the same box-like surgery. The reason there was a job space for me to join the practice was that Celia's colleague was getting married. Her groom-to-be was a German ex-prisoner of war who had fallen in love and decided to stay in England. However, Celia's colleague and friend was leaving to be a housewife. Celia recounted a happening, nothing really, but it stuck in my mind. The morning before the wedding, the bride-to be rushed in to work. She greeted Celia but rushed past her into the little surgery (thankfully not in use) and leaned close to the mirror. "Look. LOOK…"

Well, Celia looked. Over the bride's eye was the most gigantic boil (quite common in those days). It protruded green and yellow, a Mount Everest of a boil…

As Celia's story goes, the two girls got closer to the mirror to view the monster … What happened next would put anyone off their sandwich. The pressure on the eye from leaning over gave the boil only one route to take. It HAD to explode! This it did, its hideous contents trickling down the mirror in a disgusting yellow river. Joy all round, the bride-to-be wouldn't have to walk down the aisle wearing sunglasses after all!

Boils on the neck were prevalent in the years after the war. There were no easily prescribed antibiotics, so I suppose a pimple could become infected and turn into a very painful boil. Tony suffered many a boil.

Apparently, some cooks put bicarb in the greens, to make them bright green, but the bicarbonate of soda just killed off all the vitamin C, hence the boils. This MAY be an old wives' tale… but boils were very common in the forties and fifties. Mum wasn't guilty of this but, like most cooks at that time, she would boil cabbage until it became khaki. School cabbage was even worse.

DENTAL NURSES' MEETINGS

Occasionally all the dental nurses would meet up, usually to exchange ideas, have make-up demonstrations, and have a good gossip. One evening, a representative from M F, a worldwide cosmetics company arrived.

The meetings were always at our surgery, in the waiting room, which was large enough to accommodate up to perhaps twenty-five. At this meeting, volunteers were asked for by Mr M F to have a 'full make-up'. One smiling girl was chosen from a row of waving hands. I was organizing the tea and biscuits so never got a chance to offer my scrubbed face. The rep opened his box, and it began. Well, if he had been a plasterer working on an exterior wall, the workman couldn't have slapped the plaster on thicker. The dreaded panstick, a brownie-buff tint went on first, but it was the eye make-up that astonished me. Eyelids the brightest blue, lashes clinging together with the blackest of black mascara. Then, completing this mask, he applied a post-box red lipstick to the poor guinea-pig's now unsmiling mouth.

I felt heartily glad that I had missed being chosen. The girl underneath the paint looked as though she was straight off a street corner in the town centre. How he expected any of us to buy his products (which were probably all right when applied with care) was a laughing matter. (Will I be sued by M F now that I've said this?)

The next meeting was all about hypnotism in dentistry. A well-known local dentist demonstrated, using his nurse as his 'demonstration model'. Mr T was a very rotund man, his face red and his hair Brylcreemed. He began by just clicking his fingers in front of his model's face. We expected his nurse to fall asleep, or at least look drowsy, but she just sat there, awake, smiling.

This was eye opening. Mr T then proceeded to stick needles through the front fleshy part of her lower arm, in one side, and out the other. Ghastly, but totally amazing. His nurse didn't flinch. "There will be no bleeding," Mr T said proudly as he withdrew the needles. And, to our astonishment, there WASN'T!

He then 'regressed' her back to age five. Again, amazing… no stunt.

The whole performance was truly astonishing to all of us. Apparently, hypnotism was already being used in the children's dental clinic. A disc with all the colours of the spectrum on it would be spun very fast, so that the colour changed to white. The child would watch intently and become accepting of treatment.

After this startling 'show', whilst having a cup of tea, a fellow nurse leaned over and whispered, "They're 'like that' you know." She twisted two fingers together.

"Like WHAT?"

"You know… they…" she mouthed, "…do it."

"You mean…" (this is where a bit of Les Dawson comes in handy) "REALLY?" I mouthed.

"Haven't you heard? Most of the nurses are having it off with their bosses," was her whispered reply.

Shock! The thought had never entered my head. After this revelation, all sorts of 'news' seem to come my way. The next bit was as shocking… One nurse in a well-known practice was ferreting in a drawer to find something. Hey presto – condoms! Apparently, her older nursing colleague and mentor was intimate with the boss, had been for years. Whether his wife found out, I'll never know.

Even one of my friends, who used to pop down to have lunch with me, made no secret of her affair with her dentist boss. I didn't in all honesty twig that she was, mainly because I didn't know her boss's forename, so when she kept mentioning 'Harry', I truly thought she was referring to her practice mechanic/technician. It turned out that it was her BOSS, an extremely handsome man, a heart-throb for looks, but he was married. His wife was much older, wore tweed skirts, had hair twisted into two 'earphones' – even in those days that hairstyle was reserved for the over-seventies – and her brogue shoes matched the rest of her. They had no children, so I suppose the ties in their marriage might have been tenuous. So my friend became his nurse cum mistress. Eventually, he divorced his wife and married his young love. They lived happily ever after, had two children and a big house in the countryside.

I only ever met up with my friend once after they married, and that was in a butcher's. She had changed, I thought, taking the role of a surgeon's wife very seriously. I felt a bit of a pleb when talking to her.

My co-nurse friend Celia was getting married. Celia introduced me to the advantages of an engagement, and all the sexual adventures that went on when in that estate. I can only say it was an eye-opener. In Celia's household, Friday nights were 'Music Nights', a programme avidly listened to on the wireless and enjoyed by thousands. Celia's parents would sit, ears glued to the set in their back room, whilst Celia and her fiancé made merry on the front-room settee. I was astounded. I was sure that nothing so secret would or could happen in our very public front room (always too many people drifting around in 249 to do anything so cheeky). However, they said they DID.

Paul, who was asked by Celia's intended to be his best man, certainly took his job on with verve and vigour. Paul took the fiancé out in his car (no buses required now Paul had bought a little car) for a celebratory drink before the happy day. When they had stopped to let the groom alight, Paul launched into a 'sex after marriage' homily, very seriously delivered, which afterwards amused the happy couple. It was good of Paul, who was at that time very happy in his marriage to Ellen.

A BEDROOM GUEST

Life at 249 had brightened. I no longer shared my bedroom with Pat, so I could use ALL the drawers in the very ancient dressing table, also the single wardrobe, which sported a full-length mirror. This blissful state didn't last long, though.

Brother Tony had made friends with a nursing sister. Her name was Jean, but she was known to everyone as Billie. Tony and Billie met out in the Staffordshire countryside where Dad, during one of his many illnesses, was seconded. Billie was nursing at the convalescent home, a rather lovely old Victorian house near to Cannock Chase, a beauty spot. Billie became a regular visitor to 249, staying on her off-duty days. But unfortunately for me, the only bed available was Pat's old one, so my privacy had been stormed.

We got on well, although of course Billie was years older than me. I don't think there was ever much of a romance between Tony and Billie, but having somewhere to use as a base, and becoming a member of our rather weird crew, suited her. Her own family were in Scotland, so really her 'home' was the convalescent home.

The home had a cat, a Siamese, very ancient, but with bright blue eyes, which were crossed, as some Siamese cats were in those days (I think it has been bred out now). Everyone loved him, including visiting doctors. The cat would sit outside and 'welcome' the medics and visitors. Regular visitors would say "Hello, Ming, how are you today?" Ming would immediately pop his pink tongue out for inspection… I think dear Ming lived until well over twenty.

A café in Wolverhampton called the Café Royal was somewhere Billie had an occasional lunch, and one day I was invited. It doesn't sound in any way exciting today, but it felt so thrilling and grown-up to me. For some reason, the mushrooms on toast were SO good, the café SO refined and tasteful, the tablecloths SO white, and the silver-coloured teapots luxury! I loved the whole afternoon.

Billie was a boss-boots to Robin, though. She would run up the dark terrible stairs to the attic bedroom and lay down the law about his failure to appear downstairs because he was feeling ill. Bowels were another bee in her bonnet. "When my men (she only nursed men) tell me they 'haven't been' I insist that they at least TRY. If you don't sit and try, your bowels will NEVER move." I think Robin in particular was a little scared of her. I'm still not sure about Tony, he was a closed book to me anyway.

We did have some laughs, though. I was woken up early one morning by Billie whispering something. "Hey… look at this."

I looked across. There on her chest, sitting up washing its tiny whiskers, sat a little house mouse. Billie didn't flinch, and the mouse, seemingly oblivious of our presence, just continued his or her ablutions, then scampered off, probably to its home behind our skirting boards amongst the brick dust. (There was always a gap of inches between floor and wall, a hidey-hole for small creatures, frightening spiders, and silver fish, which would appear every night around the black-leaded grate in the breakfast room.)

Billie went even higher in my estimation. No fearful screaming on finding our little house 'guest'. To be truthful, so old and decrepit was our house that mice and creepy-crawlies were our bedfellows, this time literally.

I have to end this part of the story by saying that Billie fell in love with Dad's under-manager, the man who I had accidentally shown the love-making dogs to earlier. They became engaged, so at night a beautiful solitaire diamond ring was placed in its box on the side table between our beds. When Billie married, I was asked to be her bridesmaid. I was, but Mr Fullelove, the under-manager, WASN'T at the wedding. Another groom walked confidently down the aisle. His name was Don and he became Billie's husband and father to their two children. They went to live out in the wilds of Shropshire, but unfortunately didn't live happily ever after.

A BIT OF GLITZ

The Gaumont was becoming extra busy with live shows and talent competitions. I was allowed to go to see what talent there was in Wolverhampton. There was plenty! I watched from the wings as, one by one, young men and girls strutted their stuff, singing the songs of the time. On particular young woman was exceptionally dazzling. She wore an orange balloon-shaped dress, the height of fashion, and proceeded to belt out a song, plus actions! The song went, "I was walking along, minding my business, when out of an orange-coloured sky CRASH, BANG, ALACAZANG. I took one look at you. One look and I yelled 'TIMBER!'" Well, she certainly didn't need a microphone, but she looked so glamorous and sophisticated I envied her. The stage curtains were golden and luminous as they swished around her but, having finished her song, she suddenly gave in to stage-fright and ran off the stage. To everyone's surprise, she could be heard sobbing in the wings.

So Dad was into all THIS. I had never been interested in show biz, far too dodgy, and the dancing at school amongst the autumn leaves was still an embarrassing memory, but I loved the glitz.

The big show at what we all called 'Dad's' was Bill Haley and the Comets, plus Little Richard, always standing up whilst playing the piano. It was a surprise to us all that Mum and her sister Ve wanted to go to see them perform. But then came another surprise. I wasn't allowed to attend. Oh misery me! I would have given a back tooth to see them and MEET the rock 'n' roll band. (I think I would have drawn a line at the tooth bit.)

All Dad could say was, "No, you can't meet him because he's into coke." That meant nothing to me. He drank Coca-Cola? So what? I truly didn't know, and still am not sure, WHAT Dad really meant. I could only think that perhaps Bill and his band drank straight out of a tin and didn't not pour the contents into a glass, something I was brought up to believe was the height of bad manners.

Drugs were for very ill people or period pains. I really don't know NOW what Bill drank or took. Perhaps it WAS Cola? Oh innocence.

Mum and Ve seemed to enjoy the show, although neither of them had any liking for rock 'n' roll. The theatre was bursting at the seams, every seat filled. Everyone stood up and jumped up and down in time with the music. Dad became very worried about the balcony, it shook with the stamping feet. At the end of the show, there was a terrible crush trying to get out to catch buses. Mum remembered some police arriving to see order. Quite exciting for Mum and Ve; they were holed up, unable to go out, as chaos broke out and panic set in. I missed all the fun and was pretty unhappy. Mum and Ve topped the show off with a walk up to the Fire Services Club where Dad hung out (I never worked out why the fire services were his bolt-hole).

RUTH

Life at the surgery rolled on in its hectic busy way. The time came for me to ask for a rise, having been there a year or so. Mr K was still senior partner, so it was he I had to ask, if I dare.

I went into the little cell-like surgery. He was just reading the paper. I have always found money a tricky subject, even then, so I was inclined to leg it. I did, however, pluck up courage to ask him for a small raise to add to my two pounds a week.

He just peered over his glasses. "So… you want a rise, nurse. Well, let me tell you, nurse, your work this week hasn't been satisfactory. You didn't replace my cardboard dispenser yesterday, so…"

I waited, hardly believing what he had said. The cardboard box was a little square with a cross-shaped slit on top. It had to be assembled from flat and one box was always placed ready on the marble worktop, so that cotton wool, bits of food extracted from between patients' teeth, and other saliva-soaked items could be poked through. I had forgotten this once in all the time I was there.

Mr K must have seen how upset I was, and grudgingly said, "You can have five shillings, that's all." He went back to reading his paper.

The five shillings were added to my wages packet, but unfortunately that extra cash put me into the tax bracket, so I had to pay the taxman three shillings, leaving me with two shillings extra. So for lighting fires, braving the snow, helping to pack filthy underwear, let alone all the duties, reception, nursing, and telephone, I was earning the princely sum of two pounds two shillings per week, still a fortune to me. I gave Mum some money for housekeeping every week, as did Robin and, I assume, Tony.

Some time after the wages debacle, I was just crossing the hallway to get a patient when I saw Ruth sitting on the flowery sofa in an inglenook in the corner of our rather posh entrance hall. I had lost touch with Ruth. She was always busy with her job. And also with boyfriends; I had heard about her latest from her sister Jean… He was an older man, owned a flash sports car, and was taking Ruth around at great speed. One night they had spun off the road, landing in a ditch, battered but not badly hurt. I believe they split up after that, but as Jean stated, "Nobody liked him anyway."

247

So seeing Ruth here at work, although not a patient, was a great surprise. Celia was already talking to her, grimacing as she listened to Ruth tell of her badly aching back. "Too much lying on wet grass," Celia laughed. Indeed we all laughed... I was never sure why Ruth appeared that day. She must have felt like a chat, worried about her shoulder and back pains. But we took it all lightly, and it was very good to see her, so a few days later I wasn't surprised to receive a phone call from her on our seldom-used telephone stationed in the cold front room at 249.

The call shook me. Ruth had been diagnosed with TB, which could be caught by family and friends who had been in close contact with a sufferer. The pain in her shoulder and back was the TB in her lung. All her friends had to be X-rayed as soon as possible, just in case. Ruth was hospitalized straight away, into the dreaded New Cross Hospital for treatment.

My X-ray was fine, no trouble, a great relief, but Ruth was still in hospital weeks later. I had reports from Jean, and occasionally from Mrs Brickman. I decided to visit her if that was allowed, so one weekend I was shown into a small one-bedded side ward. Ruth was propped up wearing a frilly pyjama-top looking so much better than I had expected.

It transpired that the staff were brilliant. They had washed her hair, always long, slightly wavy and dark. The young nurses had made her up, so that she looked good, so great care was being given to their young patient. The main trouble was that she had to bed-rest for several weeks.

The next time I visited, Ruth had been moved into a general ward, which was not so good. It was a ward for the very elderly and confused. I found it depressing but, to her credit, Ruth never complained. After months, she was sent home, but had to take vast amounts of what was probably steroids. These came in hat-box-shaped wafers, the same size as communion wafers. Each 'hat box' was full to the top with powder. How Ruth swallowed them I'll never know, but she DID, and recovered.

We began to keep in touch again. Her mother had moved back to Wolverhampton and was working in a coal-yard office, as secretary. A coal-yard and Mrs Brickman made strange bedfellows!

Ruth left the telephone job and became a receptionist at a large and prestigious hotel in Tettenhall. We often talked about boyfriends, sex, and 'would you do it?' We talked once at great length about a certain part of a man's anatomy. Oh, shudders and giggles all round! So it was a huge and breathtaking shock when, a few months later, Ruth told me she was pregnant!

Ruth disappeared from my life for some time. She married, and they went to live in Wales. Her husband was quite a bit older than her and had already been married. They had met at the hotel when he was on a business trip. We never really discussed anything about her pregnancy or quick marriage, but letters did eventually fly from Wolverhampton to Wales and back. Ruth had grown up in an instant, but I was still pretty dim about affairs of the heart. I HAD ditched the pocket-sporting knickers, though.

About this time, Robin joined the Wolverhampton Technical College Badminton Club. I was very keen, so also went along.

BADMINTON AND BILL

I took to it like a duck to water. I loved playing, as did Robin. Friend of the family Harold was there too, a good player, but always looking adoringly at a new conquests. There were many of those, looking pretty in their white pleated skirts and equally white knickers.

I made friends with the crowd, all keen players. Sometimes the evening would be wrecked by a new member who was a beginner. Everyone had to start somewhere, but if badminton wasn't their forte the next-on-the-court list wasn't exactly 'fixed', more engineered! Otherwise it was a stop-start affair.

Romance was top of the agenda (alongside bashing the shuttlecock across the court), with couples going out with their beloved, then next month going out with another member, also a 'beloved'. It was a hotbed of lust… with in between, some very good games and away matches, and a post-badminton get together down in the basement of the Café Royal, the restaurant that served those delectable mushrooms on toast with long-lost Billie.

The Café Royal was really a drinking hole, but mainly a convivial meeting place. Young and old would stand at the bar being served by a friend to all, Doris. Doris, rosy-cheeked, middle-aged, and cheerful, became a friend to most of the badminton club. This friendship became a fixture, and Doris and her teenage daughter joined us on many a narrow-boat trip down the canal, and extended to them both coming with us on camping weekends. Robin and a friend even went to Austria with Doris. This sounds strange, but she joined in all the badminton club's 'doings' except badminton. She never played. Harold's mother Ethel even asked Harold what was going on. Ethel then push-biked up to town to view this unlikely friend. This must have taken some guts, because Ethel had never set foot in a pub, but her son's welfare could be at stake!

Doris remained a friend to all for many years. She was my travelling companion on my very first holiday abroad, to Spain, but that is another story. She did have a husband, but he had thrown himself into church bell ringing; he certainly didn't 'throw himself' into his family. He and Doris divorced after it was discovered that he had become keener on 'belles', but not the church kind.

Romance at this time with anyone from the club wasn't on my agenda, because I had met someone. Oh dream. The man in question was one of the ushers at Celia's wedding, and his name was Bill. (His name was not actually Bill – I have changed it, too embarrassing.) I was probably looking my best gliding gracefully around in a very beautiful dress made by a tailoress Celia knew. Looking back, I think the making of this must have cost Celia and her parents a fortune. The buttons from top to bottom of the back were each covered in the dress material and what would be button-holes were small loops through which the button slipped. The colour of the brocade was a delicate turquoise, embroidered with a dark pink thread, a dress for a princess! I felt a million dollars. So I suppose the tall usher was perhaps seeing me in a good light that day.

There was a let-down, however. When the groom proposed a toast to the bridesmaid, I apparently broke all the good-manner rules by standing up and DRINKING the champagne too. When I tell you that this was explained to me by Bill himself, you will understand that mortification stepped in, and I thought I was going to be cast aside as the country bumpkin he probably thought I was.

Bill lived in Liverpool, which was where Celia's new husband came from. I hadn't even danced with Bill at the wedding; there had been no contact except a small exchange of polite chit-chat and the oh so red-face-making homily about accepting a toast sitting down, and NEVER actually drinking to oneself! Writing this, I realize what a pompous thing to tell anyone, but I took it as a lesson from a 'man of the world'. So when a few weeks later I opened a letter with a Liverpool frank-mark, I did a mental somersault. Yes, Bill HAD remembered me. He was coming over to stay with the newly weds, who were living in a very damp- smelling flat in Wolverhampton.

Bill DID visit, and we got on well. It was the start of a very strange romance between the Wirral, where he lived, and Tettenhall. I had by then had another stupendous rise in salary, to four pounds a week. This was because I had become head nurse, as Celia and her husband had designed and bought a golden-stoned house 'down south' and were going to move there shortly. Celia's husband was in the wine trade, so I guess they were comfortably off. So although I still gave Mum some housekeeping money, I was able to afford a trip to Liverpool, then on to the Wirral, Cheshire. Trouble came when Bill and his friend and his friend's girlfriend Joan wanted to visit me for my birthday. I told Mum, who had never asked anything about WHO Bill was, what he did for a living or if he was 'respectable'.

I have to add here that Bill lived with his good school friend and the friend's parents, as Bill was parentless. He did have a step-mother, who he was on good terms with, but who lived too far away from Bill's workplace, which was in a bank in central Liverpool. His father had died some years before. Bill was born on the high seas between Liverpool and Ireland. Apparently his birth on the boat at sea meant his nationality was of the country nearest to the boat when he arrived on board! I never found out WHAT his nationality WAS, Irish or Liverpudlian.

The proposed visit didn't go down too well with Mum, who was always a bit ashamed of our very old, dilapidated house. Also she was literally terrified that Dad would appear the worse for drink and spoil everything. The visitors were only going to stay for an hour or two before taking me out to the Grand Theatre for a birthday treat show, (which happened to be *The Chalk Garden*, a play I never got to grips with), but to Mum's credit, she prepared a high tea, salad and ham, with some home-baked meringues. Mum's fear that Dad might arrive home having had too much beer and 'chasers' never materialized, but her reasoning was good. Dad's ill health caused by stomach ulcers, a dodgy heart valve, and the beginnings of liver trouble, were all taking their toll; Dad couldn't 'hold his drink' as before.

I must add that none of us had, even in those days, ever seen Dad legless because of drink. Certainly never at 249. In fact, Dad never drank any alcohol inside 249; he would have a 'fizzy' drink of lemonade in the early morning. Bottles in the sideboard, given at Christmas, were quite safe from Dad. I think he was a social alcoholic.

Anyway, Dad DIDN'T appear on the scene, and the friends arrived. The tea was appreciated, the table looked daintily laid, and Mum's Indian tree patterned china (a great treasure, as she had saved pennies to gradually buy just a cup and saucer, then a plate, and so on, until she had a full set!) was brought out from its hibernation in the sideboard. The napkins would all be embroidered with a crinolined, bonneted lady, walking in a flowery garden, again amongst the usual hollyhocks! We all ate our splendid tea, no Marmite in sight, and caught the trolleybus into town.

Little did my three friends know that the plaster under the window behind the table had suddenly decided to part from its wall, possibly caused by several sacks of coal being tipped down into the cellar beneath, shaking the already perished plaster, which now lay in a pile at the back of the table, shielded by the tablecloth. We were very good as a family at appearing completely at ease, in genteel sometimes 'gracious' surroundings, but we were all rather like the proverbial swan, serene above the waterline, but paddling like the devil underneath. Also, the walls in the room had been very quickly emulsioned with 'buff', THE colour of the post-war days, and some weeks earlier I had painted the whole bathroom pale blue! All this seems ridiculous now, but it was SO important to me.

Days before the visit, I set out to transform the bathroom. Nothing escaped my brush. The lion-footed old iron bath was given multiple coats of blue gloss paint, never mind the risk of lead poisoning to anyone who dared to lie in it for more than a minute. During the bath painting, I had knocked a can of gloss in a great puddle on the boarded floor. So the floor also became a victim of my ardour. Also the very obvious and complicated water pipes couldn't shrink from the treatment. Neither did the tongue and groove walls, and as for the lavatory seat, well, THAT took the paint like a trooper. It was only when I tried to lift it that the truth dawned, the seat was stuck to the bowl.

So all THIS for a two-hour visit. It was all especially disappointing as nobody had asked to use the loo. I don't remember either parent saying a 'thank you' for transforming the bathroom into the 'Blue Grotto'.

During this time, Pat had given birth to another baby, a girl. All went well, again. The birth had taken place in a private nursing home opposite 249, an old house converted, first into a home for single mothers, now for better-off ladies.

One of the head nurses was Harold's amour. I had often peered out of our front bedroom window to view Harold waiting around the corner astride a Vespa scooter. I thought Harold's waiting around the corner was to meet his girlfriend, but as it turned out much later, he was there because he was suspicious of her whereabouts, and was doing a little bit of sleuthing.

Harold was regular visitor to 249, sometimes arriving at almost midnight after a night out. One night he arrived just as we were eating a late supper, Dad tucking into a crab or a mackerel, brought back from his friend and drinking colleague Mr Cod (not his real name, as you can guess). Harold would sit in a very down-at-heel basket chair, his often bare legs splayed. Athletics were his forte, javelin his strength, hence the strong thighs. "You know, Harold's legs are like tree trunks!" was Mum's observation.

The letters were still whizzing back and forth between the Wirral and 249. Some I ripped up in case Mum or Pat ever read them. One letter contained what I thought was a very cheeky and slightly dirty account of a dream that Bill had had. I was on a desert island with him, and to his delight, I apparently appeared from a hut, wearing nothing on my top and, just a grass skirt! Oh, shock HORROR!

I burnt the letter in the little bedroom fireplace. I expect people would fall over laughing now, but in those days I was very much a greenhorn, a goodie; far too good, in fact. I must have been a very wet blanket.

Although I was keen on Bill, I had accidentally met up with a very likeable young chap called Tony, who was at art school a year ahead of me. He was studying architecture. He and a friend Jim had clubbed together and bought an old London taxi-cab. With Jim's girlfriend aboard, we would all four whiz around the Shropshire countryside in this black very roomy cab. We used to stop at a country pub. I had never done anything like that before. We had laughs, lots of fun, and a happy time. There was no romance, though, just the odd peck now and then.

I had, when at the art school annual dance the year before, danced with Tony, mainly because we turned up in the same fancy-dress costume, Roman togas, made from sheets. I think he was drunk, because he had suddenly turned to me and had given me a kiss with a TONGUE! Tony's kiss had repulsed me at the time, but, as he didn't now seem to connect ME with his unknown Roman dancing partner some months earlier, we seemed to be on an even footing, and nothing was ever mentioned of THE dance, or the amorous kiss, thank goodness!

A SMALL HOTEL ADVENTURE

Meanwhile, Bill had bought a car, just a small Austin seven. He was coming down to the Midlands, could pick me up, and we could have a couple of NIGHTS in London and the home counties. I didn't tell him of my rides in the taxi, he might not have understood, so I kept quiet. I contemplated hard and long about going off with Bill. I had stayed quite a few times at his 'digs', the home of his friend Ray, but this was different. It took me all of five minutes to write 'yes'.

Bill arrived at 249, looking rather handsome, something I hadn't noticed before. He was tall, with wavy brown hair; I was looking at him anew. We drove to Maidenhead (a rather appropriate name I decided afterwards). He had booked two separate rooms in a big hotel. Even the swish wrought-iron lift was a new experience. The bedroom was small, a single bed, and across the corridor was Bill's room, probably laid out the same as mine, not that I ever saw it.

I had a little black dress. A friend's mother had made it for me and it was so well made, it fitted like a glove. I felt SO glamorous wearing it. I dabbed some Ballet perfume in all the right places, checked teeth… no spinach or lipstick attached… Good… blew into my palm to test my breath, and waited. This was IT!!!!

There was a knock at the door. I draped myself on the narrow bed. "Come in."

Bill appeared, dark suited and handsome, not exactly a Rock Hudson, but close. Well, reader, I lay on the bed, dizzy with Bill's after-shave, and we were DEFINITELY on the way to love-making (the word sex wasn't used much, everything was still secretive!).

I never DID find out just WHAT we were on the way TO! Because, after a few chaste kisses, Bill suddenly sprang up and said breathlessly, "If I stay any longer, I will end up doing something I shouldn't!" Having delivered this very 'Noel Coward' statement, Bill strode to the door and vamoosed back to his lonely bedroom. WHAT A BLOOMING LET-DOWN!

What was I doing wrong? Well, I thought, Mum needn't EVER worry about her younger daughter, because she would never err from the straight and narrow, but not for the want of trying. 'THEY' certainly wouldn't get

255

me this time, I was all dressed up for NOTHING!

We had a nice two days, I was introduced to his London landlady and her parrot… But we remained just slightly more than friends. I arrived home at 249 the innocent flower I had been before I left.

Bill had left the Royal Bank of Scotland, and was now training to be a manager of M&S, so he would stay in London then travel back to Liverpool when he could, so he had become familiar with the London layout, something I would never have mastered on my own. We always had a happy time; he was charming and funny.

We had many other times together in Liverpool. Bill and Ray were in a drama group, so I was able to take up position in the audience on a couple of occasions. In one particular play, a Scottish one (I've quite forgotten the title), Bill appeared all kilted up, very fetching. The next was a chorus part in Bizet's opera *Carmen*. This was a lesser part as a mountain rebel-gypsy, so there was much scrambling over cardboard mountains and waving of swords, whilst singing rousing choruses.

We first-footed one new year's eve in Liverpool. There were no restrictions on drinking and driving in those far-off days, so after Bill had imbibed at every house in the area, we found ourselves in the early hours just sitting in the car, cosy and so close. Those small cars meant that you felt very intimate, sometimes a bit too intimate if you didn't know your passenger. There was ice on the pavements and glistening roof tops. We really could have stayed out for the rest of the night, it was probably 4am by then anyway.

Well, we didn't stay. In fact, within minutes Bill started the car and we chugged back to Ray's. Would it be letting the side down if I state that I felt completely fed up. The statement 'lack of intimacy' crops up here; there was a question mark over Bill.

Staying at Ray's house had its scary moments. His Mum, a very strong character, was averse to any 'hanky-panky'; even hand-holding was a sin in her eyes. Our wrists were smacked on one occasion just for holding hands across from one chair to another. I also committed a deadly sin at the tea table. There was a slab of 'best butter', so I reached over, and with my knife I gouged a piece off the slab. Oh DEAR. All eyes turned. "We don't do THAT," Ray's mother said crossly, pulling the dish towards her and out of range of my knife. She then proceeded to demonstrate the correct way to help yourself to butter in THEIR household. The knife had to skim across the butter, shaving off a very thin almost see-through curl, which was evenly spread onto the bread. I found this a bit degrading at the time, but now I realize that money was scarce, and so there were rules. I HOPE I gave Roy's mother some money for having me, it wouldn't have been any more than a pound. Perhaps it was cheeky of Bill to ask me to stay.

(I often caught sight of a big blue dish on a shelf in the pantry, laden with a joint of beef ready for Sunday dinner, but I was never asked to stay for a cooked meal, and I sometimes felt 'miffed' about that. Ray's mother wasn't going to waste a slice or two of succulent beef on Bill the lodger's girlfriend. So the beef would be cooked after I had gone home.)

Shortly after one of my weekends on the Wirral, I had a phone call from Bill to say that he wasn't staying on to became a manager with M&S, and he had re-joined the bank. The next bit was such a surprise: not only was he changing jobs, he was changing countries! There was a position in Africa, on the Gold Coast not too far from the famous Timbuktu. Bill was to be the manager of a small branch which was virtually in the desert. He would have just one helper, a 'runner' (whatever that was).

We did say goodbye. The parting took place in a train carriage on Birkenhead station. Bill stayed in the carriage with me for so long, I thought the train would start with him still on board. Lots of amorous kissing, but nothing that would upset Mum! We waved and blew kisses, and my last sighting of him was of a tall, fair, curly-haired young man, looking very thin and somehow vulnerable.

I experienced a small heart-wrench, but my heart wasn't broken. However, weeks later, I wrote a little verse about our parting. Here it is.

TRAINS OF THOUGHT.
WE SAT CLOSE TOGETHER IN THAT THIRD-CLASS CARRIAGE
ON BIRKENHEAD STATION, ALL STEAM AND GRIME.
WE CLASPED EACH OTHER, AND I THOUGHT OF MARRIAGE.
(BUT THE TRAIN-DRIVER ONLY THOUGHT OF THE TIME.)
THEN YOU JUMPED OFF THE TRAIN, WITH A KISS OF GOODBYE
THROUGH THE MIST, AND MY TEARS, YOU LOOKED THINNER
THEN THE TRAIN STARTED OFF, AND I THOUGHT I WOULD DIE!
(BUT THE TRAIN- DRIVER ONLY THOUGHT OF HIS DINNER!).

———————◆———————

Life resumed after Bill had departed, and I could concentrate on my badminton. I became a reasonable player. In my short pleated skirt, pretty knickers (always whiter than white), and white 'pumps' (certainly no 'trainers' as now, liquid whitener was daubed on the pumps before wearing), I must admit I rather fancied my chances with the athletic male players, especially my badminton partner at the time, who had the most muscular calf muscles ever.

I did go to a dance with him. In those far-off days, people would drink AND drive and he HAD been drinking. We sat in his car (quite 'something' in those days) right opposite 249. Well, of all places to make a great lunge in my direction, gentlemanly he was NOT! It just wasn't the time or place, OR right. I could just imagine Mum looking out from the bedroom window and seeing the scene of lust. Needless to say, I made a hasty escape, before 'THEY' got me; the 'SEX' police could be viewing this scene too.

We are still friends sixty years on. Both of us have grandchildren. The drunken fumbling was probably forgotten by my badminton partner, and it has never been touched on since, thank goodness. But I still remember how frightened I was. So I was a true 'GREEN', and I stayed one really because 'THEY' were always lurking in the background.

(There are still 'knicker police' waiting to cart me off if I dare to let any grey or disgusting underwear lie in the lingerie drawer. What a burden, and all because I was brought up to be aware that 'THEY' would get me should I stray from ANY path, be it cleanliness or 'hanky-panky'.)

The club was better and more efficient than any dating agency. Affairs of the heart were being played out faster than a set at badminton; lust, love and laughter prevailed. I will draw a veil over the amorous 'goings-on' because I may offend someone near and dear. The badminton was good. There were matches between the tech college and various clubs. I was in the team and my partner was a very good player. He was a very good-looking man. I fell for him, but he looked on me as a 'jolly good partner and friend' nothing more, so I rather worshipped him from across the court.

If you did well at sport, the College Students Union gave out what were called 'Colours', an embroidered badge with the college crest on it. Quite a few of us received these one evening at an STU dinner. I didn't have many accolades, so this was good.

The club became a big part of my life. The Tech (now the University of Wolverhampton) was a great place, and the building had (and still has) an entrance hall which has always been called THE MARBLE because of its rather splendid floor. The marble is where I met Harold for the second time, although HE thought it was the first!

As well as playing badminton there twice a week, Robin and I had enrolled for a German course. I'm not sure WHY, because we were hopeless. Most of the class were teachers, or ex-teachers, so their knowledge of basic English set them apart from us two lesser educated siblings, and we struggled from the first day.

I think we both realized that we were so much better at badminton, so we dropped out from the German lessons. We stopped long enough to utter a polite 'Auf Wiedersehen'. (The only conversation I had learned was 'I will run around the sports stadium', and 'That is the train station'.)

There were many social events organized by the club. One was a November 5th party at one member's house. Everyone turned up at George's, in suitable gear, trousers and stout footwear, all except George's then girlfriend, who appeared in three-inch heels and a lacy blouse. She got on very well with George's elderly mother. Girlfriend and mother sat in the front room, playing the piano and singing hymns, not quite what I had expected on bonfire night. However, in the back garden, all kinds of demented behaviour was going on. One of our group, Don, had made a giant firework by rolling up a *Radio Times* magazine and filling it with explosives. (I suppose he used gunpowder or something highly dangerous.) Don then attempted to light it!

I think panic reigned in the garden as the paper was lit. A dustbin lid was also involved. To say that the 'rocket' worked is an exaggeration. It spluttered and spat out flames, before dying unceremoniously to everyone's half relief and half disappointment, but nobody dared go near to the smouldering paper for fear of being blown to pieces. Very silly looking back, but such good fun at the time.

FIVE GO CAMPING (AGAIN)

A camping trip to the Lake District was arranged for the next summer. Don the rocket-maker, two girls from the club and Alfie. Nice Alfie was a very good player, he was studying at the Tech but his home was in India.

We intended to cheat a bit and stay at a couple of youth hostels en route, which meant hiding Don's car round a convenient corner, as in those days you couldn't stay at a hostel if you were travelling by car. I hated the hostel's dormitories and communal eating, as well as scrubbing tons of potatoes for the evening meal. It was not my scene.

However, we did eventually find a farmer's field in which to pitch our very basic tents. The rain had started, so we were wet and tired, but we three girls snuggled down into our sleeping bags. During the night, the wind got up, so did WE. With great speed. The whole of the tent just blew off into the air, leaving us lying on the groundsheet staring up into the night sky, soaking wet.

Same disaster with the men's tent. The tents went hither and thither into a far-off hedge, never to be reassembled. The only building in view through the sheeting rain was a derelict pig sty/barn, so we struggled across the wet field to that, as at least it provided a roof. This pig house became our accommodation for almost two weeks. The grumpy old farmer charged us a nightly fee for this salubrious hostelry. We hung the groundsheet up between the girls and the chaps – all very above board.

There was a hole in the stone wall at one end of the house, and every now and then a large snuffling animal would back up to it to scratch its bottom against the rough edges. It was probably a Mr Piggy-Wiggy wondering why we were blocking his way into his comfortable abode. We decided that he probably wanted his home back. Jokes were made about slicing a rasher off his rear when Mr Piggy-Wiggy's bum appeared. We talked a lot about food. The only decent meal was one made from rice and two tins of tuna, a sort of risotto, so bacon was always on our minds. Mr Piggy was living dangerously!

The trouble with this rather bohemian life was the loo or, more to the point, where to dig a hole, out of sight and away from any passing rambler. (I suffered a very bad bout of constipation due to this daily toilet routine.) The other two girls were much more relaxed about it, but loos had always been, and still are, a big worry. There is nothing more buttock clenching than crouching over a shallow hole trying not to get one's private bits stung by the nettles, then hearing the sound of walking boots coming your way and the chatter as a rambling club picks their way along an adjacent path.

Alfie was a stalwart, always twinkly eyed, smiling and fun. He was a Sikh, so wore the turban, which was a source of interest. He gave us all a demonstration one morning on how to construct this headgear. I had no idea that Sikhs never cut their hair or beards, so seeing Alfie bare-headed was a shock. His long beard he wound round and round into a tight curl, then tied the ends on top of his head along with his topknot of hair, which was already in a bun. The long cloth making the turban was swept up in a trice, and like magic, there it WAS, a very smart blue turban. I thought it was the eighth wonder of the world.

Alfie also played an Indian pipe. One morning (I guess the rain MUST have ceased sometime), he was sitting crossed-legged on the grass, playing his pipe, when suddenly, from behind a stone wall bordering the field, there appeared a row of faces all looking astonished at viewing such a weird happening in the middle of nowhere. (I often wonder how often they told this to friends back home.) In the early sixties even seeing an Asian wearing a turban would have been a first, so seeing Alfie, turbaned and piping away, must have made their day, if not year.

Towards the end of our stay in the five-star 'hotel' we saw posters up in Ambleside announcing that the Young Farmers were holding a dance in the village hall. Of course we went (although not Alfie, dancing wasn't his 'thing' culturally or religious-wise, and Don stayed with him, glad of the excuse to avoid what was probably in his mind a 'night from hell'). Trouble was, I had only brought a very dingy brown skirt and my sandals were the sort that children wore, punched leather in a pattern across the toes and a buckled fastening. I would wear these with ankle socks. One of the girls, Joyce, was always very smartly dressed, and would put on make-up every day; she always looked fine. Mavis, the other 'wielder of the spade', wasn't too bothered what she wore anyway.

We set off across some fields and entered the fray. The small hall was crowded with young folks, mainly male, their faces ruddy and weather-beaten. I think we three strange girls suddenly turning up in their midst was manna from heaven. We danced most of the night, and I didn't feel too out of place in my ankle socks. Whilst jogging around with one young farmer, he asked if I would ever think of MARRYING a farmer. I stupidly said that I loved animals and nature and yes I had thought of it. How stupid can one get? "Would you marry ME?" was his question. I'll never know what he was thinking of. Perhaps he was so hard worked and lonely, probably isolated and far off the beaten track, that ANYTHING wearing a skirt was a possibility! I danced on, not knowing what to say, but in the end I said nothing and took it as a joke, which of course it COULD have been (I hope).

We left and trailed 'home' to our pig house. The rain was still bucketing down, but it had been a happy evening, with some very jolly people AND food!

A very pressing problem arose after a week, that of personal hygiene. We washed in stream water, but the mud got everywhere. One morning we drove down to Windermere where there was a very superior-looking hotel on the banks of the lake. We must have looked a bedraggled group as we trouped into the café cum restaurant. We ordered drinks (tea and coffee) and mulled over how to get a bath. I don't know WHO actually asked if we could pay for the use of their bathroom, but it worked because a genteel-looking lady appeared. "Would you like to follow me, the bathroom's off the first landing."

Well, we DID, all of us. The bath was a deep old-fashioned one on claw feet, and the taps were bulbous and stiff to turn. Don had a go, followed by everyone until I tried. And hey presto, water in full flood. (The fact that I have Popeye arms is something I had inherited from Mum, who was able to wring a great bedsheet out until it was almost dry.) I shouldn't really brag about my prowess at tap-turning.

Oh, the ecstasy of a bath! Rather than waste the hotel water, we trooped in one by one and used the same water. After the fifth lot of ablutions, the water resembled brown soup, with 'croutons' of ferns and general debris floating amongst the scum. But OH BLISS! The hotel, to their credit, wouldn't accept any money for this wonderful few hours. I'm not sure any hotel would do that these days.

The Lake District holiday was an adventure that would have pleased Enid Blyton.

There were many more happy weekends camping in Wales with the badminton crowd, days spent on Black Rock beach near Porthmadog, and walks up Snowdon on the Watkin Path. We stayed at William's Farm, a favourite spot at the foot of Snowdon, where, to my horror, the camp loo was suspended over a stream. The sheep dogs were penned during the day. They barked a lot and would bite if given half a chance, not a farm where working dogs were loved and cared for. I hope things have changed now.

One of our very favourite campsites was Cefyn Gwyn in Snowdonia. The tents were close to a fast-running stream, which ran down into a deep clear pool, just right for bathing and swimming – always cold but crystal clear. Romance was always in the air, and many partnerships were forged on the slopes of Snowdon, or in a very wet windblown tent surrounded by ferns and sheep. The times spent there were damp but magical. (I believe Pat was swimming there nude with her three children, only to espy walkers on the bank. True to Pat, she didn't try to collect her brood and run, she stuck it out… Pat was always braver and less self-conscious than me.)

THE EXAM AND NEW STAFF

The old boss, Mr K, eventually decided to retire. Paul was now the only dentist. I suppose I did miss the evening revving of Mr K's car as he tried to back out onto the road from our garage, but I can't say I missed HIM or his underwear.

It was around this time that I took the Dental Nurses Exam. It was a very scary day. The examination was in the School of Medicine in Birmingham University. We had to complete three written papers, and then there was a viva, which I dreaded.

The written work went well, but when I waited my turn to go into the viva, my heart was thumping, almost jumping out of my bosom. Then "Will Valerie Lloyd-Davies please enter."

Three very old men sat behind a raised wooden table-cum-bench. The man in the middle wearing a gaudy bow-tie was holding a human skull upturned in his hand. He passed it over to me. "So, what are THOSE?" He pointed to the inside of the skull. Well, I peered in, and launched off into a great diatribe about the sinus cavities holding the nerves, veins and arteries. It must have impressed, because they all nodded approval. Later there was a practical exam in which we had to mix Zelex, the pink rubbery stuff that was used to make moulds of the teeth and jaws in readiness for dentures being fitted. One poor nurse dropped the pink powder all over the floor, and after cleaning up the floor and benches, she resembled a giant blob of candy-floss. After that, she lost the plot altogether. I never found out if she passed (but surprise, I DID!).

When I opened the post and delivered the good news, I don't think I was showered with back slaps and praise from Mum, who always expected the worst about me and exams. (Many years later, when I passed my driving test first time, I'm afraid all Mum did was shake her head in amazement and say, "Well I NEVER thought YOU would pass." What a deflating statement, especially as she had never seen me drive, let alone been a passenger in the car when I was driving.)

The difficult task arose at the surgery, as we had to have another nurse, so an advert was placed in the local *Express & Star* newspaper. Quite a few girls applied, and we chose Miss A. Miss A was a very glamorous young lady, blonde, and well spoken. She fitted in well and was pleasant to patients. Her parents lived close by, so she could have popped home, but she chose to eat lunch in the office. This lunch was ordered and delivered by her father. I could never believe my ears when Miss A telephoned her father and expressed a wish for a sausage sandwich or other savoury delight. Minutes after her call, 'Dad' would arrive smiling and windblown, clutching the said sandwich.

One particular lunchtime, Miss A peered into the bag, looked in disgust at its contents and threw them into the waste bin. I can't remember WHAT was wrong, but it didn't meet with her approval. This was her way of life. She smoked at break times, and no sooner had she lit a ciggy, than she stubbed it out. I don't recall her ever finishing a whole cigarette. In a way, I would have swapped MY Dad for hers. I just couldn't imagine Dad ever doing anything remotely like that. Miss A was much-loved but a very spoilt young lady.

The uniform worn in the surgery was a white high-necked coat and a starched deep belt, with adjustable holes for a metal clip to go through. These belts certainly showed one's waist to advantage. Our amorous mechanic would view our waists approvingly. "Wasp waist nurse, yes I'll bet your measurements are under 20 inches. I'll get a tape measure." We always outwitted him, or outran him, so he never got the tape around my waist! I suppose today he would be reported to the authorities for 'sexual harassment', but we just shrugged it off.

One morning when putting on our coats, I saw Miss A expanding her belt by using a different eyelet. I gathered she was putting on weight, all those sausage sandwiches. She went on gaining weight, though, so a trip to her doctor was in order. She came back to the surgery looking puzzled. When asked what the doctor had said, she replied, "He thinks I'm having a baby, but I can't be because my boyfriend has never made love to me, so how can THAT happen?" (We are back to the Immaculate Conception!)

Her boyfriend wasn't known to us. She had mentioned him once or twice, but we didn't think she was seriously going out with him. We chatted, and from the information she confided, certainly nothing HAD happened, well not enough to make a baby. Another trip to the doctor's confirmed that she was indeed pregnant, but she still insisted that they had never 'done it'. Well, they must have done SOMETHING! because weeks later she asked me to go with her to the local women's hospital for a check-up in the 'baby department'. I don't think her mother could (or would) have accompanied her, she had a very responsible job, so no time for her pregnant daughter.

We sat amongst rows of ladies heavily pregnant, all called out one by one to be examined. When it came to Miss A's turn, instead of just calling out her forename and surname, the callous nurse called, "Will MISS A come this way." I thought it terrible! In those days, the late 1950s, to be an unmarried mother was a sin to most people, but to give Miss A her due, she seemed to hold her head high.

A few weeks later, after leaving us, Miss A gave birth to a little girl. She had an easy birth (if there is one), but sadly had to give her little daughter up for adoption. Later she showed me a small photograph of her daughter, all that she had left. She could still smile and laugh, however, and once told me, "If you ever marry and have baby, don't do what I did, and keep your nightie ON, it gets terribly messy." I admired her grit. No doubt she was heartbroken, but never lost her smile.

We then had a succession of junior nurses There was a dark-haired olive-skinned Italian who seemed unable to spell. Next was a very religious young lady, who was always in a clinch with her boyfriend. She surprised me by telling me that when she and her boyfriend were at her house one weekend, her father had become very annoyed. because he was trying to mow the lawn around them as they canoodled on the grass! There was also a lot of jumping out of bedroom windows, and climbing across sloping rooftops. He certainly was an agile young man. She was a nice bright girl, who stayed for some time, but left to get married to the Romeo of the rooftops. True to form, they had four children straight off, and we kept in touch for years.

At 249, Dad had been very ill again and was in the Royal. Everyone knew him due to the Christmas present round and also the many times he was admitted as a patient. Somehow this was different. Pat decided to come with me to visit him. She was expecting number three baby. We entered the side ward, and there was Dad, having had an operation to sever some nerves, I think they are called the 'sympatric' nerves. I suppose it was to help with the pain from his stomach and liver. His hands were spread out in supports, and lay on top of the sheet. He looked ghastly. Pat walked in with me, only to be taken all over faint, so she was made to sit in the corridor.

I did feel sympathy for Dad, but not the love I should have felt. This is something I have not forgiven myself for. (I think Mum's daily dose of bitter-aloes about Dad and his 'doings' somehow killed any real feelings. It's a very sad reflection.)

Dad came home after a couple of weeks, and resumed work, and drinking, not to mention the sixty-plus cigarettes a day. He was killing himself slowly, but I didn't realize that at the time. "I think your dad's organs must be pickled with all that drink," was Mum's observation as she made the umpteenth trip upstairs to tend to Dad.

I heard regularly from the Gold Coast. Bill was in charge of a tiny hut which deputized as a bank. He had the 'runner' working for him, and some females somewhere near his tent. He once mentioned his 'black velvets', which I gathered were his girlfriends. I wrote back with updates on the daily goings-on in the UK, and of course 249. His letters became amorous – definitely the 'burn-in-the-grate' type. One of his billets-doux was from the legendary Timbuktu. I had never known where that was, so I lived and learned, but all became fodder for the fire in the little bedroom grate.

Whilst Bill was perusing his dark-skinned ladies, I was busy getting the surgery ready for a move. We were leaving the town and moving out to a Victorian pile on a road only a stone's throw from 249. How wonderful not to have to spend money on the bus every day. There was a big drawback, though, Paul and his wife were moving in upstairs, and would live above the practice. Ellen was expecting a baby.

Soon after we moved, we were joined by a very pleasant junior nurse. She was getting married, oddly enough, to a boy I was at art college with. He had shown great promise and had attained his ATD, Art Teachers Diploma, and was already teaching. He went on to become a headmaster.

Patients came and went, as did a fellow dental nurse who worked for a dentist nearby. She would appear hot and flushed, at the front door. "The boss has run out of oxygen (or sometimes nitrous oxide)… can you spare a cylinder please?" she'd say breathlessly. If we HAD a spare, we would manhandle it down the front steps and into her workplace, and so their gas session could begin. It all sounds very Heath Robinson now, and it certainly was! Somehow no patient was lost during the general anaesthetics.

One nurse did put the wind up one patient who was told that he had to have an extraction. "Would you like GAS or ELECTRICITY?" was her question to an extremely terrified man!

MOVING SURGERY

The new surgery close to home had big worries. The loo arrangements were far from private, something that I found difficult. The back door actually opened into the loo. So anyone coming in from the small back garden or separate boiler/washroom still frequented by Mrs Stokes, who did the weekly wash, could suddenly appear in mid-knicker-pulling-up! There WAS a lock, but it was rarely working so visits to the loo were lightning dashes. Paul never did understand, being a man, so ablutions were performed at Olympic speed.

The next and more important worry was the fact that Paul and Ellen lived upstairs in a large very comfortable flat. Ellen's pregnancy was going well, but she was very tired, so I was quite happy to occasionally pop upstairs and wash up their lunch dishes.

If only helping out had stopped there. The baby arrived, a son, in hospital, and, after a couple of days, Paul asked me to accompany him to the hospital in his car, to fetch his wife and son home. I never dreamt that I would be the person who would be handed the little bundle and then sit alongside Ellen in an ambulance, whilst Paul drove home.

From here on, everything at the surgery went haywire. Ellen was not too well after the difficult birth, so I was asked if I would pop upstairs and bath little James, then give him his bottle, whilst his mother rested. The trouble with this was that it was always after work in the early evening. Having worked a long day, and eager to get home to dinner or go out to play badminton, this disrupted my schedules and my relationship with Paul. I wasn't paid, so it was supposed to be a friendly help, but only when life was hectic for them, not on a regular basis. But this bath and bottle became a daily occurrence, and I began to feel 'put upon'. So, with trepidation, I applied for a job at the Wolverhampton Central Dental Clinic, where myriads of children over the years would trek with fear in their hearts and a scolding parent goading them forward to receive what was in those days was sometimes a basic dose of dentistry, as I was to find out later.

I received a phone call from a woman I had met many times at dental nurses' meetings. She was head nurse at the main clinic. She assured me that Mr L, the head surgeon, was keen on me getting the job, so I could expect a letter asking me to an interview.

I foolishly told Paul. I didn't mention my 'upstairs' life as the reason for my leaving, I just said I needed a change of scene. When he asked how much I might get per week, I told him truthfully that I would be earning eight pounds before tax, which was almost twice what I was getting. I can't say our relationship soured from then, but Paul did bring me into conversations with patients. "Oh nurse MAY be leaving me soon," Paul would say, with a stare at me, and an atmosphere probably felt by the immobile patient in the chair, who would just raise their eyebrows, unable to say anything because of the wodges of cotton wool and a noisy saliva-sucker in their open mouth.

Another rather amazing episode had happened. Harold and his then girlfriend often made a four up at bridge with sister Pat and her husband. With three little children, a babysitter was needed, so I would step into the breach. After one of these late nights Harold and girlfriend would drive me home in Harold's small Austin seven. He would always walk up the narrow path leading to 249, between overhanging ferns, to the front door. However, on this particular night, he bent down, kissed me and said, "I'm going to marry you one day." Never mind his girlfriend sitting in the car on the road, oblivious to his ardour! (I can hear Mum saying "well, I NEVER did. Fancy THAT!")

All this sudden passion from Harold I treated with great suspicion and I shook it off mainly because I was about to accept an invitation to a night out with an extremely pleasant young patient. His reason for asking me out may have been pure sympathy. The day of his appointment, I had argued and fallen out with Mum. I don't know what it was all about, but I had cried buckets and made it into the surgery looking puffy eyed, red nosed, and with no make-up on. I had tended to all the young man's needs, proffered the usual tissue for wiping mouth, and watched him spit into the bowl, delicately, I must add, no noises off. He was a keen cyclist, and we had sometimes chatted, but this particular day he asked if I would like to go out with him.

I immediately thought it WAS because I was looking so distressed that he was feeling sorry for this bedraggled girl. I said thank you but no straightaway, which I regretted because he looked so crestfallen and embarrassed. He seemed a decent lad, and I felt on the same 'wavelength' too. His next appointment was for the following Thursday. I was determined to accept if he asked me again, but now some sort of intimacy from Harold, who had only ever been a friend, just made life so complicated. I was altogether mixed-up, and being a 'dogsbody' upstairs didn't help.

AN INVITATION

Then, on top of all the personal chaos, the phone rang very early about 5am one morning. It was Bill. He apologized, realizing his mistake, forgetting the time-zone difference and so getting me out of bed. I thought I had misheard the next bit. Bill informed me that he wasn't ringing from darkest Africa, he was ringing from Nassau in the Bahamas! The phone call was such a shock… Bill asked if I would go over to stay with him in Nassau, just like that! Quite out of the blue.

When he said STAY with him, I felt he really meant LIVE with him. He then added that he had just taken part in a James Bond film that was being filmed out there, as an extra. "I am just a man sitting drinking in a bar," he said. I wasn't interested in his film debut, I just felt completely dazed. He had everything worked out. He would pay for my flight over there, and my hotel, the lot! Not only was the call a shock, it was also the first time I had spoken to ANYWHERE out of the UK on the telephone, so that was in itself was a first. The contents of this transatlantic call were bewildering and left me red-faced, heart thumping. Bill said that there was no rush to say YES. (He didn't mention the word NO!)

I put the phone down shaking from head to toe. I may have told Mum, but I have a blank, because I can't remember any answer, good or bad, from her. I may have told Robin (not Pat as she was very busy with her three little offspring), and Tony was DEFINITELY left in the dark. However, I DID tell Paul that morning in the surgery. He wasn't at all happy about me going off to a strange land, but said it was up to me.

Next to be told was friend of the family, Harold. He was all for it. "It's an opportunity not to be missed," he said cheerily. What sort of reply was THIS! I felt sad and disappointed that my friend of years, badminton player and sometime partner, was so keen to say 'farewell' to me. So the "I will marry you one day" was just a joke after all?

(I don't know NOW what to make of Harold's support for me going off to Bill, like a lamb to the slaughter. I don't think it was a 'call my bluff' statement… or was it?)

I had time to mull it all over. Life at home was eventful to say the least. Visions of an island paradise, palms and azure seas were extremely appealing. Also it would end the nursemaiding I was doing most nights at work.

The odd thing about it all was that nobody in the immediate family seemed to care a dickie-bird about me going or not going. Were we a dysfunctional family? Oddly, we all seemed to carry on as per usual, battling through giant waves and catastrophic storms; life at 249 didn't get rocked by anything. Nobody said I would be missed. I felt they thought it was a bit of a romance, possibly enhanced by me. I don't think Pat ever knew, she was busy with her little family. Robin may have said something, I'm not sure. Tony would probably say 'good riddance', and Dad… well, I can't say. He wouldn't be let into the 'Bahamagate' intrigue. I don't suppose he heard anything about my possible adventure in the sun.

I lay awake at night thinking about the trip. I had never set foot on a plane, I didn't have ANY money, so I would have to rely on Bill for everything, and that probably would be EVERYTHING!

During the 'mulling' time, I had a letter asking me to attend an interview with Mr L, the boss at the children's dental clinic. The interview went very well, and senior nurse Janet was very positive. I seemed to fit the bill. She was sure I had got the job.

It wasn't long before I received an envelope with an NHS logo on it. I knew it was from the clinic, and I couldn't wait to open it. Pride comes before a fall, however, because I had NOT got the job. They were very sorry and all that, BUT…

I was devastated, perhaps something was telling me to make the trip to Nassau. Was this a sign?

I was at a rather tricky crossroads. I felt that if I DID go I would be in Bill's debt and would have to be more than a friend. He might expect that, and IF I decided to come home, how could I pay the return fare? I was in a cleft-stick. Also there was the thorny issue of a work permit. As someone pointed out, that wouldn't apply if I was to marry him out there and become a 'kept woman'. I didn't love him, but thoughts of sun, sea, and a life of luxury would make their way into my head.

He rang several times, and it was getting to be a great burden. I didn't want to end up a married woman who had only married because of the climate, beaches and lifestyle. I remember crying a lot in private, probably in the bathroom, the only private room in the house (except the outdoor loo, which was too dark and cobwebby to sit and cry, so trips to the 'blue' bathroom became a regular bolt-hole).

Well, I didn't go! I wriggled out of it somehow, leaving Bill (hopefully) disappointed.

I later heard of Bill via my friend and ex-nurse colleague, Celia, who was happily married in Wiltshire. Bill had moved from the Bahamas to

Canada and met a girl there. That is all I know of Bill. He lost contact with Celia after a year or two, likewise his school friend Ray.

I look back on our friendship with mixed feelings. I still have a small cross-stitched little manicure set and a 45 record of *Carmen Jones*, one of the films we saw together in Chester. I hope life has been good to him. (I also had a photograph of him standing beneath Cologne Cathedral, but in a fit of pique, I ripped it up and burnt it!)

So, back to the surgery, and the evenings ministering to the little chap upstairs.

Some time after I had resumed normality, I met the senior nurse who was present at my interview in town, and what she told me rather stunned and angered me. Apparently, Paul had rung Mr L to tell him that I had received a call from a boyfriend in the Bahamas, so I MIGHT be going over there soon, making any position with the clinic a short-lived one. SO I had been dropped from their list! A rather dirty trick. I tried not to let it cloud my relationship with Paul, but it did.

As a post script, the cheerful, rather wholesome young patient who had asked me out DID turn up for his appointment, but I was off ill, and I never saw him again (violins out)! He had lovely cycling calf muscles, I have to say that, and I DID fancy him, not that he ever knew!

FIANCÉES AND JOURNEYS

Back at 249, life was looking up for Tony. He had been courting a girl for months, it turned out, but we never were allowed to ask about her or where she lived. I did find a postcard from Torquay addressed to Tony. Of course I read it, and showed it to the rest of the assembled family, it was signed 'LOVE' and a scrawled name. This was his beloved! We replaced it back on top of his books, hoping that he would never know that we had all perused it!

Some months later, to the surprise of everyone, he brought his lady-friend home to see Mum, and to introduce her as his fiancée – they were engaged to be married.

According to his wife-to-be, when telling the story years later, Mum had been typically gracious and had chatted (china cups out). When the time came for Tony to take his fiancée home to her flat, Mum had proffered her hand and said, "Do come again, won't you?" As if this visit was a one-off.

Dad didn't find out until later in the week. "Nobody tells ME anything," he had said. Dad was never at home to be asked anything, and Dad and Tony were still not talking anyway. I don't think they ever DID engage in any conversation again.

Robin also had a steady girlfriend, a doctor's daughter. Her father was Indian, her mother British. In the fifties and sixties, the colour issue was high on the agenda. We all got to know her well. She came along on canal barge trips with the badminton club and many camping trips with a crowd of us. She was training to be a doctor like her father, and was studying at Leeds University. Robin was smitten. He would take her home from 249, which was seven or more miles away from her house, then walk home in the early hours. True love.

Again I had to share my bedroom, but only occasionally when it was too late even for Robin to get her home. I had never encountered a bedroom-sharer who knocked on the door before being invited in, but K always did.

She was extremely pleasant, and we all liked her, but being half Asian made her sensitive and sometimes aggressive about the mixed-race issues of the day, especially after having a drink, which was often, and sometimes too much. She had a chip on her shoulder about her mixed parentage. She suffered bouts of asthma too, which were frightening. I never saw her during an episode.

Robin and K became engaged, much to the delight of K's mother, who was (we all felt) rather too keen on her future son-in-law. Again a solitaire diamond ring graced the bedside drawers and letters flashed from Leeds to Wolverhampton and back. Robin sometimes visited her there.

What happened, we'll never know, but K suddenly called the engagement off. Devastation all round. She qualified as a doctor, and very soon after, married a journalist. K and her husband had a little girl, and K seemed to settle down. She became a GP. We didn't see her again.

What happened next was a very black time for Robin, who was always the quiet sibling, never being vindictive or showing animosity to Dad or to anyone. Wrongly, K's mother still kept Robin informed of her daughter's and granddaughter's lives, which was not good, as she must have rubbed salt into Robin's wounds. We were right in thinking that she was keen on Robin, and probably missed him. She was a pleasant and friendly woman, but her feelings for Robin led to an evening that shattered Robin's life.

I gather that, one day, K's mother rang Robin to say that it was K's second wedding anniversary, and "would Robin make up a four for dinner at their house as K's husband had been sent to Africa on an assignment so wouldn't be there?"

WHY K's mother EVER did such a stupid thing can only be guessed at!

Of course, Robin jumped at the invitation, so turned up at their house. Dinner was all set out, and they began to eat. K excused herself from the table to go to the bathroom, and when she didn't reappear again for some time, her parents went to find her. When her parents entered the bathroom, K was dead.

I can't put any emotions or details into this, as I really don't know what went on, and none of us at 249 ever asked Robin. He did tell us some time later that her doctor father had administered CPR on his daughter for a very long time – hours in fact – but sadly all was in vain.

The funeral must have been the last straw, because whilst K's husband was on his way back from faraway Africa, K's mother again asked Robin to carry out something ridiculous… she wanted him to stay with the coffin in the church – a sort of vigil. This my brother did. The coffin's top apparently had a wreath or spray of lily-of-the-valley, and the perfume was strong. Robin can't stand the smell of lily-of-the-valley even fifty years after this sad and traumatic event. My gentle brother was never the same again.

K's parents brought up her little girl. I would guess K's widower also had a hand in his daughter's upbringing, but we didn't want to hear anything, it was all too dreadful.

Robin suffered a mental breakdown soon after K's sudden death, and it was a very difficult few months for everyone at 249, watching a loved member of the family go through anguish, self-admonishment and depression. It was terrible.

We did find out later that K's death was caused by an embolism, possibly the result of what was then the early contraceptive pill.

One of the songs on the radio at this time was a song from *My Fair Lady*, 'My Old Man's a Dustman'. This Robin would sing constantly, even when running upstairs. This went on for months; I can't describe how upsetting this was. I didn't then appreciate how depression can affect people. He must have gone through hell, but in spite of all this, 249 and its family rattled on along a bumpy disorganized path. Mum never spoke of Robin's breakdown. Friends from badminton were supportive; many had had their doubts in the first place about K and Robin. A few friends didn't like K – her drinking was legendary, and her post-drinking behaviour wasn't good – but to me she was always a nice polite friend.

Months after his breakdown, Robin decided to go walking in Italy and Spain. So off he strode with rucksack and strong boots, off into the sunset for weeks going into months.

A WIN, AND A CONVERSION

Meanwhile, life at 249 was brightening with the news that Pat had won the pools!

She pushed her baby son Peter in the pram, with the other two toddlers trotting alongside, up the Tettenhall Road and into 249 clutching a cheque from Mr Littlewood for £400! Excitement all round. Wisely, she and her husband Ray decided to buy a caravan. This they purchased, and it was transported to a small site near Porthmadog.

Harold helped them set it up, and although it was only small compared to today's 'mobile homes', it served them well, and many happy holidays were spent there.

Another 'happening' was the conversion of Tony! Tony found God. He had married his fiancée and settled locally about a mile away from 249. His wife was a very religious girl, a 'born again Christian', I believe, who had been to hear Billy Graham, the American evangelist, in London, during his tour of Britain. The transformation for Tony began almost immediately after their return from their honeymoon, spent in Pat's pools-win caravan. There was no longer blaspheming or swear words; they seemed to have disappeared as soon as his groom's grey suit was taken off. He became a sidesman in St Jude's church and, according to his wife, they "prayed on their knees together beside the bed every night". Tony had given his heart to Jesus, his spouse announced, and we believed he had…!

Robin was back from his mighty walk around Europe, feeling refreshed and ready for work painting his posters and hanging up billboards. Whilst in Spain, he had joined a group of people, mainly Americans, and found himself on board a large yacht, owned by Truman Capote, of *Breakfast at Tiffany's* fame. Truman was on board, but what went on whilst Robin was there, I don't think we ever asked. Truman Capote wasn't all that known to us in those days; it's only since that I have become aware of his strange lifestyle.

I can't see Robin in that particular set of people, but he WAS, and didn't seem impressed or otherwise. Probably life HERE at home had been far more traumatic than anything he had seen or heard on board the yacht. K's tragic end was with him all his life, and only now, as his memory dims a little with old age, can he mention her name easily. His wife Gwen would hear him calling K's name out loudly when in the bathroom. This went on for years, and none of the family ever mentioned her to his face – too upsetting, this was all a long, drawn-out episode in Robin's life.

I was still at Paul's, in charge, and working with some very friendly and pleasant girls. I had a new boyfriend, a member of the badminton club, alias dating agency! The boyfriend had a Vespa scooter and was an enthusiast. We joined a Vespa club, driving all over the country, taking part in rallies and obstacle courses for riders of Vespas from all over the United Kingdom

The boyfriend was of mixed race, his mother from Pakistan, his father originally from Leeds. However, his father had gone over to Pakistan when working for the railways, and he'd stayed there and fathered boyfriend (I shall call him D) and several more children. D had the most wonderful blue eyes – I suppose that's the Jewish bit!

We visited boyfriend D's granny in Leeds. She was very ancient, but nice and welcoming. Once in her flat, she managed to get us lunch. She consulted her cupboard and produced a tin of strawberries and she also made custard. I downed it all whilst telling lies about how much I had enjoyed it. (I'll never get to heaven!)

After tea, granny went over to a huge metal trunk, opened it and … "Now, my dear, here are all my sets of bed linen, all hand embroidered. It's for YOU, your bottom drawer." So she THOUGHT we were engaged. I tackled D later, and YES, in his eyes, we WERE engaged. Silly me!

National conscription was going still in the UK, and D was called up for National Service, first at Catterick camp and THEN Aden, in the Gulf. Letters again flashed across the seas, in which D mentioned "when we are married" etc. I was dismayed… he even said he hoped we would be able to go over to Pakistan to live!!!!!!!

Oh DEAR! I can say that 249 and all its failings suddenly became a home of warmth and comfort. I tried to say that we were never REALLY engaged (and there was certainly no ring to display), but his letters became more fervent than ever. The time for his return got nearer. I dreaded his arrival.

I had, whilst D was absent, been going out on occasions with Harold. We had been to the cinema, courtesy of Dad, and 249 was a popular venue for Harold to spend time playing cards with the gang from badminton, and we were enjoying each other's company.

D arrived back and there was a very awkward meeting. He stayed for an evening meal – he had gone back to living in his old digs in Wolverhampton. During the meal someone mentioned a film showing at the Gaumont. I tried to ignore the chatter, but suddenly 'blabbermouth'

Mum said, "That's the film you and Harold saw the other night, wasn't it?" I gave Mum a big kick under the table. "Why are you kicking me?" said Mum with absolutely no tact.

Well, it was OUT!! I HAD been with Harold when I should have been 'saving myself' for D! Mum wasn't even conciliatory; she couldn't see anything wrong with her question!

All the bother over the cinema-going seemed to blow over for D, although I was desperately trying to wriggle out of the relationship. I did a lot of 'wriggling' in those far-off days.

THE BIRTHDAY CAKE AFFAIR

My twenty-first birthday arrived.

The surgery celebrated my day. Paul opened a bottle of sherry (no champagne in those days) and the girls gave me their super presents, and Paul and his wife produced a small red leather suitcase for my travels, hopefully NOT to Pakistan!

Boyfriend/fiancé D was picking me up from work on the Vespa, and we were going to 249 for tea. Earlier in the day, I had been given cards from Robin and Pat and family. Not a sausage from Dad, who was, it seemed, completely oblivious to my birthday. However, there would be a good tea, and, I HOPED, a CAKE. I waved farewell to the girls and Paul, and we drove off down the road feeling excited.

"Do you think Mum will have a cake?" I asked from the windy pillion seat.

"Of COURSE she will. Don't worry. EVERYONE has a cake on their twenty-first," came the shouted reply. So we reached 249, my heart joyous.

Tea was laid, the Harvo loaf (buttered!) came out, as did the Marmite, but NO CAKE! Oh disappointment, and hurt. I still harboured a fancy that Mum would suddenly appear at the scullery door and produce one like a rabbit from a hat… but nothing appeared. I felt so empty, all excitement gone, it was such a kick in the teeth. I hated D for getting me all hyped up for something that never happened, although NOW I realize he was only speaking what he thought was the truth in most families. He obviously hadn't quite understood OURS! Ours excelled in understatements!

Worse still, I remembered Pat's cake on her twenty-first. Dad had got a chef to make one, AND ice it. To me, who was only fourteen at that time, THAT cake was marvellous. There was a rose made from icing, AND (and this was somehow doubly wonderful) a REAL fern-leaf against the flower, truly magic. This sounds ridiculous now, but to me it was truly wondrous!

I did receive some lovely gifts, a Dansette record player from Pat and husband. I played records on this for years, it was a generous gift. I received two Chopin piano records from D, very nicely thought out, as I loved Chopin, and could play a little Etude and 'pieces', but for my ears only. (Still 'for my ears only'.)

Although no cake weeks later, Mum did pay for me to have a very posed photograph at a posh studio. I picked the photos up and felt pleased. The canny photographer appears to have air-brushed some stray hairs out and possibly lines around the eyes, but they were complimentary. I HOPE I thanked Mum for them, but somehow I don't remember doing so, so I may have still been bitter and twisted about the non-existent cake.

Not long after my twenty-first, I had been somewhere with D, and we arrived back at 249 late at night. We walked up the dark narrow path and, to my horror, there was a body lying across the path, feet sticking out from the ferns. It looked like a man.

It was Dad. He wasn't dead, but he was dead-drunk, and was in a dishevelled mess. I suppose I shouldn't say this but I do, because D was a true gentleman. He dragged Dad up onto the steps, no cries of "How dreadful" or "DISGUSTING!" D just helped him slowly into 249, a very gallant act and one I shall remember for ever.

Mum was distraught, and family life crumbled for an hour or two, but it quickly got back on the rails as it always did. (Dad wasn't really injured, no bruises or blood.) Mum gave her observations. "When people are drunk, they just 'slump' to the floor. Drunks never seem to hurt themselves."

At the time, I was horrified, upset and furious with Dad, but now it's a feeling of sadness that he had become so reliant on alcohol. Also, he was ill, very ill, and who knows he may have collapsed with illness and the drink. This combination could have been a bad mix.

I'm afraid, for all of D's help and understanding, I couldn't go on with our rather serious romance/engagement/affair! So weeks after he had been an angel on our doorstep, I told him we were never going to be happy together. This was difficult because we both still played badminton, and that meant D had to watch as Harold and I began a romance after being friends on and off for over six years.

ALL CHANGE

This romance didn't last, though! The club was rather like a merry-go-round, with members continually changing partners. Harold met up with my junior school friend, who was a good runner, very sporty, but who hated to lose and would throw a 'wobbly' pretending to be injured if she was overtaken on the track. Harold upset my apple-cart when picking me up from babysitting at Pat's one night. "By the way, you were with me last Saturday at the Droitwich spa." I hadn't been anywhere NEAR the spa, but Harold HAD, and he had taken his new amour (who was engaged at the time), so I was made the BIG alibi. TUT-TUT! Loads of tut-TUTs!!!!!!!!! I agreed, but nobody ever asked anyway. But it was thumbs down for Harold! An extremely naughty thing to do. Writing this now, I wonder what was the matter with ME – I should have been really angry, but I just took it on the chin.

Meanwhile, Alan, a member of the club, who was a very good photographer, asked if he could take some 'snaps' back at his place. Of course, vanity got the better of me and I went. His house was in terraced row, at the back of the Gaumont, in the 'red-light' area of Wolverhampton. It was a cosy, lovingly looked-after property. Alan showed me into his sitting room or 'back room'. His bounciness and sparkle seemed to suddenly leave him, though, as we walked into the room, probably because there, sitting by the fire, was his MOTHER... "Oh Mum, I thought you were out?"

Soooo... it clicked with me. Was I heading for a photo session with a difference? Or possibly something a little more risqué? I never found out, because his very nice old Mum made us tea and cakes, and so endeth the photo shoot that never was! I never did get a peek at his photographic equipment. We remained good friends, though, and he married a lovely girl, Mary, and DID live happily ever after.

Back at 249, the neighbours living next door in the White House were Hungarians living in Britain after fleeing during the uprising. There were quite a few families living in rather squalid conditions. I don't recall WHY I was standing in their hallway, but I remember looking down at the once beautiful mosaic tiles, only they weren't visible any more, there was a layer of walked-in dirt covering them. Oh dear!

The occupants were very friendly, though. But their treatment of their chickens was rather basic! I was in the bedroom one morning and heard loud squeals and cackles coming from the yard next door. I peered out, just in time to see a poor chicken having its neck wrung or chopped off. I couldn't bear to wait to see what method was used. It was being held over the yard soak-away drain. I suppose it was no worse than Tony doing the same and watching the headless bird stride up the yard all those years before. But we had moved on from those days.

Dad's days at the Gaumont were coming to an end. He was far from well, so whether he was gently retired from J Arthur's band of managers, or whether he was pushed, we don't know. However, Dad did do a locum for some smaller cinemas in the West Midlands.

Robin had bought a little red mini, and would take and fetch Dad on occasions. Robin had also got a girlfriend, Gwen. Gwen was a very good badminton player, and she worked in the offices at Guy Motors but had been on the stage! She had appeared with some famous names of the time. Gwen didn't sing or dance, she was part of a threesome. Her two partners were gymnasts, acrobatic showmen. In their act they would perform various moves involving throwing Gwen from one to the other, Gwen contorting herself into very back-bending shapes in the process! This part of her life is somewhat misty. I don't think Gwen's mother could have heard Noel Coward's ditty about NOT putting your daughter on the stage, because she had been instrumental in Gwen appearing at local clubs, from her teens, and was always keen on Gwen treading the boards. (We never mention this time in her life, she has moved on.)

Tony had become a father, and had now progressed to being a tutor of apprentices at Hobson's Engineering. He was confirmed into the C of E church and became a regular member of St Jude's congregation. He still tinkered with bits of cars and motorbikes, and was a good friend to many. I still wasn't too sure if his 'born again' life was just to please his wife but, for whatever reason, his old life was behind him. He was still interested in guns, however, and collected a few old firearms. This led to a knock on his front door one evening. It was the police. They were checking on everyone who had a gun licence. Apparently, there had been a murder somewhere in the Midlands, so every gun-owner was interviewed! I think it was the time of the Yorkshire Ripper case, but I'm not sure.

Pat was very busy looking after her three young children and spending all the summer at her little caravan. The caravan was a bolt-hole for years, but eventually it was replaced by a low-doored and ceilinged cottage on the Lleyn peninsula, still North Wales. This was at the bottom of a small mountain, Garn Fadryn. Many happy weeks in the summer holidays were spent there.

Pat became friendly with the local village folks, and even found herself being cajoled into their annual sports day against a neighbouring village. So, one sunny (or rainy) day, Pat was at the end of a long thick rope, pulling for all she was worth in the tug-o-war team for 'her' village. Her side won... But because all conversation was in Welsh, Pat suddenly realized that she had been pulling for the opposing village! However, most holidays were spent there, Ray visiting at weekends whilst spending his weeks working in accountancy, and being looked after by Mrs Price, Pat's twice-a-week 'help'. Pat had married certainly not into lots of money, but a man who worked hard and was in a very good financial position, ending up chief accountant and director of a very big Wolverhampton firm of paint and varnish makers, Mander Bros.

Mander Bros. eventually rebuilt the centre of Wolverhampton shopping area, one of the earliest 'shopping malls'. Not a forward step, but that is just my personal view.

I finally decided to leave Paul and work for the county dental services. It was hard, and I did miss everyone, including patients, but it was difficult working downstairs below the family. Everyone said their goodbyes, and I was given some very nice presents. Paul's was a large vase, very much of its era. I still have it (although many years later, a neighbour's little girl knocked it off the hearth and so it's in many pieces badly glued together and never going to hold water again).

Oddly, I can't remember being very sad about my moving on. The mechanic Jim found space for a long-awaited hug and kiss, so he was happy. I took it on the chin (or cheek).

I got the job, but it wasn't starting until the end of the children's summer holidays, so I took some locum nursing work. I went to work for a busy practice two bus rides away. Not knowing the district, I found lunch hours long and boring...

I was in the main high street walking past a very old, beer-and-smoke pub, when a voice called my name... It was Linda, with whom I had lost touch after her marriage. I knew she was teaching in Shropshire somewhere, but this was Willenhall, a very industrial town, not very salubrious. Linda's husband's auntie ran this rather down-at-heel public house, and Linda and her husband were 'pub-sitting' for her during the summer holidays.

Not only was it nice to see Linda and catch up on her married life but, joy of joys, I was invited to spend the lunch hour with them. So I found myself sitting in a room behind the bar, eating bacon and eggs, whilst Linda and husband sat and smoked copious 'ciggies'.

I had lunch with them several times, and so, as a present for having me, I bought what I thought was an appropriate gift – quite a few packets of cigarettes! Non-U now, but all right in the early sixties.

I didn't see Linda again. I met her mother (she still frightened me) and she imparted that Linda had two children, a boy and girl and, to her mother's pride, Linda was now a headmistress 'somewhere down south'.

My lunchtime venue became a source of many questions. Nobody could envisage being seen in the pub in daylight, too grim and old-fashioned, but it became a haven for me, which got my dentist boss shaking his head in amazement. Perhaps he thought I was a stoic and a good 'all rounder' because he asked me to stay on in a permanent position, but I had to decline his kind offer, as I had already got another two-week job, yet another bus ride further on, in Walsall.

COMINGS AND GOINGS

This was a different practice, rather up-market, in a very quiet and leafy area near the local arboretum well known for its winter illuminations, a sort of very mini Blackpool, but more refined!

The boss was a handsome man, but oh dear, he was a controller of the first water. I thought the job was in the surgery, but I was surprised to be told that I was on the reception desk, as head typist, sender of reminders, NHS form 'filler in', booking in patients and, although I was used to hard work and being busy, this was ridiculous.

All this, plus answering the telephone, etc., etc.! The first day I sat at the desk, only to be told by the nurses that Mr S didn't allow us to have our handbags with us, so could I leave mine upstairs in the so-called staffroom? (I say 'so-called' because it was a huge room, with a couple of chairs, no comfort whatsoever – not that I had any time in the staffroom. I have to add that the waiting room was luxurious, palms and conservatory-type chairs – comfort!)

There wasn't a lunch hour proper, though I did manage to get out some lunchtimes to the arboretum up the road, but that was just for a few minutes. I was really feeling the pressure. If I did have a moment to spare, I was also expected to deal with all the X-rays taken that day, so I spent time in the dark room too.

I remember sitting typing. I was no good at typing, and I had never mentioned that I was any good at it during the interview weeks before, but reminders had to be sent out, so I found myself typing about fifty envelopes in between patients. All this was made worse by the knowledge that Harold was on holiday in Norway/Sweden, meeting up with a crowd of folks, girls included. For several months, we had been going out seriously. Auntie Ve knew this, and one night when she stayed over and shared my bedroom at 249, I told her that Harold was going to Scandinavia without asking me to go with him, and anyway, I wouldn't be able to pay anything towards it. "Take my advice, dear, DON'T marry Harold!! He SHOULD take you AND pay for you. He has a very good job, so THAT'S mean of him, dear."

So, after working all hours, upset and feeling disappointed with life in general, I departed, waved off by now 'rebellious' nurses. I never heard if they won their appeal for more comfortable working times and arrangements. I hope so!

Years later, I heard that Mr S had suffered for some time with a brain tumour. I felt very sorry and wondered if the tumour was there at the time, so perhaps he was viewing the world differently.

This was a time I hit rock bottom.

Back at 249, Mum had lost another brother, Tom. All her menfolk seemed to pop off early. I don't think any of her brothers made sixty. Her three sisters were still very close and there were regular trips to see them in Stourbridge. Also Auntie Glad now had the use of a friend's car, so the three aunts would arrive in splendour. They were all big ladies and squashed between them in the back seat was little Uncle Arthur, Glad's husband. He was as small as they were large. He was never allowed to sit in the front of the car, and was NEVER allowed to drive it! The fact that he drove giant lorries across the desert in Africa during the war seemed irrelevant to Glad, she knew best!

We all thought she was rather bossy with Arthur about driving, but later, at a family 'do' one day, Arthur was heard to say, "I really don't know WHAT wing mirrors are for. I have NEVER used them." So Glad was right about Artie and his driving – no need for wing mirrors in the desert, I suppose, but there might have been a passing camel!

'TREASURE' AND SLIDES

Whilst waiting to join the county dental service, I decided to try to reshape 249's front garden. There were too many ferns shielding the way up the narrow path, and the beds had become less defined. Mum was in agreement, so I started, and enjoyed the challenge. The London Pride stayed in situ – there were too many and they were too traditional. I didn't really like them, but 249 wouldn't be the same without them.

I was clearing a corner just over the brick wall and under a laurel bush next to the pavement, when, OH SURPRISE, a metal box, an old biscuit tin, was lying almost hidden by shrubs. A passer-by must have thrown it over the wall. My day had come! I was about to find my treasure, a dream I'd had from childhood. Glittering diamonds, sky-blue sapphires, and ruby necklaces, not to mention cash. I pulled it out from its hiding place, and opened the rusty lid. I had the BIGGEST let-down possible! It was stuffed full with condoms, USED ones at that!! I just stood feeling that somehow that box and its contents, summed up my life.

To make matters even worse, Harold was anxious to show his colour slides of his holiday to all and sundry, something I would rather he didn't do. But he was excited and Norway and Sweden, mountains and wonderful scenery, were new to most of the assembled crowd.

So we all gathered in the front room at 249, chairs arranged theatre-like. Harold set up his automatic slide viewer, and he was off. Not half as 'off' as ME! The scenes were snowy mountains, sparkling rivers, AND Lilamor, a Swedish girl, a beauty, wearing a spotted headscarf wrapped casually around her lovely blonde hair. Next there was Lilamor, half dressed, washing by the side of a stream… Lilamor in shorts walking, and a snap of the grass roofed 'house' where ALL the crowd were staying. Lilamor appeared to be doing bloody everything!! I hated her with real venom!

How I sat smiling through that, I'll never fathom, but I did! Harold meanwhile was totally unaware that everyone was gawping at his 'jolly' snaps, whilst I was going through a VERY humiliating hour.

We had two 'showings' of his slides, so humiliation doubled. Harold couldn't understand my fury and embarrassment. He still doesn't!

CHILDREN'S DENTISTRY

To be a dental nurse working for the county, I had to be measured for a uniform, all navy, very boring. A 'measurer' chap arrived at 249 and sized me up. There was going to be a brimmed navy hat too.

My mind wasn't really on my new assignment. In a way, I dreaded it, but the pay would be so much better. When I had my interview, the chief nurse, a grumpy, plump woman, told me that because I had my Dental Nurses Examination, my salary would be a few pounds more than given to a nurse who was still studying, so I was excited about the princely sum of £8 and 12 shillings a week.

I started, but getting to the clinic where I was based was a three-bus ride. The clinic staff were all departments, baby clinics, women's health, and the dental suite.

My first surgeon was a Mr J. He was as old as Methuselah, with a quite bad tremor! The schoolchildren flocked in, mainly from primary schools in the area. Mr J's dentistry was even worse than old boss Mr K years before. Fillings were horrendous, although usually in baby teeth.

The children were terrified stiff and sat rigid in the chair. Mr J's banter consisted of "Does your mother love you?" When the child replied a faltering "Yes", "Good job SOMEBODY does," Mr J would say. This remark was standard chat to all the quivering children. He wasn't unkind, merely of his age. He once told me during a break (of which there were many, so unlike working for a private surgery) that his grandfather remembered the last public hanging, back in about 1823, so dark-age stuff, but that's how old he was.

He wore a homburg hat, always ate at lunchtimes in the same café, a mile away, driving there in a little Morris car. "Goodbye, nurse," he'd say as he put the lights and heater off, regardless of me left in the empty surgery and too far to go anywhere for my lunch!

We would visit schools, where the children would line up, open wide and be dismissed. But on one occasion, fillings were given at the school. Mr J had a portable drill, worked by a treadle, the same as a sewing machine. This archaic instrument of torture would grind spasmodically in time with Mr J's foot.

There were many other surgeons, very varied, but all working fewer hours. Sometimes during school holidays, half-days and full days with no patients became the norm. The gas sessions were still in full swing, with children treated rather like a conveyor belt of misery.

I became friendly with a very gentle and refined anaesthetist, a lady GP, who was helping at gas sessions, I think to ease into retirement. This doctor was a lovely person, very caring, with a grown-up family. She lived in Stourbridge, so another nice point! We often chatted over newspaper filled with fish and chips at lunchtime.

(My trip to the local chippy meant standing in a lunchtime queue behind some nearby works 'runner' who had been sent out to get the whole factory's lunch! "Thirty regular chips, ten with cod, and twelve with haddock, please, luv! And... oh yes, two roes. Yes, vinegar and salt. Ta luv.")

The pleasant colleague told me that when newly married she had actually MADE a stair carpet! This miracle carpet was hessian backed using the same method as the punch-through rugs, short strands of wool threaded though the canvas and looped to hold them in. What a feat of endurance, and love.

I liked her immensely, but unfortunately she was no good at administering oxygen and nitrous oxide! Children were sometimes turned upside down when their colour changed from pink to a bluey-black-hue. Panic seemed to reign when my nice colleague was working and I remain amazed that no little patient was ever harmed during these sessions, although of course they may have been harmed psychologically and hated anything to do with dentists from then on.

One day a week I assisted a young, rather handsome dentist who had just returned from his honeymoon. One morning, when alone, he purposely invaded my space, making me dodge into a corner. Alarm bells rang! I couldn't imagine why he would make a pass at me, when he SHOULD be musing on passionate encounters at home with his new wife! He even asked me why I had refused a lift in his car earlier, a very sporty red MG. I was too much of a coward to tell him. I was a goodie-two-shoes, and 'THEY' would have got me.

He was a good dentist, good looking but a womanizer. I must admit he was the only dentist to see me almost pass out whilst he was carrying out a complicated bit of surgery on a teenage girl. I'd seen blood and gore during the session back at Paul's when the poor patient very nearly bled to death, and that hadn't made me feel queasy, but this particular day when he cut through the skin that joins the top lip to the gums, I suddenly had to go out.

Afterwards it gave him an excuse to get close and become touchy.

(Perhaps he thought I had done that 'swooning' act on purpose, but I hadn't!)

(I have heard recently that he is still happily married, with four or more children, so was I being too prudish and green, taking offence when none was meant? Somehow I don't think so… but I will never know, and who cares anyway!)

My journey to and from the clinic was a bind, especially in the bad weather. The winter of 1962/3 was particularly bad, with frost and deep snow. This is when I became a martyr. So full of zeal for doing the right thing and never letting the side down, I decided to walk to work. I think I may have taken bus number one to town, as the main road was passable, but buses two and three were a different matter. I set off very early. It was baby clinic day, the health visitor and staff would be there to set up the scales, baby changing facilities etc.

I trudged for what seemed forever through the snow, actually quite enjoying the stillness and quiet, and the beauty of the snow, and the crunch of my boots. I reached the clinic well before opening time, so I walked around, to keep warm. The snow outside the door was pristine, not a foot mark, so not even the caretaker had been to open up. Nine o'clock came and went, but not a soul turned up. No phone message to say that all clinics were cancelled… so I trudged back to 249, but repeated the experience next day. Only two staff turned up, so a wasted day.

I was helping a dentist at a special school in Tettenhall, about two miles away from home. This time I enjoyed the walk. The frost was so sparkly and the trees, especially the evergreens, made everywhere look like fairyland. Icicles hung from the boughs glistening and magical, so it didn't matter when I arrived at the school to hear that the dentist had rung in to say he couldn't make it due to the weather.

I had a warm cup of tea and returned home to a fire lit in the black-leaded grate in the kitchen, and oddly WARMTH, not an everyday occurrence in a rather draughty old house.

The winter snow and ice continued. Magical and wondrous, but it made travelling to work very difficult and hazardous. The fire in the kitchen was stoked and rewarded the family with tepid water in the frozen bathroom. I could imagine Dad's dentures, which were deposited in a glass on the bedside drawers, would probably be frozen in! Jack Frost made leafy patterns on the INSIDE of the windows and there was chaos on Tettenhall Road. Trolleybuses were stuck, sparks coming from their overhead wires. Residents were out in force digging channels in the snow so that a vehicle could pass if necessary. Shovels and spades were the order of the day. Robin had to dig a great trough the length of our back yard to the back loo (although it was frozen up, so not much action there) but he also laboured making it possible for our animals to venture out.

The cats hated getting their feet wet, but Flossy the terrier loved snow and would roll in it with delight. All the animals were catered for, but the heaps of snow either side of the channels probably looked like Mount Everest to them. Nobody thought of the poor birds. I realize that now. I suspect thousands died during the big freeze. We didn't have bits of bacon, biscuits and mixed seeds as today to throw out, those were fed to the cats and dogs. We never saw tinned animal food, instead they ate scraps from plates, sometimes boiled lights (this was a smell from hell, truly awful when boiling away on the stove, but the cats particularly loved them. Yum yum). Nothing but a few crusts for the birds. Crusts HAD to be eaten up. (I did, but MY hair never curled.)

PIGS AND FISH

The winter and spring of 1963 also saw some very disturbing events going on between the United States and Cuba. The Bay of Pigs stand-off, the Cuban crisis between President Kennedy and Fidel Castro, was in full swing. Not only was I a martyr, I became a hypocrite too. At the back of the clinic a little walk away was a church. I haven't got a clue what it was called. I had passed it one day on a little excursion, trying out a quicker route home. (I had stopped going to St Michael's and All Angels, the centre of choirboy watching and, giggling romantic 'goings-on'.) I thought I had become an agnostic, but somehow the threat of nuclear war looming sent me rushing into this church, sometimes during lunch break or after work. I remember sitting as usual, alone, watching and listening to sparrows fluttering around arched beams on the ceiling trusses. I didn't pray, but I spent time wishing with all my might that these men would see sense, so I suppose it was a bit of a prayer to someone I didn't really believe in… but I probably silently said 'Please God'. What a hypocrite!

Dad had retired completely and was looking very ill. Although he should have been at home at last, I don't think he DID stay around the house for long. He had ulcers on his legs which never healed. Great dollops of black gunge were sloshed on every day, then his legs were bandaged by Mum. He had always used wintergreen ointment on his back, the bedroom had the smell engrained into it – 'my horse liniment' Dad called it.

Robin was still courting Gwen, and had grown a dark beard. Tony was still a convert to Christianity, a state that we at 249 couldn't grasp, and we always suspected that Tony had chosen the lesser of two evils!

Several more families of Hungarians had piled into the White House and seemed happy. The Greenhams' house was now being rented by a young couple, both out at work, so Mum didn't have the opportunity to chat and be friendly.

The end of the three houses, where old Mrs Bradshaw and her middle-aged daughter had lived all those years before, was now home to a couple with two children and a bouncy boxer dog called Dom. The family were something to do with Jensen car manufacturing, I think. The mother in the household was a horse owner, who preferred horses to anything domestic. A neighbour visited once, popped their head round the kitchen door and saw newspaper on the table deputizing as a tablecloth, and just chunks of bread and cheese laid out ready for a lunch, no plates. I'm afraid the newspaper bit shocked the neighbours. I know it wouldn't matter NOW, but in the early 1960s it was viewed as slovenly housekeeping and almost a sin. Mum would have died rather than put paper on the table. There was always a nice cloth and doilies, and if visitors like her sisters came for tea, usually napkins of well-ironed linen. The Roberts clan would always put on a great show of middle-class gentility.

So many changes around 249. The gardens belonging to the rented houses became overgrown, and Mum was finding it a challenge to cut back the hedges. The privet hedge was invaded by the plant that has snow berries and is poisonous. The real name escapes me. Mum's primulas and peonies flowered with vigour, and the William pear tree gave wonderful fruit, in spite of the many pellets in its bark (I hope the lead didn't poison the fruit. There was a hint of madness in the family sometimes – was lead to blame?)

Mum's stolen cuttings of hydrangea flourished against the now crumbling brick wall. The pond had developed a crack, so Mum had fished out the goldfish and rehomed them in an old very large stone pot that lived by the back door. One fish didn't make the move. It developed a list to starboard and was unable to swim upright, passing silently away… Glug…glug! Mum took on the role of 'fishy pathologist' and performed a post mortem on the draining board. She looked up from her dissecting, holding a wobbly bit of 'something' dreadful. "I've found out what it died of." She held the wobbly bit up. "It had something wrong with its bladder!" Mum had become an authority on fish innards!

She also became an authority on the innards of the television set. Mum would quite happily unscrew the back of the telly and poke about inside. "Yes," she'd say, "as I thought, a valve's gone." More tinkering, and the odd knock or two, and hey presto, SOMETIMES the picture would reappear, none the worse for Maude's intrusion! We all told her that she was doing an extremely dangerous thing, poking around inside a TV set, but it didn't deter 'sparks' Maudie; she took no notice of our warnings.

If anything went wrong with any appliance and Dad was anywhere near, it would warrant a sharp kick, accompanied by an expletive, so Mum was always the chief repairer, decorator, scribe, to mention just a few of her talents. As for her pathology work, she was probably correct, as we now know that fish have swim bladders and if these go wrong, it's either a life of floating upside down or on their side, or fishy heaven, having been flushed down the loo!

My school friend Barbara didn't surprise any of us friends when she became engaged to her first and only love, the head choirboy at St Michael's. The week before the wedding Barbara asked her fiancé, his friend Charles from church and me to her house for a pre-wedding drink – tea, none of us knew much about alcohol. I don't think we even found the Christmas bottle of sherry which most families kept in the sideboard!

Afterwards, fiancé, head choirboy, piano-player, organist, and alto-singer, gathered up his trusty bike and walked me home. We got to the gate of 249, and I was about to say cheerio, when he launched into a very upsetting diatribe about not loving Barbara and voiced his thoughts on their coming marriage. Most upsetting. He then said he had always loved ME! I told him it was just the usual pre-marriage nerves… NO, he had ALWAYS loved me. Those few minutes were the most awkward and sad episode that I had encountered in my twenty-something life.

Barbara's intended eventually cycled off down the road, and the next time I saw him, he was standing with his best man turning to look at his bride beside him. Bride and groom were smiling as they walked down the aisle of St Michael's and All Angels church.

The wedding went off well, and the incident outside 249 was never ever mentioned. They went on to have two sons, and their marriage lasted for several years. But things all went wrong, a neighbour's wife was involved in an affair with Barbara's husband, and he left the family home and his two children, seeing them occasionally. Barbara embarked on years of single parenting, working when she could, always cheerful, not bitter, so when in her late forties she was diagnosed with cancer of the breast, the unfairness of life made my atheism even stronger.

Only NOW do I feel I can mention the heart-rending episode outside the gate of 249. The distraught 'intended' and me, completely muddled, feeling a bit of a traitor to Barbara, my best friend. I never told Barbara, even though her ex was never really forgiven for his extramarital affair. Telling Barbara would have turned a knife in a very raw wound. We were chalk and cheese, but good friends for many years.

AN ENGAGEMENT

By now, aged 25, most of my friends were married. I had been a bridesmaid five times. I can't remember Harold actually SAYING anything about plighting our troth, but somehow we knew we were going to get married.

To catch the last of the three buses home, I would walk past Samuel's the jewellers. I would stare at rings, wondering, would we? wouldn't we? I liked one ring in particular, a sapphire and diamond one. It sat on its plinth, and each night I peered at it. The sapphire was a lovely delphinium blue. But we had never looked at any rings together, so I just admired it from afar. However, I had said to Harold that I had seen a wonderful ring, but Harold didn't say anything about an engagement, or even that we would have a look at rings. Somehow it was an unspoken truth, very weird...

I never thought that the beautiful ring might be sold and disappear from its place. However, one evening I stopped as usual, and HORROR, it HAD been sold! There was another diamond ring, a solitaire, in its place!

I felt disappointed, and when Harold came round to 249 in the evening I related the loss. We were standing in the kitchen in front of the fireplace, and Harold pulled something from behind his back. It was a small blue box. I opened it and, to my great astonishment, THERE was MY coveted ring. It was a VERY romantic thing to do, and I was truly surprised and very happy. Mum was in the back room. I displayed the ring, flashing it around to catch the light. I wish I could remember WHAT Mum said, but I can't! There certainly wouldn't have been a joyous hug or kiss, but in Mum's eyes, the sun did shine out of every orifice where Harold was concerned.

I can relate what Dad said, though, when he was told about the engagement. "Nobody tells ME anything," was his reply. I hope he said something nice, but I suppose he thought Harold should have asked his permission to marry his younger daughter. Somehow feelings never rose to the surface in our family.

Next morning I rushed to the clinic and told Mr J that I was engaged. "That's nice, nurse, but marriage isn't all it's cracked up to be."

I don't know if being in a state of engagement gave Mr J some sexual licence, but that lunchtime, before he departed for his usual lunch (having switched off ALL electrical appliances before driving to the usual café), he turned, homburg hat in hand, and related a tale about a friend of his, whose wife had told Mr J (in confidence) that she was frightened to bend over, even in the kitchen, for fear of her husband grabbing her from behind. "What do you think of THAT, nurse?"

I didn't know what to make of the scenario. I tried to laugh as if I understood just WHAT he was saying. I still don't, but Mr J obviously got all excited about his friend's daring sexual exploits in the kitchen! His always shaky hand probably shook even more over his cooked lunch (always lamb chops).

Preparations for the wedding, which was only six months after our engagement, went ahead with a casual air. No worry about the venue for the reception, just a phone call to the Piggot Arms eight miles away in Pattingham, a nice little village in Shropshire. No need to book years ahead in 1963. We decided on a buffet. This was frowned on by friends and some relations, as a wedding breakfast, a 'sit-down do', was usual.

I chose my wedding dress using up more or less all of my national savings. It cost thirty-two pounds, plus a veil, and a hired diamante crown headdress. (If I remember correctly, the crown was 12s to hire.)

Gwen was bridesmaid. Her dress, in turquoise satin, was made by a friend of hers. The little bridesmaid was Pat's six-year-old daughter Sue, wearing delicate pink (made by Pat).

Flowers for the bouquet and bridesmaids' headdresses were Harold's financial contribution to the finery.

THE 'DO'

The September day arrived, dull and cool. Gwen was so nervous she was sick into Mum's hydrangeas, and Dad was so ill he couldn't bend to tie his shoelaces (Mum usually did them up for him). So Dad was wandering about aimlessly, laces dangling, looking grim, arms outstretched for someone to fasten his collar studs and cufflinks.

The three aunts arrived like galleons in full sail, and immediately took up time in the blue bathroom, all cramming in together. Marj was heard to say, "Hurry up, Maudie, it's nearly time to go." There was laughter as they all jostled to get to the mirror to dab on more panstick.

Never mind the fact that the BRIDE hadn't even spent a penny yet, or glammed herself up. The bathroom was completely out of bounds, filled with four big ladies, all weeing and laughing and powdering their noses. It verged on mayhem!

There was nobody to help me dress, as Pat was busy with crying daughter Sue, who had looked in the mirror and realized that her navy knickers showed through the skirt of the pink dress. Daddy Ray was sent off to find white ones from the drawer back home. He didn't know where to look, so the delay sent everyone into a panic! I eventually got into the bathroom, had a quick wash, and applied just lipstick and no other make-up.

Everyone except Auntie Glad left in the first car, leaving Dad upset because the button-holes had all been taken by other menfolk and he was without one! Someone had kindly fastened his laces at last, so off we set. So we set off down the narrow path, Auntie Glad walking behind holding my dress off the ground, Dad at the rear, walking very slowly and wobbly. A rather motley line of anxious people all trying to look happy and relaxed on the big day.

We reached the gateway, and there were our Hungarian neighbours, all the families, smiling, clapping and cheering us on our way. A very nice send-off, very unexpected but heartening.

I hardly remember the actual service, it was as if I was in a dream. There is a black-and-white photo of us emerging from the church. I look like a rabbit caught in someone's headlights! I NOW know that Harold had

297

a small brandy flask in his pocket, 'just in case'. Everyone lined up on the church steps – we were a strange crew, but happy.

The reception went well, very informal. Dad who was very ill (and had had to sit down during the church service) suddenly had a great spurt of energy when he espied a bar at the far end of the reception room. So we were all surprised when he zoomed past us at Olympic speed in a desperate effort to get his first drink of the day.

I had made my going-away hat from just a bit of brown net, with a giant artificial orange rose in its centre. I thought I looked the cat's whiskers but, looking back, I'm not so sure! Green suit – not my colour, but I was stuck with it for years after the 'do'.

I felt Harold's mum and dad were rather disappointed that Harold had chosen a girl with a slight heart problem. I think his mother always thought I wouldn't be strong enough to bear Harold's children, so the 'violins were out'. However, they saw us off with smiles and good wishes. The aunts all looked statuesque and 'posh'. Mum, the smallest of the sisters, wore a powder-blue suit. (This blue was always called the 'Roberts blue' by the aunts for some unknown reason.) Her hair (which had never seen a hairdresser's since the thirties, when she had endured a permanent wave involving electrical 'plugs' and the fear of imminent electrocution) was slightly blue too, to match her outfit. Mum always used a hair-dye called 'A hint of a tint', and so it was!

Maudie looked very stylish and happy talking to all her relatives and friends. Also, she was probably rather pleased that I was now being cared for by Harold, who could do no wrong in her eyes. The fact that he was 'comfortable' rounded it all off!

I had ordered a bouquet of flowers for Mum, to be delivered after the wedding day. I hoped these flowers would say 'thank you' to her for whatever trouble I had been over the twenty-five years. She never DID say if she received them. I had to ask after our honeymoon if she HAD got them. Yes she had, but she was somehow too embarrassed to say anything nice. No hug or greeting kiss or praise, and worse, no thanks for the bouquet, which at the time didn't upset me, but later it somehow contrasted with other mothers of the bride.

There had never been a motherly hug to her departing younger daughter, and there wasn't a hug on my return. I suppose if she HAD, I would have been rather surprised and embarrassed, although she and her siblings were all very tactile, and hugs and kisses were the norm between them.

(The difference showed up when we arrived home from honeymoon and dropped in at Harold's parents. Ethel kissed us both, and was so delighted that we had enjoyed our honeymoon.)

I stood red-faced, totally embarrassed, and I remember saying to Harold that night, "I felt AWFUL facing your mother today, she must have known WHAT we had been doing." I can laugh now, but, to me, parents and sex never mixed.

However, THE day was a truly lovely day. Most of the badminton club were there, ex-girlfriends and ex-boyfriends, all together, chatting and looking very happy. Paul and Ellen were there too, and ex-nursing colleagues.

I don't think I ate anything at all during the reception. I was too nervous and excited, but we cut the cake that Auntie Glad had made and iced for us.

On top was a little silver flower-holder, courtesy of Auntie Ve via her wealthy friend Doss, who owned an antique shop, filled with sweet peas. Auntie Glad told us how worried she was, because the last time that she had made a wedding cake for another niece, she had kept the cakes on the cellar shelf, and OH, when she cut it to level it off ready for a layer of marzipan, a veritable regiment of ants had marched out… so it was with bated breath that she watched us slice into our cake…

Not an ant in sight!!

So that endeth the wedding, and the holiday beckoned.

I was a bride with absolutely NO money. I had drawn every penny out to pay for my dress and veil (which I'm ashamed to say, ended up years later draped over the gooseberry bushes to keep the birds off). I couldn't have bought a cup of tea en route! So Harold hadn't married me for my money.

In fact, our total bottom-drawer items were just two dessert spoons made in Sweden, sold at James Beatties the 'posh' shop in town. Even these were not mine, Harold had bought them in anticipation of home-cooked puddings.

I'm convinced that people didn't express their feelings and emotions back in the 1960s. Certainly not as they do today. Harold never said that his bride looked gorgeous or beautiful (… perhaps I DIDN'T!). Year and years later, I asked him if he thought I looked 'OKAY'.

"Yes, I remember your teeth shining through your veil," was his reply.

Oh well, thank God for Colgate toothpaste, is the only answer to that statement!

THE GETAWAY

The honeymoon started in Cheddar, in a big hotel with cold bedrooms, squeaky boarded floors and a bathroom down the corridor, with a great bath sporting bulbous taps.

I had a nervous time unstopping the bath plug-hole, as so much confetti had stuck to my skin and congregated in a great blob in the drain that the water remained static. I suppose young brides today would be IN the bath with their beloved, or at least they would call the groom to help gouge out the confetti from the plug-hole. But this bride was far too green and innocent to be seen naked even by her new husband. I suppose this reads as rather ludicrous, but in 1963, there WAS a sexual revolution, but I wasn't part of it! I don't regret this. The excitement of the honeymoon's first 'proper' night together was hilarious, lots of suppressed giggling, and a happy time... Anyway, 'THEY' couldn't get us for sleeping together, because at LAST we were MARRIED.

Next morning, an embarrassing event took place. Harold was sitting on the edge of the marital bed putting his socks on, when BANG! the bed took a dive, as one of its legs broke in two pieces. To his credit, Harold braved the staff's obvious mirth as we left after breakfast for the next bit of our two-week trip. I hid in the car, almost crouching below windscreen height, avoiding any contact with anyone. The receptionist had reassured new husband, saying, "Oh THAT leg has been stuck back on twice already, so PLEASE don't worry, Mr Hampton." Mr Hampton wasn't very worried, it was Mrs Hampton who felt embarrassed at the thought of all the smirks going on amongst the cleaners having swept up piles of confetti and seeing the poor old bed demolished!

The honeymoon progressed well. There was a treacle tart to die for, home-made by a chap called Rex who ran a B&B near Falmouth. A fishing trip 'made for two', during which we caught two shiny rainbow-striped mackerel. We didn't know WHAT to do with them, so we dumped them on a cottage doorstep where we had previously seen a very thin cat.

There was a two-night stay in an annexe of a super posh hotel in Port Lowe. The annexe turned out to be a terraced house up a nearby hill, run by a retired hospital matron of the old brigade. The bedroom had a wash-hand basin in one corner, with a large notice over it proclaiming that 'NO HAND WASHING OF CLOTHES IS ALLOWED IN THE BEDROOM'. In one corner there was a partitioned cubicle, the loo. Every tinkle of wee was audible in the bedroom, and trying NOT to pass wind was a constant worry to me who was new to an intimate life, and trying to keep buttocks clenched at night spoilt the two nights for me. (How an hotel with a good reputation could allow the annexe to be so basic was a mystery.)

We ate our meals in the hotel, and were just about to bash the top of a boiled egg when two residents from the other side of the room suddenly waved. The man was an old school colleague of Harold's with his wife, someone I knew by sight.

"SAW A PHOTO OF YOUR WEDDING IN THE *EXPRESS & STAR*!" they shouted. All eyes turned our way. This drew the attention of a member of staff who had said earlier with confidence that he could 'spot a honeymoon couple a mile away'. Obviously we had so far got away with anonymity, but not from that moment on! Congratulations were exchanged, so we had been 'rumbled'.

Halfway through the holiday, Harold thought we should ring to check that our rented bungalow would be all right and to confirm our dates of return. This bungalow belonged to one of the very old and rather shaky school dentists. He and his very nice wife Marjorie were going on a six-month round-the-world trip so they had asked us if we would like to rent their bungalow for the six months, as the date of their holiday exactly coincided with our wedding and first months of married life. It was a perfect solution, as we had bought a house that was extremely run-down and needed a lot doing to it, so the six months fitted perfectly.

So, six days into the honeymoon, Harold rang Mrs Dawson. After the usual chat and good wishes, Mrs Dawson enquired, "How's Mrs Hampton?"

Harold hesitated then said, "Oh, I ASSUME she's all right. Well she certainly WAS all right at the reception, but I haven't seen her since."

WRONG Mrs Hampton! He had only thought of his mother, Mrs Hampton senior. Apparently, there was a pause at the other end. I never DID find out what was said then. Mr and Mrs Dawson may have wondered what was going on but they would definitely have laughed.

A BUNGALOW AND FRIEND

The bungalow in a village near to Wolverhampton was quite luxurious, three bedrooms, breakfast room, centrally heated, which was something neither of us knew anything about. So no more frozen glasses of water by the bed.

We were paying Mr Dawson 3 pounds 5 shillings a week to look after the house and garden, plus a very beautiful Siamese cat, Tai Lu. We fell in love with her straight away. She was cross-eyed and she sported a slightly kinked tail. The Dawson had a very old Alsatian dog too, but their son Richard was taking care of her, which was just as well, as the old dog died soon after her 'Mum and Dad' left for their mammoth holiday. So by caring for Tai Lu, we began our love of Siamese pussies.

The house was full of antiques, and one piece of furniture in particular, a Queen Anne table, became my project. The whole oval top was covered with grey rings caused by putting hot pans etc. down straight onto the wood, something quite terrible in my eyes.

The Dawson were not house-proud. The whole house lacked what Mum would call 'elbow-grease'. Nothing was polished, the bathroom tiles were thick with grime, and the joints between each tile were black and revolting. In fact, it was several days before I could bring myself to slip down into the bath and THAT was only after having a scrape and scrub around the taps and soap dish.

We had been there some weeks before we realized that there was a small hillock in one corner of the large living room. We lifted the carpet to disclose a great pile of Dawson family photos. Mrs Dawson obviously didn't know what to do when a multitude of holiday snaps arrived back from Kodak, so until she could get an album going, she had just shoved them all under the edge of the carpet, out of sight and out of mind! I don't think the album ever materialized!

What WAS an absolute bonus was something neither of our homes had provided, alcohol! The antique cabinet was full of spirits, liquors, sherry and gin! I can't say we 'hit the bottle', but the Drambuie was a favourite little drink, and a small tot became our regular evening tipple. Of course we knew we would have to replace anything, but the day of reckoning was six months away!

We had a party in the bungalow, with all our badminton friends, who wondered at our luxury home. We Hoovered and cleaned the whole place, and the table was slowly brought back to something bordering on lovely. Although it was a bungalow, it did have one small bedroom up some stairs. We kept all our wedding presents in there.

This was a very happy time in our lives. It was also the scene of some 'upstairs romance' as I never liked being downstairs in bed in full view of the senior school children passing the bedroom window.

Paul had asked me to work part-time back at the surgery. I was pleased to be back, although the times were awkward and included Saturday mornings. I had left the county dental service very disgruntled, having been assured that because I had the State Registered Dental Nurses Examination (in the first batch of nurses to have it under her belt, as it was relatively new) that my salary would be £8 or more. But this never happened, and even after asking the head of department about the delay, the subject was rather avoided and I never did rise up to the dizzy heights of £8, but I was still earning more than when working for Paul, so I didn't pursue it.

My sister Pat had three children under ten by now. She would bring the family over to visit us, driving her little Morris seven car (apart from Auntie Glad, she was probably the only female in our close family to drive). Her three children would stampede in and head for the cellar, where the central heating boiler was. They were fascinated with the cellar, its darkness seemed to thrill. However, it wasn't in the same league as the cellar at 249, which WAS spooky, cold and smelled of damp. This was cement, with electric lights, and dry!

Tai Lu wasn't used to little ones, so would jump up into her favourite place, the third shelf of the airing cupboard, which was in the breakfast room. She would peer down imperiously. One day we had quite a worrying time over Tai Lu. She must have jumped down out of her cupboard 'perch' and banged her nose, which rose up into a large bump and she began to snuffle with restricted airways!

I was so worried I kept her in a cardboard box IN our bed, for two nights so that I could watch over her. It was a constant anxiety that 'something' disastrous would happen before the Dawson arrived back. She was fine, and soon back to her loud rendering of 'please let me in' when clinging on to the windowsill by her front claws… The putty was deeply marked all along the window, caused by her desperate quest to be let into the warm room. She could never stand the cold weather!

She was, like most Siamese, very keen on sitting on top of doors, even balancing precariously whilst the door swung open – she never did fall off. The wardrobe was a very popular sitting place too. In fact, any high vantage point was a 'must' for Tai Lu.

Her toilet habits have to be mentioned here. One working day, we had left her in the house for rather a long time. We didn't have a litter-tray. (Had they even been invented?) At 249 we probably had what we would call a 'dirt tray', just a box filled with earth, but Tai Lu had neither. The time inside must have proved a problem, so, being the intelligent feline she was, she found the fire grate in the breakfast room. There were cinders in there from a coal fire and also a plastic beaker that had been thrown in to burn later…

We arrived home, rushed in to let her out, only to see that she had 'been'. The poo was placed on the ash and cinders, and she had weed INTO the beaker, which was half full! She sat 'smiling' down at us from her high shelf, VERY pleased with her neat work!

Very occasionally, Mum and Dad would arrive, brought by Pat or Robin. It was sad to see Dad looking so unwell. I don't remember him commenting on our rather splendid temporary home, but I'm sure he did, And I think I made a meal for them. This would probably end with a sweet. Just a packet of Angel Delight, a real favourite in those days… caramel flavour was the best! Our venture into the Orient was a ready-made packet of Vesta Beef Curry or a packet of Chow Mein! We thought this cuisine was quite daring, and certainly it was no trouble to cook!

The aunts all came to visit too. They all knew the Dawson family, who were originally from a village near to Stourbridge. Also, the friend of Auntie Ve's who ran an antique shop in Stourbridge had sold most of the furniture to the Dawson. This furniture, especially the table, began to look 'cared for'. I enjoyed polishing the wood and seeing the colour gradually return and the grey rings disappear.

TWO DEATHS

We had been married almost three months and were playing badminton in the college gym when someone came in, breathless.

"President Kennedy has been shot… he's dead!"

It IS true that everyone remembers when and where they were when this news reached them. It was so shocking, out of the blue, and it was the only talking point in everyone's lives for days and weeks.

Just after President Kennedy's assassination, Dad became ill again. He looked very yellow and was in pain. He was ill so often that I didn't feel too alarmed. He was in his favourite ward, Mallet, in his favourite hospital, the Royal, where he had for many years given out gifts at Christmas time. The sister in charge at the time was Janet, an ex-girlfriend of Robin's. She seemed very grim about Dad and told us that he had been 'seeing things' and hallucinating. He had survived so many bouts of serious illness during my lifetime, so somehow I wasn't as worried as I should have been.

We took it in turns to visit Dad, and one evening we rang Mum to ask who was going. She told us that nobody could make it so we drove over to the hospital to break up his lonely evening and pick up his pyjamas etc. for Mum to wash.

Dad was sitting up, propped on pillows. His breathing wasn't as bad as I had heard in the past, but he was very yellow. He leant forward and, after chatting a bit, he suddenly whispered, very confidentially, "President Kennedy came to visit me today." Dad was convinced that Kennedy HAD visited; the drugs were making him hallucinate. It was almost funny. We chatted on, telling him useless bits of the 'goings-on' back at 249.

He listened and then said something very disturbing. He leaned towards us and said, "Do you think I have been a VERY bad man?"

It took us aback. "Of course NOT," we reassured him, but it seemed to worry him greatly.

He then added, "One of the cleaners here, who used to be an usherette at the theatre, said that I wasn't a bad man… she thought I was a good, but I don't think so… do you?"

What a sad, befuddled question, and I can hear his voice now. How terrible that he had to ask that intimate question of a lady he hardly knew.

We muttered and mumbled something, about "of COURSE he was good and HAD always been a good man and all was fine."

I kissed him goodbye, and Harold shook his hand, and he waved weakly as we left the ward. There was no knowing what was going through his unsettled and drug-filled mind. I have felt sadder about his question more and more over the years. Who knows what we would have done in his shoes?

Very early in the morning after our hospital visit, the tenth of December, three months to the day since our wedding, the telephone rang. Harold shot out of bed. I could hear his hushed voice in the hall, but I still didn't think anything was wrong.

Harold returned and sat on the bed. "That was your Mum on the phone. I'm afraid your Dad died early this morning."

Well, my Dad, LD, was gone.

I was so glad that I had visited him on his last night on earth.

The old Welsh saying AN ANGEL AT THE ROADSIDE, BUT A DEVIL AT THE HEARTH fitted my Dad, LD, to a tee.

Of course, we jumped in the car and drove over to 249. A strange blank floats in here. I can't remember WHO was at the house, except Mum, who was as stoic as ever, but I could see that she had been crying. No doubt Tony, Robin and Pat would have hurried there too to be with Mum, but because Dad had never dwelt for long IN the house, his absence wasn't apparent in the days after his death.

I think we all questioned ourselves silently over our relationship with our father. Difficult as he had definitely been at times, had we ever REALLY understood his illnesses and what it must have been like to undergo many varied operations. His death was caused by heavy drinking and smoking. He had smoked from his early teens, so it was his abused liver and lungs that eventually gave up on him, so I suppose he killed himself, in a way.

Dad's death was announced in the *Express & Star*, a column and a half, quite an obituary. He was so well loved by ex-staff, drinking friends, and non-drinking friends. Also the nurses and doctors at the Royal Hospital where Dad would spend Christmas Day handing out presents to the little patients. The Limes TB hospital also remembered LD for his many trips, loaded with gifts for the children on their wards. These presents were all bought with kind donations from cinema-goers, and I think Dad was one of the first managers to do this. I think it was his idea originally, then taken up by other cinemas.

I never found out what Tony thought of his father's death. They hadn't really spoken for many years, the animosity over Tony's savings being 'bagged' by Dad never went off the boil, and Tony couldn't forgive Dad. (Or perhaps Tony DID when he became a Christian, fully confirmed, and a sidesman in St Jude's church?)

Robin was elected to arrange Dad's send-off. Again, this was in St

Jude's, where all our christenings, marriages and funerals took place.

So twelve weeks after walking slowly down the aisle hanging on to his daughter's arm, Dad was carried down, with full ceremony, to be cremated afterwards at Bushbury near Wolverhampton. Dad's older brother Reg's grave was also in the graveyard at Bushbury. His grave is still unmarked, just a number, and a small unevenness of ground where he lies.

Years later, when I was depressed and had to visit a psychologist, I mentioned Dad, and all the rather callous thoughts about him that I occasionally harboured. I felt sorry about everything that had passed, never saying we loved him, never actually hugging him, how we sometimes laughed AT him, not WITH him.

She listened and then came up with an idea that I felt was rather silly and quite dotty! She asked me to write my long-dead Dad a letter, explaining everything that had been wrong in our relationship. Also to write how much we DID love him and had forgiven him everything. Then to BURN IT, letting the ashes go up the chimney and away into the air.

Well, I DID, and felt so relieved afterwards, so strangely it worked. I didn't tell any of my siblings about this rather crazy letter. I know Pat would have been very sceptical and tetchy about it. Her relationship with Dad had been very 'formal' and not good. Robin was much closer to Dad, and was never caustic or vitriolic about him as we sometimes were. I think Robin missed Dad most of all.

Widowhood appeared to suit Mum, who had never had the nerve to travel on her own. In fact, all forms of transport would give her a panic attack. The Midland Red bus to Stourbridge was a terrifying journey for her. She would clutch the seat in front with white knuckles, hardly able to speak.

However, shortly after Dad's demise, Maudie boarded a black-and-white coach and was whizzed down the motorway to Cardiff, where Dad's younger brother Ray and his wife Cissie lived. There she stayed for a fortnight, before being whizzed home to 249, none the worse for her adventure. In fact she was rather blasé about the whole thing!

We were astonished! Suddenly her fears of anything on wheels had evaporated and she became 'Maudie the traveller'. Nothing TOO far, certainly NOT abroad, but with sister Glad driving and Marj and Ve alongside, and little Arthur perched between them in the back, Britain became her oyster (or as a family saying goes, her lobster!)

Life back at our luxury abode was very happy. Tai Lu the cat was a wonderful, if rather loud, companion. I was hardly working, only Saturday mornings, dealing with the piles of NHS dental forms. There were columns and columns of figures to add up, every dental procedure had to be charged, so looking back, I'm surprised I managed it, as my maths was and IS terrible!

RUTH

Friend Ruth had given birth to her fourth child, a boy, so she now totalled three boys and one girl, Bryony. They still lived in Wales, but we corresponded regularly, as was usual in the sixties. I loved letter writing, as did Ruth. (I have always suffered from 'verbal diarrhoea'.) I became godmother to one of Ruth's boys, Adam.

Not knowing anything about small newborn, I held him over my shoulder during the church service. Adam did what most babies do when upturned. He was sick all down the back of my new and precious suit. Later, I took it to the cleaners, but even then, if I turned my head, a slight whiff of milky-sick rose up from the shoulder area.

Ruth became a rather strange mother. She admitted that she adored the baby stage, but not the toddler or older stages. She ruled them ALL with a rod of iron, and on one occasion when she was reprimanding her youngest son for waking her up because he was crying with toothache, her scolding and then the march to the bathroom to get some soothing gel struck fear into both of us, who were sleeping downstairs in a sleeping bag on the floor. Instead of gentle motherly words, Ruth was shouting, and angry at being woken up, blaming Adam for his toothache – very disturbing.

On another occasion, we were eating lunch with Ruth, the children and her husband. Suddenly, "ELBOWS OFF THE TABLE!" Ruth bellowed. The children AND both of us did as ordered, and quickly! Meal times were strange, because Ruth never ate anything. She would clear the dishes and busy herself, but ate very little, and her treatment of her brood was not a comfortable one.

I can't say too much, but we think now that Ruth was suffering from some mental malady unrecognized by us newly weds. This was confirmed years later.

Robin was now engaged to Gwen, so a wedding was planned for a year ahead, a registrar office 'do' as Gwen was a rather 'lapsed' Catholic, and Robin didn't think they could promise to bring any offspring up as Catholics. So Mum and Robin jogged along together in 249, which was now a rather quiet house, so different from all the previous years.

(Can a house have a 'soul'? My feelings are that the bricks and mortar, and linoed hallway and sash windows that never worked, or when they DID, would threaten to chop your head off if you hung out of the window, MUST absorb something? The sound of children's feet running, the lifting of latches, and then the banging of ill-fitting doors, the shouting, the arguments, the laughter, and lots of tears, must stay, perhaps only as echoes.)

Mum embraced widowhood, not only with travel but with cooking! She became the 'Queen of Meringue-Making' and was famous amongst the family for her golden, cream-filled delights. Along with her crocheting, she also 'tatted', a form of crochet-work. She would diligently 'tatt' around bought linen hankies, so for birthdays and Christmas we ladies received two or three neatly folded and delicately tatted ones, which we usually kept for best, too nice to blow one's nose on! (We have some still!)

There was still an invisible barrier, a glass wall around Mum, so hugging and a kiss on the cheek was reserved for her brothers and sisters, who visited regularly. I would sometimes pop home on a nice summer's afternoon, and there they would be, Ve and Marj, having arrived by the No 1 Tettenhall bus. And hostess Mum (not always Auntie Glad. "Artie always expects his tea on time!" was her excuse. Glad was a stickler for "looking after one's man".) So the other trio of ladies would all be lying back in deckchairs, facing the burning sun, their necks and arms red, beads of perspiration on their brows. As always with the 'Roberts girls', decorum prevailed, so there would be a small 'tea table' covered with an embroidered or 'drawn-thread' (hand done, of course) lace-edged cloth, delicate china plates and cups and saucers that you could see through if held against the light. The plates would be displaying remnants of either a meringue or a very naughty AND expensive Kunzle cake, pink-topped with icing and obligatory cherry! All the 'girls' liked their cakes.

Occasionally, Mum and Ve would go to town and stop off at Patersons, a very select teashop in Lichfield Street, where they would partake of dainty little cakes served on three-tiered cake stands. There was always an air of Victorian/Edwardian gentility about all the Roberts family, and I think they felt 'special', although their young lives had been the kind that the NSPCC would frown on.

Their errant father Ludd hadn't given them anything tangible except genes, and had treated his children extremely badly, but the 'girls' in particular felt a bit upper-crust. I don't know why, but it dwelt in all the Roberts family, though perhaps not quite so much in the brothers, although Doug in later life would order a 'case' of wine, never a single bottle, even when in straitened circumstances.

Grandma Ada, Mum's mother, although from humble stock, also had gentility and refinement. Auntie Ve once told me that some friend of Ada's noticed how thin the girls' legs and ankles were. "I breed race horses NOT carthorses" was Ada's sharp riposte!

All was well at the bungalow. The Drambuie was going down at a fast rate, and so were the packets of Vesta Chow Mein, plus other shop-bought items of food that would probably have had the aunties feeling very superior, especially Glad, who was such a good cook that she used to tell us all "I will be Queen cook in heaven one day, girls." Nobody could make pastry like Gladys. In her later years, a good friend brought Glad some mince pies. "I've BOUGHT the short-crust pastry, Glad… can't waste time making it." Glad ate it politely, in fact polished it off, but as soon as her friend had gone, "NOT a patch on home-made pastry. Fancy BUYING it!"

The garden at the bungalow was very wide, with a good lawn and beds. I loved it, and worked on the flower beds with pleasure. Harold's caretaker at the office also helped occasionally with any difficult jobs. The Dawson had treated the garden as they had the house, with a lack of 'elbow-grease'. However, a lot of that went into it during our six months there and it began to look well cared for.

Outside the front door was a very old walnut tree. It never had even one walnut whilst we were tenants, but its shape and gnarled bark was to me (who had never seen one before) to be pointed out when we had visitors. It resembled one of those trees popular in ancient Asian paintings.

The house we had bought, or rather Harold had bought, with the help of Syd, his father (who very generously loaned us a thousand pounds), was a wreck, so needed a lot of work to get it vaguely habitable. The buying of this 1935 house was unusual, to say the least, as were all the houses prior to choosing one because I didn't view ANY! I wasn't part of it!!! Again, I didn't feel any animosity about it, I had no guidelines to follow.

Harold, his dad, plus Roy, a friend and colleague from work, met up on many occasions and went on the hunt. I remained oblivious. I had never known what a partnership was! I truly felt that the husband WAS in charge, so ignorance was bliss! It wasn't until years and years later that I suddenly felt hurt and angry. After all, even a male blue tit or wren shows their 'intended' several likely abodes, hoping his beloved will choose one.

My beloved would tell me that he had looked at 'this and that' house, advertised in the *Express & Star* newspaper, but he would say, "I don't think it's a viable property. You wouldn't like it." So when he DID take me to look at the outside of a house of interest, we just sat outside in the car and it became evident that he and Roy and Syd had already viewed it inside and out during one of their lunchtime trips. "There's a brick wall just outside the kitchen window so it's dark, the ceilings are cracked, bomb damage, and the garden's got a great hole dug in the lawn, probably for a pool. I don't think it's suitable at all," said new husband. I liked it, though, so persuaded Harold to ask for another viewing, WITH ME this time.

Harold was right, it WAS a total mess. The very nice Irish family who were selling up and moving back to Dublin showed us round. The fitted kitchen was a very small room, and the fitted bit comprised a worktop which could be dropped down with the help of a great lump of lead on the end of a rope. The kitchen cabinet was a wooden chest of drawers, with round wooden knobs. Each drawer was painted as traffic lights, red, orange, and green! We walked on. Where the fire grate should have been, there was a pile of small broken bricks. (THAT was the advertised 'Brickette' grate!) The bricks lay around in a heap on what was the hearth. When we reached the bathroom, the lady of the house did make a remark that was supposed to cover the peeling paint on the walls and ceiling. "We keep the washer up here. My sister lives with us, and we have a little girl, so there's lots of washing to be done."

We walked out into the garden and, sure enough, in the lawn was a giant kidney-shaped hole. "Oh, my husband was going to have a fish pool," she sighed. The rest of the very big garden was a wilderness of weeds, dominated by what looked like rhubarb, but was a weed that took over everything in sight. Then, at the very bottom of the garden were wooden stakes and a wire fence, and a railway line, still working as a freight line! All in all, it was untenable... So of course we bought it, and 200 Henwood Road became ours!

We paid £3,450 for this run-down but homely abode.

Harold's Dad Syd enjoyed helping with carpentry jobs in particular. The bathroom airing cupboard had to be extended, so Dad Syd undertook the task. This he did so well, with strong thick wooden beams, that everyone then (and since) decided that, if there WAS an atomic bomb dropped anywhere near, the house itself would be obliterated, but the airing cupboard would be intact, free-standing, defying destruction! Syd did things properly!

The bungalow was still our cosy bolt-hole, still full of surprises. For some reason, we had to move a huge and heavy wooden dresser. Of course, the dusty spider's webs were looped like material, but it was the fat-looking carrier bag that lay there that drew our attention. We lifted it out. It was heavy and some of its contents spilled out. It was a kind of treasure trove, hundreds of coins, all copper, pennies, twopenny bits, threepenny bits and halfpennies, any copper coin minted in the last thirty years was there. Why the Dawson family hoarded these, we never dared ask. We just cleaned the floor and skirting and replaced them; they probably remained hidden for another thirty years!

The six months were almost up, the garden was all done, pansies planted, and the house was pretty spotless., The Queen Anne table looked good, pot rings almost eliminated, just a few engrained ones left.

The house in Tettenhall was still a mess, but we could move in if we used the back bedroom as a sitting room and the tiny box room as our bedroom. We managed to get a double bed into the room – no space around it, though. We had two easy chairs, a wedding present from Harold's firm of quantity surveyors, installed in the upstairs larger bedroom. No stair carpet, and no curtains anywhere, but it was habitable.

On the last day of our stay in the bungalow, Richard Dawson, the family's son, and his wife arrived to check that everything was all right. They both stared at the malt-coloured shiny table, sans rings. "Oh look, Richard… look at your Mum's table!" They both ran their hands over it, looking amazed. I DID feel proud of my work. (Mum was right, you HAD to put lots of 'elbow-grease' into any worthwhile job. "If a job's worth doing, it's worth doing well," Mum's regular sayings echo even now. Well, I DID do a good job on that table.) I couldn't understand Mrs Dawson not bothering with such a lovely old piece of furniture. I would have given my back teeth for such a bit of history, and certainly would never have placed boiling hot saucepans down on to the wonderful amber-coloured wood.

The day of reckoning was also here! The Drambuie had to be replaced, which proved very expensive, and anything we had used up was bought and popped into the larder. I was so sorry to say goodbye to my friend Tai Lu, her loud voice, her bright blue eyes slightly crossed, and her kinky seal-pointed tail.

Mr and Mrs Dawson came home from their travels around the globe. We didn't meet up until months later when we went to the bungalow to settle up and tie up some financial loose ends. They were very happy about our stay, and we had a cuddle with Tai Lu and a look at some photographs. (Were they destined to end up under the carpet, I wondered?)

We had to settle the money etc. in the breakfast room… We walked in, and OH HORROR! The table had reverted back to just as we first saw it! Grey rings and marks abounded, so it was back to page one! I felt disappointed. Mrs Dawson was an educated, well-read woman, bright, but rather hopeless on the home front.

UNCLE DOUG

Everything back at 249 was going well. Mum had more time for her garden, and there were numerous visits from her sisters and one remaining brother, Doug, Wendy's father. Doug was Mum's youngest brother. He and Auntie Glad, who was two years older than her brother, had a very unhappy life when young. After their father left the house, leaving the children, he lived with his mistress May in Worcester. Ludd must have had a conscience so he decided that the two youngest children could live with him and his partner in Worcester. Both little children hated May, and also hated being apart from their siblings, so they decided to run away.

This they did. Doug was five, Glad about seven. They walked all the way from Worcester to Stourbridge, probably around ten miles. They arrived home, were greeted by all their siblings, and were promptly taken back to Worcester to the frightening lady who hoped to be their step-mother.

Neither child was sent to school, something that Glad never forgave her father for. They endured life in Worcester for years, until May and Ludd moved to Wolverhampton. The move to Wolverhampton was a good one for Glad, as Mum was newly married and living in a downstairs flat close by. I think Glad must have been working (although only around twelve), but Doug was still at home and not at school.

According to Mum, May used Doug as an errand boy, getting him to shop for her. One day, Mum was in the window and she saw Doug trotting past. He was on his way to buy wool for May to knit up. It was winter and bitterly cold but poor Doug had ill-fitting down-at-heel shoes, cramping his toes (which caused Doug to 'suffer with his feet' all his life). Mum told me this next bit so I haven't wrapped it up, but it's difficult to understand. She opened the window, leant out, and handed the frozen Doug some biscuits. "I COULDN'T ask him in, my landlady didn't allow visitors."

That was Mum, even a young brother in trouble, cold and no doubt hungry, had to go on his way clutching and eating the biscuits. It wouldn't have crossed Mum's mind to disobey her landlady and haul him up into the warmth. It wasn't done, 'THEY' might get her! Astonishing, I think, and an extremely sad story.

Doug and wife Dot had moved away from Wallasey and were now living in Malvern. Dot was deputy matron of Malvern Girls' School and Doug was manager of Elts shoe shop in the town. Wendy's younger sister Judy had been living at the farm in Fockbury, staying with Seonee and very 'grunty' Uncle Henry. Judy loved horses, in fact, all animals, and I remember when she was a very small child telling us all that "when I grow up, I am going to marry a COW"!

Actually, she married John, and they rented a cottage in the village that was the fictional village of Ambridge in *The Archers* on the radio. Judy had a mixed 'lot' of pets, golden pheasants, a peacock (according to Judy, peacocks have tiny brains and are impossible to train), also a horse, and two or three dogs… so her life was going well. John and Judy also added two daughters to their flock, Stephanie and Rebecca, or Becky as she became known.

Wendy was now teaching, and had met a very acceptable, handsome young man, Rolie. Rolie had always been a choirboy and server in Liverpool Cathedral, so the cathedral was the setting for their wedding.

(I'm ashamed to say that I think I WAS invited, but, for some reason, I was feeling at a very low ebb, and couldn't go, but it was a very dignified wedding, and Mum was pleased to see her youngest and dearest brother give his very fair and beautiful daughter away.)

HOMEMAKER

The Henwood Road house proved to be a challenge.

Once again, we had to clean a pretty gunged-up bathroom. The grouting between the small white tiles was quite a long job. We had to scrape the blackened old grout out and refill – this was my job.

Mum turned up one afternoon, a rare visit, and threw herself into cleaning the huge, cast-iron bath. Mum didn't seem too keen on walking down from 249, although it was only ten minutes away from Henwood Road. I realized that her arthritis was getting worse, mainly in her ankles, hips and knees. Her knees were flattened and out of shape. When we mentioned this, she replied, "It's all that scrubbing and polishing of floors…kneeling… I don't suppose the Queen Mother ever has had to do that. No wonder she can wear high heels!" As an afterthought, Mum added, "She uses some sort of arsenic-cream on her face, you know, AND the Queen does too!" She wasn't a royalist, but I think Mum would have curtseyed with the rest, should Her Majesty suddenly appear at the door of 249. Rather unlikely.

Marriage in the sixties for most women wasn't a partnership as it is today. An evening meal was always ready whatever time your husband arrived home. Everything to do with the kitchen was a female pursuit. Husbands worked hard, for long hours, and some wives stayed at home, so fair enough, they were the homemaker. Although the saying 'the hand that rocks the cradle' is true to a point, it wasn't so evident in 1963.

There were not many kitchen gadgets, though we eventually bought a washer with a separate spin dryer. This would almost take off when in full spin. It would start at the hall end of the kitchen, but would spin and wobble itself over to the back door… possibly trying to 'leg it', as I used to cram sheets, clothes, anything that didn't move into it! What a boon, though Mum never had any help, just strong arms, muscles bulging, as she twisted sheets almost dry before hanging them on the line.

I gardened most days, with vim and vigour… The giant rhubarb weeds, hundreds of them, had completely taken over the lower end of the garden and continued up the railway embankment. I devised a plan to dig out about twenty a day. The great kidney-shaped hole in the lawn was now filled with builder's rubble from the removal of a kitchen chimney.

Neighbour Gwen would see me digging away, so a cup of tea would be pushed through the privet hedge, or she would invite me to squeeze though the hedge to her garden, and sit on their swinging settee. On one memorable occasion, Gwen kicked the settee into almost 'swing-boat' mode, chatting, laughing, and sipping tea from her china cup. I began to feel sick – I think that was possibly when I was just pregnant, but I'm not sure.

We had a television. This is where the male side of the marriage partnership really came into its own. Having prepared dinner, I would pop the television on and await the master's return. As soon as my beloved got home, he would stride to the set and change to another programme (no remotes in those days). No asking if I wanted to see the end of a programme. This caused silent teeth gritting, ending in a slightly more silent dinner. Harold never really noticed it; men did that.

They made all the big decisions, too. I can't say ALL men DID, but certainly I gathered it was perhaps a Hampton thing, but I abided by it; to me it was normal.

The house shaped up. Harold built a very long slate fireplace to replace the pile of bricks. We went over to a slate mine in North Wales to purchase the slate. The slate was coloured, greens, dark purples, very nice, roughly riven, odd sizes. It was a truly complicated jigsaw of different shapes and shades… but it was lovely.

Harold turned out to be a very good 'hands on' husband, especially with wood. He helped to make our house very comfortable, and it gradually became home.

TAI LU NUMBER TWO

I must pop a paragraph or two in here. I had never lived without animals. We'd always had dogs and cats, plus the short-lived goat, and the many rabbits and hamsters, so the house felt empty without four-footed friends. So we bought a Siamese cat, a seal-point, very like our charge in the bungalow. We even called him Tai Lu, although the meaning of the name was 'Princess' (or so we believe) and this little cat was a male. I don't think he ever found out about his girlie name's meaning! We picked him up from a cat breeder, who showed us her latest litter of Siamese. Jane was a girl devoted to her cats. Her house was immaculate and SO clean. The mother cat and her little family lived in a downstairs bedroom, bedecked with fleeces, all snowy white. Proud mummy puss lay surrounded by her unruly brood, all play fighting and gambolling around, a happy healthy bunch of adorable cream kittens, with just a hint of the seal points on their ear tips and tails, and genitals! The journey home would probably have frightened him, so I opened the bottom of my jumper, and he climbed up onto my chest (flat in those days). The dark and warmth seemed to do the trick. We got him home to Henwood Road, and there began the next decade of fun, dismay, trouble and joy, and heartache. Very different from other breeds, Siamese respond to a whistle, rather like a dog, and have the most beautiful blue eyes. They are, like most felines, very clean and fastidious in their grooming and loo habits.

Tai Lu settled in very well, though he did sustain a slight injury when Harold's brother Bob dropped him onto a pottery nut bowl, giving Tai Lu a distinguished Roman nose. This stayed with him for life.

His life (and ours) revolved around chasing, being chased, and hiding behind doors to leap out at passers-by, or sitting balanced on the narrow edge on top of a door – he loved heights! He became very adept at retrieving small squares of carpet. We'd throw them and he would bring them back, even though his 'catch' was bigger than him. All trees were climbable – our tall cherry tree was his favourite mountaineering feat. After surveying the landscape and other people's gardens, he would descend backwards, carefully and with precision.

We were his staff, and he knew it, but was gracious, never biting or

317

scratching people, just doing his manicure on the very scratchable chairs (the material was looped and rough, so an ideal claw sharpener), or washing his Mersey-tunnel-type ears and very long whiskers.

He lived with us (or rather we lived with him!) for thirteen years. One autumn day, we became worried because his normally raucous voice became very throaty, and he had a job keeping his tongue inside his mouth… something nasty was happening. We took him to our vets. An operation was needed to see what was going on, the vet advised.

We sat at home waiting the verdict. The phone rang. "This is Mr Thomas here. We have Tai Lu anaesthetized on the table, and we have carried out an exploratory operation. I'm afraid we have found a growth in his throat. We could bring him round and then give him a course of anti-cancer drugs OR we could give him a drug that would put him to sleep, without waking him up."

I managed to say that we wouldn't want him to suffer any more so don't wake him… I put the receiver down feeling like a murderer.

We all loved Tai Lu dearly. Tears all round, and still more tears when I remember him leaving us, looking at me and trusting me, as he was taken out to what became his final hour. I never said a proper 'goodbye'.

TO A FRIEND
GONE FROM OUR HOUSE, BUT NOT OUR HEARTS.
THE SUN-FILLED WINDOW IS NOT SO BRIGHT.
PRIVET SHADE WHERE SLEEPY HOURS PASSED.
THOSE LEAFY SHADES ARE UNSEEN NOW.
NO MORE THE GENTLE HOLLOW ON BEDSPREAD
NOR THE SOFTEST TOUCH OF PAW UPON OUR FACES.
NO VOICE OF MORNING GREETING, IN THE SUNNY KITCHEN
JUST THE HARSH NOISE OF BREAKFAST PREPARATION.
OUR FRIEND THROUGH OUR SORROW AND HAPPINESS.
YESTERDAY YOU HEARD SAD VOICES, NOT UNDERSTANDING.
FAREWELL, GOOD COMPANION, FRIEND OF TWELVE YEARS.
WE SALUTE YOU, DEAR FAMILY CAT!
OUR LIVES ARE DARKER WITH YOUR PASSING.

After our four-legged companion had died, the family decided that another Siamese would be very welcome. This time we had a little female. She was a seal-point like Tai Lu. We called her Emma.

Emma was a dear little soul. We loved her to bits. She was very loud, in fact (if possible) even louder than old Tai Lu. She was a tree climber, and every tree on the old railway bank at the bottom of the garden was scaled. But once up amongst the leaves, she would cry for help! I was due at the doctor's surgery one morning, but Emma was shouting from a sycamore tree. I couldn't leave her there, so clambered up and carried her down. When I arrived at the doctor's, the GP asked me the usual questions: "How's your back these days? Are you getting about?"

I told him I had just climbed a tree and rescued a cat. He laughed, his questions answered!

One half-term morning, we let Emma out as usual, but she didn't return. We all searched. She might be locked in somewhere, the children said tearfully. On the second day, still no Emma. I was with my daughter Louise and we were walking along the old line, poking about in the brambles, when we saw what looked like a length of cardboard lying amongst the undergrowth. It was Emma, lying stretched out, with a bullet hole through her forehead. Some monster had shot her at close range. They must have seen that it was a cat, NOT a rabbit. She had probably run towards them, she loved people (not that I can call the murderer a person).

We were devastated… she was buried in the lawn with tears, copious flowers, tenderly wrapped in her woolly blanket, near to the children's swing.

MORE CATS

Months later, two more Siamese joined the Henwood Road crew. William, a beautiful blue-point, and his half-sister Sophie, a seal-point, equally beautiful. William had been with us nine months when Sophie arrived. She was so tiny, in a way, I think, perhaps too young to part from her mum. She adored William. He wasn't so enamoured, but was gracious in his acceptance. They would lie together in the basket, Sophie contentedly sucking on a bit of William's fur, using it as a dummy. He tolerated his little half-sibling, and eventually they became good friends. The joy these two cats gave us all is only explainable to cat lovers.

They got into scrapes, fought my big fur hat as they would a rat, got stuck on roof tops, trees and flat roofs, disappeared, reappeared, woke us up in the morning with a damp nose pressed into our faces.

The cat breeder we bought them off was a great cat show contestant. She rang one day to ask if I would allow her to 'show' William, so handsome was he, with a super-duper pedigree. I'm still not sure I should have let him go round the shows. He did win lots of rosettes, 'Best in Show' and 'Best in his class' etc. He didn't travel well, though, and I would think that his breeder would have had to wear ear-muffs for the journeys to places as far as Wales.

I used to get up about 4.30am to get him ready for Ann, his breeder, to pick him up, always VERY early morning. His claws had to be clean, and certainly NO FLEAS! I brushed talcum through his silver fur to make it shine, AND he had to have a lunch box put up with food for his dinner. This consisted of some dried cat food, and his VERY favourite nosh, Marmite on buttered toast cut into tiny squares. This sustained him through the endless boring hours sitting in his (very posh) cage, awaiting the judges' decisions.

William's show appearances came to an end. He had begun plucking the fur off his back. We thought it was hormones, and so did one vet, but then when all medication failed, we realized William was feeling stressed. Retirement from his celebrity status relieved the plucking, and the bald patch (shaped like a butterfly) grew fur again.

Sophie stayed a very small cat, endearing; we all loved her. Her voice was louder than her brother's, and most mischief was 'set up' by Sophie. One day, I had put some lamb chops on the grill pan, ready to cook later. Both cats saw me do it so I watched from the doorway. Sophie jumped up onto the pan, and delicately lifted a chop in her mouth. Positioned underneath was Will. Sophie dropped the chop into Will's mouth and prepared to do the same with the next scrumptious chop. For the sake of our dinner, I had to intervene. I have to admit washing the chops, and we ate them. Waste not want not. That was another of Mum's sayings.

Sophie lived until she was thirteen. The vet came to the house to put her to sleep. She had kidney failure, a sad time, and I can hardly bring myself to type it…

William lived on for years. He was just about to get the key to his cat-flap, aged twenty, when he caught a chest infection. We watched over him for days. He slept on our bed in the warmth. We became heartbroken as William got frailer. He could still muster a purr, so he received lots of strokes and gentle cuddles. A very sympathetic vet came to the house and, without moving William from his place under the duvet, he kindly put William, our dear old companion, to sleep.

Both little cats are buried in a nice shady spot under a rhododendron bush. Occasionally a small jam jar appears on their graves, filled with mixed flowers. It isn't the fairies.

In a way, I wish I didn't love animals so much. There is heartache when they have to go…

I wasn't going to add this 'cat' chapter – too upsetting, but I'm glad I have. All these animals have enhanced my life and the lives of our family. They deserve a chapter all to themselves!

Our wedding

Tony's wedding

Pat's wedding

Robin's wedding

Louise and Lance on their wedding day

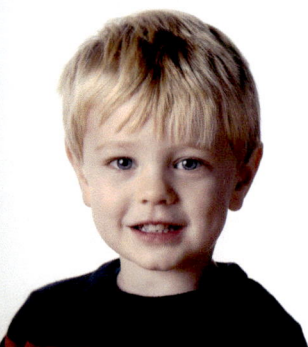

Cameron

Robin and Helen's Wedding, All Saint Church, Lindfield

Benji

Robin at Caernarfon Castle

Louise

A young Anna

My Mum at 88 years old

Anna all grown up

Val and Harold

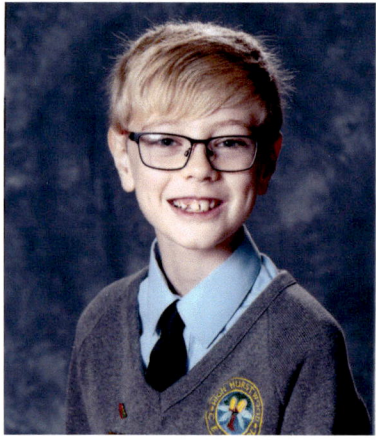

Cameron aged 8

Louise and partner Stuart Moncur, Wales, 2020

Benji on his first day at Skinner's School, aged 11

WEDDINGS, BIRTHS, AND A DEATH

G etting back to life in 1964, celebrations of all kinds were to the fore. Pat had the three growing children. Her house was only half a mile away, so she visited regularly.

Tony had been married a year or so, and they were expecting their first child in July. I accompanied Joan to the Women's Hospital (I will write a page or two about THAT hospital). This was about June. What I DIDN'T tell her was that I was also in an 'interesting condition', but seven months behind her.

The date for Robin's wedding to Gwen was set for August, a month before our baby was due.

Mum was happily widowed, her sisters, the aunts, visiting most weeks and taking her out to Stourbridge or further afield. I don't know where this took place, but Auntie Glad told us, years later, that the three sisters visited a lighthouse. They managed the many steps, Mum with difficulty, and the guide started his chat about the history of the building. Auntie Glad was listening intently, when she noticed out of the corner of her eye that Mum was slightly slumped, red-faced, sweat in beads on her brow. Years earlier, Mum had suffered from claustrophobia. She hated anyone shutting living room doors, she felt trapped and sick. Well, here it was… poor Maudie almost fainting, right up in the top of the great light part of the lighthouse. How she got down, and who helped her, I never found out, but Glad would tell this tale with a little bit of scorn in her voice. Almost an "Oh dear, Maudie's being weak and dramatic again."

I know that Mum couldn't help it – blood, glass lacerations, and confined spaces were her Achilles heel. How she dealt with Dad's many haemorrhages I never worked out. "There was more than a bucketful of blood. I emptied it into the bath to show the doctor" was one rather brave remark from Mum, after another of Dad's many blood-curdling illnesses. Burst duodenal ulcers happened more than once, and Dad's heavy drinking only accelerated this bloody happening. Mum must have coped by shutting her phobia of blood out, such was the emergency.

I used to be very intolerant of Dad's behaviour, his drinking, lending friends money, money he should have been handing over to Mum for

327

the family. But now, well, I don't have an axe to grind with Dad. He suffered bad health, had a job which was partly showbiz and PR for J Arthur Rank. He mixed with people who were heavy social drinkers, plus some who were hangers-on: "LD is good for a loan." That was his world, and of course it WAS difficult being part of it; however, I feel we should all forgive him. I have, but it has taken years. Tony never did, and Pat is still unforgiving.

I have always hoped that no child of ours would ever tread the boards or have ANYTHING to do with showbiz.

In July of that year, Joan gave birth to a little boy, who they called Jonathan. Joan was taken in to the Women's Hospital and, according to Tony, he could only visit during visiting hours (which was usual for husbands in those days). Apparently, Joan shouted and screamed out when in labour so much and so loud that a nurse had to push her bed along with her, from ward to ward to pacify her distressed patient. We all knew that Joan had a very low pain threshold. Mum would say that "To Joan a pimple is a boil." Joan did manage it, though, and came home two days later.

Mum's story of this was that Tony drew up at their house, Mum in the back seat holding baby Jonathan. Joan had been hysterical all the way home, a journey of about fifteen minutes. So distressed was the new father with his wife's suffering, he dashed round, opened the front passenger door and escorted a tearful Joan into the house. He then closed the front door, completely forgetting Mum and the new baby! After a very short time, the front door opened, and a harassed father emerged and let Mum and her new grandson out of the hot car and into the fresh air.

For the next two or three weeks, Mum was a home-help and baker of little cupcakes (at Joan's request for the many visitors that called to view the new arrival). Mum also became head laundry mistress and general dogsbody. She stayed the nights, and walked the midnight hours with Jonathan.

Joan couldn't feed him herself, so bottles were on the go. I must say, Mum did well. She loved tiny newborns, and in her later years she wrote poetry about them. Mum wrote a great many poems and fictional stories later in life when she had more time on her hands (this I will write about later!).

When I was about five months pregnant, I learnt to drive. Harold taught me and I only had one lesson given by a professional driving instructor, and that was on the day of the test. Harold was patience itself. I only jumped out once and threw a 'wobbly' and THAT was almost certainly after I had made a mistake, not Harold being bossy.

I passed the test, and afterwards whilst signing forms, I told the examiner that I was giving birth in September. He looked very surprised. "We have just had a baby, so no sleep. I should have matchsticks to keep my eyes open," he moaned.

We sat in the warmth of the car, me happy… him tired!

When I told Mum that I had passed the test, she looked up from her crocheting. "I never thought YOU would pass," she said. Mum had never seen me drive or heard any reports of progress, so I did take a psychological blow when she said that.

I have been driving ever since, but still hate it. To me the combustion engine is a mystery. The bonnet has always been 'the lid' to me, and any new knobs or dials are a great worry and not to be touched. I have never wanted anything flashy, no open roadster for me, just a reliable motor to get from A to B. I have no sense of direction anyway, so all in all, driving ANYWHERE slightly off the beaten track is a no-go area. Driving is a great worry, so a chauffeur would be very acceptable. I know there's a hint of 'Roberts family' snobbery there.

The day of Robin and Gwen's wedding arrived. I don't know who decided that 249 should be the wedding breakfast venue, but that is where the post-wedding get together would be. The house was still in a state of dilapidation, as Mum still rented the house from a firm of house agents who didn't do anything to improve its steady decline. The garden was always well kept, hydrangeas abounded along the path in the front garden. The ferns had been ditched by me (a bit silly, as we had nowhere to put them). The London Pride had become quite invasive beside the privet hedge that divided the middle terrace house where Horace and Tita Greenham lived. The White House where Uncle Reg and Betty had lived was no longer a house for Hungarian refugees; now it was a home for battered wives and had expanded into the next-door attached large semi. This was the other half of the White House where, years before, the Dace sisters had lived and fought and, in their insanity, chopped down interior doors. It might have been for firewood, but I don't think the authorities thought the same. Shortly after the chopping episode, both sisters died. (Rumour had it that one was battered about the head by her sister, but it IS just a rumour. It had always been a sad gloomy house.)

Now, in1965, it became even more sad. The battered wives were occasionally pursued by their terrifying partners/husbands. Police got involved and all that goes with what should have been a 'safe house'. I don't think Mum knew as much as us about all this mayhem. Just as well really, she might have been frightened, although it took a lot to frighten Maudie, brought up in a rather bizarre household.

Of course hosting the wedding breakfast must have worried Mum. It was only going to be a small buffet, and a three-tiered cake. The cake was a job I undertook, which was fine, although being pregnant made leaning over for hours decorating with fancy lattice patterned icing uncomfortable.

(I had been told by a consultant that the baby was in the breech position but this might change later on. However, after two tries at turning the baby by Mr F, both uncomfortable procedures, the baby wasn't for turning!)

The food seemed to appear from nowhere. I think Pat probably provided most of it, she was first class at improvisation and imaginative bits and pieces. I can't remember, but no doubt Mum would have baked dozens of meringues, still her forte.

The big upset came a week or so before the wedding date. Mum had taken over Tony's little rough-haired Jack Russell cross, Flossie. She lived a quiet life alongside her human 'Granny'. After his marriage, Tony had become a traitor and had bought another Jack Russell dog, a male called Lucky. So Mum was in charge of Flossie from when Tony left home. She loved dogs, and Flossie was a sweet, very quiet soul. Black and white, long-haired, dropped-over ears, a dear little thing. However, as she became old, her coat and teeth began to smell.

This is where I wonder what I was doing. I loved her, so why didn't I help with her grooming and general hygiene? I could have popped to 249 and carried out a spot of brushing and sprucing. I'll never fathom that out! Flossie was ancient, scruffy, about fourteen, and to Mum, a great source of embarrassment when visitors came. So hosting a wedding breakfast party threw Mum into a quandary and, I hope, some deep thought. What to do with Flossie? I don't think Robin and Mum mentioned anything about this to me. One morning, Flossie was popped into her collar and taken on the local bus to Wolverhampton centre. The PDSA was in the centre of town. This was where, after all the years of companionship and trust, dear little mongrel Flossie was detached from her collar and lead and put to sleep.

Mum apparently left a donation, and spurned the offer from the vet to take the lead and collar home. She left it there, along with its owner. Robin found it heart-breaking, but there was an exciting event soon so it dimmed too much angst. What Mum thought or did, I don't know. I suspect she did shed a few tears, but in her eyes, 249 had to be clean and fragrant for the many guests arriving for the 'do'. I was told a day later about Flossie's demise.

I feel sadder now than then. Somehow life seemed to be bowling along too fast, the wedding, the imminent birth, now with problems that didn't seem to be improving, and THE cake, so I didn't do too much mourning for the dear little dog.

I decided not to go to the wedding ceremony. I was only three weeks off the birth date. The cake tiers were on rather unsteady surfaces, and the food needed unwrapping, plus other excuses. When Pat knew that I was going to stay home, she asked if it was all right to leave her youngest, Peter, aged about five, with me. That was fine by me.

Mum wore the same outfit that she'd worn for my wedding two years before. A lovely soft forget-me-not blue suit with a real fur collar (not at all PC these days, and I agree). She looked really nice, she always had wonderful skin (thanks to Pond's face cream).

Robin looked very smart in a grey suit. He had grown a dark beard, which suited him, and he looked happy, which was a great relief to all of us.

All went well, about thirty guests appeared and had a good slap-up buffet. The cake looks pretty level on the wedding snaps, and the tiers stayed upright, thank goodness. The thin columns holding the three tiers up worried me – there might be a collapse! I had never made a tiered cake before, so I was pleased with the result and the fact I had managed to finish it before 'the event' in a fortnight's time…

The children all played out in the garden, running up and down the blue-bricked yard, the damp walls in the front room nobody noticed, and once again, 249 became a house of children laughing, friends chatting, and lots of friendly exchanges.

I really believe that the walls absorbed the happiness, the long red-linoed hall once again felt the throb and comfort of feet jumping and dancing along it after years of quiet steady footsteps. Do houses have a soul? I think they do, but then, I still believe in fairies.

For the next two years, Robin and Gwen lived with Mum at 249. They had their first baby there in 1967. Mum did moan sometimes, she was getting very arthritic, but no doubt having Robin's little son David (although wearing) was a comfort. He was a beautiful boy, dark hair with huge blue eyes. Gwen entered him into a 'Most Beautiful Baby' completion in the town hall. If I remember rightly, David won a prize. I'm not sure what rank! He would probably blush now upon hearing about the contest, but he was a super-looking little chap, with very blue eyes and a bright happy countenance. Mum was very proud of him, and loved him to bits.

THE HOSPITAL FROM HELL

I am putting this to paper, because it became a time of great upset when it should have been a time of great joy. I had been backwards and forwards to Mr F the gynaecologist for several months. The baby was still the wrong way up, so he decided to turn her (this is Louise, born September 1965).

I had two 'turning' sessions, but she revolved back after each session. The Women's Hospital just off the Tettenhall Road, only half a mile away, was a Victorian red-brick building and was the only hospital that would take me. There was a wonderful Royal Airforce hospital, at Cosford about eight miles away in Shropshire. A lot of my friends had given birth there, and it excelled in every way. However, my GP (the marvellous Dr Sayers, an old-fashioned but great doctor, who would carry out home visits if his patients were upset, despairing, and ill or, I suspect, just lonely. There truly hasn't been a better doctor since he retired.) phoned Cosford, only to be told that I was an 'at risk' patient, so it was a sorry, but no.

My last check-up with Mr F (who years later, I found out EVERYONE disliked, but he was very good to me) showed that I had high blood pressure, and the baby was still in the breech position, so the birth would be 'induced.'

I entered the Women's Hospital holding hands with Harold, wearing a very nice maternity dress, borrowed from my friend Ruth's sister Jean, who was "NEVER going to have another baby". I was happy, optimistic, and an absolute dope! It was a lovely late summer day, beds of formally planted rose bushes led up to the green double doors, and with happy hearts we entered, very excited, with absolutely no foreboding of things to come.

It turned out to be the Hospital from Hell.

Harold left me there. It was the seventh of September and the baby was due on the tenth. I was immediately told to lie in bed in a ward with four other ladies. Opposite was a very friendly girl, whose husband arrived that evening with a posy of sweet peas. He found a vase, but was reprimanded by a nurse. It wasn't a vase, it was a baby listening stethoscope!! Funnel shaped, so an easy mistake. The patient opposite was the only smiling face with welcoming, reassuring words.

It was decided that I would need an induction that evening. This was done by Mr F and it was a painful procedure, with no explanation about what would happen. Everything was just an intrusion into the body, quite roughly carried out. I was frightened. The fear gripped me then and stayed for the next few days and weeks.

My waters broken, I was then told to 'stay in bed', no friendly nurses, no smiles or jokes. I looked out of the window at the darkness outside, trees and leaves fluttered, and I longed for the fresh air, it was stifling in there. I had a few frightened tears. I hadn't thought any pessimistic thoughts about the birth, and no fear, until then.

Suddenly the teddy bear wallpaper, little baby clothes and good wishes from friends and family back at home, all seemed to be no part of this miserable place. I felt in the doldrums, but tried to appear happy. There were nurses flitting about, a lot of action, but I have never felt so lonely.

The night was long, nothing happening except discomfort. The day came and went. One of the other patients was an Indian lady. She usually sat, legs crossed in the lotus position, her head covering obscuring her face, her Koran in her hands. She silently read her sacred book, as far I could see, all day and night. She didn't speak to anyone, and seemed to be detached from the world.

I marvelled at her composure. I never knew what happened to her, because I was examined, again not told what was happening, just the thrust of a nurse's hand. Then, without so much as a word of comfort, I was taken in my bed to a small ward with just one other patient in a bed opposite mine. She was asleep, looking very pale and ill.

What happened next reads like something from the middle ages. A nursing sister (who I learned afterwards was a Sister W) strutted into the room. "Right, I've got to do this to you."

With that, she carried out an internal examination that was beyond anything I had ever felt. Searing pain and rough man-handling, plus a ripping feeling. She seemed to be reaching up into my chest! She obviously had to do something drastic. I think it was trying to force the baby's head round, but because nobody said WHAT was happening, I was terrified.

I felt like a piece of meat on a butcher's slab to be prodded and mauled until I thought I would pass out. When this was over, she glanced at my tears. "Sorry about that," she said, half apologetically, but then she disappeared out of the room, leaving me bloodied and dripping with perspiration, and stiff with fear.

This next bit is a mystery, but VERY real at the time.

I was in such pain after that intervention, my body wasn't mine any more. I didn't even notice the lady opposite. Whether she had gone through the same experience, I didn't know, and didn't care, I was so tearful and terrified.

The small room had a window high up covered in metal mesh, rather like a prison cell. It was now dark outside… Suddenly, a great fiery cross appeared in the window! The sort that the Klu Klux Klan used in their ceremonies. Flames leapt around the cross, a burning crucifix. I know now that it must have been the pain and possibly the drugs (although I don't remember being given any drugs). Of course, the vision was a hallucination. I wasn't in any way religious, but to me, it was absolutely REAL.

After about a minute, the fiery cross disappeared and the pain got worse. I was going to die, or so I thought. There wasn't a bell to ring, or any way of contacting anyone. I was just abandoned on the bed, bleeding, and distressed. Hours passed, or so it seemed. Two nurses appeared; not a comforting kind word to me, they just rolled me onto a trolley.

It was decided to take me into the pre-delivery room. When there, I was shuffled onto a bed, rather like an operating table. A tall man came into the room, dressed in green operating garb, hat, gown mask. It wasn't until he was leaning over me that I saw it was HAROLD. He had been detained in the corridor when trying to visit. He had had to empty his pockets of money and anything that could possibly cross-infect me. He was instructed to put the outfit on and not stay long. I was in so much pain that all I could think of was, "when will he stop talking and GO".

This no visitors, and certainly NO father anywhere near his wife during the birth, was usual in those dark days, and so I don't think Harold found it disturbing. Goodness knows how long I lay there after he had left, alone in great distress. I was checked occasionally by an unknown nurse. I lost any idea of the time, or what day it was. It was a terrible nightmare.

I think it was early evening on Thursday the ninth of September that I was wheeled into the delivery room.

A GREEK TRADGEDY

The room seemed crowded, everyone in green gowns and masks. (Apparently, there was a team of anaesthetists there, in case I needed a Caesarean. Oh JOY.)

Legs akimbo in stirrups, a gas and air mask was placed on my nose. A swarthy-looking man appeared and began peering in at the action end. This doctor was a Greek. He didn't seem to know WHAT to do, so the registrar was called. Louise had now moved sideways, and was presenting an arm.

An attempt was made by the Greek deliverer to pull the baby out. He was sweating, wide-eyed, and quite unable to deliver her. The Greek did something, I didn't know WHAT, but he seemed to think that strength was the way forward

Suddenly, there was a quick movement from the registrar, standing to my right. "DON'T DO THAT, YOU IDIOT!! YOU'LL BREAK ITS BLOODY ARM OFF!!" he shouted at the sweating man.

It was at this point that I decided that I WANTED to die. I didn't think of my little baby, or Harold or anything or anybody. Death was better than this. I can't say how long all this mayhem went on, but eventually Louise arrived, legs first, a poor little thing, very white and floppy.

She didn't cry, which I thought was unusual. I had seen it on film and TV. Everything seemed quiet. I was shown my baby, and told to confirm that it WAS a girl. Then she was rushed off to WHERE? Nobody said anything. I suppose she was put in the special baby unit. That was the last I saw of her for two days.

This was one o'clock on the tenth, her allotted birth-day. Harold had been asked to ring at 1am. I do remember someone telling me to "hurry up… your husband is ringing soon."

Little did I know that Harold had gone to bed and slept right through the night, no phone call, nothing. I'm glad I only found out months later! I feel that this is unusual for a new father, but life seemed to be like that, never conventional. I am still hurt by his sleep whilst his wife was going through what I felt was a very nasty nightmarish 'accident', certainly not a jolly and joyous birth.

It HAD been a scene from hell, so perhaps the flaming cross that I had witnessed, although a hallucination, was a warning of things to come.

(One strange happening that has never really been explained was that two nurses arrived, just as the afterbirth was delivered. They gathered it up, took it to one side and obviously wrapped it up safely. I didn't really care at the time, but later when home, I read that some afterbirths were used in cosmetic creams. I'm hoping that's not true.)

After everything was over, the registrar disappeared and I was left bleeding badly internally and externally, and all alone with my Greek deliverer. Try as hard as he could, he didn't seem to be able to stop the bleeding. He shouted that he needed help. I found out afterwards that there had been several babies arriving all at the same time that night so no nurse was available as they were under-staffed.

He had the suture needles, but they were the wrong size. He was sweating, and mumbling probably Greek profanities. He threw a packet of needles onto the floor. The door opened, and, oh relief, an Asian nurse appeared. She leant over and said quietly, "So sorry, but we are busy, I can't stay with you." With that, she passed the new needles to the Greek and went.

My sweating Greek now began crying. He was holding a suture needle up in the air, it was threaded. So desperate was I, that I half sat up and asked if I could help. This seems bizarre, and IS, but it's true. "You are NOT sterile!" he shouted, still with tears running down his cheeks. Stitches were inserted, the sweating and the tears of frustration went on. What had happened I really don't know, I can only guess…

After the internal stitches, he 'sewed' me up externally… only to find that the internal ones hadn't stopped the flow of blood. He was completely alone, no help, so although I didn't think so at the time, he MUST have been terrified. He had to redo the first sutures, and I suppose, looking back forty-eight years, he must have been in hell, trying to do his best with no assistance, and probably no experience of this blood-bath kind of delivery.

Eventually the stitching was over. I was wheeled down a long corridor. There was a whirring noise, and I remember asking the trolley nurse what it was.

"Never you mind. It's nothing to do with you, my love."

That was the extent of conversation with anyone.

I arrived back into a different ward. It was night-time. I lay half-dozing. I felt that this must be a dream. Where WAS my little daughter? What had happened? No mobile phones to call Harold, no contact with the outside world. I viewed the whole birth as a nightmare, and still do. No mention of what had happened to my baby by anyone.

Morning arrived, and a plump young trainee nurse stood beside the bed.

"I've come to wash you." She held a small bowl of water. This warm water was poured over my stitched area. It was heaven. She took some time, and the relief was wonderful. I asked her how many stitches. "Oh don't ask." Then she added quietly, "About twenty-four."

I did find out what had happened to Louise. Later that morning, a passing nurse, a very nice red-haired girl, stopped when I called. It wasn't her department. "I'll find out for you." With that, she left, and reappeared quickly.

"She's in the nursery in a special cot. You can't visit her today, though, because Dr E-J will be seeing her sometime. Babies delivered breech have to be watched. I'm sure they will let you see her soon." The nurse was sympathetic and embarrassed that I was so 'in the dark'. This wasn't even her ward, but she stopped long enough to try to give some help, so a great comfort of sorts.

The weird part of this is that I somehow went along with this. I still felt completely dominated by the old building, the silent staff, the comings and goings, alien to me. I started to sweat. Perspiration ran down from my chest and soaked my nightie and the bed. I felt unclean. There wasn't a baby to feed so water leaked out of my breasts and ran amok. Communication wasn't the flavour of the day, and I was naïve, trusting, and a bit if a dope for not asking and insisting on information. I didn't know HOW or whether 'THEY' would get me if I DID enquire or cause an upheaval, how silly.

Later, when talking across the ward to another new mother, who had her baby by her bed in a cot, I mentioned the Greek doctor. "Oh HIM," she shouted. "Sister Woodward gave him a right good kicking for some reason yesterday."

I suppose I should have felt some sympathy for him, but I didn't.

(Oddly, after eventually getting home, I wrote to Ruth, who had not long before given birth to a little boy. This was in North Wales. Her reply surprised me. She had also had a Greek 'surgeon' deliver her last child, Jon. Whether he was THE same one, I'll never know, but she did say what an inexperienced butcher he was.)

There were three other new mothers in the ward. All but one and me had their babies brought in in the morning to be fed. The patient without a baby was smiling across, so I asked if she had a baby.

"Yes, but they showed me her spine. There's a red mark on in it, halfway down. They're seeing to her now." At that time she wasn't too upset, but later in the day, after a (I suppose) a consultant had been talking to her, she was sobbing. I know now that her little child had Spinabifida.

I think the fact that the husbands or partners were kept away from the hospital, and could only visit for an hour in the afternoon and an hour in the evening, was routine in those unenlightened days. Home births, if possible, seemed to be a family affair, and although the new dad had to stay down in the kitchen boiling the water and fending off visitors or looking after the older children, it must have been less stressful.

I have to bring Harold in now. He did ring, but it was SIX am, and to this day I don't know what 'they' said. He apparently got in touch with my Mum, his parents, and Pat. There was rejoicing in 249. Mum had played cards, Solitaire, for hours, having had four very painful births at home years before.

Certainly my dad was never there for our births, he only came home to wet the new baby's head and drink to the new member of the household, bringing his noisy 'cronies' home too (Mum's words). They would all stand around the bed drinking and laughing, a happy sociable occasion for the men, but it must have been very difficult for Mum. However she always had her weeks 'lying-in' so she did have time to get to know her baby.

She told me a very funny story about managing, after a month or so, to go to a dance with Dad, whilst still breastfeeding one of us. The current fashion was for Russian boots… Apparently, she danced in her splendid boots with Dad for some time, but felt and heard a 'sloshing' coming from her foot area. She investigated, and found that, as it was past feeding time, her milk had overflowed and had run down, right into her boots, so she was squelching around in milk. I'm surprised she DID tell me this rather odd and funny story, because normally she was very embarrassed about ladies' parts. Breasts were really a 'no-go' area and only whispered about, but she DID tell me, to my embarrassment! I wonder if she had been at the sherry.

Harold visited in the afternoon. What I didn't know at the time was that a nurse had taken him down to the baby unit, and from behind glass, showed him Louise, asleep in a cot, the head end tipped down, feet end up, I suppose to let blood flow into her head. Harold was ecstatic, father to a little girl, exciting. He didn't appear worried in any way. Harold has never really talked about that time. He isn't given to very deep intimate post mortems. I was never able to talk about the birth. I felt I shouldn't, everyone would think I was 'a baby'.

Many years later, when I DID tell a friend about the terrible birth, I began to shake. It was as though I had been through a road accident and had seen and heard and felt things that shouldn't be experienced by a human being. This feeling has never truly left me.

The morning following the birth, I awoke to see the face of the vicar from St Jude's. He was leaning earnestly over me, hands clasped in a praying mode. I was like a grease spot dripping with perspiration. Waking and seeing him praying over me made me more frightened than ever. I was in the grip of anxiety from then on.

He said that sister-in-law Joan had asked him to come, as I and the baby were very ill. I didn't know that I WAS ill, and I certainly didn't know how Louise was, but it did strike at my heart that Joan had told the vicar about us both. I think she had done a 'boil rather than a pimple', as Mum always said she did.

I think she HAD, because neither of us was 'at death's door'. There were big complications, but certainly not worthy of a prayer. It was not a good start to the day.

The hospital became a prison to me. The matron was a woman who struck fear into her staff and her patients. The ladies' bathroom and lavatory was filthy. I hated it. One morning the wash basin had spat-out blood in it, someone's gums must have bled. However, it was a room where we could have a conversation with other mothers. One very nice Asian girl, who looked about sixteen, had been through a long labour, partly because she had thought that the pushing, and bearing down was going to result in a poo! So she had held her buttocks together for hours, too scared of the humiliation if she should soil the bed.

Back in the ward, another new mother was dressed in a wispy black see-through nightie, and her visiting husband couldn't contain himself. He kept (to the amusement of the onlookers) kissing and fondling her. She seemed to enjoy it. "I'll be back here in ten months' time. He can't wait," she laughed.

All carnal 'goings-on' were so far from my mind, I just gaped at her. How could she even think about it? I found out she had several children already, and I suppose she may have gone on to have lots more.

Harold came in the afternoon. He was holding a paper bag, in which were two dishes of the most creamy and wonderful caramel cream, made by his mother Ethel. (I hadn't eaten anything, as yet, as we were supposed to sit at a long trestle table. I did manage to get there, and tried but couldn't sit. The dinner arrived. Nobody knew what it was until someone told us it was supposed to be chicken stew. There was a watery fluid lurking on the plate, in this floated some grey peas, a carrot slice or two, and some white meat. Nobody ate much, it was rubbish, and certainly not fit for new nursing mothers, who needed a healthy diet.) So to me these small and tasty caramel puds were a life-saver. How nice of Ethel to send them. I asked if he had seen Louise. Yes he had, but he gave no details, and again I somehow didn't expect any. Shocking, isn't it? He did say she had her cot tilted, head down, but nobody had explained anything to him either; he just viewed through a glass screen then walked down a corridor to see me.

I didn't find out until much later that, behind the scenes, some family squabbling was going on. Mother-in-law wanted to come with Harold to visit me, but the rules stated only one extra visitor, and Harold decided it should be MY mum, so it was very nice of his mum to make these goodies instead of seeing her little granddaughter.

After Harold had departed I was determined to see Louise. The nurse who had been very friendly earlier was passing, I asked if she could get me down to the nursery. "Haven't you been, luv?" She looked amazed. "Of COURSE, I'll get a wheelchair." I was shaking (this trembling went on for weeks). This she did, and I sailed down, pushed by a 'human being' at last. Corridor after corridor, it seemed, then… there was my baby!

We still had to view from behind a glass window, and I had to be told which baby was mine. There were three in there. Yes, the cot was tilted, and I couldn't see very much, but she looked like all babies, just a face in view. I was so relieved, but happiness didn't flood over me and I didn't feel that I MUST pick her up and hold her close. Separation at birth can do strange things, and I certainly felt detached at that time, but thankful.

Louise did have a dark patch of dried blood on her crown. I just thought, as did Mum, that nobody had washed the baby's hair. However, she still had this crusty, and by then almost black, scab, when we eventually left the hospital, over ten days later. (A nursing sister who lived a few doors away peered at the black scab, and told me that sometimes a fontanelle test was done on breech babies. We were never told anything about any test, so it's not definitely true. Nobody today would attempt any procedure on a child without talking it over with the parents, but we parents were just non-existent forty-eight years ago.)

I suppose this kind of treatment was handed out all over the UK. How wonderful that time and knowledge have stopped all this medical secrecy. (Well, not quite, as I will relate later.)

Physicians and the medical fraternity in those days (and before) were held in tremendous esteem. They were not to be spoken to in some instances, and every bit of dialogue was through an accompanying nurse. It took Auntie Ve to put the medical clan in their place. "Just because they've got their higher school cert., they think they are GOD! They all go to the toilet, just as WE do. They are NO different, dear." Then she added. "Even the Queen has to 'go' so we are all the same underneath." How true!

After two days, Louise was brought to my bed, and there, looking like a yellow daffodil with jaundice, she lay fast asleep, legs straight out, as some breech babies do, having spent weeks in the womb in that position. I thought she was the most beautiful baby I had ever seen.

Mum arrived with Harold, and there were no motherly kisses or hugs. I think she would have liked to, but restraint got the better of her, so she just gazed down at the cot. She loved babies, especially new ones, and she loved this little fairy-like child.

I haven't mentioned the dreadful matron. She was of the old school, "stand by your beds" did apply. One day she strode into the ward. First she told a mother (who had several other children, so was an old hand at baby care), "DO NOT SWADDLE YOUR BABY!" Matron then snatched the poor unfortunate baby up and unfurled it from its wraps. "You will give her a heat rash, Mother." (Everyone was called 'Mother', we didn't have names!)

Matron then strode over to me. She peered into the cot and at the locker. She bent down over Louise, so I thought I would tell her about the jaundice. How stupid of me!! Matron looked gimlet-eyed at me. "I can SEE THAT, Mother." She turned. "Now, THIS rail on your locker is for baby's towel, THIS…" she spun the locker around (the locker had wheels so could be turned) "…THIS RAIL is for YOUR towel. Do you understand? We can't have THIS untidiness, Mother." It was as though I was back at school, being told off for some misdemeanour.

I sat back on the bed. THIS was also a terrible sin. "And DO NOT sit on your bed!!"

Where we were supposed to sit, God only knows. So that was matron. Years later, during a family gathering, for fun and a laugh, the family were asked, "If you were James Bond and could assassinate anyone, who would that person be?" I probably answered something like Hitler, but Matron of the Women's Hospital, Wolverhampton, would be my target, definitely!

She had never married, had certainly never had children, and I doubt whether she had indulged in romance, or sex. She was a dried-up old spinster. I can say this NOW, because I suppose she's gone to the great hospital in the sky, to bully all the angels up there, and probably God himself.

I stayed in that hospital for two weeks. Each day, Dr E-J would give the babies a once-over and say which child was well enough to go home. I had almost given up, so I decided to ask. Every other baby had gone, all the mothers had changed, new ones were bedded down in the ward with their offspring.

I managed to catch the eye of a passing nurse. "I'll go and look at the doctor's list." She disappeared, but came back in minutes. "NO, sorry, your baby isn't on today's list." Tears that I had held in for weeks just burst out. I cried like a banshee. Seeing my distress, the good soul said she would look again and see if there was a chance of Louise being passed over on the daily round. The now-flushed young nurse almost ran back into the ward. "YES. They made a mistake, luv. Both of you can GO HOME TODAY!"

As I write this, I can feel that elation. It was as though I had been in Wormwood Scrubs, but now I was about to escape from the gallows…

In the afternoon, Harold brought my clothes in, and home beckoned.

I remember particularly a suspender belt (stockings in those days, no tights). I fastened it up without difficulty, and the mother in the next bed marvelled at my thin waistline. No wonder, I had hardly eaten anything for two weeks. A friend who worked in pathology did bring me some chicken sandwiches, which I realized were her lunch, and family had sent in nice delicacies, and of course those dreamy caramel creams from Ethel.

Two weeks previously, I had walked into that building, an excited mother-to-be, holding hands with Harold, apprehensive but happy. Now, I walked out a different woman. I had heard, seen, and experienced some terribly bizarre events. It was as though I was a 'changeling'; my whole perspective on life altered in those two weeks. I had to pretend to family and friends that all was well, but it wasn't! In hindsight, I should have raged against the treatment, but nobody questioned medical procedures, unlike today.

These unhappy two weeks were a turning point, not an upwards turn, though, quite the opposite. Life at 249 had been very difficult. There had been traumatic events, dire illness and anguish and discomfort, but I had managed for twenty-five years to just accept everything, and was always positive. I had been converted, not to North Sea gas, but to pessimism. To use an old 'up North' expression, I felt that "The devil had his clog on me". Today it's called "baby blues", but in 1965 there wasn't any of that nonsense! So I hid it, and have up until now. So I hope you will excuse this medical bulletin. Like wind, it is "better out than in"!

There were problems when home. Louise was what was called delicate. The midwife called regularly. I didn't tell her anything about the birth. She knew about Louise being breech, but otherwise I couldn't tell anyone. Harold was so overjoyed with his little daughter, he didn't appear to want to know. Pat was all excited, and anyway, I couldn't have told Pat about the traumatic two weeks, and Mum was, as usual, a bit distant. When I did say something about the birth, Mum had replied. "Oh, I know. I had to have my pelvis 'scraped out' when one of you were born." So I shut up, and just carried on perspiring and trembling my way through, trying to let it just be 'water under the bridge'.

Harold's mother was very helpful. Oddly, I had always thought of her as cool towards me, but she would pushbike it down to the house, get her sleeves rolled up and wash and iron the little baby nighties. Nappies were all terry towelling, no disposable ones, so there was a pile of washing every day.

After being home a few days, the midwife said I could pop baby in the bath. Ethel was there at the time. The midwife had gone, also on her trusty bike. We got the plastic bath half filled with, nice warm water. I supported

Louise's head, very nervously, but somehow she didn't seem to respond to the warmth. THEN, her eyes closed and she went very white. I pulled her out and wrapped her in a towel. Ethel was distraught. She dashed to the door. I remembered that the midwife was going two doors down where a neighbour had recently given birth at home. So Ethel ran round to the neighbour's. The midwife returned with a very flustered Ethel. She took one look at Louise, and laughed. "SHE's ASLEEP. It's probably been too much for her."

Oh, relief all round. Sure enough, Louise was asleep, snoozing in the comfortable water. Panic over.

As a post script to this tale of callous medical ethics and brutal treatment, years on, when Louise gave birth to her own daughter, the medics found damage to Louise's pelvis. One member of staff asked her if she had suffered from rickets as a child, which of course she hadn't, so when that was obviously NOT the cause of her pelvic trouble, the next question was "have you been in a very bad car accident?" Well, she HAD been in a very nasty birth 'crash'. I feel we were so lucky to have a bright and beautiful daughter. Nobody helped or mentioned physio for Louise's straight legs, but every time there was a break in jobs, one of us would carry out a pedalling action on her, bending and stretching. They might have bent correctly anyway, but we were all in the dark, as usual, but our very amateur efforts were rewarded.

Here endeth the medical disaster section.

I had to write it all down, even if I decide to obliterate it later. It's helped to actually put into words the birth experience, the aftercare, and how medicine and midwifery have thankfully moved on since 1965.

Other medical mistakes have occurred since. I'm not sure whether I can put them on paper. I'll see. I don't think being born on Friday the 13th is responsible. No doubt many people could write similar stories of medical disasters and lack of care and arrogance amongst the 'upper-crust' very arrogant surgeons of those days.

CARRYING ON

Mum was still trying her best to manage garden and a cold, crumbling house. The aunts visited her regularly, Auntie Glad borrowing a car now and then.

I did once walk with the pram around to 249 and deposit Louise with Mum and Auntie Vera. I almost ran down Tettenhall Road to the hairdresser's. Oddly, they were now situated where, years before, the very posh dress shop had been. This hairdo was almost the stand-up job that I had endured all those years before. I did sit down, though, but felt it was the electric chair, so worried was I, as I hadn't left Louise before (and didn't very much afterwards). A quick haircut, and I hared it back up the hill, to be met by two red-faced ladies, holding and rocking a bundle of screaming sweating child. They couldn't pass Louise back quickly enough!

I don't know how I could have left this bit out, but I will pop it in here. My piano and I were reunited shortly after getting the house habitable. It was placed in our front room, back against the hall wall, in exactly the same position as in the front room at 249. It probably felt at home again, after a very bumpy ride to Henwood Road. I played most days, just for my own enjoyment. The boogie-woogie that Joy had shown me came in handy, though I lacked the short drooping fag balanced on the lower lip that Joy usually sported, and the half-closed eye, as the smoke wound its way upward.

We hadn't heard any more from cousin Joy since the letter from a social worker had landed on the mat at 249, telling Mum that Joy had given her Auntie Maude as her next of kin. Mum thought that Joy was hoping to return to stay with us, but that was far too much for an already worn-out Maudie.

I have only just found out that Joy went on to work as a secretary in the civil department of a military office, somewhere in London. She had become stone deaf, so to achieve this secretarial post was a positive move. She was a fast typist in her younger days and she was very well read. Robin has books on poets, writers and politicians, the life of Disraeli and some weird 'mystics' in his bookcase today. The children's story, written when she was in her thirties, is still in our 'throw-it-all-in' wardrobe in the spare room, never having seen a publisher.

344

Joy was a strange woman, very masculine, hair always short, a man's hairdo, but I look back on her as fun, daring, quirky, talented, and a 'one-off' woman. Life had been hard to her. She died in the 1980s, unbeknown to us, in a home for retired military women in London. On her death certificate, the witness was a lady member of staff.

Where WERE Joy's three half-siblings? Ruth was now an eye surgeon, Mansel no doubt working in some white-collar job somewhere 'down south', and Barry, I believe was a bursar /purser to an independent school near the New Forest.

Mum never heard from any of Reg's children, except Joy, but even Joy couldn't communicate after about the late 1970s. We always feel that we were best forgotten by the Gittoes-Davies clan, but Joy had always been closer to the family at 249, but not close in any way to her three half-siblings. So we seemed to drift apart; the Gittoes-Davies clan and the Lloyd-Davies clan became strangers.

Life at 200 Henwood Road was busy. Louise was thriving, a golden-haired charmer. Tai Lu loved her, and was most distressed when Louise cried. He would rush into the kitchen and try to tell us she was crying. We used to place the carrycot on top of the sideboard, and Tai Lu would jump up onto the sideboard if he heard just a deep breath or whimper coming from the cot, then jump down and rush over to us. Contrary to what some friends said, he never lay on top of her. "Cats and babies don't mix" some old relation told us with foreboding, expecting Louise to be smothered any minute.

The neighbours were, as all our neighbours have been, and still are, lovely, friendly people. An elderly couple, Bessie and Arthur, lived one side. Oddly, Bessie had always worked in the antique shop at New Bridge, owned by Chas Brickman, Ruth's father. The shop had been taken over by a young woman, but Bessie stayed on when Chas died. Every day, Bessie (looking very glamorous, flowery hat well hat-pinned onto her greying ginger hair) would mount her trusty steed, and pedal off up the road. Her bike was so ancient it had a basket on the front and a semi-circular 'crossbar', so it was with some secret amusement when one morning we found poor Bessie standing on her drive, looking perplexed. Someone had stolen her bike! The thief must have been in a hurry to get somewhere, then dumped it!

Arthur played golf and went to the Whitmore Reans Working Men's Club every lunchtime. His car was a Morris Minor, no bikes for Arthur. They were good helpful neighbours. Their garden at the top end was open, no division between us, and on wet or windy days, if my line of washing took a dive, Bessie would rush out and get the (mainly nappies) in, and vice versa. Recipes changed hands, and if Bessie had baked for a family party, leftovers were brought round.

We had a telephone, but Bessie hadn't, so we took many a call from their friends… "Could you hang on a minute?" I'd then make a dash across to number 202 and Bessie would breathlessly take the call, sitting on a stool shrouded in coats, umbrellas and general rubbish in the cubby-hole under the stairs. (This cubby-hole telephone station was still going strong forty years later. One friend would always ask, "Are you STILL sitting in the cupboard?")

In those far-off days, we were on a party line. Our 'party' was two doors away. This family had two cheeky young lads, who thought it very funny to listen in to our conversations and giggle and make smart remarks throughout.

GOODBYE TO 249

Although Mum was still mobile, she was in pain with arthritis, so she decided that the time was right for a move. No. 249 was gradually crumbling, was draughty and cold, and the long back garden was getting too much for her. Somehow to Mum this move-to-be wasn't a painful thought, but it was to us.

Pat's husband had a very good job as a top accountant for Manders, the stain and varnish company, in Wolverhampton. If Mum saw a house she liked, Pat and Ray would help her financially. It was Pat who suggested it, but I think Ray was all right about it (he could be terribly mean with money…or 'tight' may be a better word).

So, the search began for a smaller, warmer place to live out her last years, having slogged away for over twenty years on floors at 249 that would have brick dust scattered over from the perished bricks disintegrating behind the skirting boards, and the endless trips carrying hot water upstairs to pour into our strange blue-painted bath.

Pat and Mum found just the right place, a little cottage almost opposite Pat, black and white, about as old as 249, so no change there, but a smaller back garden, and hardly any front garden – no long trudge up the path to the front door carrying shopping. It was what the doctor ordered for Mum, but a sad parting from a dearly loved house by us three siblings, particularly me, as I was the only one actually born there. So farewell to twenty-five years of discomfort, frozen water by the bed, but happy and sad memories.

So we began slinging anything that Mum couldn't take to her new abode. The giant stag's head (Mum's first piece of furniture!) was taken off to Tony's. There was a burnt-out incendiary bomb in the pantry, along with a heap of brown-edged glossy photos. They were Uncle Reg's, the ones given to him whilst working in PR for Paramount Films, which had hung around the walls in the dining room of the White House Hotel, now out of their frames, damp and going brown.

There was a huge bonfire burning away in the middle of the once green and daisied lawn. THEN, to our horror, the bundle of photos was thrown unceremoniously onto the fire. They shrivelled up, the faces of many famous film stars shrivelled into oblivion. Cary Grant, or Archie Leach as Reg knew him, was on the pyre, as were Mae West, Errol Flynn, and a host of other film idols. All signed 'To Reg'; some had signed 'with love'. They were all just ash. It was something Pat and myself felt sad about, but I suppose they WERE only pictures!

Years later, Mum was unrepentant and her excuse was, "Well, they were damp and mouldy in places, and curled. Anyway, who would want those old photos?"

The contents of a house which had been a family home for years were vast, and weird! The skeleton of the incendiary bomb was dumped, along with the scaly preserved skin of a baby alligator, which took up the whole hearth in the front room. The old rugger ball, laces rotted, also disappeared into the dustbin. Pairs of leaky wellies, garden tools that had lost handles and had rusted almost into the earth, along with general junk.

The cellar was always full with bottles from Mum's wine-making days, old boxes for long-gone gas masks (where DID those go, we wondered). I expect the bonfire was going strong for days. There was an ashtray that Dad had brought home one night, a hideous thing. It was a skull and cross bones, in plaster, nicely finished, with the inscription MEMENTO MORI around the edge. Robin bagged that, and still has it.

Mum's new abode was only tiny compared to 249, so she couldn't take much. We really left it to her to sort and choose. I suppose the new owner of 249 would sling everything left behind; he was going to turn the dear old house into four or more bedsits.

After weeks of ditching, slinging, and laughter over some long-forgotten rubbish, Mum was all ready for the move. So the stained-glass front door, with its roundel showing a river bank with a little boy fishing and a statuesque heron looking on, would be just a memory. The noisy mice behind the skirting boards, polished black lead grate, and the dreaded long, dark-red-linoed hallway, along with a host of memories, would soon be thrown into a skip.

We all stood looking for the last time at the garden, the blue-bricked yard where so many games had been played. We did cry, it was such a sad farewell. Well, it was for US, but not for Mum, who couldn't get away quickly enough!

MUM'S COTTAGE

Mum probably thought 'good riddance' to all that floor polishing, frozen water, and a scullery which was all right in the 1700s but was hell to work in; not exactly the black hole of Calcutta, but a draughty, dimly lit workplace for Mum for over thirty years.

Mum never did look back. She welcomed the warmth and comfort of her new home in a terraced black-and-white cottage that had been updated a year or two before. It had one sitting room, a 'modern' (well to Mum it was!) kitchen with a walk-in pantry, and a manageable back garden. Upstairs there was one very spacious bedroom. The other bedroom had been made into a large bathroom. The upstairs was reached by a winding staircase (later called a 'lighthouse job' by an ambulance man, and so it was).

The first thing done when Mum had finally moved a small portion of the furniture from 249 was to start revamping the long thin strip of back garden. Single-handed, she reconstructed a lawn, admittedly a little uneven in places, but quite an area. I think a few of her originally stolen hydrangea bushes, once small stolen cuttings from Nevin, North Wales, were the first plants to be installed in the narrow borders. She added primulas, lupins and a myriad other plants. The far end of the garden was a bramble area. I helped her cut it back and we found hidden raspberry canes, a bit wild now but nurturable. A slab stone path was laid by Mum. I'm not sure where from or if I'm correct, but she may have had help. The rough overgrown privet hedges each side were clipped back and brought under control. She would come into the kitchen almost purple faced, perspiration dripping onto her nose… but happy.

Mum had done the right thing. The move from 249 was good; she never looked back. Her sitting room was cosy, and a small bow window ensured that her potted 'spider-plants' were in the light. The two-bedded bedroom was also a warm and comfortable room, a haven when the stairs had been negotiated! A luxury bathroom, certainly to Mum, not all that up to date, but OH GOODNESS, an immersion heater, so HOT WATER on tap. What more could anyone want?

The bus to town also ran on the road outside, so she could make trips to get her groceries, no longer from the rather posh Masons, which had long gone, but from the less desirable Tesco's. Mum was moving with the times.

Shopping or even visiting the local post office required a tweedy ladies' trilby-type hat, coat to match, gloves (she wouldn't be seen dead without those) and a handbag. Her hair was beautifully trimmed by Maudie herself, and the Pond's face cream was administered every morning, along with a piece of 'shammy leather' which bore traces of her lipstick, so made a very good substitute for rouge. She would dab this on accompanied by a solidified powder, never panstick, which she considered 'common'!

So Mum settled in really well; no lingering thoughts of our crumbling but endearing 249. We all missed it, but Mum never spoke of it again.

MR A GOES A-COURTING

The new garden was giving up its soft fruit – the almost wild raspberries, and some gooseberries also found hidden amongst the weeds – so of course Mum made jam. Unfortunately, she would usually over boil it, and so the jam became almost toffee, but was nice anyway.

She had loads of visitors. One in particular she didn't need, but again this is Mum's version of it, so a rather 'romantic' view…

One of Dad's drinking friends was a Mr A, a single man, who had never married. (Hearsay has it that it was because his fiancée had died young and he had never got over it.) He was always walking to town from his digs in Tettenhall. He would have a packet of Spangles (fruit sweets) in his overcoat pocket, so any child walking past would get a sweetie. I suppose in today's world he could have looked like a child 'lurer' or pervert, or paedophile, but to our knowledge, he was just a rather gentle old man.

One Christmas, we invited him here for Christmas dinner. Mum came too, as Pat and Ray had bought a little cottage in North Wales, so always went there for the festive season. Of course Louise had the customary Spangles after the meal, and Mum and Mr A chatted about Dad and his 'cronies'– I'm sure Mum would say 'friends'.

He was rather like Mr Punch in looks, with a rather large hooked nose, a shock of white wavy hair, and always a buttonhole in his lapel, next to a starched shirt collar, courtesy of his landlady, who 'did everything' for him. I don't think he would know how to cook anything, not even egg and bacon, he was a serial lodger!

In the new year, Mum received a visit from Mr A. His hat would be doffed, and no doubt Mum would offer him tea in her Indian tree patterned tea-service. The visits became a weekly thing. Mum would moan a bit, as he would turn up when she was either baking or watching a soap on TV, or whilst crocheting. One visit, though, made her sit up and reach for the phone. She rarely used it except in an emergency, so I knew it was just that!

Apparently, Mr A had either given her a friendly hug or held her hand – this was going right over the top for Mum. "I think he wants to marry me. As if I COULD." She was quite upset.

Whether Mr A had actually asked her to marry him, we'll never know, but from then on, Mum didn't like him going round to see her, and she would try to avoid him if possible. Poor man, he still walked everywhere, the Spangles were still offered willy-nilly to all and sundry, adults included. I think he realized that somehow Mum was no longer the happy hostess, so his visits became less frequent.

(I'm afraid to say, that even when he was friendly with Mr A, after a drinking session, Dad, when home but not dry, would say, "Been to the club with 'A', he's a right old pouffter". I don't think Mr A preferred men, I just think he was a rather sad old man, not loved by a woman, having lost the love of his life, so he acquired a rather effeminate manner, not really Dad's cup of tea. But Mr A did like his drink, so, birds of a feather DO flock together, although these two birds' catalyst was alcohol.)

Life back at Henwood Road was going well, but life at work wasn't for Harold. The practice, Henry Vale & Sons, was under stress financially. Harold had always been very happy there, but there was talk of redundancies. One day, he was called into the office for a 'chat'. I had said goodbye to him outside our local playgroup's premises, dropping Louise, then aged four, for the morning. Harold jokingly said, "Do you think I should be wearing a black tie today?"

We waved him off and somehow I thought all would be well. He had quite a senior position and was liked by Trevor and Adrian, the partners. At lunchtime, Harold drove into the drive. "I should have been wearing that tie. I HAVE been given notice, redundancy and all that." What a blow.

A new chapter opened for Harold. He started a practice in Dudley, eight miles away, in the heart of the Black Country. Harold and a colleague who was a civil engineer bought a Victorian property together, his colleague having rooms on the ground floor.

Eventually, years later, his ex-boss Trevor Vale came to work for Harold and Harold's partner Ray, so it was a complete turnaround. Trevor was a very nice person. He had recently split from his wife of many years, so was feeling at a loss, and I think working in a small practice was helpful to him – no pressure like the years working in a family firm with high expectations and burdens. Trevor's younger brother also left the family firm and opened a toy and games shop in South Wales. Henry Vale & Sons struggled on but has now folded. Trevor had a very sad and untimely death. He was a kind man with problems that became too much to bear. He is remembered with great fondness.

CATS, COTTAGES, AND RUTH

Our holidays were usually taken either in Pat's caravan, or later in her one-storied fisherman's cottage on the Lleyn peninsula, just a few miles on from Pwllheli.

We decided to take Tai Lu on our next holiday, although he hated being in the car. Robin and Gwen and their children (another offspring, a daughter, had arrived) were going with us to the cottage.

We arrived and set up 'home'. The whole of the journey we had been regaled with a miserable howling, which was very upsetting. Louise cried, I cried, and I would think Harold was crying silently… it was a journey from hell.

It was a strange place, low doors, an outside loo, so you had to brave the elements and some steps when the need to 'go' arose. One night we opened the back door to be confronted by a cow. She was blocking the door to the loo, and it took some shooing to get her to go backwards. Tai Lu meanwhile was out every night. We could hear his yowls and screams as he fought off farm cats. Our bedroom window was always open so that he could jump in, and this he did, leaping onto and off the bed all night. There would be a few minutes of calm, we would try to nod off… THEN, having got his breath back, he would leap through the window, and there was another punch-up. Later in the holiday, Louise caught some bug or other, and was hallucinating, seeing 'creatures' crawling up the wall. Well, we felt as though WE were going 'up the wall'.

It was decided we could never take Tai Lu with us again, but of course we DID!

A year or so later, we decided to head for Pat's cottage, mark two… This was a lovely house, two cottages that had been knocked into one, many years before, overlooking the Porthmadog estuary and virtually the whole panorama of Snowdon. We couldn't leave our loud but endearing blue-eyed friend, so, very stupidly, we popped him into the car, where he sat on the back shelf looking very scared.

Over an hour later, we were about to reach Llangollen, when all three of us just couldn't listen any longer to his distressed wails. I held him on my shoulder as we drove into the village of Chirk. We stopped at traffic lights, and a crowd gathered around my window, children pressed their fingers to the glass. I suppose Tai Lu was unusual but somehow it was the last straw.

Ruth lived with husband Roy in Llangollen, just up the road, so we drove there. I'm not sure what we thought we were going to do. However, Ruth and her four young children were so excited to see us (mainly Tai Lu). "We'll have him," Ruth said, to the delight of the children. Bryony, their eldest, wheeled up her doll's pram and Tai Lu was popped into it, wrapped in a blanket, and pushed off down the garden. The canal was at the bottom of their large garden. I had a heart flutter thinking about it. The last we saw of him for a week was a small dark face, no ears showing, and his blue eyes peeping out from under a pink crocheted doll's hat, being wheeled up the path in the little pram! We all heaved a sigh of relief, our ears still ringing with Tai Lu's loud cries.

We decided that we must try to get Ruth and family a present for her kind gesture, but what? In the end, we bought a large, ready-for-the-oven chicken. Looking back, it's a bit strange, but with all the family there, and I knew that financially they were struggling a bit, so a chicken it was! I hope they enjoyed it. It was a small gift for such a very kind deed. Tai Lu was fine. He had been prowling around in their steep garden, hadn't fallen into the canal as I thought he might, and all the family loved him and were sorry to say cheerio.

As I mentioned earlier, but I didn't know at that time, although Ruth loved the children when they were babies, she had little patience with them when they got older. She became a very strict mother, too strict for me. Her children were forming their own characters, and were no longer immobile babies completely under their mother's control, so they had to be slapped and reprimanded for the tiniest mistake. If a child walked into the room and we were chatting together, the 'intruder' would be told to "GET OUT, WE ARE TALKING!" No explanation from the child would do. The "GET OUT" was repeated, and they HAD to make a hasty retreat.

Later, Ruth got a job in a children's home in Wales. Why she chose to look after other children when she found her own brood not to her liking, I will never know. She worked nights sometimes, and not being able to drive, she relied on Roy to take and fetch her. Her family fell to pieces years later when she left home with her youngest son, leaving Roy to look after the other three. We once visited Ruth in her tiny ex-chapel home in the town, as we were passing on our way to Pat's cottage. She was happily working for a local seed merchant in the office. No explanation was given about her separation, and the conversation was stilted and guarded.

We did correspond now and then. Ruth did write that she was in and out of hospital… something about her throat. She felt that something was stuck. Nobody in her family told us what DID happen to Ruth at this time.

I met her sister once in Wolverhampton town centre, but she was guarded too, so I was reluctant to ask. However, later, I met Mrs Brickman in town. She appeared very worried about Ruth. "She's a little better now, but months ago she weighed under six stone." I can't say exactly what was the matter, and I can't blame the family for keeping it dark. Mental illness was a most embarrassing illness. It was shrouded in mystery.

Although Ruth had left three children in the care of Roy, the children were still very fond of their mother. It did surprise me, as Ruth meted out some harsh treatment at times when they were young, particularly to her daughter Bryony, who still talked kindly of her mother. One instance of strange behaviour from mother to daughter stands out.

We were at Chester Zoo. Bryony was about thirteen or so. The monkey house had a glass frontage. A notice stated DO NOT BANG ON THE GLASS. Bryony didn't bang hard on the glass, but she did touch it. In front of everyone, Bryony was bent over her mother's knee and smacked hard on her buttocks. I can't forget this, it was quite out of order and left Bryony embarrassed and tearful. I should have known this was NOT the normal chastisement given to a young daughter and alarm bells should have rung, but, unsettling as it was, and upsetting, we felt unable to intervene.

Bryony married young and seemed happy and fulfilled. We were asked to take Ruth's awful mother to the wedding over the border in Wales. I took a phone call from Mrs B prior to the wedding. True to form, Mrs B hadn't got a good word for Bryony's groom. "He's as common as muck, dear," Mrs B said in her plummy accent. Mrs B was a snob to the end.

Ruth's three other children were friendly with her too, and I think popped in to see her. For many years, Ruth was admitted to hospital. Occasionally she wrote to me, saying that she was under investigation and having tests on her stomach. "I feel as though I have a feather stuck in my throat," she once wrote. We were never informed by Mrs B or Ruth's sister, but we gather that there were many hospital visits and stays. Whether Ruth had anorexia, we are not sure, but we know she had years of medical treatment, but we didn't know what for.

Years on, we received an invitation to Ruth's wedding. She was marrying a retired psychiatrist. It was a surprise, but I was pleased that she had found happiness. We went to her wedding, and she looked really well. Her weight was as I remember it, and she looked very happy. The newly weds settled into the groom's family home. He was a widower with a grown-up family, and was a grandfather.

We corresponded often. Both of us liked writing and receiving the written word. I felt Ruth had found her haven, after a few years of stormy and rather troubled sea. The most surprising part of her new life was that she and her 'new' husband took up bridge, a game that she had said she would never NEVER play, due to her parents always arguing and shouting at each other after a bridge session!

This isn't the end of the story of our friendship, but I'm not sure if I should, or could, put it down on paper. I will just say… I think Ruth DID find happiness for some years. Latterly, cards from me seemed to fall on stony ground and Ruth didn't reply – not like her. She (like me) was a very keen letter-writer.

In the last year, I heard that Ruth was living near to Wolverhampton, in a nursing home. Nobody had told us, I gleaned the information from Ruth's nephew. We visited her one sunny summer's day. The home was like a four-star hotel, very gracious living, all pale green drapes. A very friendly lady took us into a lounge, where there were elderly ladies sitting, some half asleep. I was walking past one lady, when Harold tapped my arm. "That's Ruth," he whispered, turning to an elderly lady. The lady in question looked to me. I felt I was looking at Ruth's mother, but of course it was Ruth. She smiled and I held her hand. Her fingernails were beautifully painted bright pink. So the staff must have cared.

When I said who we were, she smiled again, but I knew she hadn't a clue WHO we were. "I'm waiting for my darling husband to come," she said, looking expectantly at the door… "He WILL come," she said. But somehow we didn't think he WOULD come. We had heard that her husband was very ill and housebound.

I was still holding her hand, marvelling at her nails, but all of a sudden, she pulled her hand away and said very curtly in her 'elbows off the table' voice, "Off you go, then." And she turned away.

We waved goodbye… but she didn't watch us go.

I have spoken to Ruth's older sister since that visit (again through a bit of research into her son's telephone number). During the conversation, her sister said, "Ruth has been mentally ill for a VERY long time."

I knew what she meant, and looking back now, I understand. However, we were good friends when young, and had many a happy hour laughing and crying over boys, sewing rather strange frilly dresses and exchanging secrets.

HAROLD'S PARENTS, SYD AND ETHEL

I must add some history of Harold's family

Ethel was from a small village in Norfolk. She was one of about nine children, and her father was a policeman and bailiff. In a rural community many of the girls were taken into service, at the 'big house'. Ethel was one of these girls. Possibly only fourteen, she was taken on as a kitchen maid. After a year or so, when she was around sixteen, the head cook in the big house got a job as a cook to a rich family in Canada. She asked Ethel if she would like to go with her. We don't know much more about how or why Ethel said 'Yes', but she did, and so began a life in Toronto, Canada, and then in the USA.

Thinking back, it must have been a huge and daunting step to leave her family and the village that she had never ventured from, and then spend weeks on a liner with an older woman. This she did, but we don't know much about the journey. Harold never asked, and Ethel wasn't forthcoming.

Canada was wonderful, and she did tell us a little about it. Also there are snaps of Ethel, smartly dressed in 1920s' gear, cloche hat in place, with friends, probably on her day off.

The family she worked for took to her, and she became a cook proper. The young son of the house was very frail. Ethel never knew what was ailing him, but he was put on an invalid's diet, which she had to prepare. This consisted of jelly made up from the boiled feet of chickens. It was thought to be full of goodness, which I doubt.

For the adults, pheasant was often shot and hung… "They would hang them by the neck until the neck rotted and the body fell to the ground," was one of her tales of life below stairs. The little chipmunks were a delight to her. They would visit the kitchen door, I suppose for food thrown out. There was no Fairy washing-up liquid then, so earth from outside would be used as a scrub for saucepans and metal dishes, the gritty soil doing the trick, but I do wonder if anyone ever picked up bacteria from this rather basic dish washing.

What happened to her head cook from England, she never said. Also, what did happen to the poor little boy who had to suck down that pale grey chicken's foot jelly?

Ethel stayed there for many years, and on her marriage, her employers gave her a wonderful silver teapot, sugar and milk set, engraved with the combined initials of S and E and H. So Ethel would be greatly missed after her marriage to Harold's father Syd, who, although from Liverpool, met and married Ethel in New York. How or why Ethel was in New York is a complete mystery, never to be solved. Syd was there working for the shipping line Cunard, owners of the White Star Line, much in the news in 1912 as the owners of the ill-fated Titanic. However, this was about 1931, so long after that disaster. Syd worked as a clerical officer, I believe.

SYDNEY CALLOW HAMPTON

Syd was born in Liverpool in 1896 to a ship worker, Robert Hampton, the eventual captain of a dredger, and mother Florence, who hailed from the Isle of Man, whose family name was Callow. There are a few relatives named Christiansen, possibly descendants of Danes who had invaded the island hundreds of years before.

When Syd was in his early teens, his father was seconded to Spain, in charge of the dredger. He took his wife Florence and Syd's two older sisters and a brother with him and they lived in Spain for some time. Syd's older sister, May, went to school in Spain, and was able to learn the language. Not many of her family knew much about this time in her life; that is, until May was very ill at the end of her long life. According to her daughter, she would sometimes lapse into Spanish. Remarkable, as she hadn't spoken it for probably seventy years!

Syd stayed home until 1914/15, when he was called up or volunteered to fight in the First World War. He was sent to France as a foot soldier, we THOUGHT, but searching on an ancestry site, we uncovered the very unbelievable fact that Syd was placed in the horse division. Anyone who knew Syd would be speechless with surprise, as Syd wouldn't have known which end he had to feed and which end produced manure! What he DID with the horses in his care we will never know, but his war came to an abrupt end later on, possibly in 1917, when he was shot in the neck and shoulder. This he never discussed with anyone, certainly not Harold or his other sons.

There is a hiatus here, but I do know that in his mid-twenties Syd decided to sail to the USA. He states on the record (just uncovered) that he wished to take up FARMING when in the States. Nobody would even think or dream that Syd, a Liverpool 'townie', could possibly know (or care) about anything vaguely rural. We think he had to give a reason for his passage, so he hit on farming. It's funny, as all his life he couldn't tell a flower from a weed. Ethel was a wonderful gardener.

He appears to have returned to the UK a year or so later, and again we have unearthed some lists of passengers and crew. THIS time Sydney Callow Hampton was on the crew list as A CHEF! How that came about is bizarre! Later in life when widowed, Syd showed no aptitude for cooking anything more than egg and bacon. All these different personae must have been a means to get to and from the States.

Syd must have gone back one more time, because he met and married Ethel in the late 1920s. Ethel's engagement ring bears the mark of a New York jeweller, as does her wedding ring. How they met isn't known, possibly at a dance.

Syd and Ethel rented a flat in Queens, New York, and this is where Harold's older brother Douglas was born in in 1930. Harold followed four years later. Douglas was christened in New York, but Harold wasn't. (He had to put up with a christening when about ten years old, back in the UK. By then he would possibly be taller than the vicar!)

The family lived many floors up in a skyscraper building, and Ethel related how she would have a job getting the pram into the lift. It must have been a strange life.

Syd's younger brother Bert had also been roaming around Canada and the States, and he was best man at the wedding, as he did his best to get to New York at that time. We think he was in the Canadian Mounties at some time, so another member of the Hampton clan to get friendly with the horses!

I believe Syd made quite a lot of money when in the States. At one time, just before his marriage, he had been a 'passenger PR' on a cruise ship to the Caribbean – the Bahamas and the ports around that coast. Some menu cards and passenger lists are with us now. The Churchill family from Britain were on board. We have the menu and list today. We are pretty sure these people were THE Churchill family. This was about 1925.

Bert Hampton married just before the Second World War. After two weeks of marriage, Bert joined the navy and became a crew member on the boat HMS *Hood*. After just a short honeymoon, his young wife Jess was widowed. HMS *Hood* was blown up by the Germans, and as it was carrying explosives, it was completely destroyed. I don't think there were many, if any, survivors. Jess lived until her eighties. She never remarried.

Ethel made one trip back to see her folks when Douglas was about three – very brave, as she was alone; Syd had stayed behind due to work. Ethel returned, and all the family eventually sailed home, Douglas six, Harold two. Two little very smartly dressed boys, so the older relatives said. Doug, who had been so used to lifts not stairs, was puzzled. "Where's the elevator?" he asked an auntie, to their amusement.

The family settled for a while in St Johns Wood, London, where Syd invested in two properties. Financially he was 'comfortable'. Later when the War Bonds came about, he gave quite a large amount to help the war effort. Years after the war had ended, his money had gone down to a fraction of its original amount. What a cruel ending to a generous gift.

Ten years after Harold was born, and fourteen years after Doug's birth, Ethel became pregnant. This was terribly embarrassing for her. Not only was she just beginning to enjoy life, as the two boys were growing up, but worse, she was forty-two, and beyond 'all that'. She told me she rode her pushbike until the nine months were almost over, well covered up, so that the neighbours wouldn't see her enlarging figure.

Nature did its bit, though, and another son arrived, Robert John Hampton, called Bobby by the family, but Bob in later life. I think the song 'I Want to Be Bobby's Girl' was around at that time too, so a very trendy name!

So Syd and Ethel had three sons. Ethel was a gardener, growing all their vegetables, and turning up trousers, letting them down again, and working very hard indeed to make ends meet. I used to notice her stained and work-worn hands. Ethel thought that the family were rather struggling financially, so keeping three boys in uniforms and sports equipment must have been a great worry to her. She suffered from 'tummy trouble' on and off. She said she thought it was the stress and strain of bringing up the family and constantly trying to 'make ends meet'.

Syd had never told Ethel 'his business'. Everything financial was a closed book to her. Eventually, Syd did buy his hard-working wife a small fridge. (Later years revealed that Ethel had struggled needlessly, as they were better off than she thought.) She was always home cooking and a loyal member of the local Co-op, with a number that Harold can remember to this day. Her pushbike was her trusty steed for many years.

Ethel Hampton was a worker. She was a member of the WI in Codsall, Staffordshire, and amused us one day by telling us that Peter Casson the hypnotist had given a demonstration one evening. She had been chosen from the crowd. She couldn't say WHAT she did on the stage, but whatever it was, she enjoyed the experience.

Ethel's tummy trouble began to worry her so she consulted a gastric surgeon, who immediately sent her to the hospital. An operation was performed. I can't say what it was for, really, because nobody has ever said anything concrete. Cancer has been mentioned since. Whatever it was, Ethel survived, and for a few weeks afterwards, an aunt came to look after the boys, especially little Bobby.

Harold won a place at the Wolverhampton Grammar School. He had wanted to go to Doug's school, Brewood Grammar School out in the countryside, about four miles away, but Syd was adamant. He wanted Harold to get the best education, so he wrote Wolverhampton Grammar down as top on his list of possible schools. Harold hated the idea and cried that his mates would think him a sissy… it was too 'posh' so he DIDN'T want to go THERE!!

361

Harold DID go there and it was the best thing a father could have done for his son. Harold was bright, also very athletic – cricket, athletics, he loved it all, and did very well academically too. Wolverhampton Grammar School was, and still is, a wonderful place of learning, and a good grounding for any child. The school now accept girls. (Harold thinks he was born too early.)

Harold's older brother Doug grew up a tall handsome young man. He joined the police force but had to leave to do his National Service. During his two years in the army, he was sent to Kenya. After his stint in the forces, for reasons unknown, he didn't go back to the police. Instead he applied for a job at Henry Vale & Sons Quantity Surveyors, the firm that Harold joined later and worked for many years.

Just before Doug's twenty-first birthday, around Christmas time, he felt very unwell, and after a few days was admitted to the Royal Hospital. He was a patient there for several days. On the 3rd of January 1951, Doug died. The medics said it was rheumatic fever, but Ethel always maintained that his spell in Africa was the cause of his illness, "I think he must have caught one of those native germs out there," she once told me.

This was something that must have changed Ethel and Syd's life forever. Ethel would lay a place at the table at Christmas and other 'high days' and holidays. I was afraid to mention his death, but I really wished I had plucked up courage, as I think mother-in-law Ethel especially would have been glad of the chance to talk about her firstborn. It's only since I have had my own children that I now fully realize how devastating it is to lose a child. I didn't think too much about it all when young, and Harold didn't say much about the ordeal, except that he NOW feels he didn't pay enough attention to his parents' grief. It's a young person's way of coping, I think.

Syd and Ethel cut off a small lock of Doug's dark curly hair, and it's been in an envelope ever since. We looked at it the other day, and can't bring ourselves to throw it away. Bobby was seven when Doug died, so Ethel had a young child to look after, which may have slightly eased her sadness.

When Louise was four years old, Ethel fell ill. She had stomach trouble, something she had suffered with all her married life. She was admitted into the Royal Hospital in town for an operation to remove an obstruction.

After the op, we were visiting one evening, when a nurse popped her head round the ward door and beckoned Harold out into the corridor. I sat with Ethel for a few minutes, and then Harold reappeared. Harold told us he had known this young nurse, and on meeting him again, she had wanted to get up to date with news of family. So we all went on chatting, quite happy, as Ethel felt that her operation was over and done with.

What Harold didn't tell me until later when back home was that the operation was never done. The surgeon had opened her stomach but found that the tumour was inoperable, so he had closed her up, unable to help her any further. Harold had made up the nurse-friend story so that Ethel wouldn't suspect that anything was awry.

Whilst in the two-bedded ward, Ethel was befriended by a woman in the other bed, who had undergone minor surgery. Ethel did strike up an 'all in the same boat' friendship with Mrs T, but would tell me later that she was 'NOT my sort at all'. But of course they had exchanged stories of their families, as two women incarcerated together would. Mrs T certainly WASN'T Ethel's sort, but Mrs T and her husband seemed to impress Syd.

Ethel returned home and was nursed in her bed for weeks, always hopeful of recovery. She must have guessed that she was very ill, but the word cancer was never mentioned. It was when I was sitting by her bed that she told me how hard she had worked all her life, particularly when the boys were young. She told me that Syd had money put away all that time, money earned in America, money that he never told her about, so her scrimping should never have happened, as they were always comfortably off. I was shocked. I felt angry at how Syd could have watched Ethel trying her best to cope financially. It wasn't a nice Hampton trait, and I felt differently about quiet, smiling, Syd after that.

Ethel Rachel Alexandra née Yaxley died at home, having been nursed by Macmillan nurses. Syd's sister May also travelled over from Liverpool to stay and help out, and neighbours both sides were extremely good, watching over Syd. Ethel was buried in the same grave as her firstborn son Douglas.

THE ACCIDENT

Louise was about five when I discovered that I was pregnant again. Louise Jane was a lovely golden-haired child. Her slightly wavy hair was a delight to Mum, as all Mum's sisters and her own two daughters had very straight hair, but all the 'boys' (Mum's brothers) had wiry very curly hair. Very unfair, I think.

"Look, she's DEFINITELY going to have curls," Mum would say, winding a wisp of hair around her finger.

Louise loved school (I think), although she has since told me things that I had no idea of her real feelings about. In fact, she has told me that as a mother, I was naïve, but I think she means when she was older, a teenager or beyond!

I have no idea what I said when I told Louise that she would be having a baby brother or sister – no scans in those days. I thought I had prepared her well for a sibling's arrival, but again I must have completely messed it up, because apparently I didn't!

The new arrival was due just after Christmas, so in the summer, when I was about three months, we decided to go to Wimbledon to see the tennis, as we might not get another chance. Harold had been a lucky winner in a tickets out of a hat-type draw for seats. We had Centre Court ones, which was very exciting. We left Louise in the care of Pat, and off we set. We had probably rarely been out on our own in the car, so it was a treat.

We enjoyed the day, and did what everyone does, the strawberries and cream bit, and felt the thrill of seeing famous stars of tennis. Rather hard seats, even with the little cushions provided (or hired?).

We set off home, along the M1 motorway. It should have taken about three hours but this time it took us about eight. I had never drifted off in a car in my life, but I DID let myself fall asleep on this journey (I was the passenger, I must add). How I wish I hadn't, because when I awoke I thought I must be in a terrible nightmare… we were being lifted up into the air.

I didn't know it at the time, but we were crashing into a lorry.

Just off the M1, at a large island, a lorry's brakes had failed. The lorry then hit a small white van, which in turn ran into us, which then pushed us back into the out-of-control lorry, so a bash both ends. It was a very nasty accident, for the car. The front and the back were completely wrecked, only the centre bit, the cab and front and back seats, were untouched.

It was all over so quickly. I awoke to feel the car rise up, lots of noise, and a lot of shouting. The passenger door my side had been bent inwards with the impact, so I could only open it a few inches. Harold shouted for me to get out. This I did, managing to squeeze out, no bump as yet. Harold thought that the van had driven into us and knocked us into the lorry. He hadn't seen the lorry hit the van first. There were some F-words from Harold (never heard before or since) to the van driver, then an apology when he heard the van driver's explanation.

The lorry driver was sitting out on the grass verge, head in hands, thinking the worst. What a mess. The police arrived on the scene. By then, we were sitting on the grass verge, and when I told them that I was pregnant, I was quickly ushered to a police car, and made to lie on the back seat. We watched as a lorry with a crane picked up our car, which was by now just a cab. I felt all right, shaky and a headache. Harold was the same, shocked but ok.

Then a strange thing happened, and I don't know if it was very good policing. The police were receiving messages in the car all the time whilst interviewing us, but one message came in which must have been VERY urgent, because, without any ceremony, I was told they had to dash off to another 'worse accident', so would we go back and sit on the verge again until our 'rescue' driver picked us up!

The rescuer was Pat's husband Ray, who arrived in his pyjamas under his trousers, as by now it was the middle of the night. Talk about abandonment! At the time, I didn't worry too much; we were safe, and so were the other drivers but, looking back, WHAT a dreadful let-down by the police.

I did have a little bit of 'trouble' pregnancy-wise the next day and also a headache, so we consulted the doctor, our lovely Dr Sayers, my hero, who sensibly told us that if a baby is healthy and well, all would remain in situ, but if it was easily moved, then 'let it happen', because the pregnancy wasn't a strong one.

All WAS fine and the next day we went to Pat's children's school fete, none the worse for wear. I can't say the same for our car, though. That was in the breaker's yard within hours. "It's only a car" everyone said, and how right they were.

Although this was really nothing dreadful at the time, this accident did have tremendous repercussions for us later, which have dragged on for years.

I must put a small chapter in this saga about our late neighbour, who became part of our lives.

WELSH KATHLEEN

About this time, the early 1970s, we had become friends with a near neighbour, Kathleen, a retired domestic science teacher. Kathleen was born in Cardiff about 1908. Her father, a teacher, was a clever man but had been thrown out of Aberystwyth University for burning some furniture, supposedly for warmth. Her mother was Scottish and a lady who had four offspring, but would spend her days sitting behind a screen reading, so letting the hired nanny/help bring up her children. The days in Wales sounded rather haphazard but good fun. The visits to Tenby, running around and playing on the beaches, and nude bathing in the sea, were all spoken about with affection by Kathleen.

Kathleen became a teacher of domestic science in Wolverhampton. The subject was very different in the 1930s, from what I gather, not so much actual cooking but much more scientific than today. Also the cleaning and laundry work seemed to be part of it.

When she was in her early twenties, Kathleen was desperate to get back to Cardiff for some family function. Flying was in its infancy, and passenger flights were not usually available. However, they WERE to the indomitable Kathleen. I'm not sure HOW she procured it, but she became the only passenger in an aeroplane flying from Birmingham airport to Cardiff. "There was only ME and the pilot. It was very windy up there, and only a flap-type- thing to protect us from the elements," she related. I think she had to wear a helmet kind of headgear, but THAT may be my imagination! I could always picture her with a dark-brown leather close-fitting helmet and wearing goggles. That attire would fit Kathleen; she never conformed.

When in her middle twenties, Kathleen married Vincent, a senior school teacher, a man troubled by demons, mentally unstable, and a great worry to Kathleen. Vincent never wanted children, so they were denied a family; he was very adamant about it.

When I say I was friendly, it WAS a friendship that lasted until she was ninety-nine, but Kathleen was a very dogmatic and at times an extremely difficult character. She played bridge at the local club, and made friends but also a lot of enemies. She spoke her mind, when really she should have said nothing, but THAT was not her way. Her Welsh voice was strong as though addressing her class of teenage girls. I came in for a lot of 'teacher-to pupil' admonishments, as did other friends and one particular neighbour.

It was years before we realized how ill Vincent had become. Apparently, he was seeing people following him, so he would hide when walking home from school, to get away from 'the followers' who were lurking behind lamp posts. He must have been mentally unstable for many years.

Kathleen did say once that Vincent was always called for when a boy in a colleague's class was disobedient. "Let Vincent deal with him," which meant that the unlucky lad would be caned, by Mr Price, who must have enjoyed it or got some sort of gratification from hurting a child. Kathleen didn't hide that fact; she was almost proud of Vincent's ability to bring fear to all the boys who didn't toe the line.

When Vincent was retired and ill, Kathleen bought a car, a bright egg-yolk yellow one (can't say what make as I am car-blind). We named this car the Yellow Peril. So bad was Kathleen's driving that one day when driving into a hospital car park, she demolished someone's wing mirror. Then, when exiting the same car park, she managed to scratch and slightly dent another hospital visitor's pride and joy. She was always unrepentant. One 'slight' accident became a police case, and she was summoned to appear in court for breaking someone's wing mirror off and not stopping or reporting it. Kathleen somehow escaped court, but was fined. She was a little more worried about this, but she resumed driving straight away. We used to watch her back out of her drive, our eyes half shut in fear, ears covered, waiting for the crunch of metal on metal. But she did manage to carry out this manoeuvre without too much harm to her car or others. Definitely more luck than judgement.

Vincent died one November day. My friend Jane the nursing sister, who had only met Kathleen twice, was summoned to the house where Vincent was lying. Kathleen wanted to lay her husband out, something that Jane thought was rather cheeky, but it was typically Kathleen. "He must be wearing his good suit," were the instructions.

I heard the story from Jane and we did have a little giggle about it. The fact that no undertakers were called but the laying-out procedure was hours after the death, so poor Jane had quite a job to fit him into his best attire. Rigor mortis had set in, and that didn't help.

Now widowed Kathleen didn't let the grass grow under her feet. The Yellow Peril travelled as far as Brecon, in Wales, but most journeys were NOT without incident.

Visits to us were frequent, and not at all dreary. She liked Robin and Louise, and always asked what they were doing at school. If she had been given some delicious Thornton's chocolates, she would almost 'hop and skip' round to present me with one or two. Her Christmas cakes were made to an old recipe, then placed in a deep bowl half full of alcohol. "Any will do, whatever you have left over." The cake would then gradually 'suck up' all the sherry/brandy/whisky. (I have taken a leaf from Kathleen's book and the old recipe lives on.)

She attended communion every Sunday. Later, when she had given up driving, she would ask a neighbour to drive her to church, usually to morning matins. Kathleen would insist on being driven into the churchyard, and then (usually late) she would stride with her friend in tow through the big noisy doors to the very front row of pews, much to her good friend's embarrassment. Then if the sermon went on too long, she would drag the friend out well before the last hymn, to the amusement of the congregation. Most of the people there knew Kathleen well, she was known for her eccentricity.

Kathleen liked her clothes. One winter's day, she arrived here in an outfit befitting a royal. A blue-mink coat and a matching hat, very expensive looking, rather out of date, but a talking point. I had never seen mink before, let alone BLUE mink. I did have a shudder thinking about how many dozens of minks had been sacrificed for this, but they were long dead. All kinds of 'dress parades' were acted out in our house. She loved the colour red, so she would walk the 'catwalk' in our sitting room like a turkey-cock. Last but not least were Kathleen's rings. Most were opals. Although she had never been to Australia, she loved the changing colours of the stones, and sometimes there would be four or more rings adorning her hands.

There was a friend in her life for a little while. A fellow bridge player, he would arrive in his big white van (not really to Kathleen's liking, but this van got her to the bridge club, so she endured it). The bridge sometimes went on almost to midnight, too late for her colleague to drive home, so some mornings the white van was still in her drive. We smiled about this, and all sorts of suggestions were put forward by the family, about whether the friend R was so arthritic (he walked with a stick or sticks) it was too much to expect him to drive miles home, or perhaps they were playing again next day… This went on until one sunny morning, when looking out of our bedroom window, we saw on Kathleen's washing line, blowing in the gentle breeze, a pair of long johns. This was a regular occurrence and the long johns were joined on occasions by a woolly vest and various other male garments. Good for Kathleen.

The little romance didn't last long. Apparently, according to other members of the bridge club, Kathleen appeared one morning holding a bundle of clothes. Without a word, she threw them onto a table where R was sitting then made a dignified exit. She never told us what had happened, but we think it was a bridge move by R that stopped them getting a rubber, a crime never to be forgiven.

As the years rolled on, we slid into being part-time carers for Kathleen. She had never suffered fools gladly, so sometimes 'word arrows' were shot towards both of us, mainly at me, because she still preferred men. Harold became her driver to bridge and general light-bulb changer.

FROM A TWO-SEATER TO CONCORDE

When Kathleen was in her eighties, her niece suggested a trip to Morocco. Of course Auntie Kathleen was delighted; she would definitely go.

The means of transport was on the super streamlined aeroplane Concorde. It couldn't have been more different from her maiden flight in the little 1930s' plane. She wasn't in any way nervous; she was a stoic, and her aches and pains caused by arthritis were forgotten.

We eagerly awaited her return a week later. Oh ALAS, it wasn't all good. When reaching the airport in Morocco, her suitcase was not amongst the other passengers' luggage. So no clothes or toiletries. To find underwear for an eighty-year-old lady in Morocco was impossible.

"I had to wash my knickers every night and hang them over the window sill. And as for other clothes, I just bought a great big kaftan and wore that all the week."

The suitcase never materialized, 'lost in transit'. Kathleen had lost not just clothes but a Swedish gold brooch, her mother's. That did upset her, but the loss of her clothes wasn't the end of her world; she quite liked striding around the narrow streets in her flowing brightly coloured kaftan. That was Kathleen.

The actual flight wasn't mentioned much, she had taken that in her stride.

Months later, Kathleen received a bottle of champagne and some flowers from whoever 'ran' Concorde. I don't think she got any money back for her lost items.

Life went on, with all the trials and tribulations, deaths and births.

Kathleen had a nice old lady, a cleaner she had employed years before, and her friends from bridge called and sometimes played bridge there with Kathleen. It was difficult to get a 'four' as many of her friends were very ancient, in their eighties and nineties.

Lots of water under the bridge later, we were shopping, preparing meals, and going round to visit Kathleen every day. She stayed in her home in spite of two burglaries. One in particular was sinister. She awoke one night to see a masked man by her bed. He didn't speak to her or move towards her, he just fumbled for her handbag and left the bedroom. It transpired that he had drilled into an old wooden window in her breakfast room and lifted the window pane out. Our phone rang, and we called the police. They were very helpful and supportive of Kathleen, who they viewed as a frail old lady who would be traumatized by this assault on her privacy. They didn't know Kathleen. She bounced back and didn't feel fear going to bed, or being in the dark; she just got on with her life. The thief was never caught.

A second intruder entered her house in the daytime. A young lad climbed onto her waste bin in the side passage, and then through a window and down into her room. Kathleen was in there reading. "Give us your handbag." The handbag wasn't given, but the youth grabbed it and, looking frightened, he ran out.

This still didn't put Kathleen off. She continued, with help, until her nineties. There is a lot I could say, but I will draw a veil over it. She wasn't the easiest of women, and at times she made life very uncomfortable for us all. I think 'tearing hair out' covers it!

After a lot of visits to nursing homes, we found one close to Henwood Road, and Kathleen resided there, in a single room, staying in there most of the time, not eating downstairs with some of the other residents. It was not ideal. The nursing was all right, but the room was paltry, and there were no real napkins, just thin white paper ones at meal times, and no china cups, just thick bog-standard cups, or sometimes mugs. The name tags we sewed on to her rather expensive clothes didn't deter the staff – we would find Kathleen wearing someone else's skirt or top. Her wool dresses, which were so smart, became mini dresses after they had shrunk in a too-hot wash. They became unwearable.

Kathleen's ninetieth birthday loomed. We and others said, "You may get a telegram from the Queen. You're nearly one hundred."

"I certainly DON'T want to live to see THAT," she would say, with feeling.

Well, she didn't see a hundred. We went to sit with her one sunny afternoon. She was curled up in bed, in a foetal position. She didn't open her eyes and just said, "Go away, and leave me to die."

We waved her goodbye, and her plea to be left alone was answered.

We had a phone call that evening to come to the home; Kathleen was fading. We dashed to see her before her demise, but she had beaten us to it. Kathleen was curled up, looking as though she was asleep. There was a nice smiley black lady by the bed who had been sitting by her charge's bedside, so Kathleen wasn't alone when she made her last journey.

Harold was her executor (he had been give power of attorney many years before). Kathleen was a generous friend. She left me her largest and most expensive opal ring. Robin and Louise received one hundred pounds. Lastly, Harold was left a very nice gift of money.

Difficult was Kathleen's middle name, but we admired her guts, and we became very fond of her over twenty years. We visit her grave on 1st March, St David's day, and leave her some daffodils.

I just thought I would pop in this piece about a stalwart, sometimes very rude, old friend.

BACK AT THE WOMEN'S HOSPITAL

As the birth of my second child approached, I found myself back at the Women's Hospital. I hated the thought of walking into the place where, over five years earlier, so much unhappiness and pain had changed my outlook on life. Unlike five years before, now I walked in with fear and dread in my heart. I still had to keep a happy countenance. I had the feeling that somehow Louise's birth traumas should be 'hushed up' and were possibly my fault.

Harold did know that I was very fearful and scared. This pregnancy had been better, but… and it was a BIG but… Harold got me into bed, new nighties to the fore, and then he left. Six years on, and still fathers were not allowed to attend their child's birth. (But I must add that, even if dads had been allowed to be present, Harold would never be there – he didn't like the thought of all that blood and gore. Neither did I!)

It was the same ward as five years earlier. Six beds, all but one occupied by a mixture of mothers-to-be. There were smiles all round from the patients, and the atmosphere felt lighter and less rigid. I couldn't believe it when in the evening a nurse arrived bearing gifts…

These were a whole box of sanitary towels! "Here you are, ladies!" She plonked the box down. I can't remember WHAT we DID with these, but it was a sort of packing and wrapping job. We sat in a small circle, laughing and chatting, so in a way it was more relaxing.

I was due to be induced in the morning by Mr F the gynaecologist. Not a pleasant thought, but I was tired and not too unhappy. The bed opposite was empty, but in the late evening, nurses escorted a Caribbean patient to her bed and settled her in. Her husband came in and sat beside her, but his wife didn't speak, she was busy reading the Bible and mumbling quietly. There was some rushing about, and the husband was earnestly talked to by sister. It appeared that this lady had given birth earlier, but would not see or talk about her baby. She was disturbed and began swaying, then trying to get out of bed. She was restrained, and the poor husband began crying, desperate to talk to his wife. She just flung herself about and began shouting, very loudly – very heart-wrenching.

A young girl in an end bed was visibly frightened. We exchanged scared

373

looks. Eventually, the husband left the ward and we tried to settle down. This was too difficult so three of us ended up in the bathroom down the corridor. Two ladies were smoking (in those far-off days, smoking and pregnancy was not a sin, as today). We all chatted and generally hung around, scared to go back to the ward

The lady was still shouting and trying to 'leg it', so at about 3am, on the morning I was supposed to give birth, I was leaning against a wash basin, in the women's loos, chatting in a cloud of smoke.

Back in bed once more, we all tried to get some sleep. I was the only patient with a bell above the bed to call for help. Suddenly, the young girl in the next but one bed cried out, "Ring for help. She's trying to steal something out of my locker!"

We all sat bolt upright. The frightened unstable lady was beside the young lady's bed, trying to pull something out of her bedside locker. It was as if she was sleep-walking; she didn't show any fear or emotion. Nurses arrived. They put the wanderer into her bed and did what they could, but she wouldn't accept a drink or talk to them.

We all drifted off again, only for, "HELP! Ring again, she's trying to get INTO bed with me." The unfortunate young girl was out of her bed and the coloured lady was in it! This episode was so unsettling for all in the ward. We DID get some sleep, but not much. I think the disturbed husband was by her side when we all woke up.

I awaited the call for the induction. I asked a young doctor if I was to be 'done' that morning. "Oh NO... It won't be. So sorry, but Mr F's on holiday, so I'm not sure when or who will do it."

I had only seen Mr F a day or so before, and he had definitely told us that he would do the procedure. I felt it was all going awry, yet again.

My bed was looking straight down the corridor and, to my relief, I saw Mr F, dressed in what looked like his gardening clothes, walking up to the ward. He was giving up an hour of his holiday to help me, so the young doctor was wrong. I felt really grateful, but still scared silly.

This time the method of induction was with a small anaesthetic, a horrible procedure, followed by a drip providing hormones to hurry labour along. There was still an enema, and shaving... I decided to carry on knitting whilst in labour. Still, it was a lonely labour, just me and a cleaner. Nobody to talk to to take my mind off the pain, which was extremely intense. So knitting it was – a little baby jacket. The funny part of this WAS that as a painful contraction took hold, the stitches would become erratic, leaving a ribbed jacket, but between contractions, normal smooth work... then loose dodgy stitches when pain arrived, a truly uneven garment! I can laugh at this now, and I intended to keep the weird piece of knitting, but I think it was binned years later.

Robin arrived at teatime, a healthy dark-haired and 'dark'-skinned little chap. The post-birth care wasn't as bad as six years earlier, but was still very basic, and some of the nursing was still very formal and not comforting.

Robin was face up when delivered. "Sunny-side up," one of the nurses said. Some 'repair' needlework had to be done shortly after Robin's appearance. Echoes of what was left over from the Greek tragedy. No myths, though. This was carried out by a very kind, gentle doctor, so different from years ago, so all was well, and after this reasonably smooth birth, I felt excited and thankful.

There was still the 'old guard' of nurses. As one particularly glamorous sister was going off duty, she looked in from the doorway. When I asked for towels because I was bleeding a lot, she was extremely rude. She was "Going off home, SO don't ask!" She flounced out without even looking to see if I was bleeding to death!

I just lay in a 'state' most of the night: the bed resembled a place where someone had committed hara-kiri the night before. The treatment of the previous night, with the mentally disturbed new mother, was an event that I hope would be managed better now. She would have some sort of counselling. I never saw or heard her again. It was a sad episode.

I was glad to be sent home after three days. Henwood Road looked pretty good to me. Home again, so 'all's well that ends well'.

As a maternity obstetric and gynaecological unit the Women's Hospital was a grim, soulless place, run by a matron from hell, who should never had been dealing with new mothers and their babies, or anyone. A neighbour who subsequently was admitted to the hospital suffering from breast cancer, and later died there, was (according to her friends and family) treated kindly by staff, but she died a sad death, very frightened, and for days she tried desperately to 'escape' from a cot-sided bed. According to her good friend, "Doris was like a little bird trying to get through the bars of its cage." There was not much, if any, sympathy from her gynaecologist, who turned out to be my consultant Mr F, who I thought was so kind. Well, he was to me, but he did go down to bottom notch on my list of 'goodies' after hearing about that terrible scene and Mr F's lack of empathy.

Robin was a cheerful little baby. He was plagued by tummy problems, resulting in us having to take him to hospital to see the paediatrician. I should have known that the same consultant who had been so remote and who was arrogant enough to conduct tests on Louise without mentioning it or even seeing me when Louise was born, was still working. He carried out his examination and spoke through his nurse. Not once did he look or talk to me. The nurse was like an interpreter, passing on questions from this rude man to me. It appeared Robin was intolerant to dairy products. His sleep was punctuated by stomach pain, we were like yo-yos in and out of bed.

Louise viewed her little brother with suspicion, Tai Lu behaved like a nursemaid, dashing into the room, making sure that we had heard the baby. He would get quite agitated. Can cats look worried? I suppose they can't, but somehow Tai Lu did convey worry to us humans. He still stood on the top of open doors, and hid behind them, jumping out, paws outstretched when some unsuspecting person walked though. We needed earplugs, though; his 'voice' was deafening. But Robin's was even louder.

Louise never showed any jealousy, no pinches or pokes to Robin when we were not looking. However, I'm not sure NOW, because years later, she admitted that to start with, she didn't really like him very much. How naïve I was. I always thought she adored her little brother! So much for good parenting. When he was about eight months, we nicknamed him 'the Buddha', so chubby and smiling was he. (He is still the smiling Buddha, but much thinner.)

FIVE GO CARAVANNING (but NEVER again)

Harold was busy at his office in Dudley, near to the famous castle zoo. He could hear the lions roar and the elephants trumpeting.

Mum was enjoying her self-made garden. We would sit outside on her 'home-made' lawn, crunching through her meringues, or her very thinly cut cucumber sandwiches. Her lupins stood like church spires, not just blue – now other colours had sprung up, pinks and yellows joined in the colourful borders. We bought her rose bushes and clematis; her little garden was thriving and she loved it.

The stairs were getting difficult for her, her knees and hips actually creaked like the timbers of a rowing boat, audible to all. All her sisters visited regularly, but all but one of her brothers had died early deaths (only one of Mum's brothers got to over sixty). There wasn't a photo of Dad anywhere in the cottage. I have only just realized that whilst writing this.

Auntie Glad in particular had never liked Dad. She would say some very derogatory things about him, which did hurt me, but I felt I couldn't say anything. In those days, answering aunties back wasn't done. It was not genteel to be stroppy with an elder. 'THEY' would get me if I dared to intervene.

One summer's day, all three sisters, plus Glad's husband Arthur (Arty to Glad) asked if they could have a week at our caravan (this was on a very quiet site in North Wales, near Porthmadog). This holiday, taken in August during a heat wave, almost finished a very happy sisterhood.

With Glad driving, the 'girls' decided that diminutive Arthur, all of five feet five, was to take a place in the back seat, sandwiched between Maudie, not too large, the smallest of the sisters, and Marj, very portly, and six foot tall. Ve, also almost six foot tall, sat like 'Queen of the May', statuesque, in the front passenger seat.

Our caravan was at the end of a very long pot-holed and steep track. "Too much weight in the back, Artie, you had better get out. My back-end won't take it!" shouted Glad.

So poor rather downtrodden Artie did just that, and the three ladies drove slowly on, leaving him to walk, stick in hand, up the perilous path. Arthur's weight would only be a quarter of the girls' weight, but Glad thought that the removal of Arthur might save her 'back-end' from being wrecked on a boulder.

The weather was extremely hot that week. The caravan slept four, six at a push. I never did make out the exact sleeping arrangements, but whatever they were, they proved uncomfortable and caused stress, particularly for the bigger aunts. The allocation of beds or 'pull-down' beds became a huge issue, and quarrels started. I've no doubt that Mum would have been moved from bed to bed, without complaint, that is, until afterwards. She was well known for her martyrdom.

The obligatory deck chairs and loungers were set up on the little front lawn in the day and the ladies relaxed in the burning sun. Rather silly, but it was a chance to get some colour and have afternoon tea. I'm not sure they liked drinking their tea from mugs and not china teacups, though – not a 'Roberts' way of having afternoon tea.

By the end of the week, poor Ve and the others girls were decidedly red with sunburn. I don't think Glad drove the car once during the week. Not only was her 'back-end' trouble, this was joined by "My exhaust won't take it, Artie love." During the week, Arthur did go for the odd walk to stand looking over the small bays in Borth-y-Gest, and to get away from the (by now) arguing ladies.

The catering arrangements were not mentioned, which for the Roberts girls was strange – they all loved their food. (Glad always said that when she died, she would be 'Queen cook in heaven, my dears'. She WAS a very good cook, so her place in heaven WAS probably to be in the kitchen kneading endless loaves of bread, frying the multitude of fish, and doling out manna.)

The journey home to Stourbridge began badly. Ve automatically got into the front passenger seat. She had the most horrible feet! Some toes had been amputated in earlier life, due to hammer toes, so her balance was affected. (I have only just thought that this may have been the reason Ve could never dismount elegantly from her pushbike.) Marj was furious; she had had to endure the back seat squashed "like meat in a sandwich", so Marj kicked up a fuss…

Very reluctantly, Ve climbed out and sat in the back, huffing and puffing. Again, Artie wasn't allowed into the car, he had to make it down the hill on foot. He probably didn't mind, in view of the girls' squabbling. Once on the open road, all seemed well, when suddenly Ve burst out crying. Her rather mangled feet were painful and she was purple with heat. So Glad stopped, and all hell was let loose. Ve was crying, Marj sat defiantly ram-rod upright, trying to ignore Ve's cries. Mum was, as usual, very stoic, and was "Quite all right, thank you" but clearly wasn't! Artie tried to pour oil on his troubled sisters-in-law, but his advice was totally ignored by all, so it was stalemate.

They continued their journey, nobody talking to their fellow travellers, and again Ve started weeping, so Marj decided, very reluctantly, to squeeze into the back… and a relieved Ve hobbled into the passenger seat.

This holiday took some getting over. All the Roberts family were normally very united, and close and had never vaguely fallen out, but somehow this hot, uncomfortable week unsettled their friendship, and apparently, according to Mum, it was a silent, 'no hugging', farewell at the end.

I'm pleased to say that this discord didn't last long, though, and they all regained their sisterly love for one another. For weeks afterwards, Uncle Arthur recounted his part in the fiasco with gusto, always seeing the funny side of any event. I know they would never entertain going to our lovely but cramped caravan again. I think they viewed the week as an endurance test not a holiday.

ALL EARS

Not long after Robin was born, I began having weird and bizarre hearing problems. I could hear my eyes moving in their sockets, a sort of sandpaper rasping noise. Also bodily noises were amplified. Movements of my spine and head, or in fact any joint in the body, would echo and drown out 'normal' sounds. Chewing was like thunder, and walking made each footfall rumble – I could never hear anything said by a companion beside me on a walk, but I would pretend I had heard, and laugh or scowl in (what I thought were) appropriate places. If I stopped walking on some pretence, although the roaring background sounds were still there, I could pick up most of the conversation from my walking friend. At times heart beats would be so loud that I would suffer vertigo. Bizarre is the word for this, and my life was moulded around the 'noises', and for years I felt I was going mad.

A visit to the hearing consultant decided that my Eustachian tubes were blocked, and he performed a rather terrifying 'blow out' without sedation.. This was done twice, and eventually, after no success, I was admitted to hospital for a day to have grommets fitted to equalize the pressure and so drain away any fluid present.

I woke up after the operation and heard the consultant talking to a lady in the next bed. He was telling her the grommets would do the trick, as some fluid had already drained.

He walked over to me… "Sorry, Mrs Hampton, the grommets are in, but there isn't any fluid. But don't despair, we will have to wait and see."

I waited for months, but eventually Mr J the consultant decided to remove them. This he did in his room. "Oh dear, Mrs Hampton, you seem to have lost one already." He didn't enlighten me as to whether the grommet was floating behind my eardrum or had just dropped out! He then proceeded to peer into my other ear… there was tremendous pain, and then, "That's got it!" He held the minute grommet up triumphantly. One out and one who-knows-where?

"What I think you have, Mrs Hampton, is arthritis of the neck. I'm sending you for an X-ray. You may have damaged your neck when you had your accident in the car."

The X-ray done, I trotted back to Mr J. He showed me the X-ray, and sure enough, I showed signs of arthritis in one or two bones in the neck. There appeared to be a bit of bone detached, too.

"I think we may have solved it, but I'm sending you to a neurologist, the enlarged vertebra may be pressing on a blood vessel, and that may be affecting your hearing. It's called pulsatile tinnitus."

In between the appointments with the surgeon, I had booked appointments with a lady in Kinver who was a chiropractor. I would pop Robin (who was about four years old) into my old blue VW beetle, and off we'd go. I got on well with the young lady, who was the vicar of Kinver's daughter, I found out later. She decided that stretching the neck might lessen the pressure on the blood vessels. So, this is what she did. I attended these sessions for weeks. They were not too uncomfortable but quite expensive. But if the treatment worked, it would be worth every penny. Unfortunately, nothing changed.

As the appointment with the neurologist loomed, I cancelled my last appointment with the chiropractor, suddenly fearing that too much pulling and stretching MIGHT be fatal. She was not amused. I was surprised how sharp she was on the phone after I had cancelled the next session on the 'rack'.

All this was happening when Mum was getting more crippled by her arthritis, Louise was in the last year at St Michael's and All Angels junior school, and Robin was to start school.

I didn't say too much to Mum – she was having a struggle. And of course the children didn't really worry about their mum being in hospital for a day or so. My strange hearing wasn't something I could talk about anyway. I don't think anyone knew. HOW could I explain? So the family were ignorant of what was going on. I regret not divulging any details, because trying to hide the symptoms made eating out, travel on public transport, and all kinds of social activities a 'no-go' area for me.

Harold was a great believer in 'keeping one's counsel' where illness was concerned, another regret. I would have liked him to have been an advocate for me, and explain to friends why I didn't always cope with loud noise, and sometimes had to drop out of evenings out or parties, where loud music would make me feel off-balance.

The garden was my saviour. I had also taken on an allotment in Tettenhall, which was such a help to me, and also had the bonus (after a battle with the terrible overgrown ground) of fresh organic vegetables. I loved all the digging, the earth looking dark and fresh. The potatoes, leeks and a host of other vegetables made my heart sing, and still does. (I am still there, same plot, forty-two years later, producing most of our vegetables.)

The weird sounds got worse. I could still hear my eyes moving in their sockets, and every movement of my body still resounded. Eating was a nightmare, the sounds were so loud, drowning out any table-side conversation; celery was a killer. Walking was still a big problem. To everyone, I had tinnitus. That word became my explanation to everyone. I even wrote to the MP Jack Ashley, who was almost completely deaf, but was reported as having continuous tinnitus. I thought he might help in some way, perhaps suggest a help line – I was VERY desperate. He never acknowledged my letter, though, so I felt extremely let down.

I did go to the doctor's, in fact many times, but when I told the GP I could hear my eyes moving, a look of amused disbelief would take over his face. I can't blame him really, it WAS so ridiculous. When I said that the only relief was when I bent over double (all sounds became crystal clear in that position) any medic would stay poker-faced, but underneath, he/she may have thought I needed mental help rather than physical. I feel that a quick appointment with a psychologist or psychiatrist was what the doctor thought would be the next step. "Mrs Hampton is 'losing it'." I should imagine that is what the GPs said when meeting up for their monthly meeting.

The deep sounds like thunder behind a cloud continued day and night. I invested in headphones for night-time, with 'white' noise to drown the others out. I gave relaxing tapes a go too, but nothing lessened the droning. Touching the skin was loud, and a playful thump on the back was like a thunder clap. Going to the dentist was hell, the noises so loud I would feel I was passing out. I still didn't tell anyone. How stupid. I think it was the difficulty in getting anyone, even someone medical, to believe my symptoms, so bizarre were they.

MEDICAL COCK-UPS

Harold came with me to see a Dr R H in his rooms. I had all the neurological tests. Finger on the nose test, and my eyes following his biro pen which he moved across my face from side to side. Again the very hygienic biro on the soles of my feet… and lots of stethoscope on my neck, listening in to any abnormality in the blood vessels.

"Who told you that you have a bit of bone out of joint?" Dr R H asked. I told him Mr T, the ENT surgeon. "Well, I can't see anything like that." So drawn swords amongst the medical men. "BUT I can hear your noises." Dr R H appeared as excited as me about it! "I think you have something going on with your blood vessels in the neck. It's probably the result of your car accident when you were pregnant. Blood vessels are more dodgy when you are pregnant." He then asked, "How old are you?" When I replied 'forty', he looked cheekily at me and said, "Forty is a VERY dangerous age." What he meant I will never know, but he had a twinkle in his eye when he said it.

He then said the dreaded words, "I think we should get you into Smethwick Neuro Hospital and have some tests done. We have to rule out A and B."

The thought of leaving the children, and Mum (who was relying more on Pat and myself) was daunting, but the possibility of a cure and normal hearing was too good to miss. And anyway, I might have a life-threatening brain tumour.

I can't remember saying goodbye to the children. We kept it all on a low key, and I shouldn't think they were in any way worried. I entered Smethwick hospital, slightly scared, but hopeful. After all, I was only in for tests. I settled in. The ward had about six beds. The bed next to mine was occupied by a young woman called Frances. I got to know her well during my stay in hospital. She had had a brain tumour removed, so had had her head shaved and was wearing a mob cap. She was very nice and welcoming.

I was to have a test that involved injecting dye into an artery in my groin, and the radiologist would watch and see if there were any obstructions. Really I suppose it would rule out a tumour or aneurism. The dye would go into my brain.

I had only been in bed an hour or so when the lady opposite called over, "What are you having done, luv?"

I told her. "Oh, I have just had THAT, it's the most TERRIBLE test… They inject you with a big needle in the neck, and then you look at the screen to see the dye rising… there's no anaesthetic, so you feel everything. It's the worst thing I have ever had done!"

Talk about Job's comforter. She sent a shudder of fear through me. Would they not give me a general? And would it be a great needle in the neck? Now, what had been something not pleasant but bearable, especially as I hoped I would be asleep, became a frightening prospect.

"Take no notice. Silly old woman," Harold said when he visited me that evening. "She's only trying to frighten you." Well, she certainly DID.

Next morning, there were the usual blood tests, but the girl from the pathology lab had to take a sample twice. "Just a mix-up" she smiled. During the time between the bloods, I had been startled to see a man pushing a trolley which displayed the yellow atomic logo! He headed for me. "Don't worry, I'm injecting you with the radioactive dye. You are to go down to have a body scan." So three jabs, all done in succession. I did wonder if this really WAS the top neuro hospital in the Midlands.

Unlike today's CAT and MRI scans, the patient had to be strapped, head tightly bound, on a table in a room. This dark windowless room WAS the scanner. There was a glass-fronted 'hatch' high up on the wall with faces peering down.

Nobody said much, although they were friendly, so when I shed a silent tear, the young radiologist probably thought 'what a bloody baby'. The scan involved the scanner above going backwards and forwards for possibly an hour. It was bearable, but lonely and very hard not to shuffle under the body straps. You had to keep perfectly still.

That night I put a photo of Louise and Robin close by on the locker and settled down. Suddenly, there was a figure standing over me, shaking my arm. "Hello, I'm Bridie. Nobody will tell me anything." This was a young Irish girl from the end of the ward. She lived in some remote part of Ireland, very plain and old-fashioned. She was a slightly strange and unsophisticated country girl. Possibly what, in those far-off days, would be called 'simple'.

She sat on my bed, holding my hand, and kept repeating that nobody would say anything to her. Frances called the night nurse, and poor frightened Bridie was settled back in bed. I lay awake for hours. It was history repeating itself, echoes of the night before Robin was born.

Next morning, Frances took me down the corridor to the lecture room, where we viewed glass cases containing all shapes and sizes of brains, all floating in preservative. They were all around the walls, a 'library' of brains. Somehow we managed to laugh. Frances was 'doing very well' after her operation. No trouble moving her arms or legs, and her intellect wasn't impaired at all, she was an example of good spirits and positive thinking. She brightened my first two days. Her husband visited her, a very handsome young man. They had two small children, and Frances was a Brown Owl in their local Brownie group.

Later that day, a Friday, the sister arrived and stood at the bottom of the bed. "You can go home, Mrs Hampton, we don't carry out any radiology tests at the weekend."

So, wearing the hospital plastic tag, I was driven home by Harold. Pat asked us for lunch and everything was normal, the children not anxious. The big test was scheduled for Tuesday. I did cry when in the car.

When I arrived back in the ward, Frances and two other women greeted me like a long-lost sister. We were allotted our own toaster so that we ladies could get our own breakfast or afternoon snack. Very Heath Robinson looking back, but fun, during a ghastly time.

"We will carry out your test tomorrow," said the sister. So, I was all prepared, and had 'nil by mouth' above the bed.

Frances's husband walked into the ward that evening, along with a very pretty young blonde, quite a stunner. The contrast with poor pale, horn-rimmed specs-wearer Frances, sitting in bed, no hair, and a mob cap pulled down to her glasses, was rather awful. I don't think Frances noticed, but I did.

This attractive lady, who the husband introduced as his secretary, made for unease. The husband and the blonde seemed too close in their body language. I decided that the husband was extremely insensitive bringing his secretary along. Perhaps Frances didn't mind or feel any anxiety. Perhaps I was being too critical.

Next morning, I was all prepared mentally for the catheter in the groin job. Nothing happened in the morning, no clank of a trolley. I was SO hungry. We all took it in turns to do the toast, but my turn had to be postponed. The smell of the toast was so good. Afternoon arrived and there was still no activity on the operating front. I was about to wither away with hunger when a nice smiling nurse arrived. "Sorry, Mrs Hampton, they seem to have forgotten you."

Yet again I had to ring Harold at work. By now, his secretary Margaret was as fed up as me, but very sympathetic. Harold was cheesed-off.

No explanation was given by the sister or anyone. (I had felt very upset earlier with the sister on duty. Each time I had arrived back she had taken my beta-blocker tablets, needed when a tachycardia attack came on. "Oh you DON'T need THESE," she had said as she marched out of the ward with the bottle. I know we couldn't keep them with us, but it was definitely a rebuff for thinking I had cardio trouble, which I'd had since the age of sixteen, and still have.)

I was told to stay in overnight, then go home until the following Monday. I stayed another night, chatting with the happy Frances. Frances had been given good news. She was doing well and could go home the next day. She was so excited, we even went down to the TV lounge. There was another Job's comforter in there watching. Again he asked what I was going to have done. "You're not having THAT, are you? Oh poor you. I had that, but it didn't work, so they drilled a hole in my head." He was in a wheelchair – not a good outlook!! I was scared to death.

A tall middle-aged patient was also there. I had seen her previously in a one-bedded room down the corridor. She was very cheerful and made us laugh. She showed us a painting her youngest child had done for her with a 'GET WELL' on the top. The picture was of a church, and miles of graveyard, with lots of crosses and floral wreaths. We all saw the funny side.

We must have become very blasé, because we giggled away constantly. This place was in a different world, all brain ops, head injuries and nasty tests… but laughter.

When visiting time came, Harold arrived, followed by Frances's husband, alone this time. They chatted, laughed and sounded so happy. As the husband left the ward, he waved and turned to talk to a nurse. They talked for a while in the corridor. Then the husband came back to the ward and stood in the doorway, quite a long way from Frances. "Frances, you can't go home tomorrow, you have got to have some radiotherapy." And with that, he left! Tact or empathy were NOT his middle names.

This rather confirmed my suspicions. What good husband would just stand yards away and deliver bad news? I thought it callous of him. Frances just burst into floods of tears and was so distressed. A young doctor was called. He held Frances in his arms whilst she wept. I heard him telling her it wasn't the end of the world, a precaution in case the tumour returned. He was so kind, as were all the young doctors in this very strange and ill-run centre of excellence.

I watched next morning as Frances was wheeled to the door to be driven to another part of the hospital. She was going to have a lead helmet constructed to measure, with a hole left open over the operation site, so that the radio waves could penetrate her head and shrink any tumour left behind. The window behind my bed looked out on the ambulance in the yard outside. I wanted to wave but didn't because as she was being loaded into the ambulance, she fell onto the car park. Someone had lost their grasp. She was all right, but shocked. This looked and felt like a nightmare.

So home again, home again, jiggetty-jog. The coming and going was stressful, but I was so happy to be with the children. We all went out with

Pat and Ray to a stately home in Shropshire, me still wearing the wrist tag. I felt very low, but we had a good afternoon watching toads and frogs in tandem, mating. There were hundreds, the males taking a piggy-back ride, much to the children's amusement.

Somehow Mum wasn't particularly worried about her youngest child. Harold wouldn't tell anyone any details, so I was under a cloak of secrecy. Again I wished he HAD told someone because I couldn't explain to friends – it was all such a debacle.

Tuesday loomed, and back we drove to dreadful Smethwick (birthplace of my Dad!). I was on a different ward this time, no Frances to keep me brave. She had gone home after radiotherapy. This new ward was originally an isolation ward, almost a pre-fab hut, now joined to the main Edwardian red-brick hospital proper. The friendly patient in the next bed was suffering the aftermath of a rail crash.

Up went the children's photo, and the books I had never had time to read were piled on the bedside locker. Opposite was a patient who had been crushed under the rubble of her parents' house during the blitz. One side of her head was almost missing. She was now middle-aged but a wonderfully cheerful soul. I kept thinking my test was nothing compared to her trauma over the years. Counting one's blessings is a good idea, but somehow the blessings evaporate away into a mist of fear. I did feel sorry for myself in spite of trying to be brave.

Shaving was the order of the day. I was given a form. I was about to sign when I realized that it wasn't the lower end that the form was for, it was to give them permission to shave my head! I hoped THAT would never be on the cards. Why I was given the form was a mystery – one of many.

I waved goodbye to everyone in the ward, and felt that at last I would find out what was going on 'in head-office'. No needles in the neck, just a general anaesthetic, and oblivion. I do remember waking up in the operating room, lots of activity, then nothing.

I did eventually find I was back in my bed in the ward. I couldn't see, but could hear… "WHAT shall we tell her?" Then a whispered conversation… I opened my eyes to see the sister and a nurse standing at the foot-end of my bed. Well, that's IT, they HAVE found a brain tumour, I thought, having heard these damning words.

The sister spoke, from the foot of the bed, no hand on shoulder or intimate one-to-one. "I'm afraid they haven't been able to do the test, Mrs Hampton. You are a very nervous person, so that transmits to your blood vessels. So I'm afraid your veins closed and shrank and the radiologist couldn't get the catheter in. Sorry, but you will have to come back in a few weeks to have it done again." And with that, she turned on her heels and disappeared.

The dark nurse didn't go. She looked at me, shaking her head… "We'll give you time to get over this, then try again." She was definitely sympathetic, almost embarrassed. No wonder!

Shortly after, the lady opposite called across. "Where HAVE you been? We all expected you back in an hour, but you have been down in the theatre well over six hours."

Sure enough, I had been away for a long time. I didn't question this. As usual, I accepted that I had proved a difficult patient. I felt heart-thumping disappointment, and was down in the depths. Later, when a bit more compos mentis, I felt my left hand begin to swell, also my forearm. I investigated my groins; both groins were stitched and painful.

I felt a total failure, a wreck. I felt that I was useless, causing all this worry for my family, and all because of my nerves! All the ladies were very supportive and kind. The blitzed lady sat with me and helped me through a tearful time. I contacted Harold's secretary Margaret. She was very upset. "All your comings and goings, and NOW you have to go back." Margaret was very understanding, as were the staff (bar the sister, who never talked to me again during this visit).

An elderly nurse came and sat by me. Every now and then, she would feel the pulse in my feet. She stayed for the rest of the day, rather nun-like. I was treated with care, more care than I thought I should command. I was so well 'watched over' – very strange, but nothing untoward dawned on me or Harold. I just felt I was a nervous shambles, having given everyone here and at home extra worries. In fact, a complete and utter failure! I got back home, feeling lower than low; the messed-up test was all MY fault.

Next morning, my arm was very painful. I couldn't lie on it or touch it. Also it was red to the elbow. "You have phlebitis," announced Dr S the GP during a hurried visit. "The blood vessels in your hand have been under stress so are inflamed." He asked me how I felt about not having the test carried out and I did have a tear in his surgery, something I never usually would have done. And he responded with a sympathetic smile. He didn't know what had really happened. I had the arm bandaged and returned home, dodgy in the groin area, stitches pulling and, worst of all, feeling disappointed with MYSELF, a nervous shambles of a woman, even my blood vessels were cringing and scared! This is not recommended as a help to self-confidence.

I had the groin stitches out a week later, but my arm was still painful and bandaged for many weeks.

Life back home was great, and the children, as usual, were life savers. Robin was at St Michael's and All Angels, doing well, no longer worried about going as he had been for the first weeks. Louise was also great. She and her 'best friend' Joanne played the piano, had sessions playing with an old tape recorder, singing their version of a pop music radio station.

Robin was recorded singing his version of 'Down Amongst the Deadmen' and nursery rhymes. I cherish these times together. I have the old tape still, carefully labelled "DO NOT THROW!"

Mum didn't ask what had happened to me in Smethwick, and I didn't burden her with any details, especially as I was, in her eyes, a failure anyway, So THIS would have been another event to add to her list of my under-achievements.

I think Harold kept his counsel. This is something I wish he hadn't done. To talk of hospital 'doings' was (and still is) deemed to be letting the side down and causing the stiff upper lip to relax into a grimace, and possibly a hint of 'blartin' (Black Country slang for crying).

Everyone was 'stiff-upper-lipped', all except a nurse friend a few doors away. She was shocked and surprised. I could tell Jillian everything, so I DID! She couldn't see HOW all this mix-up had occurred in such a wonderful hospital. She became a confidante and later a great help and a pseudo whistle-blower.

I awaited the call-back to hospital for another test. I dreaded it. Would my veins and arteries close up with fear again? It had been confirmed what Mum had always thought… I WAS a great failure all round.

Mum really was tired. Her garden was great, and she continued to make her jam. This latest batch was turned into strawberry candy! She would boil and boil it, thinking it would be more solid. Well, solid it WAS, but there was one thing in its favour, it would lurk around in jars for years and never go off! Her little pantry was stacked with jars.

There were still sessions of tea and sunburn in the garden. The aunts were now travelling in a car actually owned by Glad – all her other vehicles had been borrowed from friends.

About this time, their youngest and dearest brother Doug died from a heart attack. Such a blow to his sisters. Doug was the last of their brothers alive and over sixty. Doug had been out to visit Wendy and her husband and two children in New Zealand. They had enjoyed time together, something Wendy valued as she had been living so far from everyone for some years. His funeral took place in Malvern, where he and Dorothy had lived for many years. He died in his sleep from a heart disturbance then failure.

When a lad in Stourbridge, Doug had become the 'runner' and delivery boy for a famous shoe shop in town. The shoe-shop owners would pay a visit to homes of the wealthy, measure their feet, get the details, then, either have them made, or find a fitting pair. Someone had to deliver and fetch, so young Doug would walk miles with his precious shoe-boxes. Doug had slowly risen through the ranks and had become manager of a large shoe shop in Liverpool, then eventually Elt's shoes in the lovely town of Malvern, the Malvern Hills being the favourite place of Edward Elgar, a wonderful place of quiet and tranquillity.

All the family attended the church service. The friend who gave the eulogy about Doug was a famous radio actor who had for years been Walter Gabriel of *The Archers*. Mum and the sisters had known him as a young boy, and he was in the same scout troupe as Doug, so they were thrilled that he spoke about Doug, who was liked by all. Doug's ashes were scattered on the Malverns, much later that year, as Wendy and husband Rolie wanted to be in the UK for their last goodbyes to their much-loved father.

A few weeks later, I had a call from the neurologist's secretary, would I come in and discuss any worries with Dr R H. Then he would get us up to date with what would happen now.

The same happened.

"Well, Mrs Hampton, I'm afraid nervous patients have nervous blood vessels", etc., etc. "Smethwick will send an appointment for the same test to be done again."

I slunk out, wondering how I could be less nervous next time. I felt a wimp and ashamed.

I had to say cheerio again to Louise and Robin, but they were not upset, so good were we at hiding everything. Harold became a master of the 'keep it all in a brown-paper-bag' mode.

The dark yard and drab buildings of Smethwick Neuro didn't beckon. I was settled in the same pre-fab-type wards. Again, I was greeted by nice gentle smiling young doctors. They must have been hand-picked for their bedside manner.

It was a teaching hospital, and I had agreed from the first day that I wouldn't mind observers or young doctors trying their hand at diagnosis. One or two had a good go at diagnosing my condition. I had to lie naked, but with certain areas covered with a red blanket. The young nervous man would ask all kinds of questions. Once I jumped the gun and told him some information. He covered his ears. "I'm not supposed to hear that. I have to work it out myself, so no help please."

All this was done with the utmost dignity, thank goodness.

The cheerful dark nurse was my particular nurse. When we were chatting, I mentioned the last failed test. "Don't you worry! ALL MEN ARE PIGS!" She said it with such venom, spitting the words out. I was in the dark, but even then I didn't associate her outburst with me... the penny never dropped. I thought that perhaps she had a vicious husband or boyfriend.

Nil by mouth, the shaver out, back-fastening gown that had only one tie, so I would show my wobbling buttocks when walking, all preparation for THE frightening procedure. I glimpsed the same radiologist when I was wheeled into an ante-room. He wasn't gowned. He wore a check shirt, which I thought rather casual.

All went well. I was out and back to the ward in less than an hour. Just one groin was stitched. So all I had to do was lie back and wait for the results.

There were still very disturbed patients in the ward. One middle-aged lady was the mother of an acquaintance. For some reason, she targeted me, saying that I shouldn't be there. I had nothing wrong with me. The staff told me she had a brain tumour that had changed her personality, and not to worry.

There was, however, light-hearted chat and many laughs on the ward. The food was still inedible, so Harold brought in bananas. I consumed quite a few. When sitting with a fellow patient one morning, we were laughing about the shaving – mainly heads – and we jokingly got to the subject of my hairy arms. I showed her my thick black fuzz…"Too many bananas," she quipped. Only a silly little joke, but I could laugh. I was on the 'up'. I still didn't sleep much, but the nightly Horlicks was good, and I would be home soon.

Two days later, I was told Dr R H would visit and tell me what they had found, if anything. I sat perfumed and talced, I had even put lippy on. He arrived, late in the day. "So sorry. My cellar is flooded so I have had to deal with that… apologies."

He then delivered the verdict. No tumour found, that was ruled out. However, two small blood vessels had joined together, causing a kind of shunt between them. THIS was the cause of my peculiar bodily noises. "I think the shunt may have happened when you had your car accident. Blood vessels are very 'dodgy' when pregnant. Not to worry."

It all seemed wonderful. I was almost bursting with nice thoughts of home and the family, I felt elated. He stayed for a while. He was a very pleasant chap, still the twinkle in his eye, and he gave my bare ankle a reassuring squeeze I suppose nowadays this would have been a bit too familiar, but I wasn't in any way bothered. He could have given me an all-over squeeze and I wouldn't have cared, I was SO happy.

Oddly and reassuringly, Dr R H walked away down the ward arm in arm with a jolly-looking nurse. They executed a John Cleese kind of 'silly walk'. Wonderful!

Dr R H's visit had lasted until afternoon, so it was decided I would stay overnight. I rang Harold at the office. Margaret answered the phone and she was almost shouting in her excitement. Harold would bring my clothes in the next morning. I put the books and bits and pieces into a carrier, but left the photo of the children on my locker. I felt a very lucky woman.

The nurse on night duty asked if I would like a sleeping tablet, but I refused. I was going to sleep the sleep of relief and happiness. I prepared to settle down, but then became aware of a man walking down the ward. He stopped at my bed. I had seen him chatting to the night nurse by her desk earlier. He introduced himself. "I'm a staff nurse on the male ward over the corridor." He pointed. He seemed eager to chat. I showed him the photo and told him about the family. "What are you in for?" he asked.

I told him I had had all kinds of quite horrible tests, but there wasn't a tumour there so nothing to worry about.

He then said, "We have patients here who have undergone EVERY test possible to see if they have a brain tumour. When nothing is found, they go home, but a year or so later they arrive back suffering from a brain tumour."

He left and walked back to the nurse's little office cum desk. I lay stunned. Fear gripped me, sweat ran down between my breasts. Everything seemed to crumble around me, all the nice positive thoughts, the bubbling happiness inside, that had all gone in a few seconds.

I walked down to the night nurse and asked for a sleeping tablet, but I didn't mention the conversation with the unknown male nurse. I should have told the ward nurse, but somehow I couldn't get the words out. So I could have a tumour lurking in my head, waiting to grow. I might die. I haven't told many people, friends and relations, about this. Just as I had somehow covered up Louise's very traumatic delivery and the post-delivery stay, I tried to carry on when depressed. These events somehow had put the tin lid on my life.

When home, Harold had bought flowers and made a meal of my favourite egg and chips. Everyone was happy to see me out from under the dark cloud.

"Well, thank goodness THAT'S all over," Harold said.

To which I replied, "Oh no, it's NOT over." I burst into floods of tears and uncontrolled weeping. I then told him what had happened.

My friend, the nurse Jillian, visited a few days later. What she told me made me so angry. I felt totally let down and belittled. This is what she had been told. She was at work in a local hospital, and during a morning break, Jillian sat and chatted to a friend and colleague, who was still studying, She had been seconded to Smethwick Neuro Hospital to observe the various operations and procedures. Whilst on observation she was asked to watch a test involving catheters from the groin to look at blood vessels in the brain. She had arrived back to work upset and dismayed at what she had seen during her observation duty at Smethwick.

"Some poor woman had to have this test, which should have been straightforward, but the radiologist hadn't got the right size catheters. He tried to push one into her groin, but he couldn't get it in, so he then opened up the other groin, but that failed too. The loss of blood was awful, the poor woman was very ill and she had to have a blood transfusion. She had lost so much blood."

From all this information, Jillian realized that the 'poor woman' was ME.

Nobody told me that I had had a blood transfusion, possibly the reason for the hours away from my ward (also the reason for the phlebitis in my arm – too much prodding around causing the blood vessels to become irritated). And I realised that my nice dark nurse's remark 'some men are pigs' must have meant that the staff knew what had happened but had been told not to tell me. I can truly say that the mistake wasn't the whole issue, it was the fact that everyone closed ranks and put the blame on MY nervous disposition.

I remember that after the second successful test, an hour or so later, a check-shirted man had appeared beside my bed. He didn't smile or even look at me – I wasn't acknowledged. He just peered at my legs, felt the pulse in my ankles, and walked off…

I NOW know that that man must have been the radiologist who had tried to perform the first procedure months earlier. It was his check shirt that gave the man away. What a coward! Everyone can make mistakes, but blaming it on my nervousness was a slight and an untruth that has somehow followed me ever since.

Because we didn't have positive proof about the whole botched job, we couldn't complain. (In hindsight, we certainly could have asked Jillian's friend to verify that I WAS the patient that had upset her.) We SHOULD have explored it more, but I was feeling ill, Harold had the children to look after, so we stupidly kept quiet about it all.

However Harold DID get in touch with the matron, to tell her about the male nurse's remarks the night before I was discharged. Harold had an appointment with her. She apologized profusely, and reassured Harold that she would get the nurse in and give him a grilling (I'm not sure she did). This interview with matron was a chance for Harold to tell all… but this was the 1970s, the medical profession was unbeatable, so he let it rest.

Looking back now, we were pretty wimpish, but we guessed that we would NEVER win the battle for the truth. So many mistakes and bad treatment went on, but it's only now in the twenty-first century that ordinary laymen can raise their voice when shoddy treatment is meted out to patients. Unfortunately, nowadays the 'we will sue you' has messed it all up. We WERE idiots NOT to have complained during the times when I was shunted in and out of hospital and needlessly prepared for surgery. We would never have even imagined suing anyone, but an apology and explanation would have been such a relief, and would have ended many months of self-deprecation.

The botch-up in Smethwick Neuro Hospital, along with Louise's catastrophic birth, are, to me, the stuff of nightmares. Writing this saga about these medical cock-ups, has helped enormously. They are 'water under the bridge', but muddied water.

I kept in contact via letter with both Frances and the lady caught up in the London blitz. Frances wrote how sick she was on the car journey home, and how ill she had been before she had been diagnosed. Her husband would leave for work, unconcerned about Frances's sickness and subsequent throwing-up every morning. Also he wasn't worried about her eyesight, which would sometimes make everything look red, but without any 'rose coloured' specs. Her letters stopped. I just hope she recovered well, she was such a gentle, friendly young woman. She made my days next to her in the ward a bit more bearable.

The lady from the blitz only wrote once. I know she was very ill, but I never heard what happened to her.

It's true to say that these ladies, and others (bar the patient who scared the life out of me with her talk of 'long needles into the neck') made despair tolerable… laughter often prevailed… the silly rota re who should be toaster-in-chief for the day… it all helped during those five weeks, on and off, in what was, to a lot of grateful patients, a centre of excellence.

My writings are just about MY stay, and the many mistakes and cover-ups made during that time. I wish that I could have openly talked about WHAT happened. I don't suppose any of my siblings knew just what went on over those traumatic weeks. Harold never talked about it to anyone; the same silence after Louise's birth. I'm not sure WHY we do this.

I did try to tell friends and family, but always stopped, thinking that nobody wants to hear medical details. I would be overcome with the 'shakes'. So these catastrophes remained a horror story and certainly have blighted my visits to anyone vaguely medical, even now, decades on.

Not many months after my stay in Smethwick, the hospital was closed and demolished. All departments were transferred to the Queen Elizabeth Hospital in Birmingham.

SCDS

An update on what I REALLY have – nothing really wrong with my hearing.

It wasn't until 2012 that I read a doctor's column in the *Daily Telegraph*. The doctor reported the unusual case of a man who could hear his eyes moving in their sockets, and all body movements were loud. He was also unable to hear when eating or walking. He had been diagnosed with SCDS. This is 'Superior Canal Dehiscence Syndrome, or holes in the superior canal. Through these holes the sound is relayed incorrectly, causing the weird and bizarre sounds and feelings. He had endured this for six years, and they were driving him dotty…

I was SO happy! At LAST the same symptoms, exactly. He had undergone an operation to block up two holes in his superior canal. It was a marvellous success. I can't explain how wondrous reading that column was. I contacted Dr La Fanu, the writer, and thanked him. This syndrome has only been found in the last few years, so it wasn't known at the time of my Smethwick visits. There are only a few people with this strange malfunction. The medical folks aren't quite sure how these holes occur. Some patients have thinned areas in the canal, probably from birth. Others seem to have canals that 'wear away'. I am joyous because I know NOW that I'm not a crack-pot, it's got a NAME!

I have had this for forty-three years. It has been a trial not being able to explain that I can't hear when walking, too many low noises blotting out other low sounds, and eating is so loud I dread formal dinners where strangers converse. I have to stop all head movements and certainly no chewing whilst listening.

I know that my tinnitus and low body noises began when I was pregnant and had been in a car accident, so Smethwick wouldn't have looked in the right area. It was a confusing situation. It was all blood vessels or tumours to the neuro specialists. I am too old now to have an operation, but I'm really comfortable with my very rare condition. I still think of the reaction in my GP and the gynaecologist when I ventured to tell them that I could hear my eyes moving. One gynaecologist laughed outright and obviously thought I was a nutcase, and my GP probably wrote something down on my medical records. Probably. "This lady needs help, she THINKS she can hear her eyes moving in their sockets, I advise a psychiatric appointment."

I know that in the family there is still a stiff upper lip and don't say too much, people are not interested in medical 'goings-on'. I don't think Harold has ever told anyone the full story. The brown paper bag is always there, keeping everything secret and unseen.

I did think I would leave my head to medical science, but I will keep my 'holes' to myself… but the jury are still out on that.

THE HUB OF THE WHEEL

Mum loved her little cottage. It was on a bus route, so she could still go shopping at Tesco's food store in the centre of Wolverhampton. This didn't seem to bother her. No Masons now, or the cake shop Pattisons on Darlington Street, often visited by Mum and Ve, where square delicately iced Kunzle cakes were consumed, usually on a Tuesday afternoon, followed by a walk to the Gaumont to see a film.

I would sometimes be driving up to the shops past Mum's, when I would see a very smartly dressed elderly lady wearing a dark turquoise overcoat, with matching trilby hat, curls of white hair just peeping out. I would wave vigorously, but the gloved hand would just raise slightly, in an almost royal wave, wrist loose so that the hand pointed down. This was Mum. I know she knew I would stop off later at the cottage, but this wave was somehow her signature, anything vaguely 'wild' or frantic was never in her repertoire. Mum lived all her life somehow under an imaginary authority where shows of exuberance or joy were frowned upon, so waving frantically at her daughter in a passing car, was NOT the thing to do…

Pat lived in almost opposite, so visited Mum whenever she could. Pat and Ray had bought a lovely cottage in Wales, so there were many trips up there, and their children's school holidays were always spent there.

Pat took Mum on holiday to the cottage and to west Wales. Pat's three children delighted Mum; she wrote copious poems about Pat's firstborn son, Andrew. She was a great reader of nursery rhymes, and really enjoyed all her grandchildren. Dad wouldn't have made a brilliant grandad, but he never had the chance. He died when Andrew was tiny, so never knew that he was a grandad to six more!

We often drove past 249. The chimneys had gone, so no open fires. The front door has never changed, its Georgian panels and the black knocker still remain to this day. The door colour changes every few years, though. It was always dark green when we were in residence. Even the yellow-spotted variegated laurel bush inside the front wall, scene of my tin-box find, was left alone, and languishes leathery and dusty, beside a busier than ever main road.

The strange thing was that when we drove past 249 with Mum as our passenger, we would 'dip our wings' but Mum would hardly give the old house a glance. For her, the years at 249 must have represented years of anxiety, along with a pinch of misery thrown in for good measure. Mum had moved on.

The cottage garden bloomed with Mum's beloved lupins and swathes of purple and mauve primulas. I would sometimes drop in, and there she would be, beetroot red with beads of sweat running down her cheeks; she had probably been gardening for hours, even in the hot sun.

Her sandwiches still amazed Harold. The bread was always sliced wafer thin, cut awkwardly towards her (never any blood on her see-through slices of cucumber, though).

Tony and wife Joan would invite her to dinner on Sundays, something that was kindly meant but somewhat of an ordeal for Mum. "All that door slamming, and the shouting at Jonathan and Lucky the dog," she would say. Joan even tried her best to 'convert' Mum to Christianity. They took her to St Jude's on several occasions, only for Mum to be very underwhelmed by the vicar and the service in general. "Joan actually BELIEVES in Adam and Eve, and the Garden of Eden," Mum once said, shaking her head. She continued, "When I asked Joan how Cain and Abel had children and WHO by as there WAS only their mother, Eve, Joan went all huffy and couldn't say anything. THAT GOT HER!" Mum cried defiantly. The word incest wasn't mentioned, but Mum obviously thought that was the only explanation.

I suppose hell awaits me, because I think the whole story could not possibly be true. Darwin's theory must be correct, but it doesn't matter WHAT we think. People can believe what they want to. To have some kind of faith, this can only help in life, and death. I know we are a clan of heathens, but heathens with consciences. I don't care if people worship stones or birds, in fact anything, if it helps to make life's journey easier and doesn't offend or hurt anyone. Faith in anything has got to be good.

Mum's arthritis was definitely getting worse, so Pat arranged an X-ray at the Nuffield Hospital, with a view to paying for a new hip or knee if Mum needed an operation. The X-ray done, Pat drove Mum up to the hospital to receive the orthopaedic consultant's verdict. Even getting into and out of the car was quite an ordeal for Mum. Her knees had become swollen, and one hip made an audible creaking noise rather like the creaking timbers of an old boat. The consultant was at the far end of the corridor to greet them. He called, "Mrs Lloyd-Davies, just walk towards me please."

This call seemed to fill Mum with unearthly zeal, because, to Pat's surprise, she steamed down the corridor as though the hounds of hell were after her or she was on the way to a gold medal.

"VERY good. Excellent. Come this way."

'This way' was his consulting room. Mr P held Mum's X-ray to the light. Mum may have sprinted down the corridor but the X-ray showed that her right hip was very severely damaged with osteoarthritis, and an op was the only answer. The op itself would take almost an hour, longer than most, because the socket had become so thin, rather eggshell-like, so replacing the joint was more difficult, but it could be done.

Mum might as well have said, "Well...well fancy that. I never did," because she decided against all intervention. So that was that!

Life got more difficult for her, and getting up her 'lighthouse' winding stairs was a slow process. All the family visited and helped out, and although getting into a car was an enormous effort, she did it, and would come to either Pat's or Tony's or to us.

Mum's 80th birthday loomed, also Pat's 50th. For reasons unknown, Pat and Ray didn't invite us to her party, held at their house. I was just in the middle of icing a cake with HAPPY BIRTHDAY for her when Pat arrived. "So sorry," she said apologetically. "We can't ask you and Harold, too many people to cope with. I would have liked to ask ALL the family, but…"

Unusually, I felt upset. I hadn't told her I had baked a fruit cake for her. In fact, I had the icing bag poised over the cake just about to ice in pink the number 50 as she arrived. I had thrown a tea towel over it, such was the surprise visit. Pat, unaware of any upset, rushed off, and in a trice I whipped the tea cloth off and changed the 50 into an 80. All done. So no cake for sister Pat, but a beautifully iced birthday cake for Maudie!

On Mum's actual birthday in May, we assembled rather like the 'Tettenhall Mafia'. We all sat round in the garden amongst her lupins and a riot of forget-me-nots, whilst a host of grandchildren ran amok amongst the rather overgrown raspberry canes and fruit bushes. Not 249, but Maudie was in her element, the hub of a wheel with so many spokes, all whizzing around her.

Shortly after her birthday, Mum found that she couldn't get out of bed, her knees and hip were too painful. We called her GP (who, I must say, was the kind of doctor who would, and DID, send a patient to hospital with a dead verruca or a hammer toe. This he did to Pat's oldest son, Andrew, in spite of the fact that hammer toes hadn't been operated on for many years.).

We heard that this doctor had originally hoped to be a vet. Well, thank goodness! The animals were saved, because the GP became a doctor to humans. He had been our family doctor, but now only Tony's family and Mum stayed with him (which is the worst mistake ever made by us all).

Dr X gave Mum's knees and hips the 'once-over'. "Now, my dear, stay in bed, rest your bones."

Mum ALWAYS did as the doctor ordered so she DID stay in bed… for the next six years.

The next six years proves that we were a family of lunatics. Mum remained upstairs in her bed, no gardening, no flowers to tend, no baking of meringues; she followed her doctor's orders to the letter. So began Maudie's incarceration, something we all thought was dreadful, but Mum thought was the correct thing to do in the circumstances.

Years on from Mum becoming a 'bed lady', I penned a few lines of verse about her and her love of lupins, her favourite flowers. The shrubs she loved were her hydrangeas, all started from 'stolen' cuttings many years before, and some were transported from 249 to her little cottage. She delighted in all her plants and flowers in her garden. This was a place of solitude and reflection, a place she never set foot in again.

MEMORIES

She stands, blue lupins her guardians,
Their pepper-scented pollen
Hidden for only the bee to find,
Each round leaf's centre is set
with a single diamond of dew.
And she remembers.
How often had her hands,
Child's hands with, sea-shell tipped fingers
tilted the leaves,
Spilling the liquid diamonds,
Those 'fairy-baths' of childhood games,
until they fell, sparkling onto the grey earth.
Her face so pale and hollow now
Had once glowed 'butter-bright',
Reflecting the buttercup's shiny petals
and she had burst the dandelion-clock
Sending the seeds high, towards the sun,
Her young breath blowing them higher, into heaven.
She stands, blue lupins her tall guardians,
Crystal scenes of her youth, dance upon the grass.
They enfold her stooping body, warming.
She reaches out swollen fingers, feeling forgotten textures,
And the lupins shed their diamonds,
As tears fall onto the grey earth.

THE SPOKES OF THE WHEEL

This part of the family saga is written with sadness and a little bit of 'angst'!

Mum's little cottage was ideal, well, only for lighthouse men. The stairs wound round, too difficult to have any chairlift installed, so Maudie did what the doctor prescribed, and stayed upstairs in her cosy old bed. Somehow nobody thought this weird or selfish. Her sisters all visited and almost encouraged Mum's bed-bound life.

The trouble was that the 'looking after bit' fell to Pat and myself. Of course, Robin and Tony were visitors, but they worked full time, so couldn't see Mum so often. We were female and housewives, so it was up to us to care and cherish Mum. In the 1970s that was what was expected and we DID have more time.

Every meal had to be made or brought in. Mum could still walk across the small landing and into the bathroom, so she washed and used the loo as normal. For night times there was a commode in her bedroom. However, food was always to be there on her bedside table seven days a week.

Looking back, we are amazed at these years of total home-care. No home-help was seconded. Later on in Mum's sojourn, she did have some help, but for the first few years, the family were her sole carers. More amazing now is the lack of any help from her half-soaked doctor.

Life at 249 and all its trials and tribulations probably gave us girls a good grounding. We weren't trained in servitude and had rarely had to tend to any of our siblings, and Dad never had any TLC from us, mainly because the poison was well embedded in all of us by Mum (all, that is, except Robin, who has always retained a respect for Dad).

There is a corner in my mind that feels sad about my thoughts, although Dad was very dysfunctional as a family man, and was quite at sea with anything vaguely domestic, he knew no better. He suffered physically, without so much as a kind deed or thought from any of us, "It's all his own fault" was the order of the day at 249. The poison was laid.

As the months, then years, went on, Mum's breakfast was always made the night before. It had to be All-Bran, with a handful of raisins sprinkled amongst the bran, milk in a jug, and tea in a thermos... all by the bed on her lacy-doilied little bedside drawers. Pat lived across the road, so the mornings were her time. She would try hard to get Mum to get dressed. Every effort was met with "Oh NO, it hurts too much. I'm all right." Of course Mum let us change her hand-knitted vest and nice soft-coloured nighties. A very fetching hand-knitted pastel-coloured bed jacket was worn over her shoulders, but she would never wear a dress or any 'day time' clothes. Very frustrating for Pat, but tussling or cajoling with Mum wasn't on; she was a VERY stubborn lady.

This sounds odd, but up to this time, this rather ridiculous bedridden drama never appeared to us anything but normal! Looking back, it was so stupid. It stopped all kinds of family life. (I had two children very young, particularly son Robin, and Pat had teenagers, with all the traumas that teenagers bring.) This never dawned on Mum. She was happy, taking her anti-inflammatory tablets and her dose of laxatives most evenings. Her mattress sort of 'sank' into a hammock shape! But she said all was fine, and she liked it, "It fits my hips."

There was a small amount of money really meant for carers each week. This she used to hand over to us to buy her food and toilet goods. I was chief buyer and shopper. "I do like those Bird's chicken pies." But she would add, "There isn't much chicken in them!" Also "Brown bread for my sandwiches," she'd order (did we cut the crust off? Oh dear, can't recall, so black marks).

The sun would come into the little bedroom window, and occasionally Mum would sit in her Lloyd-Loom chair, but too low to see out onto the road with its constant traffic. She never was able to view her beloved garden again, but she rarely asked about what her roses and flower borders were doing. We looked after those between us. Sunday dinner was sometimes taken steaming hot right to her bed, by a very breathless brother Tony. Tony was by now suffering from heart trouble, having had a heart attack, followed by small attacks, which left him breathless.

Christmases were hell! Pat and Ray and the three children always spent Christmas and sometimes new year at their Welsh cottage. So Christmas was our time to minister to Mum, with visits from Tony and wife Joan, and brother Robin, all bearing presents. Both boys visited Mum over the years, as did Joan, so really all of us four siblings were ever present, the 'spokes' around the rather static hub!

We now had Harold's father Syd staying with us on and off, but always at Christmas. Syd was drifting into confusion, having had some small strokes, and he had become doubly incontinent.

To say that even Father Christmas would have given us a miss is an understatement! Juggling children and Syd (who was very poorly and immobile in a wheelchair), trying to plate up a hot turkey dinner with all the trimmings for Harold to jump into the car and deliver to a hungry mother-in-law, then get back in time for his (hopefully) hot dinner, well it was a sweat-making regime.

A few years ago, I did find a school exercise book penned by son Robin, he would be about eleven. I sounded like a terrible winging drudge: "Mummy is always moaning about having to 'do things for my Nanny'". It went on in this mode… So I DID weary of the constant daily trips to the cosy cottage, as highlighted by Robin, but I don't remember, I have blocked the angst out whilst the caring was underway.

Thinking back, of course I DID have to gird my loins most days, and some days teeth were definitely gritted! Pat did too, but we never discussed it at the time, only NOW when we remember how silly we had been. Both of us were very 'green' and almost 'programmed' to look after our mother. A VERY Victorian view.

Pat had her pottery most days; she was 'in residence' at Wightwick Manor. (This local large mansion was owned by the Mander family, who were Pat's husband Ray's bosses. Wightwick Manor was later gifted to the National Trust.) She had a lovely little thriving business and turned out some wonderful dishes, cups and saucers, and in the latter years, tiny hedgehogs, unglazed but ideal for children to buy. Quite a few schools would look around the manor, then pop in to see 'Pat the Potter'.

Nobody in the social services or medical clan ever mentioned physio for Mum, or help in any way. Eventually, Mum did have a home-help, possibly twice a week, and a 'bath-lady' once a week on a Friday morning. We asked for a social worker, and one day a nice middle-aged lady arrived with a folder of papers. She sat for some time, asked Mum a couple of questions, but then, when I mentioned (for some reason) CATS, she held forth for some time. They were obviously her favourite animals, so lots of anecdotes about her two little 'chaps'. Soon after that she left, and that was IT! We never heard anything from a social worker again! So no change THERE.

Far from being unhappy in her incarceration, I suppose the luxury of being looked after and able to do whatever she chose suited Mum. She still made her face up, a touch of lipstick for rouge (a mix of lippy and Pond's face cream) and powder from her compact. She even popped her now silver hair in rollers every night, but for the life of me, I can't remember WHO washed her hair.

True to the Roberts family code, Maude Eleanor née Roberts looked good. Her skin was always smooth and unwrinkled; this nice bloom lasted until the end of her life. Maudie's skin must have been of the tough but smooth variety, because after years in bed, she never developed so much as a red patch on her buttocks. Quite amazing, so no awful bed-sores.

Mum's days were always full. She began penning (in her strange backward slanting script) very long and weird stories, fiction, but obviously based on some facts. She wrote two books whilst sitting in her hammock bed. Her poetry was legendary in the family; some was very readable and touching. Mum loved poetry. One of her favourite poems, or 'gatherings' of poetry, was the Rubaiyat of Omar Khayyam. These writings had been translated into English from the original language by Edward Fitzgerald. Mum owned three or four illustrated books. (I too love a few of the poems.)

I gave her some Conté crayons, and her latent art blossomed once again. Not so well as earlier, but she got great pleasure using the pastels. But the bed sheets got very colourful! I never found out WHY, but monks were very much her 'thing' when pastelling. Cloche-hat-wearing ladies were also around. All very Virginia Wolfe and Vita-Sackville West.

Once a week, all three sisters would arrive: Glad in the driving seat and Marj statuesque in shades of blue or teal, always sporting a hat to match, and still occasionally showing a glimpse of her shiny pink to-the-knees knickers. Vera, her large bust supported (courtesy of the Spirella Undergarment Company), would appear elegantly dressed in her home-crocheted jacket, purple, with a darker dress, her poor half-amputated toes enclosed in sensible shoes. Again usually a very acceptable hat to go with her outfit. Glad was the first to wear trousers or slacks, always the more daring of her siblings. Then Ve began wearing slacks, feeling it was VERY trendy. I don't think Marj ever succumbed to trousers, so the pink knicker-legs with elastic were viewed when sitting down. I suppose they were called 'drawers'. M&S and other stores brought in more modern underwear, but I don't think Marj ever joined the smaller knickers brigade, but I may be wrong.

Cakes were consumed, and tea always made in a pot and served in china cups (the Indian tree pattern collected by Mum). Eventually, even the Roberts girls had to use teabags when at Maude's, probably because I bought them… another lapse in the Roberts family etiquette.

I now had a little blue Beetle car, very old (it had semaphore arms for turning left or right, but these had been overshadowed by having winkers fitted – very modern!) and rather Hitler-like, with a running board and a slit for a back window. Having wheels, I could now 'do' lunches and evening meals for Mum.

The doctor would occasionally visit when Mum's repeat prescriptions ran out. He never once advised Mum to become mobile – a fact we found odd. The doctor was, in our opinion, a twit! He didn't have a receptionist or indeed a nurse. His prescription pad was open when you entered the surgery and very little examining went on. These were the days when antibiotics were used constantly, and this doc certainly used them willy-nilly. He remained Tony and Joan's GP, and they thought the world of him, plus the added marks for he and his wife attending St Jude's church. THAT 'sold' him to Joan, so he could do no wrong.

Joan could never come to terms with our lack of God following. She said to me once, "Just say you believe in God and heaven, and there will be a place saved there for you." So simple but, in my eyes, so devious and nutty! Siblings Robin, Pat and this writer are all atheists. I can say this now, because I am braver over 'coming out' over God. No doubt Maudie was a non-believer too, but was too frightened to say much, in case 'THEY' got her! She remained afraid of 'THEY', a fear that has been passed on to me. (THEY will definitely get me if I find I have paid too little by accident. I suppose 'THEY' are one's conscience…)

There are 'knicker police' lurking around corners to pop in and check my lingerie drawer whilst we are on holiday, SO I HAVE to leave all knickers pristine, no old and grey ones – they are slung out, or hidden in the recesses of the bottom drawer. 'THEY' watch to make certain teeth are brushed . The 'teeth police' are on patrol should I skip a morning brushing, uniformed officers may burst into the bathroom armed with giant toothbrushes and a prosecution document! There is ALWAYS a hand at the ready to clap down on my shoulder. Mum instilled this into us all. I don't think Pat is quite as daft as me! THEY never attempt to get HER.

The years rolled on. All kinds of unimaginable traumas, happy times, deaths and births marriages, all took place whilst Maudie was in her cosy nest.

Pat's three children were all at college or university. The oldest, Andrew, became an accountant, and Sue received a degree in Geology. The last of the three, Peter, had a few years of hippy life, sometimes living in an isolated log cabin in Wales, so basic that he could see through the logs to the outside so that the wind whistled in. He also decided that his hair would be best kept healthy by enclosing it in red clay We would hear all this bizarre news from Pat, and shake our heads, wondering what Peter was going to do with his life.

Well, the upshot of it all is that he's done a lot with his life. He eventually achieved a good degree, and is, at the time of writing this epistle, working in computers in the city, living with his partner in Islington. (That's a little update, just to prove that sometimes letting 'it all hang out' isn't such a terrible thing.)

At that time, though, the odd bit of news that filtered through to Mum about Peter surprised her, but the world outside her bedroom was becoming a world that she wasn't part of. I suppose she had experienced much stranger 'goings-on' in her life, so it ALL passed her by. There was the odd "Tut-tut" and "Well I NEVER DID!"

Mum never spoke of 249, it was a great chapter now closed forever, but we all dip our wings when driving past. I notice now, how very often the front door changes colour. It was always dark green whilst we lived there, but then a bright blue, and perhaps a year later, a black door, imposing, but not the right colour.

CHANGES AND A FALL

No. 249 is being mucked about with. The variegated leafed laurel is still there hanging over a crumbling low wall and the rusty hinge of the little gate (a gate I never saw as it was commandeered for scrap metal during the war, never to be replaced, but the hinges are still there, idle and useless). Net curtains are sometimes draped across the windows. Mum would have had a very nasty attack of the vapours over those. She hated net, and likened 'those sort of curtains' to foreigners and aliens – "Very common"!

In the 1980s Wolverhampton was changing. When we were young, a coloured face was rarely seen. Mr Oates, our lovely patient, was really the first dark person I had ever had contact with. The influx of eastern and Caribbean families was something Mum knew nothing about. I don't think Mum had ever had dealings with anyone from the Caribbean or a dark-skinned person. There WAS Louis Armstrong, who blew his trumpet so loudly and sang at full throttle, frightening the daylights out of Mum when she was on the front row of at the long-gone Hippodrome back in the 1950s. Otherwise, apart from Turner and Leyton, the singing duo (I don't know which man was coloured, Mum had fallen for BOTH of them, I think!). However, the changing face of Wolverhampton was unseen by the bedroom-bound Maudie.

One morning Mum had a fall. She injured her already swollen and painful arthritic knee. An ambulance was called and two ambulance men appeared. Seeing the spiral stairs, the first chap shouted to his colleague, "It's a lighthouse job, Jim!"

No stretcher could get down the stairs without getting stuck, so a chair was brought, and Mum, pink and blue gowned, with her lacy bed jacket over her shoulders, was (rather roughly) carried down into the kitchen she hadn't seen for many years. There wasn't time to stop and check that the kitchen was clean and tidy, I knew THAT was what Mum would look for. Were the spokes doing a good job? Did her electric second-hand cooker gleam?

She was taken to New Cross Hospital, the hospital that Dad would "NEVER OVER MY DEAD BODY" go to – his home-from-home the

Royal had closed by this time. It wasn't a first through the gates of New Cross for Mum as she had had visited the wing that was (but no longer) a workhouse when visiting Great Uncle Harry and, of course, Uncle Reg. Unhappy memories of undignified living lingered when New Cross was mentioned, not just by our family, but these thoughts were echoed by many in Wolverhampton at that time.

New Cross is a wonderful centre of excellence now. The heart and lung department is known worldwide. It's a 'town' in itself, with all departments bustling. I still view the red-brick wing that was 'home' to so many poor and destitute as a menacing building, though.

The ligaments in Mum's knee were damaged so Mum would have to stay in a while, to check her general health. By now she was about eighty-seven. Mum loved it. There were three other ladies in her ward, so we had a daily whispered bulletin of their illnesses and their families… but, to our horror, not a word of praise for them! The snobby side of Maudie suddenly broke out, guns blazing!

The lady opposite had received a visit from her granddaughter, and after her nice young visitor had gone, the patient opposite held up a photo of her granddaughter. This photo was held up for Mum to view from a distance. The photo showed the granddaughter wearing her cap and gown, she had just graduated from Liverpool University, and rightly her granny was very happy and proud.

"I don't believe that girl has got her degree," Mum whispered. "Her grandmother isn't the TYPE, they are VERY ordinary."

To add to this, the grandma opposite shouted across to Mum, "What's your name, luv?"

Mum replied (I was there, so heard her), "Maude, with an 'E', second name Eleanor (she pronounced it as Eleeeeeeenor) as in Eleanor of Aquitaine."

Embarrassment set in.

Oh dear, Mum's history was up the creek, because Eleanor of Aquitaine was a horrible woman, not the royal personage Mum would have liked. Mum no doubt tried to impress with her knowledge of history, but did the opposite.

There was a rather poignant time during her stay, when the whispered conversation was rather different. "They think I've got BO," whispered Mum.

"Why do you think THAT, Mum, because you haven't?"

Mum got closer to my ear. "I looked at my chart, and it DEFINITLY says on EVERY page, BO."

Poor Mum really thought that the BO meant body odour, and not bowels opened! We put her right!

There wasn't much communication from the staff on Mum's health or length of stay, but one day Pat and I were asked to go into the sister's office. She asked how long Mum had been in bed, I suppose thinking maybe days before the fall, or even weeks... When we said about five or six YEARS, the look of amazement on the sister's face was full-blown and mouth open! Her response was not what we expected. "YOU SILLY IDIOTS!" No "GOSH... How WELL you've done, how MARVELLOUS!" She had just a look of almost disdain AND disbelief!

Yes, she HAD got it correct. We WERE silly idiots, but without any back-up from the doctor, who was quite happy with his patient in bed being ministered to by her loving family. Also no help, except a weekly bath-lady, and sometimes a home-help so we just DID it! We lacked advice from someone who knew the ropes of the NHS, what was available, and how and where we could ask for help. In a way, these were wasted years for all of us siblings, and of course Mum. Even her sisters were complacent about Maudie – children should look after their parent! A very Victorian way of thinking. But Mum WAS a Victorian, but only just, as she was born in 1901, the year that Queen Victoria had died.

Mum's knee, although damaged and already very swollen with arthritis, was deemed to be not a bed-taking-up case. Rightly so. We were in a difficult dilemma. Mum was even more immobile, and the staff were adamant that she would need nursing. All four of us 'children' got together and discussed ideas. Paying a twenty-four-hour carer was not really an option, and where would we get one from? And there was only one bedroom. So that was dismissed. Every avenue was chatted about. At last, our ploy was to say to Mum that she needed convalescence in a nursing home, until she could take some weight on her knee. This sounds so cruel, but we decided that after several weeks, when she was settled, we would tell her that it was impossible to go home.

I feel awful and tearful about this even now, but it was definitely the right and best thing to do. She loved her little whitewashed cottage, and her hammock-like bed, her books and knitting were always close, inches away, plus her little window out onto the green leafed trees, across the busy road beneath, but it had to end. We could no longer cope.

Pat and I began searching for a suitable residential/nursing home in the Tettenhall area. We visited homes that stank of stale wee, but displayed very attractive bedrooms, all chintzy, but with pools of urine on the landing floor en route to the bathrooms. A no-no! Most homes had double bedrooms, and that was almost certainly not on Mum's agenda; she would like her usual splendid isolation. We tried not to announce our arrival in some homes on our list, and this worked, as conditions in most homes were dire, but undercover to the invited visitors.

THE 'HOME'

The residential home we hoped would fit Mum's bill was close by. It had only two residents, as it was just opened. The owner, a doctor's wife (who had been a nurse), was there to greet us. She said she had always wanted to care for the elderly, and this detached large house had come onto the market, so she was going to realize her dream.

We were introduced to the 'second in command', a nursing sister in a navy uniform, complete with stiffened belt. Although smiling, she was judged (especially by me) to be very masculine, her hair shaved up at the back. Nowadays, we would both say probably lesbian, not a word that, in those days, tripped as lightly off the tongue as it does today. The home could take about ten residents, and some more ladies were arriving very soon. There was a chef and everything was 'home cooked'. We toured the kitchen and met the chubby red-faced lady chef. There was no acrid smell. Everywhere was fresh. It was a two-bedded room, though.

THE day arrived, Maudie was on her way. We sisters sat with heavy hearts, waiting for the ambulance from the hospital to arrive. Mum arrived and was wheeled into the bedroom. She was somewhat shaky and confused about her journey from New Cross Hospital. Admittedly, the parts of Wolverhampton that she was driven through were pretty derelict, with dark foreboding run-down small works, rows of terraced houses, and a multi-racial gathering of families. Blocks of twelve-storey high-rise flats must have stunned Mum. Coloured faces abounded, wearing brightly coloured saris, clothes that Mum had probably never seen. Mum had never seen many Asian and Caribbean folks in her life, except on the television. These families were just doing their shopping, and going about their business, but to Mum it was like a dream into some futuristic world.

Apparently, the ambulance kept stopping to drop people off at their abodes, so the time taken was over an hour. I think she found the whole journey a nightmare with visions of a world that she didn't recognize. It was frightening for her. Her in-bed years had shielded her from the changes that were going on all around her little cosy kingdom. Mum had been cocooned in her little nest, happily writing poetry and long weird fictional stories. She became a little confused. A small event like that journey had somehow instilled all manner of weird happenings into her head. She would talk about 'that ride home' for many weeks.

Unbelievably, Mum settled in, though she STILL thought this was a halfway house to home.

Molly, her roommate, had only one leg. She was a very pretty elderly lady, softly spoken and smiling, with only physical problems, her mind as bright as a button. Molly was a good knitter, a delightful lady, always positive. And by coincidence, Molly's late husband had also been a cinema manager. But Mum somehow couldn't gel with her. Even the theatre or cinema that Molly's late husband had managed was frowned on behind the scenes by Mum. "I don't think he had EVER managed a 'PROPER' cinema" was Mum's whispered remark.

The deception about Mum never going back to her cottage certainly worried us, but there was no way we could carry on daily visits cooking and shopping, let alone lift her. Oddly, though, her damaged knee didn't seem to make her any less mobile. In fact, she didn't use a wheelchair, she had a walking frame, and while she didn't exactly 'zoom' from bedroom to dining room, she DID it!

To start with, the food seemed to please Mum, a small portion which suited her, so we didn't worry too much. However, one day when I was visiting at lunchtime, I peeped into the dining room and was shocked. The tablecloth was a very thin disposable plastic/paper cloth, and the napkins white poor-quality paper. In the kitchen doorway stood the lady chef, her countenance less than happy. She was looking cheesed-off, hot faced, and was eager to talk.

It appeared that she was constantly trying to make one small chicken go around about ten residents. It was the same with the small amount of vegetables she was given. She was doing her best to make do with what her budget allowed. Make do and mend should never have come into this equation.

Now we knew that corners were being cut; everything was fine on the surface, but these old folks were being given too little, on a table that resembled an institute for the poor and homeless. The chef HAD had enough, and walked out the next day!

There were two more chefs. Both were cheery ladies, and honest, so the food they were asked to cook was too little and ridiculous. I think another lady chef stayed for a very short time. I suppose Mrs Doctor's-wife took over the kitchen duties for a while.

Pat had a word with Mrs Doc. She was as charming as ever. Yes, they had had troubles with the cooks, but now SHE was in charge in the kitchen. We didn't hold our breath. Tea was a shop-bought pizza, with a piece of bread and butter. Pat viewed the ladies' tea (their evening meal) and again was upset to see old women, with perhaps wobbly dentures, trying to bite through a piece of leathery pizza crust. Mum had never even seen a pizza before, let alone eaten one!

It all got worse. Sadly, Molly died, and Mum was given a bedroom upstairs. (The one good point was that she was shown how to use the stair-lift, and DID, then shuffled into the sitting room on her 'downstairs' Zimmer.) It was a single room, and small, but in a lot of respects, comfortable.

One day, we noticed that Mum's ruby and diamond old-set ring was nowhere to be seen. "I've given it to the young lady nurse (helper and general factotum). She says she will clean it for me, it was quite dirty," was Mum's innocent reply.

We never saw the ring again. All questions s were answered by Mrs Doc with "Well, your mum is very vague and forgetful, she's probably thrown it in the bin." The 'well, she's old and is not to be taken seriously' came into play! The family should have tackled the young helper, but even WE were unsure of Mum's story. So how could we accuse her of stealing? It was all very sad. It wasn't an expensive ring anyway, an Edwardian setting and one small diamond missing, but we found out later that Mum had left it to Pat in her will. Years and years later, Pat laughed when we were reminiscing about the ring. "Well, I would never have worn it anyway." Pat never wears rings, just her gold wedding ring, never anything fancy. The young lady helper disappeared, obviously given her marching orders.

Next to vex us was the 'chocolate-debacle'. Visitors to Mum, not knowing what to bring when visiting, often arrived with boxes of very desirable chocs. Mum's memory was bad, and was getting progressively worse, so when we asked if she had enjoyed her chocs, she would look slightly vague. She thought she HAD... but the chocolates were never by her chair or in her bedroom.

I tried to find Ann, the 'sister' in charge (we found later that Ann had NO nursing experience at all). She spoke as though she was Florence Nightingale, always wore a navy uniform, and was masculine in her manner. I was a little bit in awe of her. She told me she had undergone a hysterectomy, and the next day her friends wheeled her to the pub. I felt a bit suspicious – it didn't fit with her sober demeanour. I found Mum's chocolates, high up on a shelf in the office. Ann wasn't around, so I had a good look, several had gone. Ann soon arrived.

"Oh, we CAN'T give Maude those. She gets the most awful dose of 'the runs' if she eats chocolate." We now know that the chocolates seemed to be for the staff. I don't think Mum ever saw them. But we conformed, more's the pity. We thought that if we made a fuss, Mum would be the one to suffer, so we said nothing. Also it would be Mum's word against theirs, and who would believe a senile old lady?

Soon after this, Mrs Doc told me she and Mr Doc were off. They had sold the business and were moving away. A new young couple were taking over. What a relief… we were happy to say cheerio to Mrs Doc, who had earlier said she had always wanted to care for old folks. It certainly was 'cut the corners' type of care, so when Mrs Doc said that if we were ever down her way (she even gave us her address) would we visit them, I hypocritically mumbled something but knew none of us would darken her doorstep in the future.

The new young couple took over a nice enough twosome. Sister Ann left straight away, leaving only a very young girl to minister to the old ladies. She would turn the TV on in the morning, usually to the under-fives children's programmes or Radio One, pop music, quite inappropriate for the poor old souls.

Anyone visiting from our family would turn the TV or radio to another station, hoping to find something less intrusive. Not that any of the residents watched or listened. Most were past caring, their heads on their chests. Mum, who had knitted and crocheted all her life, did attempt to knit some coloured squares, but sadly, she didn't really manage to finish them. Sometimes we found her wearing someone else's clothes. Everyone had name tapes sewn in, but there she would be, sitting in a skirt too long, or too short and badly washed. Her wardrobe held more alien outfits but Mum didn't seem to notice.

Amazingly, after years of not dressing herself, she would have a stab at dressing, though this didn't always go to plan, her vest would be in all sorts of places, but she did try. Her skin always looked unwrinkled, and she managed to put some make-up on. The Roberts way of life was still there, and she always looked pretty. That sounds strange, but Mum had a nice face, and in old age she looked prettier than in her younger days. Photos of her when she was young showed a very dark straight-haired thin, tall girl, with rather a big nose. "That's my Roman nose" she would say proudly. It's only NOW, all these years later, that I found out that YES, it WAS indeed Roman. Her great grandfather was a very famous Italian engraver, who lived here for years, and was royal engraver to King George III. His name was Francesco Bartolozzi. So THAT's where Mum must have got her light and shade drawing talent from. She would have been SO happy, as would all her siblings, had they known any of this. None of them knew much about their father Ludd, he was (and still IS) a mystery man.

The 'log-on' computer age dawned after Mum had died, so looking up the ancestors wasn't very easy. It IS now, and has given up some fantastic revelations about the Roberts/Bartolozzi/Anderson part of the family. It's quite amazing.

In fact, it turns out we are mongrels. German, Italian and Welsh. Goodness knows what other nationality is thrown in for good measure, a kind of genetic stew of mongrels.

A SAD FAREWELL

At the same time as we were visiting Mum and selling the cottage, Auntie Ve became ill. It appears that she had an infection in one of her poor disfigured toes. Antibiotics were given, but they seriously disrupted and eventually damaged Ve's stomach and colon.

She was taken to a hospital near Stourbridge. We walked up to her ward with apprehension, horrible depressing thoughts passed through my mind. She greeted us, and half sat up. I won't tell any more, except to say, when we asked her how she was she replied with surprising vigour, "BLOODY awful!" She then smiled her toothy smile, and we had a chuckle at her choice of language.

These were not her last words, though. She lay in bed for several more days, receiving good treatment (we hope). An operation to repair her punctured bowel was offered, but, true to any of the Roberts girls, she asked to be left alone, no food just water. She was prepared to die, and the hospital respected her wish.

My favourite auntie, godmother and confidante died a quiet death. Greatly loved by her three sisters, and her many nieces and nephews.

Her love of chocolate was legendary. She could polish off a box of Cadbury's in an afternoon. Her wonderful crocheting and her ability to remember verses and sayings and all kinds of bits and pieces of Shakespeare was remarkable for a young girl who left school at about thirteen. Auntie Ve also had another very special gift – she could laugh AT herself, and DID, very often.

Mum didn't show many outward signs of bereavement after Ve had died. We'd only ever seen Mum distressed once, and that was over the death of her brother Stan years before. Now old age had softened the news of Ve's death, but probably many treasured memories would fill Mum's mind when alone. The 'old' days and the strange and awful events of her years in Stourbridge had always been very alive in Mum's thoughts, but they were no longer in black and white, they were becoming misty and vague, which may be nature taking over, making life more bearable and comfortable.

Out of the nine Roberts offspring, only Mum and the much younger Auntie Glad lived on.

FAREWELL, COTTAGE

The family had to sell Mum's dear little cottage. We had got through the awful weeks of deceit, telling Mum that she was only in the retirement home until she felt well enough to live there again. It's a truly terrible lie, and we didn't feel good about pulling the wool over Mum's eyes, but we could no longer look after her, we had completed over five years of constant care. Gradually, though, Mum seemed to accept the life away from her sanctuary, so the time became right to put 6 Codsall Road up for sale.

The house sale went well, and surprisingly fast. It was sold to a single lady, and we hoped it would be a happy home for her.

Harold was Mum's executor, so we all had a peep at her will. She had written in long-hand about where all her special little items of jewellery and ornaments were to go. Pat inherited the ruby and diamond ring (that had already gone to the very dishonest young helper). Mum had mainly left all her precious little keepsakes just of sentimental value. Memories of 249, ranging from the scary skull ashtray (left to Robin), Mum's box of very old coins, some Roman, they were Tony's, and some pink glass for me, Edwardian and very pretty.

There was, however, THE naked lady oil painting, the one that had excited my old grandpa when he lived with Reg and Betty. Mum had 'inherited' it from next door, and sent a photo of the painting to Christie's. We found the reply from that well-known auction house when sorting out her bedside cabinets. Yes, it WAS very old, possibly Italian, but was part of a bigger work of art. However, whatever it was or wasn't, Mum had always wanted Robin to have it, so he did. None of us bothered who got what! All were memories of weird, sometimes sad, but also happy days at 249, the crumbling semi so loved by all of us. The cold draughts and the families of mice, Jack Frost INSIDE and buckets and kettles full of steaming hot water carried painstakingly upstairs to pour into the bath. All of us united by some unseen dusty cobwebs of times past.

There were all Mum's books to distribute. Her poetry, written mainly during her years in bed, and also her three handwritten books. They started off not too fanciful, very much in the Edwardian style, romantic (as were a lot of her poems), very dated and in parts hilarious. But there was a sad

415

undercurrent in her writings. Maudie really had a hidden part, a part that had never managed to escape when she was making ends meet and looking after everything and everyone. Her fertile imagination during her sojourn in bed became extraordinary, verging on the funny. I took charge of her writings, and still have them. The poetry is now, to me, very sad. All the feeling that she felt for her family, and particularly her first grandchild, Pat's son Andrew, were displayed out on the page but rarely expressed verbally in her life.

In today's world, she would enjoy being creative, erudite and positive, a person in her own right. She was repressed by marriage and motherhood, as were many other ladies in the twenties and thirties. Perhaps the war-work carried out by women liberated them, but liberation hadn't touched Mum. I think she would have loved to be set free from domesticity, an artist and poet, but never able to escape from her cage.

So we piled up the books. Some were cousin Joy's, very 'highbrow' philosophy and politics, biographies of statesmen, pages of tissue separating the engravings. I hate to say this, but we did have to let some books become 'jumble'.

There was some excitement, though, as we pulled books out and shook them. Mum had been busily squirrelling bank notes away between the pages, and they started fluttering out, so we then had a jolly good search, and found well over forty pounds.

Mum knew nothing of the sale. By now, she was getting very vague mentally, but still able to walk with the aid of a frame, something she had resisted for years.

The new owners of the home installed an electric organ, and for a few weeks the residents were serenaded by the ex-RAF co-owner, a rather quiet and gentle man. Also they asked sister-in-law Joan to bring some of St Jude's church choir in to 'singalong' with the old ladies. (It was ALL ladies. One man did stay a few weeks but disappeared, probably to hospital – nobody seemed to know. So it was an all ladies audience.)

The food didn't get any better, though, and a couple of cooks left frustrated with having to 'make do and mend' money-wise. Still paper napkins and even paper tablecloths. By now, though, Maudie was past caring. Napkins and lacy tablecloths were a thing of the past. Some of her crocheted doilie-type mats were on her very minuscule so-called dressing table.

A year or so after Mum was given a single bedroom, upstairs, managing the stair-lift well, she would sail down, wearing a strange combination of clothes. Sometimes not her own, in spite of the labels diligently sewn into her garments. Goodness only knows what underclothes she had on or in WHAT order! Bras over vests, and tights too big, the person who had originally worn them must have been much taller. Mum had shrunk to about five foot, a loss of about five inches.

ANOTHER FAREWELL

A very sad event happened shortly after Mum's move upstairs. Brother Tony had owned a caravan in Crickieth, North Wales, for years. He and Joan would go up there in the summer. I think it was possibly Tony's happiest time.

Joan always 'enjoyed bad health'. Her back and her allergies were legendary. Tony became a settled, rather hen-pecked husband, but a strict father to his son and daughter. Shoulder-chips emerged occasionally, but all of his siblings found him a more likeable chap. I would like to think it was Tony's conversion to religion, but we found out later that religion wasn't the answer; it became a shield from a very religious wife. So Tony had put on a very good 'show' for the sake of peace and quiet, and we think a lot DID change with his new persona, all to the good. So Tony was still, to all eyes, a 'God-fearing' man, no longer the speaker of rather pseudo-Germanic foul language or the difficult brother, viewing Robin as 'a weakling'. He visited Mum when at home in her cottage, always panting up the stairs, his heart trouble was always present.

In the summer of 1990, Tony bought a new car. It was new to Tony, but was some years old so second-hand; however, a much nicer jalopy. He drove over to show it off to us. It had a radio and a tape-player. Tony's love of Western music was still there, and I sat in the passenger seat with him whilst a jolly 'Cowboy-out-west-hillbilly' song filled the car. I suddenly felt that after all the years of angst, the tormenting of yester-year had gone. I felt sisterly love towards him. Admittedly, it had taken many moons to come to that decision, but there it was! Never too late.

Harold was duly given a viewing of the car. (I have no idea WHAT make as I am 'car-blind' and can't tell one from another, the exception being VWs, which I find easier to remember, plus the fact that I had always had 'beetles'.) Tony looked well, suntanned, still fair haired, although so much more receding at the temples. He didn't look his sixty-three years.

The next day, after his visit to show off his car, he and Joan, plus Joan's old mum, Mrs Pugh, and their family dog, were going to the caravan. There was long grass to cut, so they borrowed a friend's Flymo. I don't think it had ever been used by Tony's friend, it was a second-hand mower when the friend and her husband bought it. (I am not certain about that.)

No doubt Tony was looking forward to his holiday. He was cheerful and happy, a Tony who was very different from the 'old' Tony. We waved him off home. He was in his element, music from his tape recorder, a car that he liked – his pride and joy, and a holiday in his favourite place. He loved his caravan.

Next day, we had a visitor, one of Harold's old work colleagues. I was showing Keith my vegetable patch, the broad-beans were rather spindly but Keith grew vegetables, so it was 'gardener's world' chat.

The phone rang out in the house, so I ran up to get the call. It was Robin. He told me that Tony had died whilst cutting the little grass area around his caravan. It was very sudden. A doctor on call had certified the death.

This sounds rather cold, but I just went down to the two men, still standing by the beans, and declared that "Brother Tony is dead, a heart attack, in Wales."

Keith made to go back up the path quickly and leave us to the sadness, but I still was able be somehow unaffected. I could stop to admire certain flowers and plants as we walked up to the house. I was stunned, and felt nothing, a sort of blank numbness. I did keep thinking how well he had looked two days before. Also how cruel life was. Tony's new car, his hillbilly music. He had been very happy for a few days, at last!

(What Keith thought of my carrying on as though nothing had happened I will never know, although I have met him many times since, it has never been mentioned. Stiff upper lips are all right to a point, but this was going too far.)

This is Joan's account of what happened that terrible afternoon. They had motored to Wales, stopped off for fish'n'chips, and arrived at the caravan to find the grass was very overgrown, also wet. However, Tony decided to get the Flymo out and have a go. Joan, her mum, and their collie dog all sat in the warmth of the caravan. Tony plugged in the mower through an open window. Minutes later, the dog jumped up onto a bench and looked out of the window, barking and very agitated.

Joan rushed to the window and saw Tony lying on his back in the wet grass, beside the mower. In Joan's words. "Tony lay looking up to heaven. He had a smile on his face, as if he was seeing Jesus, who must have appeared, ready to take his soul up to heaven. We KNEW he was with the Lord."

A doctor was called by a neighbour on the site, but Tony had died, it seems, instantly, looking up toward the heavens, not falling forward clutching his chest, as would someone experiencing great pain when having a heart attack.

Heart failure was recorded to Joan and her family. A report said his death was the result of a previous heart attack, or attacks. After his first heart attack, Tony had no guidance about changing his way of life. Something 'medical' went AWOL for Tony, and no doubt others. No anti-fat diet sheet, no physical regime of exercises. In fact, nothing, which perhaps was what happened in those days, this was 1990. It is so marvellous today, so perhaps nobody is to blame for Tony being left to his own devices.

However, we siblings feel differently about the whole terrible event. Tony borrowed the Flymo from a friend, in all good faith. It wasn't tested back home but taken straight up to the caravan. There was long, very wet grass that day, and although we have no reliable evidence, we think Tony was electrocuted.

After the funeral, Pat went up to the caravan with Tony's son Jonathan to collect the death certificate from the office in Criccieth. She put the mower in her car, and it ended up in her garage at home, awaiting an electrical test to see if it WAS the hazard we thought (and still think) it was. It never got as far as the testing, however. A thief broke into her garage and stole the mower. A week or two later, it was reported in the local paper that someone had bought a Flymo from a car-boot sale and had been fatally electrocuted. It MAY have been another mower, a horrible coincidence, but we think it unlikely. We will never know.

One of the worst aspects of Tony's death was telling Mum that her eldest child had died. I went with Pat to the home. Both of us were very worried about Mum's reaction to the news. We took Mum into the dining room for quiet and privacy. Pat took one of her hands and I the other. We both told her of our brother's demise. She didn't respond to the hand-holding (but she never did anyway – never a reassuring grip back). She just looked at us in a questioning way. A big pause. Then she said enquiringly, "Tell me, which one of you was that?"

In a way, the slight dementia she had started suffering from had softened any blow, and although Tony was her firstborn, she really didn't feel upset. It wasn't the almighty blow we had imagined. Mum looked at us both (by now we were a bit tearful). "Well, he always DID have heart trouble," she added, without tears. So that was that!

Joan settled into widowhood. The two children, Catherine seventeen, and Jonathan twenty-one, had had a very strange relationship with their dad. I only heard recently how hard and strict Tony had been, especially to Jonathan. Control was still Tony's way of life, certainly to his offspring, but not to Joan, who he 'ministered' to all their married life, helping with lifting, carrying and general household chores, as Joan had, amongst many other ailments, a permanent 'bad back'.

The money side was fine for his family, as Tony had worked extremely hard all his life, and was (before he took early retirement) a tutor to engineering apprentices in the aeronautical business.

Tony was greatly loved by friends. He would do anything to help them, especially 'tinkering' with clapped-out engines or any practical task. In a way, he was a bit like Dad, perhaps thoughtless and hopeless with his children, but a very amenable friend. Dad would help a friend out with money, Tony helped out in kind; there's a big difference.

I suppose a psychiatrist would find plenty of profound meaningful work when looking into Tony's life. It would also be a field day for them should they peer into the whole of the Lloyd-Davies family. And it's a certainty that Mum's Roberts clan would keep a psychiatrist working for years, such were the weird 'goings-on'. Well, at least they were interesting in a rather surreal way. Never four beats to the bar!

For the next six weeks everything jogged on. We would pass 249 regularly, always dipping our wings when driving past. The house didn't look too different, except that Mum's immaculate front garden was now rather unkempt, but the laurels thrived, and the narrow path still had clumps of London's Pride growing out of the path's edging. The front room was now a complete through room, the wall between the lounge and dining room gone. That was visible from the front view (lots of peering, trying to look when we were passing).

Mum was gradually sinking into vagueness, not really saying anything, just sitting there smiling, but still looking smart (albeit in someone else's clothes!). She managed to put on face powder, and her white hair was washed and set once a week. Mum had finally settled, her old memories fading, which was, in a strange way, a relief.

I don't think she went a day without one or other of us popping in. Glad, Marj, and Uncle Arthur also drove over from Stourbridge. I think we were all viewed as the Tettenhall/Stourbridge Mafia.

One day in August, I stayed longer than usual, mainly because we were going up to visit Harold's cousin in Liverpool the next morning so would be off the 'see Mum rota' for the whole day. When I got up to leave Mum in the sitting room, having spent a rather silent hour or so, I gave her a little kiss and said "goodbye". Then, because we all knew the other ladies incarcerated there, and always kissed some of them 'farewell', I did the rounds. Two or three minutes later, I realized that Mum wouldn't remember me actually kissing HER first, so I went over and kissed her again. She smiled a little smile, and I left looking forward to seeing Marj 'up north' ('up north' was to me anywhere north of Stafford).

We had a nice time out and arrived back quite late in the day. As we drove up to our house, we saw Pat sitting in her car, obviously waiting for our homecoming. She stepped out and walked across as soon as we pulled up at the gate. I knew what she was about to tell us. Mum had died whilst being helped into bed. The young helper had said, "Come on, Maudie, put your leg up" and Mum had just passed away quickly and without any obvious pain (or so they told us?).

That was it… a gentle death, aged eighty-nine. She had survived her eldest son by seven weeks.

Somehow the door of 249 had closed for the last time with Mum's demise.

I am so pleased that I gave Mum two kisses and not the usual one.

No. 249 REVISITED

Some time after Mum's death, I penned a little verse about 249 Tettenhall Road, after a disastrous journey to visit ghosts of the past.

I had walked around to the end house in the terrace and into the old back garden. The garden was gone! Nothing there, just a car park. The whole building had been altered with a newly built back 'wing' resembling a prefabricated office building. There were bins on their sides, and one tiny bit of privet struggling to survive in rubble. There wasn't one flower or tree left standing, just tarmac and hard-core where the little lawn had been. Everything had GONE. German bombs couldn't have done as much damage to Mum's wonderful garden.

When home, I sat down feeling tearful, and wrote this rather sentimental verse.

A HOME REVISITED

Toadflax in the mortar, and loose bricks in the wall,
Yellow peeling paintwork (were those windows always small?)
The gate is off its hinges, and there's an over-turned bin,
Grass grows on the back yard and the privet's just a sin!
I peer through the windows at wallpaper damp,
There's ashes in the fireplace, and a broken lamp.
Oh HOW I remember each ill-fitting door,
Each dip in the step, every creak of the floor.
The laughter of childhood echoes still down these halls,
And the heartache of youth clings fast to these walls.
OH WHY did I come here to stare at this mess?
Memories so happy should escape this distress.

◆

Something I gained from Mum is the love of writing verse. I pen all sorts of rubbish when a special event happens, after the death of a greatly loved pet. I always have eyes (and nose) running when penning the latter.

The awful truth IS that somehow I CAN let the emotion out when a dear cat or dog has departed, but, like Mum, I find it hard to express my feelings and emotion when someone close dies.

One day after the death of a much-loved pet, I mentioned to sister-in-law Joan that the dear departed animal would be "running around in the green meadows of heaven".

"Animals do NOT HAVE souls, so they CAN'T go to heaven" was the caustic reply.

Well, of course they DON'T, it's just a lovely fantasy on my part.

I am a complete heathen where we humans are concerned, and being a gardener, I wouldn't mind being thrown (gently) onto the compost heap, one last act towards a greener land, a life recycled! Anyway, I have NEVER liked vicars, especially hovering ones.

(Years ago, I wrote a poem that included vicars in the last verse. To save any more embarrassment, I will forgo putting it to paper; however, I am having to resist the urge to pop it down, but thankfully for ALL, I am running out of space.)

ENDINGS

Marjorie and Gladys lived on after Mum died, Glad still driving, and carrying on all her arty-crafts. She busied herself with painting her goose eggs, crocheting little hats out of raffia for 'home' dressed dolls. Decoupage took over, and her cards for birthdays were works of art. Her mince pies were famous (still NO bought pastry.)

By now, they were living in a high-rise tower block, horrible to look at, and somehow the exterior didn't gel with the Roberts girls personae. Many months before when the aunts and Uncle Arthur decided to move to these ghastly flats, there were lots of 'oh dears' and lots of humming and ha-ing, the modern hideous buildings were right on Stourbridge's ring road, a complete contrast to their Victorian houses so full of character.

However, Marj, Glad and Unc all loved it. They had a fantastic view over Stourbridge, and Glad said they could see the Clent hills on a fine day. When we were visiting one Christmas, there was excitement. A crane driver who was working on some new buildings had got into the spirit of Christmas and had hauled a Christmas tree with lights up into his cab. This was like watching those 'interludes' that were shown between TV programmes, usually a potter, but this crane was magical (if a crane CAN be magical?). We all gazed out of the window in awe.

Uncle Arthur went regularly to Birmingham town hall to listen to organ recitals. He met other music lovers and enjoyed friendships. He played his electronic organ every day. Being on the third floor of a block of flats might have been awkward, but 'upstairs' above said that they never heard anything, so we gather the ceiling/floors were solid.

We received a very funny phone call from Glad one afternoon. Arthur's sister was staying with them so we expected news of her health. It wasn't!

"Lily's here… but something TERRIBLE has happened. You know she suffers with arthritis in her hands. WELL, Lily's just tipped a WHOLE cup of boiling coffee over Artie's organ."

The thought of poor Unc's privates being scalded brought expressions of sympathy from our end. Was Unc all right?

There was a loud giggle. "No, NOT Artie's 'you-know-what', dear…

NO the coffee's gone down inside the electric organ. We've got a hair dryer on it. Lily is TERRIBLY upset."

Marj, who had shared the flat with Auntie Ve, lived surrounded by Ve's wonderful antiques, a corner cupboard that was supposedly William and Mary, and beautiful porcelain bowls that would 'PING' when flicked.

Happy memories abounded for all the families of the aunts' houses (and we all thought of them as THAT – poor old Uncle Artie was somehow excluded). Great fun had by all inside the crumbling old houses. There were banisters to slide down and rainwater galore out of those ancient pumps at Auntie Ve's.

Auntie Ve was always my favourite auntie, and the giver of 'savings stamps' during the war. Later she gave me a leather-bound book of all of Shakespeare's plays. I'm ashamed to say that I didn't look after the beautiful book. I have it still, but minus its cover. It has not been well read, just moved from bookcase to bookcase, and very occasionally referred to when a crossword or quiz gets the better of me.

Glad and Arthur had lived a hundred yards down the road from Ve's. Their house was smaller than hers, but a very cosy abode. Always full of music; Arthur played every day on the amazingly big 'practice' organ. Their garden was quite spacious, walled at the bottom end, where the neighbours conversed, permed heads just visible above the curved blue ridge bricks. Lots of silent 'mouthing' chatter went on between the ladies, all very secret to us children.

Arthur (actually using his woodwork prowess for the first time) had put together a wooden bench that extended right round the apple-tree trunk. Here Artie and Glad would sit, feeding a tame blackbird who would arrive at breakfast time and help itself to pecks of yolk out of their boiled eggs. (Little did it know what it was eating!)

Happy times were had in this garden.

The deep, dark outside loo is remembered with almost affection, and the smell of marigold leaves crushed under running feet brings back the joy of just being able to play freely without restrictions.

So these flats were looked on with scorn by us, and it wasn't until well after the aunts moved in that we realized how difficult it had been to keep their gardens and houses going. They were all in their seventies.

The rules of occupancy of the flats stated that nobody under fifty need apply, so there were no noisy teenagers hogging the lifts or hanging around outside. Also there were gardens with benches, which would soften the blow for Glad.

Many years were spent in these high-rise flats, overlooking the new swimming baths. (The water slide afforded both Glad and Arthur happy hours watching delighted children and their families whooping and screaming as they slid down and splashed into the water.)

The lifts in the flats occasionally broke down. One day, Marj was sailing down from her seventh floor to Glad's on the third, when jolt after jolt, the lift stopped mid-floor. The panic button was pressed many times!

Along came the fire brigade…

"They were SO handsome!" exclaimed Marj (after a cup of tea with brandy).

Marj didn't have a fireman's lift, but she was carried out, and I think she secretly enjoyed being in the arms of her handsome muscular rescuer. Always the romantic, with echoes of the 'Penny Dreadfuls' she read as a young woman, Marj had a love of the risqué, along with passion, although she had never lived a life of thrills. But she could dream, and DID.

Marj lived for some time in her seventh-floor abode. It was elegantly furnished, mainly with Ve's antiques, now in Marj's hands. Marj still read, library books brought to her by friends. Frequent visits from Mike and his wife Val made her life reasonably happy. Like all the Roberts girls, she was suffering from osteoarthritis, so moving around was getting very painful, and she was getting weary.

Her sudden death, before she could be moved to Northampton to be nearer Mike, left Glad and Arthur the sole family members in these most comfortable high-rise council flats, so maligned by us, but which had proved to be a haven and a blessing.

Glad's pastry-making continued. She welcomed all her nephews and nieces with open arms, always a buffet waiting, and a seat (for anyone who could play a simple well-rehearsed one line of musical score) alongside Arthur as he played all the regular organ pieces, sometimes forgetting passages. But Bach's Toccata and Fugue still resounded around the living room, and very often the 'Rustle of Spring', played by heart… These weird duets always ended up in laughter.

These simple memories remain part of our lives, lovely times.

Arthur added another string to his bow. He became an organist at the local crematorium. His tales of the music requested by the deceased or by well-meaning relatives were eye opening. 'My Way' and once, 'The Grand Old Duke of York'!

Arthur became ninety, but wasn't in good health. He was suffering from prostate cancer. Auntie Glad knew, and accepted that her 'Arty' was going to the great organ loft in the sky. Glad looked after Artie. She had always been the boss but she would tell people it was Arthur who made the decisions. This was totally untrue, everyone knew, but kept the peace. However, she did star on the household front. Arthur was hopeless at looking after himself.

Once, Glad left him for a day to go to a flower-arranging demonstration. "Now, Artie, there's an egg you can boil for your lunch."

Artie DID, but in the kettle! He told Glad that evening that he had had trouble getting it out of the lid. So, although he must have cooked SOMETHING whilst in the desert, he had forgotten it all! Or was it a ploy to make sure he could sit back and have the joy of knocking back Glad's cakes, pies and fabulous roast dinners?

Auntie Glad, true to form, soldiered on after Artie died. In fact, she came into her own. What surprised all of us was the lack of photos or memorabilia of Uncle Arthur. There was one, on the window ledge, but that was IT!

Glad always had lots of friends. Some were her painting and craft colleagues, also her flower arrangement friends. She was a master at flower arranging – not my cup of tea, I always thought it was 'cruel' to pull the petals of a tulip out flat so that it resembled a Japanese flower – but Glad was an expert. Just another talent to add to the others. Tailoring was also her forte, and she would appear in a two-piece suit made by her own fair hands. Cushions were covered in an afternoon, always flowery in pattern, but muted colours. Adding all this, and her woodwork prowess, Gladys Barlow was a multi-talented woman.

The Roberts' osteoarthritis had been coming on over the years. Also her stomach that had always been 'difficult' was suddenly painful. We didn't know HOW 'difficult' until later. She let it out to us (Pat and myself) that she had taken senna, in tablet form, for about ten years. Never able to miss 'going' because it led to great pain and trouble.

Glad was admitted to Russells Hall Hospital for tests.

ANOTHER MEDICAL NIGHTMARE

Another medical debacle took place, but this time we nephews and nieces rebelled.

One of Auntie's tests was under general anaesthetic. Pat drove us both to the hospital in the evening. Auntie was in a small side ward. It was dark, no lights. We could hardly tell it WAS Auntie in the bed. On the bed was draped an open-work, I guess, cotton blanket. When we eventually popped a light on, we could see the blanket was a discoloured yellow. As our cousin Judy said, having also popped in later, "I wouldn't have put that blanket on my dog's bed."

Auntie grasped our hands and said in a very hoarse voice how very thirsty she was, but because the nurses had wound her bell cord around something above the bed, it was completely out of reach, so she couldn't alert anyone. She had been trying to make contact with someone for some while. We asked a passing nurse if it was all right to give liquid to Glad. "Oh yes, just little sips." She then fetched a glass of water.

Auntie had been back in her side ward for, well, we don't know HOW long, with no water, no light, no bell to call for help, her bed cover just about covering her body. Modern nursing had hit rock bottom.

Back next day on the main ward, the care was dreadful. The water jug always had its handle turned away so that Glad couldn't lift it off her bed-table and pour herself any water.

On another occasion we were there when the evening meal was served. Soup and a giant CRUST of bread, white sliced and OLD, curled at the edges! We asked the lady who was delivering these 'feasts' if we could have a fresh piece of bread. "Yes, me love, of course. I'll get you one."

No bread arrived, and Glad, so hungry, drank her supposed chicken soup. This was a powdered type. Harold had a sip, and 'yuk!' Auntie pulled a face, but manfully finished it. The bread NEVER arrived. We stayed the whole of the visiting time and saw a very unhappy old Auntie trying her best to conform.

"I think I have a bit of a sore bottie," Auntie whispered one day. Sure enough, there was the telltale signs of a bed-sore. Also her heels were shiny and red from friction. We mentioned this and pads were popped under her poor bottom. But they seemed to make Auntie more uncomfortable.

Our cousin Ann and her husband brought in nappy rash cream, and this we smoothed over. On one such time, a cheerful nurse happened to be passing. "Oh... just what I need," she said, helping herself to a great fingerful of our cream before disappearing into the next ward to smooth it onto another patient's derriere.

The obvious happened, though, and the sore skin broke, so a full-blown bed-sore. We all felt let down over Auntie's treatment. This was meted out in about 2003.

Cancer was eventually diagnosed, so Glad went back to her cosy flat for the last weeks of her life.

Christmas day was spent with a good friend, also a widow, who lived in the next-door flat. "I had a lovely Christmas, dear, we talked about 'the old days' and watched the television."

Soon after this, we found a nursing home in Amblecote, a village near Stourbridge. Glad was pleased to go. She was putting on a good show, but was in great discomfort.

To see Auntie Glad leaving her flat and all her memories was, to me, a heartbreaking time, and one of the worst days of my life. Again, Glad showed courage. "I don't want to say goodbye to Dorothy (her good friend next door). I know she will try to see me off, but..."

We knew what she meant. So we crept past Dorothy's door, Glad wearing a headscarf and no wig. All bodily finery gone, just a plain headscarf (something that Glad would NEVER have worn years before), we reached the lift. It became a nightmare.

(Seeing her without her trusty coiffure was a surprise. Auntie Glad wasn't completely bald, her hair (oddly still dark) was thin and straggly, but not a bit as we imagined it. Years of being 'under cover' wouldn't have helped her hair to flourish, but it was a secret right up until then.)

The journey to the nursing home began. It was very like the journey in the tumbrels, end point... the gallows. Glad sat looking straight ahead, holding a little bowl on her lap, "Just in case, dear." She was feeling sick. The car journey seemed endless, but we got there mostly in silence.

We were met at the door of the nursing home by the owners, a middle-aged married couple. Glad's bedroom was chintzy and cosy. The owners welcomed us, and we all had tea, no thick giant mugs, which would NOT have pleased Glad. This tray was laid with thought for the elderly 'guests', as was everything else in this truly wonderful home.

This became her home for the next week. Kindness abounded, and Glad was made very comfortable. We called in one morning to find one of the helpers gently washing their charge. There was a dusting of talc and a dabbing of soft towels to dry her rather wasted body.

Glad looked up when we entered.

"How are you Auntie?"

"In heaven dear, in heaven."

This wonderful home was the happy ending to a sad medical story. It proved to be a wonderful place for Glad to end her days. She died with Pat holding her hand.

After Glad's death, the funeral directors asked us if we wanted Glad to be 'laid out' for people to pay their last respects. None of us wanted to view her, but we thought perhaps friends might, so we said yes. The funeral director then asked, "Would it be possible for you to choose one of your auntie's wigs? We would like her to look as she was."

Somehow this was a request I had never envisaged, all doom and gloom seemed to descend. But, as Harold said, it was the last thing we could do for Glad, and of course it was.

Auntie had a few wigs tucked away somewhere, but we didn't want to search through her drawers. We DID, though, and we found a recent addition to her collection, a very up-to-date, short curly one, very chic. She had looked ten years younger when she popped it on her head. It didn't bear thinking about what she would look like wearing it now, but we had to do the last deed for a very gifted and interesting auntie. So we handed it over.

This time was very stressful for both of us. Harold was executor, so organized her will and all that comes with a death. Strangely, when viewing her birth certificate, we found that the date on the certificate stated that her birth was two days BEFORE the day she always said was her birthday! This was possibly an error by her father, Ludd, who seemed to have made so many errors in life. It was a minor one, but Auntie was two days older than anyone knew.

The night before Auntie's funeral, I was drinking the dregs out of a milk bottle (NOT a Roberts action! Everyone who was a Roberts was probably whizzing around in their graves) when I banged my mouth on the glass rim, and OH HORROR, a lower front tooth was knocked out.

Normally I wouldn't have been seen dead with a gap, but I had to be at the funeral. I was… with a bloody gap, soaked to the skin, as both Harold and Robin had used their umbrellas to shield just about EVERYONE in the crematorium, from funeral directors to gardeners, saving them from what had become torrential rain. My hair was flattened, all signs of decorum gone, toothless, and make-up washed off. I suppose all my assembled cousins thought I had 'let myself go'.

We all said goodbye to the last of the Roberts girls. In fact, the last of that generation.

Stourbridge is no longer a town to visit, and Clifton Street is almost avoided when we have to travel through the town on our way back from Wales. Memories, happy and sad, have filled some of the hours whilst I wait for sleep to arrive.

Just towards the end of Auntie's life, she had confided that, if she couldn't sleep or was anxious, she would imagine a garden with beautiful flowers, and tiny silvery fairies flitting through the roses, transparent wings fluttering in the sunshine. This sounds weird and childlike, and a bit crackers, but these scenes and imaginings must have been a place she chose to be, away from all life's worries.

Glad had never had a proper childhood, too many unhappy episodes, with the loss of her mother when she was seven, and lack of love from her father and Ludd's partner May. She had been badly treated by both… at one time father Ludd kept her at home instead of sending her to school. This was before she had escaped with her younger brother Doug. We all need a dream to escape life's unfairness, and this simple 'fairy' one was Glad's.

Shortly after Auntie's death, I asked my cousins, Ann, Mike and Judy, if they would like me to write a letter of complaint to the hospital that had so badly let Glad down. Everyone said 'yes', so I set down a list of all our complaints, all of them encompassing just general common sense, so sadly lacking where Glad was concerned. I sent the three-page letter to the chief executive of the hospital, itemizing our complaints.

We received a very detailed letter back, answering every item on my list. All bar two of our complaints were acknowledged as errors, and an apology was given. (One of our complaints deemed to be incorrect by the hospital hierarchy was that the cream we had used to help with the bed-sores wasn't the 'correct' one, and 'not used for that purpose'. Well, it didn't seem to put the passing nurse off – she had happily used it. It seemed a pretty silly remark as no other cream was available, and none was offered to Glad.)

However, we felt that the letter from the hospital was a fair one. Complaining was the last thing all of us could do for a much-loved, if at times 'naughty' auntie. (I have had to leave a little bit out about Glad's life. Suffice to say, she had sometimes been 'adventurous' in her youth!)

I HOPE that now, in 2014, this kind of poor treatment of the elderly in hospital or nursing home no longer happens, and that they are more considerate, thoughtful and kindly towards their charges. All our moans were about lack of common sense and basic nursing… But hearing and reading the latest news, I remain a pessimist.

So, I'm nearing the end of a great long story which was originally only going to be the 'bare bones' of life in the Second World War, but which has gone on from 1938 to 2015, encompassing our rather chaotic family and eccentric aunts as well as our friends, not to mention a whole wonderful host of animals (extremely varied).

Our old family house, No. 249, is mentioned very often by relatives and old friends. Everyone has some vivid memory of a 'happening' there.

After I asked if she had any special memories to recount so that I could add them to this saga, lifelong good friend Josie replied that she always remembers our front door with its stained-glass panels. "Your door at 249 was never locked. Anyone and everyone could just walk in… also that super brick wall that we used to sit astride."

This ancient crumbling old wall was the place that we children would go to discuss a possible adventure and talk about our world whilst dangling our legs, not caring a jot for the turmoil around us. I think that is what a childhood should be.

I feel that Josie's memories were a very nice compliment to a rather weird family and to Mum, Maudie, who was sometimes very distant and unable to show love outwardly to her brood of very different children.

Everyone who knew Dad, LD, liked and loved him. He contributed to his untimely death by his drinking and smoking, but there was something charismatic about him to his friends in his 'show biz' life. Dad had completed over forty years working for J Arthur Rank. He was awarded a grandmother clock on his retirement (no gold watch), and for many of those working years, LD was a well-respected employee.

One thing that has shone through all these pages of life during the war and post-war days is that none of us have fallen out! We remain always united by our rather weird upbringing and shared traumas. Pat still says that we are all 'psychological cripples'. She is probably correct.

This epistle just 'growed and growed like Topsy'. I hope I haven't spoiled any friendships by writing a hopefully accurate account of our lives through the years.

Pat said recently, when I told her about this memoir, "You always DID have a brilliant imagination." She says she remembers very little of life at 249. My tales about the old neighbours were a revelation to her. She wasn't born with the 'nosey gene'.

Certainly, most families have their 'myths' and I have tried to say that one or two events are 'hearsay', but otherwise, I hope this is as true as I can get it. 'THEY' WILL definitely get me if it isn't!

I have left out quite a few events that might hurt or upset friends and family. But I hope it's a fairly accurate account of life, and enjoyable to read, even though a few 'happenings' are stranger than fiction. I have had a few laughs whilst penning this, especially when writing about the aunties, characters who could have sprung from an Alan Bennett book.

I have never found a casket brimming with sparkling jewels or shining nuggets of gold. But, having written this saga, I realize that I HAVE found treasure – lots of it.

My memories of a childhood growing up in 249, a house open to all comers, lived in by a rather dysfunctional family, but a family full of colourful and precious gems, who all still sparkle in my memory, rather like the fairy dew drops in the lupin leaves.

Now I have my own special treasures. Harold, and my two dear children, Louise and Robin, and their families. Also in 2015, three greatly loved grandchildren. I hope Anna, Benjamin and Cameron can still find a warm, comfortable wall to sit on, faces turned to the sun, feeling the wind in their hair, their legs dangling down against rough bricks. Whispering and giggling secrets to their friends, telling of their adventures… looking up through transparent leaves, and feeling the wonder of the sky, or just watching a long processions of ants going about their daily business.

My wish is that they just enjoy having a carefree and happy childhood… and beyond.

The Moving Finger writes, and having writ
Moves on: nor all thy Piety nor wit
Shall lure it back to cancel half a line
Nor all thy tears wash out a Word of it.

From The Rubaiyat of Omar Khayyam.